T0242261

Communications in Computer and Information Science 1374

More information about this series at http://www.springer.com/series/7899

Kanubhai K. Patel · Deepak Garg ·
Atul Patel · Pawan Lingras (Eds.)

Soft Computing and its Engineering Applications

Second International Conference, icSoftComp 2020
Changa, Anand, India, December 11–12, 2020
Proceedings

 Springer

Editors
Kanubhai K. Patel ⓘ
Charotar University of Science and
Technology
Changa, Anand, Gujarat, India

Deepak Garg
Bennett University
Greater Noida, Uttar Pradesh, India

Atul Patel ⓘ
Charotar University of Science and
Technology
Changa, Anand, Gujarat, India

Pawan Lingras
Saint Mary's University
Halifax, NS, Canada

ISSN 1865-0929   ISSN 1865-0937 (electronic)
Communications in Computer and Information Science
ISBN 978-981-16-0707-3   ISBN 978-981-16-0708-0 (eBook)
https://doi.org/10.1007/978-981-16-0708-0

This Springer imprint is published by the registered company Springer Nature Singapore Pte Ltd.
The registered company address is: 152 Beach Road, #21-01/04 Gateway East, Singapore 189721, Singapore

Preface

It is a matter of great privilege to have been tasked with the writing of this preface for the proceedings of The Second International Conference on Soft Computing and its Engineering Applications (icSoftComp2020). The conference aimed to provide an excellent international forum to the researchers, academicians, students, and professionals in the areas of computer science and engineering to present their research, knowledge, new ideas, and innovations. The theme of the conference was "Soft Computing Techniques for Sustainable Development". The conference was held during 11–12 December 2020, at Charotar University of Science & Technology (CHARUSAT), Changa, India, and organized by the Faculty of Computer Science and Applications, CHARUSAT.

There are three pillars of Soft Computing viz., i) Fuzzy computing, ii) Neuro computing, and iii) Evolutionary computing. Research submissions in these three areas were received. The Program Committee of icSoftComp2020 is extremely grateful to the authors from 15 different countries including the USA, United Arab Emirates, Mauritius, Saudi Arabia, Palestine, Peru, South Africa, Pakistan, Nigeria, Ecuador, Libya, Taiwan, Bangladesh, Ukraine, and UK who showed an overwhelming response to the call for papers, submitting over 252 papers. The entire review team (Technical Program Committee members along with 12 additional reviewers) expended tremendous effort to ensure fairness and consistency during the selection process, resulting in the best-quality papers being selected for presentation and publication. It was ensured that every paper received at least three, and in most cases four, reviews. Checking of similarities was also done based on international norms and standards. After a rigorous peer review 28 papers were accepted with an acceptance ratio of 11.11%. The papers are organised according to the following topics: Theory & Methods, and Systems & Applications. The proceedings of the conference are published as one volume in the Communications in Computer and Information Science (CCIS) series by Springer, and are also indexed by ISI Proceedings, DBLP, Ulrich's, EI-Compendex, SCOPUS, Zentralblatt Math, MetaPress, and Springerlink. We, in our capacity as volume editors, convey our sincere gratitude to Springer for providing the opportunity to publish the proceedings of icSoftComp2020 in their CCIS series.

icSoftComp2020 provided an excellent international virtual forum to the conference delegates to present their research, knowledge, new ideas, and innovations. The conference exhibited an exciting technical program. It also featured high-quality workshops, keynote, and five expert talks from prominent research and industry leaders. The Keynote speech was given by Dr. Valentina E. Balas (Professor, Aurel Vlaicu University of Arad, Arad, Romania). Expert talks were given by Dr. Deepak Garg (Bennett University, Greater Noida, India), Dr. Sanjay Misra (Covenant University, Ota, Nigeria), Dr. Vishnu Pendyala (San José State University, San José, CA, USA), Dr. Kiran Trivedi (Vishwakarma Government Engineering College, Ahmedabad, India), Dr. Pritpal Singh (Jagiellonian University, Poland), and Dr. Korhan Cengiz

(Trakya University, Turkey). We are grateful to them for sharing their insights on their latest research with us.

The Organizing Committee of icSoftComp2020 is indebted to Dr. Pankaj Joshi, Provost of Charotar University of Science and Technology and Patron, for the confidence that he invested in us in organizing this international conference. We would also like to take this opportunity to extend our heartfelt thanks to the Honorary Chairs of this conference, Dr. Kalyanmoy Deb (Michigan State University, MI, USA) and Dr. Leszek Rutkowski (IEEE Fellow) (Częstochowa University of Technology, Częstochowa, Poland) for their active involvement from the very beginning until the end of the conference. The quality of a refereed volume primarily depends on the expertise and dedication of the reviewers who volunteer with a smiling face. The editors are further indebted to the Technical Program Committee members and external reviewers who not only produced excellent reviews but also did so in a short time frame, in spite of their very busy schedules. Because of their quality work it was possible to maintain the high academic standard of the proceedings. Without their support, this conference could never have assumed such a successful shape. Special words of appreciation are due to note the enthusiasm of all the faculty, staff, and students of the Faculty of Computer Science and Applications of CHARUSAT, who organized the conference in a professional manner.

It is needless to mention the role of the contributors. The editors would like to take this opportunity to thank the authors of all submitted papers not only for their hard work but also for considering the conference a viable platform to showcase some of their latest findings, not to mention their adherence to the deadlines and patience with the tedious review process. Special thanks to the team of OCS, whose paper submission platform was used to organize reviews and collate the files for these proceedings. We also wish to express our thanks to Ms. Kamiya Khatter, Associate Editor, Springer Nature India, New Delhi, for her help and cooperation. We gratefully acknowledge the financial (partial) support received from the Department of Science & Technology, Government of India and the Gujarat Council on Science & Technology (GUJCOST), Government of Gujarat, Gandhinagar, India for organizing the conference. Last but not least, the editors profusely thank all who directly or indirectly helped us in making icSoftComp2020 a grand success and allowed the conference to achieve its goals, academic or otherwise.

December 2020

Kanubhai K. Patel
Deepak Garg
Atul Patel
Pawan Lingras

Organization

Patron

Pankaj Joshi   Charotar University of Science and Technology, India

Honorary Chairs

Kalyanmoy Deb   Michigan State University, USA
Leszek Rutkowski   Częstochowa University of Technology, Poland

General Chairs

Atul Patel   Charotar University of Science and Technology, India
Pawan Lingras   Saint Mary's University, Canada

Technical Program Committee Chair

Kanubhai K. Patel   Charotar University of Science and Technology, India

Technical Program Committee Co-chair

Deepak Garg   Bennett University, India

Advisory Committee

Arup Dasgupta   Geospatial Media and Communications, India
Valentina E. Balas   Aurel Vlaicu University of Arad, Romania
Bhushan Trivedi   GLS University, India
Bhuvan Unhelkar   University of South Florida Sarasota-Manatee, USA
J. C. Bansal   Soft Computing Research Society, India
Narendra S. Chaudhari   Indian Institute of Technology Indore, India
Rajendra Akerkar   Vestlandsforsking, Norway
Sudhirkumar Barai   BITS Pilani, India
Devang Joshi   Charotar University of Science and Technology, India
S. P. Kosta   Charotar University of Science and Technology, India
Dharmendra T. Patel   Charotar University of Science and Technology, India

Technical Program Committee Members

A. Jayanthiladevi   Srinivas University, India
Abhineet Anand   Chitkara University, India
Abhishek K.   Banaras Hindu University, India

Aditya Patel	Kamdhenu University, India
Adrijan Božinovski	University American College Skopje, Macedonia
Akash Kumar Bhoi	Sikkim Manipal University, India
Ami Choksi	C.K.Pithawala College of Engg. and Technology, India
Amit Joshi Malaviya	National Institute of Technology Jaipur, India
Anand Nayyar	Duy Tan University, Vietnam
Ankush Bhatia	Qualcomm, India
Aravind Rajam	Washington State University, USA
Ashok Patel	Florida Polytechnic University, USA
Ashok Sharma	Lovely Professional University, India
Ashraf Elnagar	University of Sharjah, UAE
Ashutosh Kumar Dubey	Chitkara University, India
Avimanyou Vatsa	Fairleigh Dickinson University - Teaneck, USA
Ayad Mousa	University of Kerbala, Iraq
B. Rajkumarsingh	University of Mauritius, Mauritius
Bankim Patel	Uka Tarsadia University, India
Basavaprasad B.	Government First Grade College Raichur, India
Bhavik Pandya	Navgujarat College of Computer Applications, India
Bhogeswar Borah	Tezpur University, India
B. K. Verma	Chandigarh Engineering College, India
Brojo Kishore Mishra	GIET University, India
Chaman Sabharwal	Missouri University of Science and Technology, USA
Chirag Patel	Innovate Tax, UK
Chirag Paunwala	SCET, India
Costas Vassilakis	University of the Peloponnese, Greece
Darshana Patel	Navgujarat College of Computer Applications, India
Deepshikha Patel	Sagar Institute of Research and Technology, India
Devasenathipathi Mudaliar	GTU, India
Digvijaysinh Rathod	GFSU, India
Dinesh Acharya	Manipal Institute of Technology, India
Dushyantsinh Rathod	Alpha College of Engineering and Technology, India
E. Rajesh	Galgotias University, India
Gayatri Doctor	CEPT University, India
Harshal Arolkar	GLS University, India
Hetal Patel	Charotar University of Science and Technology, India
Hiren Joshi	Gujarat University, India
Hiren Mewada	Prince Mohammad Bin Fahd University, Saudi Arabia
Irene Govender	University of KwaZulu-Natal, South Africa
Jaishree Tailor	Uka Tarsadia University, India
Janmenjoy Nayak	AITAM, India
Jaspher Kathrine	Karunya Institute of Technology and Sciences, India
Jignesh Patoliya	Charotar University of Science and Technology, India
József Dombi	University of Szeged, Hungary
Killol Pandya	Charotar University of Science and Technology, India
Kiran Trivedi	Vishwakarma Government Engineering College, India
Krishan Kumar	National Institute of Technology Uttarakhand, India

Kuntal Patel	Ahmedabad University, India
Latika Singh	Sushant University, India
M. Srinivas	National Institute of Technology Warangal, India
M. A. Jabbar	Vardhaman College of Engineering, India
Maciej Ławryńczuk	Warsaw University of Technology, Poland
Mahmoud Elish	Gulf University for Science and Technology, Kuwait
Mohamad Ijab	National University of Malaysia, Malaysia
Mohini Agarwal	Amity University Noida, India
Monika Patel	NVP College of Pure and Applied Sciences, India
Neepa Shah	Gujarat Vidyapith, India
Nidhi Arora	Solusoft Technologies Pvt. Ltd., India
Nilay Vaidya	Charotar University of Science and Technology, India
Nirali Honest	Charotar University of Science and Technology, India
Nitin Kumar	National Institute of Technology Uttarakhand, India
Parag Rughani	GFSU, India
Pranav Vyas	Charotar University of Science and Technology, India
Prashant Pittalia	Sardar Patel University, India
Priti Sajja	Sardar Patel University, India
Pritpal Singh	Jagiellonian University, Poland
Rajesh Thakker	Vishwakarma Govt. Engg. College, India
Ramesh Prajapati	LJ Institute of Engineering and Technology, India
Ramzi Guetari	University of Tunis El Manar, Tunisia
Rana Mukherji	ICFAI University, Jaipur, India
Rathinaraja Jeyaraj	National Institute of Technology Karnataka, India
Rekha A. G.	State Bank of India, India
Rohini Rao	Manipal Academy of Higher Education (MAHE), India
S. Srinivasulu Raju	V.R. Siddhartha Engineering College, India
Sailesh Iyer	Rai University, India
Saman Chaeikar	Iranians University e-Institute of Higher Education, Iran
Sameerchand Pudaruth	University of Mauritius, Mauritius
Samir Patel	PDPU, India
Sandhya Dubey	Manipal Academy of Higher Education (MAHE), India
Sannidhan M. S.	NMAM Institute of Technology, India
Saurabh Das	University of Calcutta, India
S. B. Goyal	City University of Malaysia, Malaysia
Selvanayaki Shanmugam	Concordia University Chicago, USA
Shachi Sharma	South Asian University, India
Shailesh Khant	Charotar University of Science and Technology, India
Shefali Naik	Ahmedabad University, India
Shravan Kumar Garg	Swami Vivekanand Subharti University, India
Spiros Skiadopoulos	University of the Peloponnese, Greece
Srinivasan Sriramulu	Galgotias University, India
Sudhanshu Maurya	Graphic Era Hill University, Malaysia
Sujit Das	National Institute of Technology Warangal, India
Sunil Bajeja	Marwadi University, India
Tanuja S. Dhope	Rajarshi Shahu College of Engineering, India

Thoudam Singh	NIT Silchar, India
Trushit Upadhyaya	Charotar University of Science and Technology, India
Tzung-Pei Hong	National University of Kaohsiung, Taiwan
Vana Kalogeraki	Athens University of Economics and Business, Greece
Vibhakar Pathak	Arya College of Engg. and IT, India
Vijaya Rajanala	SR Engineering College, India
Vinay Vachharajani	Ahmedabad University, India
Vishnu Pendyala	San José State University, USA
Zina BenMiled	Indiana University, USA

Additional Reviewers

Abbas Sohail
Chronis Pantelis
Davvetas Athanasios
Kamdar Karnavee
Lataifeh Mohammad
Lee John

Mukhopadhyay Dibya
Rontala Prabhakar
Theocharidis Konstantinos
Tsoukalos Mihalis
Viriri Serestina
Zagganas Konstantinos

Contents

Theory and Methods

Systems and Applications

Theory and Methods

On the Performance Analysis of Efficient Path-Planning Algorithms for Fire-Fighting Robots

Sreesruthi Ramasubramanian[(⊠)] and Senthil Arumugam Muthukumaraswamy

Heriot-Watt University, Dubai, United Arab Emirates
{snrl, m.senthilarumugam}@hw.ac.uk

Abstract. Fire-fighting robots with the ability to detect and extinguish fires are extremely useful in saving lives and property. However, most of these fire-fighting robots have been designed to operate semi-autonomously. Using path-planning algorithms to guide the robot to move from the present position to the target position would greatly improve the performance of the robot in the fire extinguishing process. Two types of sampling-based path-planning algorithms, namely, Rapidly Exploring Random Tree (RRT) and Rapidly Exploring Random Tree Star (RRT*) are investigated in this paper. The performances of these algorithms are analyzed and compared based on the computational time taken to generate paths and the length of the paths generated in order to select an effective path-planning algorithm. After investigation, RRT* is chosen for path-planning in both static and dynamic obstacle environments.

Keywords: Path-planning · Sampling-based algorithms · Fire-fighting robots

1 Introduction

Fire-fighting robots are extremely useful in detecting and extinguishing fires in indoor environments. Most fire-fighting robots designed have a camera attached so that the user can control the movement of the robot remotely by observing the environment [1, 2]. However, since these robots aren't completely autonomous, they require human supervision. Having an autonomous fire-fighting robot that has the ability to avoid obstacles and reach the target quickly would improve the efficiency of the robot.

Some robots have been designed to work autonomously by using ultrasonic sensors for obstacle avoidance [3]. However, the robots that solely rely on ultrasonic sensors will take a long time to avoid obstacles and reach the destination. The sensor will detect the static obstacles only as the robot moves towards the target. Implementing motion planning in fire-fighting robots will give the robots the ability to operate autonomously and navigate various rooms in a floor to reach the destination quickly.

The objective of motion planning is to develop algorithms that would equip robots with the ability to decide on how to move from the start to the end position. Usually, multiple paths exist between start and goal positions. It is often essential to find the path

K. K. Patel et al. (Eds.): icSoftComp 2020, CCIS 1374, pp. 3–14, 2021.
https://doi.org/10.1007/978-981-16-0708-0_1

that minimizes that total distance for the robot to travel in. This is especially important in fire-fighting robots as time is of essence in saving lives and preventing damage. However, it is also important to consider the computational time taken for path identification. These two main factors influence the performance of the path-planning algorithms.

To implement path-planning, the position of the fire has to be first obtained. Let's suppose that the floor of a building has a certain number of rooms. The fire is detected with respect to the room using deep learning-based object detection model [4]. It is beneficial to use deep learning rather than conventional flame sensors for fire detection since the position of the fire can be obtained using the coordinates of the bounding box surrounding the detected fire in the image or video [5]. Using this position, the target position of the fire is obtained. The target position is the position a certain distance away from the fire [6]. This is so that the robot can extinguish the fire without being affected. The local target position concerning the room is used to obtain the global target position with respect to the particular floor. The robot is present at a known location and the path is planned between the two positions using an appropriate path-planning algorithm. The robot will follow the path found, move to the target position and extinguish the fire. The overall procedure is illustrated in Fig. 1.

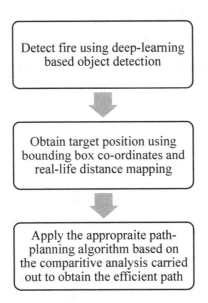

Fig. 1. Flowchart representing the necessary steps to be performed for efficient fire-extinguishment

Grid-based path-planning algorithms such as *Dijkstra's* or *A* algorithm* can be used for path-planning [7]. However, sampling-based algorithms are preferred over grid-based algorithms since they can be easily implemented. In this paper, two sampling-based algorithms, *Rapidly Exploring Random Tree (RRT)* [8, 9] and *Rapidly Exploring Random Tree Star (RRT*)* [10] are investigated. The performance of both the algorithms is analysed by using the average computational time taken for path identification and the average path length to choose an appropriate path-planning algorithm. The chosen path-planning algorithm can then be implemented in order to ensure that the fire-fighting robot extinguishes the fire in a minimum time.

The rest of the paper is organized in five sections. Previous works regarding path-planning algorithms are described in Sect. 2 and the appropriate methodologies are presented in Sect. 3. The results obtained are presented and discussed in Sect. 4. The key takeaways are presented in Sect. 5 which is the conclusion of the paper. The future scope of the project is discussed in Sect. 6 of the paper.

2 Literature Review

Path-planning algorithms have been applied in various situations to find the appropriate path. The literature review section aims to show some sample situations where sampling-based algorithms have been applied to find the necessary path and the comparison made between sampling-based and grid-based path-planning algorithms.

The *RRT* algorithm was used to perform path-planning to find the path when the road network was congested due to traffic [8]. The algorithm was simulated based on data obtained from the road network in Wuhan City. The modification made to the *RRT* algorithm was that the road segment closest to the line between the nearest node and the random point was selected. If the road network found collided with an obstacle area, resampling was performed to find a new road. Since real-time traffic kept changing with time, it was essential to re-plan the path according to the data obtained. Hence, if congested areas were found in the predetermined route, the current road was considered as the root node and the *RRT* was initialized again to find the path. In this manner, *RRT* was able to find the least congested route based on real-time data.

RRT* was used for planning a minimum dose path in nuclear facilities [10]. *RRT** was proposed for use in nuclear environments since the radioactive environment changed frequently during decommissioning and it was necessary to frequently generate a new network. The obstacles were modelled using basic geometric shapes and detected using virtual reality. The performance of *RRT** was compared with *Dijkstra's* algorithm. The path produced by *RRT** was smoother and shorter than the path produced by *Dijkstra's*, reaching the target 18.3 s earlier. The cumulative dose of *RRT** was also less by 2.74%. However, the average time taken to generate *RRT** was 341 ms more than the time taken by *Dijkstra's*. *RRT** took more time since it needed to check for obstacles at every iteration. However, the path generated by *RRT** was much better when considering all aspects. The overall time taken for evacuation following

RRT* would still be less than the overall time taken following *Dijkstra's*. Hence, *RRT** was used for path-planning inside nuclear facilities.

Devaurs et al. discussed about parallelizing *RRT* through large-scale distributed-memory architectures using *messaging passing interface (MPI)* to improve the performance [11]. They compared three parallel versions of RRT- *Or Parallel RRT*, *Distributed RRT* and *Manager-worker RRT*. They compared their performance on different motion-planning problems such as passage problem, corridor problem and roundabout problem. In *Or Parallel RRT*, each process first computed its own *RRT*. The first one to reach the termination condition then produced a termination message, instructing others to stop. If many processes managed to find the solution at the same time, the program instructed them to coordinate and agree on which process to display. The time taken for these communications was negligible when considering the overall runtime.

In *Distributed RRT*, for each iteration of the tree, the process had to first check whether it had already received new nodes from other processes. If that was the case, the node was added to the copy of the tree in that process and it performed the next step, i.e. it attempted to expand. If this attempt was possible, the node was added and announced to all the processes. In *Manager-worker RRT*, only the manager had access to the tree. The manager initially checked if it had received nodes from any of the workers. If this was the case, it added them to the tree, then computed the random node and found the nearest neighbour in the tree. It then looked for an idle worker to whom it sent the required data in order to expand the tree. These steps continued until the goal was reached.

From the results they obtained, they concluded that motion problems for which computational cost of *RRT* expansion is high can use *Distributed RRT* and *Manager-worker RRT* to lower the cost. Parallelizing can also be applied for other *RRT*-based algorithms such as *RRT**. *RRT** has a greater number of steps such as adding and removing edges after rewiring which will increase the time taken for communication. In such a case, they remarked that *Distributed* version will be more beneficial compared to *Manager-worker* version.

Some form of cost indication is required to plan paths using *RRT* on rough terrains [12]. In *RRT*, the nearest neighbour in the tree to the random node was found using the Euclidean distance. *Tahirovic et al.* used a roughness-based metric called *Roughness based Navigation Function (RbNF)* that represented an estimate of the roughness value. From the simulation results obtained, they concluded that *RRT-RT* was very effective in exploring favourable terrain regions. They observed that the algorithm produced paths that decreased the total roughness. The results also demonstrated that paths produced by *RRT-RT* did not significantly differ from optimal paths. This can also be implemented for other path-planning algorithms such as *RRT** to improve their performance on rough terrains.

3 Methodology

3.1 Binary Occupancy Map

A map represents the environment of the robot through which it has to navigate. A Binary Occupancy map is usually built by obtaining information from range sensors. The Binary Occupancy Map considered for path-planning is shown in Fig. 2 [13].

In the Binary Occupancy Map, the black regions represent occupied spaces and white regions represent free spaces. The position of the start and end locations is described in terms of x and y meters. The walls of the rooms are the obstacles which the robot should avoid and the free space is the region through which the robot should navigate to reach the target position.

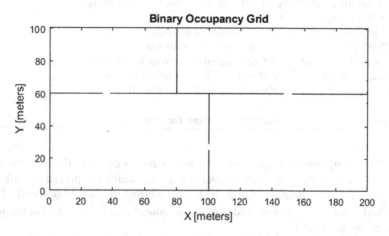

Fig. 2. Binary Occupancy Map of the floor where the robot operates

3.2 Rapidly Exploring Random Tree (RRT) and Rapidly Exploring Random Tree Star (RRT*)

In the *RRT* algorithm, a tree is generated from the starting node. Each time a random node N_R is generated in the free space, the algorithm tries to connect the random node to the nearest node N_N in the tree. If N_R can be connected to N_N according to predefined *connectionDistance*, then tree is expanded by connecting both of them. If not, *RRT* algorithm then generates another node N_B away from N_N by the distance Δd along the line between the random and the nearest node. The tree is then connected to the other new node generated. In this manner, the tree grows until it reaches the goal position.

Pseudocode for Rapidly Exploring Random Tree

N_{start} ← The start position
N_{end} ← The goal position
connectionDistance ← The allowed distance between N_R and N_N
StartTree(N_{start})   // start building the tree from N_{start}
while (valid != 0)   // until the algorithm reaches the goal position
N_R ← RandomNode()   // create a random node
N_N ← NearestNodeInTree(N_R, Tree)
// Identify the node in the tree that is closest to N_R
if (Distance(N_R, N_N) < connectionDistance)
N_R ←N_{new}
else
N_B ← NewNode(N_N,N_R,Δd)
N_B ← N_{new}
// Produce N_B away N_N by the distance Δd in the direction of N_R
if NoObstacles(N_{new}, N_N)
// If there aren't any obstacles between N_N and N_{new}
AddNode(N_{new})   // Add the node to the tree
BuildEdge(N_N, N_{new})   // Create an edge between N_N and N_{new}
if (N_{new} == N_{end})   // if end position has been reached
valid ← 0   // terminate the loop, valid =0
else   // if not
valid ← 1   // continue building the tree

RRT* is an optimized version of *RRT* which produces paths that are shorter in length. *RRT** works the same way as *RRT* but has an additional procedure called the *rewiring procedure* to produce shorter paths. In rewiring, the neighbourhood of each recently added node N_{new} is searched based on a radius value r. The value of radius r is determined by the Eq. (1).

$$r = \gamma (\frac{\log(n)}{n})^{\frac{1}{d}} \tag{1}$$

where d is the dimension of the search space, γ is the constant based on the environment and n is the number of nodes in the tree.

The neighbouring node which will make the cost to reach N_{new} minimum is chosen from all the neighbouring nodes within the radius area. If rewiring the neighbouring node to the node N_{new} decreases the cost to the nodes in the radius area compared to the older costs, the neighbour is rewired to the newly added node and the previous edge connecting the neighbour to its old parent is removed. *RRT** can produce shorter paths in this manner.

Pseudocode for Rapidly Exploring Random Tree Star

$N_{start} \leftarrow$ The start position

$N_{end} \leftarrow$ The goal position

connectionDistance $\leftarrow$ The allowed distance between N_R and N_N

StartTree(N_{start})   // start building the tree from N_{start}

while (valid != 0)   // until the algorithm reaches the goal position

$N_R \leftarrow$ RandomNode()   // create a random node

$N_N \leftarrow$ NearestNodeInTree(N_R, Tree)

// Identify the node in the tree that is closest to N_R

if (Distance(N_R, N_N) < connectionDistance)

$N_R \leftarrow N_{new}$

else

$N_B \leftarrow$ NewNode(N_N,N_R,Δd)

$N_B \leftarrow N_{new}$

// Produce N_B away N_N by the distance Δd in the direction of N_R

if NoObstacles(N_{new}, N_N)

// If there aren't any obstacles between N_N and N_{new}

AddNode(N_{new})   // Add the node to the tree

BuildEdge(N_N, N_{new})   // Create an edge between N_N and N_{new}

$N_{near} \leftarrow$ CheckRadius(N_{new}, r, Tree)

// Identifying neighbouring nodes within the radius from N_{new}

$N_{min} \leftarrow$ ChooseParent(N_{near}, N_{new})

// Choosing the N_{near} node that makes cost to reach N_{new} minimum

Rewire(N_{min}, N_{near}, N_{new}, Tree)

// Check to see if the cost to the nodes in N_{near} is less through N_{new}

// compared to the older costs

// If so, change the parent of N_{min} to N_{new}

if ($N_{new} == N_{end}$)   // if end position has been reached

valid $\leftarrow 0$ // terminate the loop, valid =0

else   // if not

valid $\leftarrow 1$ // continue building the tree

The *Navigation Toolbox* has been used to implement the *RRT* and *RRT** algorithms in *MATLAB*. The steps below outline the procedure followed to simulate *RRT* and *RRT** in *MATLAB* [14, 15]. The path-planning algorithms were simulated on a computer having Intel i7-5500U processor with 2.4 GHz and 8GB RAM using *MATLAB 2019b*.

- The Binary Occupancy Map and the start and final states in terms of x, y and theta were the input parameters necessary for obtaining the path. For example, the start state would be input as (40,20,0) and the end state would be input as (180,80,0) to plan the path between the respective positions. The theta value was always set as 0.
- The *stateSpaceSE2* object was used to store the states and the respective parameters in state-space in the form of x position, y position and theta.

- The *validatorOccupancyMap* validator was used to validate states and motions using the Occupancy Map.
- The *validationDistance* was the interval for sampling between the states and checking the validity of states. It was chosen to be 0.005 m.
- The upper and lower bounds of x, y and theta were specified using the *stateBounds*. The upper and lower bounds of x and y were set to be the limits of the Binary Occupancy Map. Thus, the upper and lower bounds in the x direction were 0 and 200 and the upper and lower bounds in the y direction were 0 and 100 respectively. The theta value was specified such that it could vary between pi to -pi radians.
- First the *RRT* planner then the *RRT* star planner was chosen to find the appropriate path. The *connectionDistance* was chosen to be 50 m.
- The tree developed and the path found were then plotted onto the map.

The computational time taken by the *RRT* and *RRT** algorithms for generating paths between different sets of start and end positions and the length of the paths generated by *RRT* and *RRT** were compared and analysed to choose a suitable path-planning algorithm.

4   Results

The simulation results obtained via *RRT* and *RRT** algorithms are presented in this section. The results obtained using *RRT* and *RRT** are then compared to choose an efficient path-planning algorithm.

The path generated by *RRT* and *RRT** between the start position (40,80) and the target position (180,65) is shown in Fig. 3 and Fig. 4 respectively. From Fig. 3 and Fig. 4, it can be observed that RRT* tends to produce much shorter paths. RRT* produces shorter paths due to the rewiring procedure.

The computational time taken to generate paths for the robot to move from one room (120,80) to another room and extinguish the fires present in that room by travelling to target positions (120,20), (160,10) and (180,40) along with the path length is presented in the following tables. The statistical comparison using the average and the standard deviation of computational time taken using *RRT* and *RRT** algorithms are presented in Table 1 to compare the performances of the two algorithms. Also, the statistical comparison using the average and standard deviation of lengths of the path to reach the targeted position using *RRT* and *RRT** algorithms are presented in Table 2.

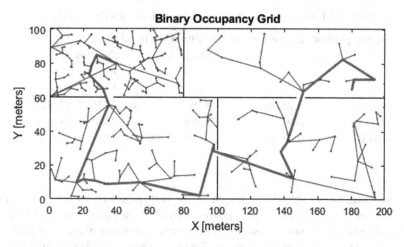

Fig. 3. The path generated using *RRT* between (40,80) and (180,65)

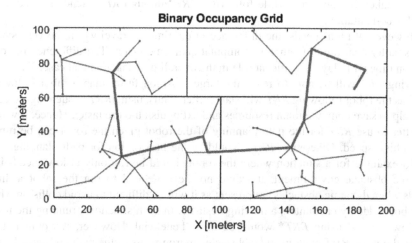

Fig. 4. The path generated using *RRT** between (40,80) and (180,65)

Table 1. Computational time taken to identify required path using RRT and RRT* algorithms

Starting position	Ending position	Computational time taken (s)			
		Average		Standard Deviation	
		RRT	RRT*	RRT	RRT*
(120,80)	(120,20)	0.5401	0.5537	0.3837	0.3971
(120,20)	(160,10)	0.3683	0.3411	0.1423	0.0532
(160,10)	(180,40)	0.3230	0.3570	0.0538	0.0411

Table 2. Length of paths obtained using RRT and RRT* algorithms

Starting position	Ending position	Lengths of the path (m)			
		Average		Standard Deviation	
		RRT	RRT*	RRT	RRT*
(120,80)	(120,20)	148.9847	135.5366	22.5957	22.6028
(120,20)	(160,10)	56.8667	61.3547	22.6800	24.5246
(160,10)	(180,40)	67.6447	49.1537	28.3458	16.8122

As observed from Table 2, the length of the path produced by *RRT** was on an average shorter in length than the path produced by *RRT*. However, since *RRT** spent a considerable amount of time in rewiring, the average computational time of *RRT** was greater compared to *RRT* as observed in Table 1. When the robot is following the computed path, the time taken by the robot while following *RRT** would be less than the time taken by the robot while following *RRT* although *RRT** tends to take more time for computation.

However, at high speeds, the difference in the time to travel would be very small, even smaller than the difference in computational time taken. The difference in computation time will play a significant role in the overall time taken in that case. The robot following *RRT* will be able to reach the target position faster than a robot following *RRT** as the robot following *RRT* will start earlier. Thus, using *RRT* at such high speeds will help to save computational resources and extinguish the fire faster. Hence, it would be better to use *RRT* for the path-planning of the robot given the robot can be run at such a high speed. Otherwise, *RRT** would be the best option for path-planning.

An example for a situation where the robot should be run only at low speeds is a dynamic obstacle environment. It would not be beneficial to run the robot at high speeds when dynamic obstacles are present as it will be difficult to avoid collision when the robot suddenly encounters a moving obstacle. In such situations, running the robot at a lower speed using *RRT** would be more beneficial. However, it would not be practical not use RRT even in static obstacle environments as the path produced by the algorithms has many turns and the robot would not have the proper leverage to turn at high speed. Thus, RRT* is chosen for path-planning in all environments.

5   Conclusion

In this paper, the sampling-based path-planning algorithms *RRT* and *RRT** were compared based on the average computational time taken for path computation and average path length to find a suitable algorithm for the path-planning of a fire-fighting robot. Choosing a suitable path-planning algorithm will help the fire-fighting robot to extinguish the fire in minimum time. Even though *RRT* produced the path faster on an average, *RRT** produced shorter paths. However, the difference in time taken by the robot to reach the destination while following both the computed paths would be very small when the robot is moving at a high speed. Hence a robot following *RRT* would be able to reach the destination faster as *RRT* has a faster computational time on an average. Therefore, *RRT* would be the best option for path planning in a static obstacle environment where the robot can be run at such a high speed. However, it would not be practical to run the robot at such high speeds since the robot will not have the proper leverage to turn. Hence *RRT** is chosen for path-planning in both static as well as dynamic obstacle environments.

6 Future Scope

In order to plan the path of the robot in a dynamic obstacle environment, the speed of the dynamic obstacle must be known. Using laser sensors or image processing techniques, the speed of the moving obstacle should be found. After finding the speed of the moving obstacle, the position of the obstacle in each second should be found. Using this, it can be determined whether the obstacle and the robot will collide and whether it is necessary to re-plan the path using the path-planning algorithm.

References

1. Mittal, S., et al.: CeaseFire: the fire fighting robot. In: 2018 International Conference on Advances in Computing, Communication Control and Networking (ICACCCN), pp. 1143–1146. IEEE (2018)
2. Jia, Y.-Z., et al.: Design and research of small crawler fire fighting robot. In: Chinese Automation Congress (CAC), pp. 4120–4123. IEEE (2018)
3. Suresh, J.: Fire-fighting robot. In: 2017 International Conference on Computational Intelligence in Data Science (ICCIDS), pp. 1–4. IEEE (2017)
4. Shen, D., et al.: Flame detection using deep learning. In: 2018 4th International Conference on Control, Automation and Robotics (ICCAR), pp. 416–420. IEEE (2018)
5. Ramasubramanian, S., Muthukumaraswamy, S.A., Sasikala, A.: Fire detection using artificial intelligence for fire-fighting robots. In: 2020 4th International Conference on Intelligent Computing and Control Systems (ICICCS), pp. 180–185. IEEE (2020)
6. Ramasubramanian, S., Muthukumaraswamy, S.A., Sasikala, A.: Enhancements on the efficacy of firefighting robots through team allocation and path-planning. In: Jeena Jacob, I., Shanmugam, S.K., Piramuthu, S., Falkowski-Gilski, P. (eds.) Data Intelligence and Cognitive Informatics: Proceedings of ICDICI 2020, pp. 139–151. Springer, Singapore (2021). https://doi.org/10.1007/978-981-15-8530-2_11
7. Hidayatullah, A.A., Handayani, A.N., Fuady, M.J.: Performance analysis of A∗ algorithm to determine shortest path of fire fighting robot. In: 2017 International Conference on Sustainable Information Engineering and Technology (SIET), pp. 53–56. IEEE (2017)
8. Hu, Z., et al.: Application of rapidly exploring random tree algorithm in the scene of road network with scheduled tracks. In: 2017 2nd International Conference on Advanced Robotics and Mechatronics (ICARM), pp. 311–315. IEEE (2017)
9. Chen, X., Liu, Y., Hong, X., Wei, X., Huang, Y.: Unmanned ship path planning based on RRT. In: Huang, D.-S., Bevilacqua, V., Premaratne, P., Gupta, P. (eds.) ICIC 2018. LNCS, vol. 10954, pp. 102–110. Springer, Cham (2018). https://doi.org/10.1007/978-3-319-95930-6_11

10. Chao, N., et al.: A sampling-based method with virtual reality technology to provide minimum dose path navigation for occupational workers in nuclear facilities. Prog. Nucl. Energy **100**, 22–32 (2017)
11. Devaurs, D., Simeon, T., Cortes, J.: Parallelizing RRT on large-scale distributed-memory architectures. IEEE Trans. Robot. **29**(2), 571–579 (2013)
12. Tahirovic, A., Magnani, G.: A roughness-based RRT for mobile robot navigation planning. IFAC Proc. Vol. **44**(1), 5944–5949 (2011)
13. Mathworks.com: Create occupancy grid with binary values. https://www.mathworks.com/help/nav/ref/binaryoccupancymap.html
14. Mathworks.com: Create an RRT planner for geometric planning. https://www.mathworks.com/help/nav/ref/plannerRRT.html
15. Mathworks.com: Create an optimal RRT path planner (RRT*). https://www.mathworks.com/help/nav/ref/plannerRRTstar.html

Automatic Image Colorization Using GANs

Rashi Dhir[1]([✉]) ⓘ, Meghna Ashok[1] ⓘ, Shilpa Gite[1] ⓘ,
and Ketan Kotecha[2] ⓘ

[1] Symbiosis International University, Near Lupin Research Park, Lavale,
Mulshi, Pune, Maharashtra, India
{rashi.dhir,meghna.ashok,shilpa.gite}@sitpune.edu.in
[2] Symbiosis Center for Applied Artificial Intelligence (SCAAI),
Symbiosis International University, Near Lupin Research Park, Lavale,
Mulshi, Pune, Maharashtra, India
head@scaai.siu.edu.in

Abstract. Automatic image colorization as a process has been studied extensively over the past 10 years with importance given to its many applications in grayscale image colorization, aged/degraded image restoration etc. In our project, we aim to generalize this process using a Generative Adversarial Network (GAN) that takes fixed size black and white images as input and obtains corresponding coloured images of the same size as output, to demonstrate GAN working and superiority. We use a special type of GAN called Conditional Generative Adversarial Network which takes a specific type of input as opposed to vectors from random probability distributions, and we primarily work on the CIFAR-10 dataset. Our goal was to build a successful CGAN model using limited resources that utilizes Google Colaboratory, Strided Convolutions and Batch Normalization to colorize images. Our resulting model is essentially a base model that beginners and students can implement and embellish to further GAN understanding and techniques.

Keywords: Deep learning · Computer Vision · Architectures · Image processing · Generative Adversarial Networks · Convolutional Neural Networks

1 Introduction

Computer Vision has been around since the 1950s and is one of the most advanced applications of Artificial Intelligence utilized in today's world [3]. The success of Computer Vision is solely due to the massive amount of data that has been generated in recent years after the advent of Machine Learning. Computer Vision is intertwined with Deep learning resulting in a wide variety of applications, through Convoluted Neural Networks (CNNs). Deep neural networks and Convolutional Neural Networks have already been extensively used in the domain of image processing and computer vision change. Many image colorization problems and applications have been solved using these technologies, but there is one major issue with it. If a small amount of noise is added in these networks, the results go haywire. For instance, supposing an image of a dog is to be classified, when noise is added to the image (even of a small magnitude) it

© Springer Nature Singapore Pte Ltd. 2021
K. K. Patel et al. (Eds.): icSoftComp 2020, CCIS 1374, pp. 15–26, 2021.
https://doi.org/10.1007/978-981-16-0708-0_2

leads to the dog image being identified as an ostrich. This led us to explore Generative Adversarial Networks as an alternative to automatically colorizing gray-scaled images.

GANs are a fairly novel subject in the domain of research. It is increasingly capturing researchers' interest due to the advantages it brings along which we have mentioned throughout. The discerning feature is that we have attempted to solve the age-old problem of image colorization using GANs with bare minimum parameters and requirements. We still got promising results which can be improved exponentially by scaling up our development environment. Although CNN models are extremely efficient with object detection, classification and a vast number of image processing techniques, they are hungry for data and this can moreover pose a problem when there is a limit to the amount of data available. GANs cover up this shortcoming very gracefully as they are capable of generating their own data which is in agreement with the original input data. In our study, we implement a Conditional GAN model on a small scale that successfully colorizes images.

2   Survey on Existing Techniques of Image Processing

2.1   Image Colorization

Image Colorization using Computer-assisted Process was brought out by Wilson Markle in 1970, his idea was to add color in the black and white TV programs or movies. In the Computer-assisted process a color mask is manually painted for at least one reference frame in a shot as a marked image then motion detection and tracking are appealed on marked images, which allows the colors to be automatically assigned to other surrounds in regions where no motion occurs and sometimes it requires manual fixing.

GANs have been extensively used in the field of automatic image colorization in recent times. In one such development, TIC-GANs were made use of which is an extension of Cycle GANs itself. It solves the ambiguity arising in coloring the gray scaled images by forming a bridge between thermal infrared and RGB images [9]. GANs have successfully made their way into healthcare as well, wherein it is deemed suitable for identifying skin lesions which indicate the onset of melanoma (type of skin cancer). The achieve this style-based GANs are used and a classification model is built using transfer learning model for the analysis of skin images [13]. Moreover, Mohammad Mahdi Johari and Hamid Behroozi in their paper [5] have used parallel specialized networks, as opposed to traditional single model networks to identify similar color themes and contexts and produce high quality images using a Cycle-Consistent Generative Adversarial Network.

2.2   Generative Adversarial Networks

The original Generative Adversarial Networks paper by Ian Goodfellow [3] defines the GAN framework and architecture, and discusses its 'non-saturating' loss function. This paper also derives the discriminator, which competed with the generator in the model.

The paper also demonstrates the empirical effectiveness of GAN on the CIFAR-10, MNIST, and TFD image datasets.

3 Comparison of Relevant Works

(See Table 1).

Table 1. Comparison of relevant technologies in image processing

No	Reference paper	Methodology	Limitations
1	Generative adversarial nets [3] by Ian Goodfellow in 2014	Internal working and concept of GANs	Generator and discriminator must be well synchronized during training in order to avoid "Helvetica scenario" There is no explicit representation of p(x) in the model
2	Conditional Generative Adversarial Nets [11] by Mehdi Mirza, Simon Osindero in 2014	How a condition is set on to both the generator and discriminator	Introductory results shown, but demonstration of the potential of conditional adversarial nets and its applications is depicted
3	Self-Attention Generative Adversarial Networks [16] by Han Zhang, Ian Goodfellow, Dimitris Metaxas, Augustus Odena in 2018	Model implementing attention-driven, long-range dependency modeling for image generation	Lack of data-set hence, lack of performance/stability. There is a more theoretical model
4	Emotional image color transfer via deep learning by Da Liu, Yaxi Jiang, Min Pei, Shiguang Liu in 2018 [9]	Mitigates the problem of unnatural coloring taking place in colorizing problems	Training is time consuming
5	Thermal infrared colorization via conditional generative adversarial network [6] by Xiaodong Kuang, Jianfei Zhu, Xiubao Sui, Yuan Liu, Chengwei in 2019	The method uses a composite objective function to produce finely detailed and	Encounters poor results with blurry or distorted image details
6	Context-aware colorization of gray-scale images utilizing a cycle-consistent generative adversarial network architecture [5] by Mohammad Mahdi Johari, Hamid Behroozi in 2020	Parallel colorization models introduced as opposed to traditional single models	Does not deal with pixel-to-pixel mapping

(continued)

Table 1. (*continued*)

No	Reference paper	Methodology	Limitations
7	Emotional image color transfer via deep learning [19], Liu Da, Jiang Yaxi, Pei Min, Liu Shiguang, 2018	Considers semantic information of images to solve unnatural color problems in images	Instability due to limited train and test sets
8	Optimization based grayscale image colorization [18], Nie Dongdong, Ma Qinyong, Ma Lizhuang, Xiao Shuangjiu, 2007	Optimization approach to colorization that reduces computational time and reduces color diffusions	Spatial-temporal approach to be developed for maintaining temporal coherence

4 Basics of Generative Adversarial Networks (GANs)

4.1 Training of Discriminator

The discriminator looks at the original images and image generated separately. It makes a distinction about whether the input Discriminator image is real or created. D(X) is the probability of input being true, i.e. P (Input Class = actual Instance Data). Just like a deep network, we train the discriminator for classification. If the input is real, then we require D(x) = 1. If not, it should hold a Nil value. Through this process, the discriminator identifies features that contribute to real data instances (Fig. 1).

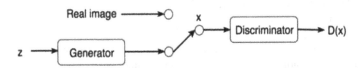

Fig. 1. Training discriminator

The discriminator sends out a value D(x) which indicates the chance of x being a real data instance. Our goal is to optimize the opportunity to recognize real data instances as real and generated instances as fake, that is to say, the maximum likelihood of the observed data. For cost choice, cross-entropy is used.

Discriminator Mathematics:

$$\max V(D) = E_{x \sim pdata(x)}[\log D(x)] + E_{z \sim pz(z)}[\log(1 - D(G(Z)))]$$

where,

$E_{x \sim pdata(x)}[\log D(x)]$ recognizes real images better

$E_{z \sim pz(z)}[\log(1 - D(G(Z)))]$ recognizes generated images better

Goal: Optimize G that can fool the discriminator the most.

4.2   Training of Generator

We construct images by the generator with D(x) = 1. Following which, we train the generator for data production instances which are susceptible to what the discriminator feels is true. On the generator side, it wants the model to have its objective function to trick the discriminator, produce images with the maximum possible value of D(x). Generator Mathematics: min $V(G) = E_{z \sim pz(z)}[\log(1 - D(G(Z)))]$.

4.3   Simultaneous Training of Generator and Discriminator

When both objective functions are established, learning takes place together using the opposing downward gradient. We patch device generator parameters and perform a single gradient descent iteration on a discriminator using the images that are real and generated. Then we switch hands. Fix the discriminator and train the generator to another version. We train all networks in turns until the generator generates images of good quality (Fig. 2).

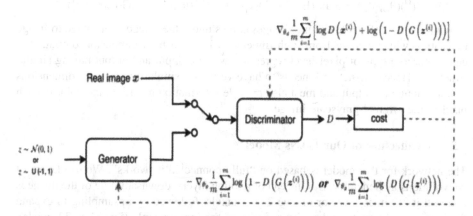

Fig. 2. Training of generator

4.4   Conditional GANs

In traditional GANs, the generator takes noise vectors of random probability distributions as input. The purpose of GAN in our project is to colorize i.e. add three channels (RGB) with relevant intensities of each color channel to black and white images i.e. images containing only one channel, hence we cannot use random distributions as our input.

Therefore, we use Conditional GANs to address this problem, which accepts grayscale images (with one intensity channel) as input (i.e. G(0 z | x), mathematically). The discriminator input is also altered to be compatible with the conditional GANs. It takes as input a pair of grayscale image and generated image, and grayscale image and original image and judges if the pair is fake i.e. produced by the generator or real i.e. original image (Fig. 3).

Conditional General Adversarial Network

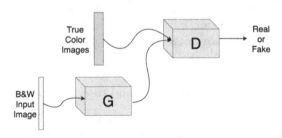

Fig. 3. Conditional GANs

Our final cost functions are as follows with above modifications.
Conditional GAN Mathematics:

Min $J^{(G)}(\theta_D, \theta_G) = \min - E_z [\log(D(G(0_z|x)))] + \lambda\|G(0_z|x) - y\|_1$

Max $J^{(D)}(\theta_D, \theta_G) = \max (E_y [\log(D(y|x))] + E_z [\log(1 - D(G(0_z|x)|x))])$

Colorization of single channel images comes under the category of Image to Image translation with mapping from high dimension input to high dimension output. It is equivalent to a type of pixel level regression with the input and output having similar structures. Hence the network needs to have very high similarity of spatial dimensions of both input and output and must also provide information regarding the color to each pixel in the original grayscale image.

4.5 Architecture of Our GANs Model

The network for this model is based on "fully connected networks". We use layers of convolutions in Generator. But instead of pooling layers, downsampling of the image is done till it becomes a vector of size 2×2 pixels, followed by upsampling to expand the compressed part to make it to the size of the input sample (i.e. 32×32 pixels), similar to the expanding encoding networks and compressed decoding networks in Encoder-Decoder models. This strategy helps in training the network without consuming large amounts of memory.

The generator takes an input X as a grayscale image having dimensions $(32 \times 32 \times 1)$. It is initially downsampled with a kernel of size 1 and stride 1. After this layer, it is subsequently compressed to image to size (2×2) with a kernel of size 2 and strides 2. This operation is repeated four times after the initial layer, resulting in a matrix $(2 \times 2 \times 512)$.

The expansion stages consist of upsampling of the matrix with kernel size 2 and strides 2 except the last layer using conv2D_transpose. Concatenation of i and n − i layers are done to preserve the structural integrity of the image. In the first and second expansive layers, dropout of scale 0.5 is done to introduce noise for robust training of Generator and improved generalization. Batch normalization is done for better training. In our model, we used LeakyReLU with slope of 0.2 as it has shown better performance than ReLU activation function. In the last layer convolution with kernel size 1 and strides 1 is done to construct an image of dimension (32 × 32 × 3) along with "tanh" activation function as it has shown to have better performance than linear activation functions. Final output is a matrix containing values from −1 to 1. The model is trained to minimize the cosine distance between the predicted and original image (Fig. 4).

Generator Architecture plan:

C1	[32,32,1]	->	[32,32,64]
C2	[32,32,64]	->	[16,16,128]
C3	[16,16,128]	->	[8,8,256]
C4	[8,8,256]	->	[4,4,512]
C4	[4,4,512]	->	[2,2,512]
DC0	[2,2,512]	->	[4,4,512]
DC1	[4,4,512]	->	[8,8,256]
DC2	[8,8,256]	->	[16,16,128]
DC3	[16,16,128]	->	[32,32,64]
CC4	[32,32,64]	->	[32,32,3]

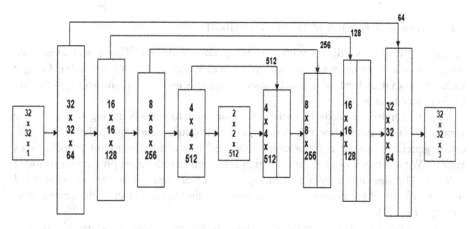

Fig. 4. Discriminator architecture of our system

Discriminator architecture begins with concatenation of grayscale image (single-channeled image) and the predicted, or the grayscale image and the ground truth image on the channel axis (axis = 3), hence it forms a colored image. We then perform downsampling of the matrix successively using a convolutional layer with filter size of (2 × 2) and strides equal to 2. Each layer has Leaky ReLU activation function with slope 0.2 and Batch Normalization is performed at every layer to stabilize the learning process. The last layer is flattened followed by a hidden layer containing 128 units, which is connected to an output layer containing 1 unit. Sigmoid activation function is used in the last layer which gives the probability of the input image belonging to predicted image class or ground truth image class, i.e. D(x).

Discriminator Architecture plan:

C1	[32,32,ch]	->	[16,16,64]
C2	[16,16,64]	->	[8,8,128]
C3	[8,8,128]	->	[4,4,256]
C4	[4,4,256]	->	[4,4,512]

Total params: 5,517,828
Trainable params: 5,513,988
Non-trainable params: 3,840.

4.6   Experimental and Development Environment

GANs differ invariably from other machine learning models, which calls for a different kind of setup as well. We have used Python as our programming language as it also provides in-built libraries for carrying out the training as well as deployment such as Scikit Learn, Tensorflow, Keras, PyTorch. Since, training is highly computationally expensive, we have made used of the GPU services provided by Google Colaboratory which was very convenient and free of cost which is really useful for students.

4.7   Training Strategies of Our GANs Model

Adam's optimizer is utilized with a learning rate of 0.0001. The model uses open source python libraries such as Tensorflow and Keras and is trained using Google Colaboratory GPU. LeakyReLU activation function is used as it is shown to give better performance than ReLU.

The Generator succeeds in fooling the discriminator into believing that the same generated output is real hence it generates similar outputs each time. Hence, the generator generates similar outputs every time and hence the generation process lacks variety. We use batch normalization which is proven to reduce the probability of mode collapse. The size of our batch is 50 images. However, batch normalization is avoided in the first layer of the discriminator and generator and the last layer of the generator as suggested by [3].

As proposed by [11], Strided convolutions are used instead of spatial pooling. Hence, rather than depending upon fixed downsampling and upsampling, convolution layers with increased stride allow models to learn its own upsampling and downsampling. This technique has shown to upgrade the training performance and helps the network to learn important invariances with convolution layers only.

5   Results

Training of GAN models is complicated and differs significantly from other machine learning models, it is difficult to identify if it is performing upto the mark but easier to know when it is going in an unanticipated direction. Our aim is to keep the discriminator accuracy as large i.e. closer to 100% and simultaneously ensure that the generator loss does not reach zero. If so happens, it indicates that the discriminator is not performing the job well. Below is a graph showing generator and discriminator accuracy losses (Fig. 5).

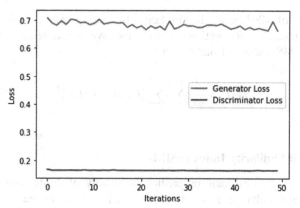

<Figure size 432x288 with 0 Axes>

Fig. 5. Generator and discriminator loss

Discriminator loss is an indicator of the degree of closeness of generated data with respect to the real data. In our case, the real data are the original colored images and the generated data are the colored images generated by the generator. The lesser the discriminator loss, the more is the efficiency of the generator. If the loss value goes below 0, i.e. negative it indicates overfitting. Additionally, the generator loss should not be 100%, as it would signify that it is being successful in befooling the discriminator with fake images. Minimax loss is used in the original GANS paper by Ian Goodfellow [3]. The generator and discriminator are the two game players and they take turns updating their model weights. Min and Max refer to the maximization of the discriminator loss and the minimization of the generator loss. The generator minimizes the below function while the discriminator maximizes it.

Minimax Loss:

Min $J^{(G)}(\theta D, \theta G) = \min - E_z [\log(D(G(0z|x)))] + \lambda\|G(0z|x) - y\|1$

Max $J^{(P)}(\theta_D, \theta_G) = \max (E_y [\log(D(y|x))] + E_z [\log(1 - D(G(0_z|x)|x))])$.

The discriminator seeks to increase the probability associated with the real and generated images. The model is fit while trying to minimize the log loss or average binary cross entropy.

As depicted by the above graph, the discriminator loss is expected to rapidly decrease to a value close to zero, where it remains in a somewhat stable fashion during training. The generator loss is expected to continuously decrease or decrease up to zero during training. Convergence failure was encountered multiple times, which can be resolved by changing optimizers, increasing learning rates, changing kernel rates and introducing batch normalization. The more we train the model, the generator and discriminator losses must converge to some stable permanent numbers, i.e. a recognized pattern.

5.1 Mean Squared Error (MSE) Equation

Lesser the value of MSE, more the similarity. Increasing values imply lesser similarities and this increases proportionally with the average difference between pixel intensities. The MSE score of our model is 1.44

$$MSE = \frac{1}{mn} \sum_{i=0}^{m-1} \sum_{j=0}^{n-1} [I(i,j) - K(i,j)]^2 \tag{1}$$

5.2 Structural Similarity Index (SSIM)

SSIM index is used to estimate or predict the quality of digital images and digital media. It depicts the change in structural information of the images. SSIM value can range between 1 and −1, wherein 1 denotes perfect similarity. It can be found in scikit-image. The SSIM score of our model is 0.79.

$$\text{SSIM}(x,y) = \frac{(2\mu_x\mu_y + c_1)(2\sigma_{xy} + c_2)}{(\mu_x^2 + \mu_y^2 + c_1)(\sigma_x^2 + \sigma_y^2 + c_2)} \tag{2}$$

Post training, once the model acquires good enough accuracy, we discard the discriminator as it was only used to keep a check on generator's performance. As soon as it is learnt that the model is capable of generating in very close resemblance with the real data, the discriminator's job is done and is thus removed. Now, the GANs model is capable to be deployed and run on unseen and new data as well.

5.3 Findings on Our Dataset

Our project involved use of conditional GAN for colorization of black and white images. While implementing our project, we realized that architecture of a neural network as well as careful selection of hyper parameters act as a bottleneck to any deep learning project's success. We realized that even minor changes in such aspects of GAN can massively influence performance of GAN or any neural network in general.

In this project, we were successful in automatically colorizing grayscale images using Generative adversarial networks, to a visual degree which is acceptable. The images of CIPHER 10 with synthetic colors by GAN looked reasonably well and similar to the original images. There were some incidences where the model misunderstood the blue sky for grass during the training process, but with further training, it was successful in coloring green color for grasses. We observed that the model faced unusual problems with red color, which it learnt after many epochs as compared to other colors (Fig. 6).

Fig. 6. The above images are the result of GAN training. From top to bottom: single-channeled image, GAN generated image, Ground truth color image. (Color figure online)

6 Conclusion and Future Directions

Generative adversarial networks are being used far and wide in medical imagery, self-driving cars, image translation and many more such areas. We tried to do the automatic colorization of grayscale images using Generative adversarial networks. The images of CIPHER 10 generated by the GANs with synthetic colors looked reasonably well and similar to the original images which supports our implementation. However, initially there were some incidences where the model misunderstood the sea water for grass during the training process, but with further training, it was successful in properly identifying the color green. Moreover, we observed that the model also faced an unusual problem with the color red which it took longer to learn than other colors so it could also be explored further. Though we have trained the model for single channel images, the model works well with black and white images as well.

Though GANs are relatively latest areas, it has been significantly working well in applications such as Image processing and analysis, text to image translation, generating pictures of people's faces and so on, which gives directions of further exploration into different application areas. Our model can be extended to video formats as well so that GANs would be made further interesting. It can also be used on converting old movies and videos to a colorized version. Furthermore, GANs model will prove to be beneficial in case of restoring distorted pictures which have tarnished due to the effects of time, mishandling etc. Thus, GANs have a potential to fit into a wide range of applications and make image processing more interesting.

References

1. Brock, A., Donahue, J., Simonyan, K.: Large scale GAN training for high fidelity natural image synthesis. arXiv preprint arXiv:1809.11096 (2018)
2. Child, R., Gray, S., Radford, A., Sutskever, I.: Generating long sequences with sparse transformers. arXiv preprint arXiv:1904.10509 (2019)
3. Goodfellow, I., et al.: Generative adversarial nets. In: Advances in Neural Information Processing Systems, pp. 2672–2680 (2014)
4. Isola, P., Zhu, J.Y., Zhou, T., Efros, A.A.: Image-to-image translation with conditional adversarial networks. In: Proceedings of the IEEE Conference on Computer Vision and Pattern Recognition, pp. 1125–1134 (2017)
5. Johari, M.M., Behroozi, H.: Context-aware colorization of gray-scale images utilizing a cycle-consistent generative adversarial network architecture. Neurocomputing **407**, 94–104 (2020). https://doi.org/10.1016/j.neucom.2020.04.042
6. Kuang, X., et al.: Thermal infrared colorization via conditional generative adversarial network. Infrared Phys. Technol. **107**, 103338 (2020)
7. Ledig, C., et al.: Photo-realistic single image super-resolution using a generative adversarial network. In: Proceedings of the IEEE Conference on Computer Vision and Pattern Recognition, pp. 4681–4690 (2017)
8. Ling, W., Dyer, C., Yu, L., Kong, L., Yogatama, D., Young, S.: Relative Pixel Prediction for Autoregressive Image Generation (2019)
9. Liu, D., Jiang, Y., Pei, M., Liu, S.: Emotional image color transfer via deep learning. Pattern Recogn. Lett. **110**, 16–22 (2018)
10. Liu, S., Zhang, X.: Automatic grayscale image colorization using histogram regression. Pattern Recogn. Lett. **33**(13), 1673–1681 (2012)
11. Mirza, M., Osindero, S.: Conditional generative adversarial nets. arXiv preprint arXiv:1411.1784 (2014)
12. Park, T., Liu, M.Y., Wang, T.C., Zhu, J.Y.: GauGAN: semantic image synthesis with spatially adaptive normalization. In: ACM SIGGRAPH 2019 Real-Time Live!, p. 1 (2019)
13. Qin, Z., Liu, Z., Zhu, P., Xue, Y.: A GAN-based image synthesis method for skin lesion classification. Comput. Methods Programs Biomed. **195**, 105568 (2020)
14. Radford, A., Metz, L., Chintala, S.: Unsupervised representation learning with deep convolutional generative adversarial networks. arXiv preprint arXiv:1511.06434 (2015)
15. Wiley, V., Lucas, T.: Computer vision and image processing: a paper review. Int. J. Artif. Intell. Res. **2**(1), 29–36 (2018)
16. Zhang, H., Goodfellow, I., Metaxas, D., Odena, A.: Self-attention generative adversarial networks. In: International Conference on Machine Learning, pp. 7354–7363, May 2019
17. Zhang, J., Zhong, F., Cao, G., Qin, X.: ST-GAN: unsupervised facial image semantic transformation using generative adversarial networks. In: ACML, pp. 248–263, November 2017
18. Nie, D., Ma, Q., Ma, L., Xiao, S.: Optimization based grayscale image colorization, 9 March 2007. https://www.sciencedirect.com/science/article/abs/pii/S0167865507000700. Accessed 29 June 2020
19. Liu, D., Jiang, Y., Pei, M., Liu, S.: Emotional image color transfer via deep learning. https://www.sciencedirect.com/science/article/abs/pii/S0167865518300941. Accessed 29 June 2020

Gujarati Task Oriented Dialogue Slot Tagging Using Deep Neural Network Models

Rachana Parikh[✉] and Hiren Joshi

Gujarat University, Ahmedabad, India
{rachanaparikh, hdjoshi}@gujaratuniversity.ac.in

Abstract. In this paper, the primary focus is of Slot Tagging of Gujarat Dialogue, which enables the Gujarati language communication between human and machine, allowing machines to perform given task and provide desired output. The accuracy of tagging entirely depends on bifurcation of slots and word embedding. It is also very challenging for a researcher to do proper slot tagging as dialogue and speech differs from human to human, which makes the slot tagging methodology more complex. Various deep learning models are available for slot tagging for the researchers, however, in the instant paper it mainly focuses on Long Short-Term Memory (LSTM), Convolutional Neural Network - Long Short-Term Memory (CNN-LSTM) and Long Short-Term Memory – Conditional Random Field (LSTM-CRF), Bidirectional Long Short-Term Memory (BiLSTM), Convolutional Neural Network - Bidirectional Long Short-Term Memory (CNN-BiLSTM) and Bidirectional Long Short-Term Memory – Conditional Random Field (BiLSTM-CRF). While comparing the above models with each other, it is observed that BiLSTM models performs better than LSTM models by a variation ∼2% of its F1-measure, as it contains an additional layer which formulates the word string to traverse from backward to forward. Within BiLSTM models, BiLSTM-CRF has outperformed other two Bi-LSTM models. Its F1-measure is better than CNN-BiLSTM by 1.2% and BiLSTM by 2.4%.

Keywords: Spoken Language Understanding (SLU) · Long Short-Term Memory (LSTM) · Slot tagging · Bidirectional Long Short-Term Memory (BiLSTM) · Convolutional Neural Network - Bidirectional Long Short-Term Memory (CNN-BiLSTM) · Bidirectional Long Short-Term Memory (BiLSTM-CRF)

1 Introduction

Semantic interpretation of task is of utmost importance in a task oriented dialogue system. Dialogues are converted into sequence labels for any machine to understand the language. Proper sequencing increases the output accuracy. Language understanding ensures identifying domain, determining intent and filling slots so that machine could function based on the aforesaid identifications. Domain identification and intent determination are treated as classification problem. Domain classification method includes Hidden Markov Model (HMM), support Vector Machine (SVM), Conditional Random Field (CRF) and neural networks. These algorithms have already

© Springer Nature Singapore Pte Ltd. 2021
K. K. Patel et al. (Eds.): icSoftComp 2020, CCIS 1374, pp. 27–37, 2021.
https://doi.org/10.1007/978-981-16-0708-0_3

achieved state of art performances [1]. The deep convex network (DCN) gave promising result on semantic utterance classification [2]. Linear SVM gave better performance for semantic feature classification [3]. Slot tagging can also be considered as sequential labelling, through that proper sequencing of word is done for any given sentence. User dialogues with N words to N sequence tags are converted through slot tagging. Labelling of each user dialogues is done to get the desired output. HMM/CFG composite models [4], conditional random fields (CRFs) [5, 6] and support vector machines (SVMs) [7] are widely used standard models for resolving the slot tagging problems. However, researchers in the recent past explore deep learning approaches [8, 9] as they provide better accuracy then traditional methods, as these methods also avoid handcrafted features.

For Gujarati language, task oriented dialogue annotated data is scarcely available. POS tagger developed for Gujarati dialect gave accuracy of 92% [10], later on NER Tagger was developed which identified Person, Organization, Location and others using CRF which gave accuracy of 83% [11]. In the same manner researchers have also done work in Hindi for Name Entity Recognition. Hindi name entity recognition was done using BiLSTM and was compared with RNN and RNN-LSTM by researchers and they have achieved ∼77.5% F1-score. [12]. Hindi name entity recognition was done using conditional LSTM and BiLSTM and researchers achieved 74% F1-score [13], similarly Hindi name entity recognition was done using deep neural network and researchers achieved F1-score 64.5 [14]. Using traditional method for slot tagging like CRF has major disadvantage that researchers should have in-depth knowledge of language, as features are classified manually, to ensure quality of features researchers need to have language expertise. To implement deep neural models, tagged data is required, which is scarcely available in Gujarati Language as compared to other languages. Researchers achieved ∼96% F1-score on ATIS English airlines data set, using Recurrent Neural Network (RNN) and combination of RNN and CRF (R-CRF) [15]. Subsequently, many researchers used variation of RNN, which includes LSTM and BiLSTM for sequence labeling, wherein, they achieved accuracy of ∼97% on CoNLL2000 data set [16]. Looking at the accuracy achieved using deep-neural network approaches in other languages [15–17], and because of traditional method disadvantages, in this paper we have implemented and compared Gujarati slot tagging using deep learning models like LSTM, CNN-LSTM, LSTM-CRF, BiLSTM, CNN-BiLSTM and BiLSTM-CRF. The result shows that BiLSTM models outperforms LSTM. BiLSTM-CRF outperforms other two BiLSTM models for Gujarati slot tagging when compared among themselves.

Segment-wise classification of the paper is as follows: Segment 2 describes the slot tagger, Segment 3 gives an overview of approaches to slot tagging. Furthermore, Segment 4 describes, Deep Neural Network models for slot tagger experiment on Gujarati task oriented dialogue and Segment 5 deliberates on paper conclusion.

2 Slot Tagger

Slot tagging is a sequence-tagging method. Slot tagging focuses on identifying a particular information depending on the domain and intent. It can tag an entity or any other information depending on intent.

In a goal oriented system, it should automatically identify the logical and required semantic pointers from the human dialogue or utterances and fetch us desired output. This would result into a machine understanding human language model (Table 1).

Table 1. Tagged Sentence Example with its Intent

Sentence	મુંબઈ	નું	સૌથી	વધારે	તાપમાન	જણાવો
Slot	B-Loc	O	B-Weather-Attribute	I-Weather-Attribute	I-Weather-Attribute	O
Intent	Weather					

Aforementioned table shows an example including slot tags and intent. This example is about weather forecast considering it as intent. Slot tagging comprises of the in/out/begin (IOB) representation. In this example, મુંબઈ (Mumbai) is a location slot value. Even the aforementioned dialogue has weather-attribute, which is required to check highest temperature of that location, સૌથીવધારેતાપમાન (maximum temperature), wherein weather-attribute is specified as the slot values.

The base for slot tagging is the input from the user in the form of a dialogue. This dialogue is a logical representation of series of words (W). Slot tagging process includes assignment of tags (S) to each of the words in the given dialogue from the user. Traditional methods for Language Understanding systems allots appropriate slots which includes the maximum posteriori probability $p(S \mid W)$. This process provides the desired output to find the semantic representation by slot sequencing.

In slot tagging one-hot encoded vector, uses one to represent a particular word in a vector and rest of the elements in the vector are zero. This vector indicates the input word value, which is defined as word embedding. These generated word embedding vectors are then provided to BiLSTM for training and testing purposes.

3 Approaches for Slot Tagging

3.1 LSTM

Long Shor-Term Memory is a deep recurrent neural network with ability to remember selected data for longer duration [24]. LSTM model consists of number of cells. Data flows from one cell state to another. Each cell pass on two states, which is cell state (c) and the hidden state (h) to next cell. It's the responsibility of cell to remember information, this is achieved using three gates present in each cell, the output gate (o), forget gate (f), and input gate (i). The forget gate mainly functions to discard unwanted data from cell state. The input gate functions to add new information and the output gate is responsible to generate relevant information from given input and previous state values. Given the input sequence A_1, A_2, A_3, ..., A_n the output vector Y_n is generated. The A_t is a input at time t. W_{ai}, W_{hi}, W_{si}, W_{af}, W_{hf}, W_{sf}, W_{ao}, W_{ho}, W_{so} are weights and bi, bo, bc, bf are bias used for computing. The output of LSTM hidden layer is computed using following formula [25]:

$$ig_t = \sigma(W_{ai}A_t + W_{hi}\,h_{t-1} + W_{si}\,cg_{t-1} + b_i) \tag{1}$$

$$fg_t = \sigma(W_{af}, A_t + W_{hf}\,h_{t-1} + W_{sf}\,cg_{t-1} + b_f) \tag{2}$$

$$cg_t = fg_t\,cg_{t-1} + ig_t\,\tanh(W_{as}A_t + W_{hs}\,h_{t-1} + b_c) \tag{3}$$

$$og_t = \sigma(W_{ao}\,A_t + W_{ho}\,h_{t-1} + W_{so}cg_t + b_o) \tag{4}$$

$$h_t = og_t\,\tanh(cg_t) \tag{5}$$

LSTM models were used for neural speech recognition [26] and for entity recognition from clinical text [27]. Figure 1 shows the working of LSTM model for Gujarati Language Dialogue.

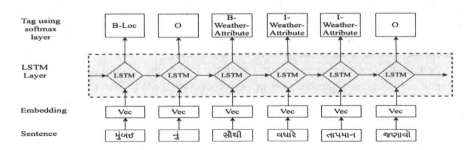

Fig. 1. LSTM model for tagging a Gujarati dialogue

3.2 BiLSTM

Bidirectional LSTM model uses word embedding features of user utterance from left to right & right to left i.e. from both the directions. This would help in achieving better accuracy [28]. The Fig. 2 shows the Bidirectional LSTM model working for Gujarati Dialogue. If the input is of length M it reads the features in N time. At particular time t, it takes inputted word at time T (A_t). Two internal states are maintained by this model to generate output sequence (Yt). The internal states are hidden (h_t) and cell (cg_t) at particular time-step T. To train BiLSTM back-propagation through time (BPTT) is used [29]. The advantage of BiLSTM over LSTM model is that it unfolds the h_t at each time step. In our implementation the entire dialogue is parsed from left position to right position and right position to left position.

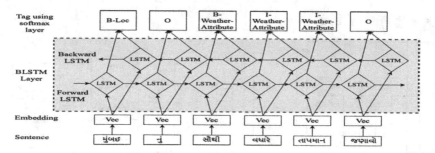

Fig. 2. BiLSTM model for tagging a Gujarati dialogue

3.3 BiLSTM-CRF

BiLSTM-CRF network model is a composition of BiLSTM network model and a CRF network model, which is more particularly described in Fig. 3. In this network model, the sentence features are inputted, wherein, firstly, it is provided to forward LSTM layer from beginning to end and thereafter to backward LSTM layer, from end to beginning. BiLSTM layer generate a vector of weight of each output tag. CRF layer is then provided generated vector as input. CRF layer learn some constraints on provided vector at the time of training. On the basis of this learned constraints CRF layer performs the final valid predictions. This prominent feature helps in increasing the accuracy which is further shown [32].

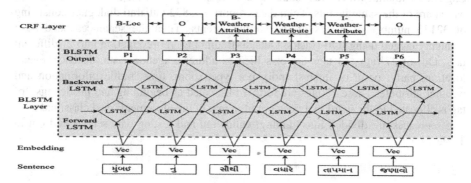

Fig. 3. BiLSTM-CRF model for tagging a Gujarati Dialogue

3.4 CNN BiLSTM

CNN-BiLSTM model comprises of CNN and BiLSTM network model. CNN layer is used for learning features of input data. CNN layer consists of two sub layers i.e. Convolutional and Max pooling layer. Convolutional layer extracts the characteristic features of the inputted data. This feature vector is passed to max pooling layer for compressing of filter. This is the most widely used methodology to perform pooling of filter. [33, 34].The feature vector generated by max pooling layer is then passed onto BiLSTM layer [35]. The working of CNN-BiLSTM model for Gujarati Dialogue is shown in Fig. 4.

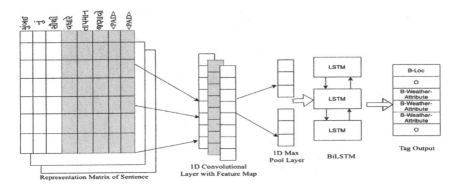

Fig. 4. CNN-BiLSTM model for tagging a Gujarati Dialogue

4   Deep Neural Network Model's Slot Tagger Experiment and Results on Gujarati Task Oriented Dialogue

4.1   Corpus

The Gujarati dialogue data have been collected keeping base as Stanford Natural Language Processing (NLP) dialogues of driver-agent, mainly consisting of 3 intent i.e. Schedule, Weather and Navigate. However, only driver's dialogues are translated from English to Gujarati which are around 1200. Remaining part of the data is self-generated which are of the same intents. Total data comprises 3832 Gujarati dialogues consisting of 32133 number of words of the similar intents. Then the sentences have been manually tagged using IOB (Inside-Outside-Beginning) representation into 27 different tags. Out of 27 tags, 13 tags are classified as address, agenda, date, distance, event, location, party, point of interest (poi), poi type, room, time, traffic information and weather attribute. These 13 tags are further bifurcated as beginning and inside tags. 'o' tag is allocated to the word that does not fit in any of the aforementioned classified tags. The sentences are divided into training, validation and testing data sets as laid out in Table 2.

Table 2. Sizes of Sentences and tokens for Training, Validation and Testing Data Set

Training	No. of Sentences	2760
	No. of Tokens	23281
Validation	No. of Sentences	306
	No. of Tokens	2800
Testing	No. of Sentences	766
	No. of Tokens	6052

4.2 Word Embedding

It is very crucial to improve the performance while slot/sequence tagging is performed. In the instant research the word embedding is created of 1620 vocabulary size. Each word are converted into 50 dimensional vectors.

4.3 Implementation of Deep Neural Network Models and Results

For Gujarati task oriented dialogue slot tagging, two main deep neural models are implemented i.e. LSTM and BiLSTM. To perform slot tagging using deep neural network model, word embedding is generated for each token of the dialogues. The generated word embedding is further fed to deep neural network model for training and testing. The deep neural network model's performances are affected mostly by word embedding and last layer of network, however, the performance is least affected by the number of layers and recurrent units [36]. The performance of the model are calculated in the form of F1 scores. Basic deep neural network models (LSTM & BiLSTM) and hybrid models (LSTM-CRF, CNN-LSTM, BiLSTM-CRF and CNN-BiLSTM) for slot tagging are implemented and compared in the current experiment. The changes which are achieved is solely because of the different network models used as a platform for research. F1 scores are calculated to measure the functioning of respective models. Table 3, shows model and its performance score.

Table 3. Comparison of F1 Score of three models

Model	F1-Score
LSTM	86.8%
CNN-LSTM	88.5%
LSTM-CRF	89.8%
BiLSTM	89.2%
CNN-BiLSTM	90.4%
BiLSTM-CRF	91.6%

LSTM model takes into consideration context of words in forward direction. From the above table it may be mentioned that CNN-LSTM model has achieved 1.7% better accuracy while comparing the model with LSTM. In CNN-LSTM model, CNN word embedding feature extraction is added in addition to forward context. Convolution on word and character helps in getting better features. LSTM-CRF model achieve 1.3% more accuracy by connecting the outputted tag with one another. CRF layer uses conditional probability, to predict current tag based on past and future tag. In CRF, the weights of different feature functions determine the likelihood of the labels in the training data. Bi-LSTM takes into consideration the word context in both forward and backward direction which give better accuracy in tagging a word.

This research also elaborates the performance accuracy based on tagging of models as shown in Table 4:

Table 4. All Beginning Tag's F1-Score for 6 models

TAG	LSTM	LSTM-CRF	CNN-LSTM	BiLSTM	BiLSTM-CRF	CNN-BiLSTM
b_address	0	0.8	0	0	0	0
b_agenda	0.18	0.5	0.86	0.8	0.8	0.67
b_date	0.88	0.93	0.9	0.93	0.94	0.95
b_distance	0.81	0.82	0.83	0.85	0.88	0.81
b_event	0.96	0.94	0.94	0.95	0.99	0.96
b_location	0.89	0.94	0.89	0.94	0.96	0.93
b_party	0.79	0.84	0.88	0.96	0.97	0.81
b_poi	0.76	0.83	0.68	0.93	0.9	0.82
b_poi_type	0.9	0.92	0.94	0.96	0.95	0.94
b_room	0	0.67	0.67	1	0.8	1
b_time	0.85	0.96	0.94	0.94	0.96	0.96
b_traffic_info	0.63	0.69	0.72	0.63	0.71	0.73
b_weather_attribute	0.94	0.95	0.91	0.94	0.95	0.97

Further, in the research intent-wise F1-score is calculated as shown in Table 5 of the given Gujarati Dialogue Data string.

Table 5. Intent Wise F1-Score for 6 models

Intent	LSTM	LSTM-CRF	CNN-LSTM	BiLSTM	BiLSTM-CRF	CNN-BiLSTM
Schedule	0.79	0.85	0.8	0.94	0.94	0.93
Weather	0.87	0.9	0.9	0.89	0.92	0.91
Navigate	0.92	0.94	0.95	0.85	0.89	0.87

In the instant research, the result shows that only the base LSTM model is affected by change in number of LSTM units, but rest of the models are not affected by number of units The Fig. 5 below shows the increase in F1-score with changes in number of units in LSTM model. Additionally it also shows the difference of accuracy achieved using two different optimization functions: 'rmsprop' and 'adam'. However, it is observed that after 500 units, if we still increase the number of units, there is no major change in performance of the model.

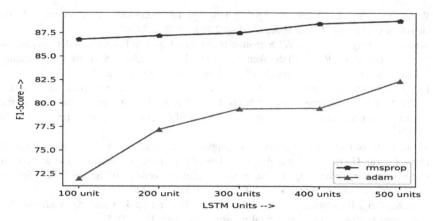

Fig. 5. Change in F1-Score with increase in LSTM units

In the proposed research, for rest of the models, number of recurrent units sampled are 100 units, even if we increase or decrease the size by 50 units, it is observed that there is no change in the accuracy level of the performing models. But, if we increase or decrease the size by more than 100 units the accuracy of the performing model is reduced.

5   Conclusion

Deep neural network models are implemented and compared using Gujarati dialogue for slot tagging. The state of art performance is successfully achieved using these deep neural network models. BiLSTM models achieved ~2.2% better F1-score than LSTM models. CNN-BiLSTM achieved 1.2% more accuracy then BiLSTM, whereas BiLSTM-CRF achieved even higher accuracy then CNN-BiLSTM by 1.2%. In view of the foregoing, it is concluded that BiLSTM-CRF gives the highest accuracy amongst all models in Gujarati Language dialogues. Better accuracy can still be achieved, if more domains are included. Aforementioned, accuracy is achieved using only limited data, however, better accuracy can be derived, if more tagged annotated data is included for training and testing.

References

1. Haffner, P., Tur, G., Wright, J.: Optimizing SVMs for complex call classification. In: Proceedings of the ICASSP, pp. 632–635 (2003)
2. Tur, G., Deng, L., Hakkani-Tür, D., He, X.: Towards deeper understanding: deep convex networks for semantic utterance classification. In: Proceedings of the IEEE International Conference on Acoustics, Speech, and Signal Processing, ICASSP, pp. 5045–5048 (2012)
3. Dauphin, Y.N., Tur, G., Hakkani-Tür, D., Heck, L.: Zero-shot learning for semantic utterance classification. In: 2nd International Conference on Learning Representations, ICLR 2014 - Conference Track Proceedings, pp. 1–9 (2014)

4. Wang, Y., Deng, L., Acero, A.: Spoken language understanding—an introduction to the statistical framework. Signal Process. Mag. **22**(5), 16–31 (2005)

5. Wang, Y., Deng, L., Acero, A.: Semantic frame based spoken language understanding. In: Tur, G., De Mori, R. (eds.) Spoken Language Understanding: Systems for Extracting Semantic Information from Speech, Chap. 3, pp. 35–80. Wiley, New York (2011)

6. Liu, J., Cyphers, S., Pasupat, P., McGraw, I., Glass, J.: A conversational movie search system based on conditional random fields. In: 13th Annual Conference of the International Speech Communication Association 2012, INTERSPEECH 2012, vol. 3, pp. 2453–2456 (2012)

7. Kudo, T., Matsumoto, Y.: Chunking with support vector machines, vol. 816, pp. 1–8 (2001)

8. Deng, L., Tur, G., He, X., Hakkani-Tur, D.: Use of kernel deep convex networks and end-to-end learning for spoken language understanding. In: Proceedings of the 2012 IEEE Spoken Language Technology Workshop, SLT 2012, pp. 210–215 (2012)

9. Yao, K., Peng, B., Zhang, Y., Yu, D., Zweig, G., Shi, Y.: Spoken language understanding using long short-term memory neural networks, pp. 189–194 (2014)

10. Okazaki, N.: CRFsuite: a fast implementation of Conditional Random Fields, CRFs (2007). https://www.chokkan.org/software/crfsuite/

11. Garg, V., Saraf, N., Majumder, P.: Named entity recognition for Gujarati: a CRF based approach. In: Prasath, R., Kathirvalavakumar, T. (eds.) MIKE 2013. LNCS (LNAI), vol. 8284, pp. 761–768. Springer, Cham (2013). https://doi.org/10.1007/978-3-319-03844-5_74

12. Athavale, V., Bharadwaj, S., Pamecha, M., Prabhu, A., Shrivastava, M.: Towards deep learning in Hindi NER: an approach to tackle the labelled data scarcity. In: Proceedings of the 13th International Conference on Natural Language Processing, ICON 2016, Varanasi, India, 17–20 December 2016, pp. 154–160 (2016)

13. Shah, B., Kopparapu, S.K.: A Deep Learning approach for Hindi Named Entity Recognition (2019)

14. Sharma, R., Morwal, S., Agarwal, B., Chandra, R., Khan, M.S.: A deep neural network-based model for named entity recognition for Hindi language. Neural Comput. Appl. **32**(20), 16191–16203 (2020). https://doi.org/10.1007/s00521-020-04881-z

15. Yang, X., Liu, J.: Using word confusion networks for slot filling in spoken language understanding. In: Proceedings of the Annual Conference of the International Speech Communication INTERSPEECH, vol. 2015-January, no. 3, pp. 1353–1357 (2015)

16. Huang, Z., Xu, W., Yu, K.: Bidirectional LSTM-CRF Models for Sequence Tagging (2015)

17. Mesnil, G., He, X., Deng, L., Bengio, Y.: Investigation of recurrent-neural-network architectures and learning methods for spoken language understanding. In: Proceedings of the Annual Conference of the International Speech Communication Association, INTER-SPEECH, no. August, pp. 3771–3775 (2013)

18. Deng, L., Tur, G., He, X., Hakkani-Tur, D.: Use of kernel deep convex networks and end-to-end learning for spoken language understanding. In: 2012 IEEE Spoken Language Technology Workshop, SLT 2012, pp. 210–215 (2012)

19. Yao, K., Zweig, G., Hwang, M.-Y., Shi, Y., Yu, D.: Recurrent neural networks for language understanding. In: Proceedings of the Interspeech (2013)

20. Xu, P., Sarikaya, R.: Contextual domain classification in spoken language understanding, pp. 136–140. Microsoft Corporation, Redmond (2014)

21. Ekbal, A.: Language independent named entity recognition in Indian languages. In: Proceedings of the Workshop on NER South East Asian Languages, IJCNLP 2008, Hyderabad India, 12 January 2008, pp3340 PDF 160KB, no. January, pp. 33–40 (2008)

22. Ekbal, A.: A conditional random field approach for named entity recognition in Bengali and Hindi. Linguist. Issues Lang. Technol. **2**(1), 589–594 (2009)

23. Sasidhar, B.: A survey on named entity recognition in Indian languages with particular reference to Telugu. IJCSI Int. J. Comput. Sci. **8**(2), 438 (2011)
24. Hochreiter, S., Schmidhuber, J.: Long short-term memory. Neural Comput. **9**(8), 1735–1780 (1997). https://doi.org/10.1162/neco.1997.9.8.1735
25. Wang, P., Qian, Y., Soong, F.K., He, L., Zhao, H.: A unified tagging solution: bidirectional LSTM recurrent neural network with word embedding (2015)
26. Soltau, H., Liao, H., Sak, H.: Neural speech recognizer: acoustic-to-word LSTM model for largevocabulary speech recognition. In: Proceedings of the Annual Conference of the International Speech Communication Association, INTERSPEECH, vol. 2017-August, pp. 3707–3711 (2017). https://doi.org/10.21437/Interspeech.2017-1566
27. Liu, Z., et al.: Entity recognition from clinical texts via recurrent neural network. BMCMed. Inform. Decis. Mak. **17**(Suppl 2), 53–61 (2017)
28. Graves, A., Mohamed, A.R., Hinton, G.: Speech Recognition with Deep Recurrent Neural Networks. Department of Computer Science, University of Toronto, pp. 6645–6649 (2013)
29. Bod, M.: A guide to recurrent neural networks and backpropagation. Rnn Dan Bpnn **2**(2), 1–10 (2001)
30. Shah, D., Bhadka, H.: A survey on various approach used in named entity recognition for Indian languages. Int. J. Comput. Appl. (0975 – 8887) **167**(1) (2017)
31. Collobert, R., Weston, J., Bottou, L., Karlen, M., Kavukcuoglu, K., Kuksa, P.: Natural language processing (almost) from scratch. J. Mach. Learn. Res. (JMLR) **12**, 2493–2537 (2011)
32. Chen, T., Xu, R., He, Y., Wang, X.: Improving sentiment analysis via sentence type classification using BiLSTM-CRF and CNN. Expert Syst. Appl. **72**, 221–230 (2017). https://doi.org/10.1016/j.eswa.2016.10.065
33. Zhao, J., Mao, X., Chen, L.: Speech emotion recognition using deep 1D & 2D CNN LSTM networks. Biomed. Signal Process. Control **47**, 312–323 (2019). https://doi.org/10.1016/j.bspc.2018.08.035
34. Wang, J., Yu, L.C., Lai, K.R., Zhang, X.: Dimensional sentiment analysis using a regional CNN-LSTM model. In: 54th Annual Meeting of the Association for Computational Linguistics, ACL 2016 - Short Paper, pp. 225–230 (2016). https://doi.org/10.18653/v1/p16-2037
35. Guimar, V.: NER with Neural Character Embeddings (2014)
36. Reimers, N., Gurevych, I.: Optimal Hyperparameters for Deep LSTM-Networks for Sequence Labeling Tasks (2017). https://arxiv.org/abs/1707.06799
37. Wu, C., Wu, F., Chen, Y., Wu, S., Yuan, Z., Huang, Y.: Neural metaphor detecting with CNN-LSTM model, pp. 110–114 (2018). https://doi.org/10.18653/v1/w18-0913
38. Kulkarni, S.: A survey on named entity recognition for south Indian languages, vol. 167, no. 1, pp. 11–18 (2017)
39. Bhatt, S., Patwa, F., Sandhu, R.: An access control framework for cloud-enabled wearable internet of things. In: Proceedings of the 2017 IEEE 3rd International Conference on Collaboration and Internet Computing, CIC 2017, vol. 2017-January, pp. 328–338 (2017). https://doi.org/10.1109/CIC.2017.00050
40. Graves, A., Schmidhuber, J.: Framewise phoneme classification with bidirectional LSTM and other neural network architectures. Neural Netw. **18**(5–6), 602–610 (2005). https://doi.org/10.1016/j.neunet.2005.06.042

Energy Efficient Aspects of Federated Learning – Mechanisms and Opportunities

Shajulin Benedict[(✉)]

Indian Institute of Information Technology Kottayam,
Kottayam 686635, Kerala, India
shajulin@iiitkottayam.ac.in
http://www.sbenedictglobal.com

Abstract. The role of machine learning in IoT-enabled applications, most predominantly in societal applications, is instrumental. That the active researchers take a series of steps utilizing innovative technologies to override emerging challenges such as data privacy, latency, scalability, energy consumption, and so forth. Federated Learning (FL), a subset of machine learning paradigm, has shifted the mindset of researchers, including system architects, in recent years while solving the existing challenges of the inclusion of machine learning in applications; it has taken a more distinct shape in terms of handling learning mechanisms in a decentralized fashion. In fact, energy-efficient mechanisms need to be incorporated into the FL frameworks/architectures. There is still no work that expresses the energy reduction opportunities of FL algorithms or architectures. This paper has primarily focused on revealing the energy-efficient aspects of FL. Besides, it is reinforced with the discussions on the recent developments of FL and prominent future research contributions in various application domains with an emphasis on energy efficiency. The article would benefit researchers, more specifically the system engineers or tool developers, who deal with the inclusion of FL for applications.

Keywords: Energy efficiency · Edge/Fog/Cloud · Federated Learning · IoT · Machine Learning

1 Introduction

Machine Learning (ML) renders innovative solutions for traditional services considering a large amount of data. Applications that predict the user experience of web data, drug discovery, COVID-19 patient movements, shared mobility, and so forth, which surpass from geographical diversification to organizational distinctions, have marked a sudden surge in the inclusion of ML approaches while influencing a wide range of researchers/practitioners such as

This work is supported by IIIT-Kottayam research fund and OEAD-DST fund.

K. K. Patel et al. (Eds.): icSoftComp 2020, CCIS 1374, pp. 38–51, 2021.
https://doi.org/10.1007/978-981-16-0708-0_4

system engineers, algorithm designers, and performance analysis tool developers in recent years. Obviously, research opportunities have evolved; and accordingly, addressing the existing challenges of ML algorithms or frameworks/architectures, including energy inefficiency, have considered to be a primordial task among researchers/practitioners.

In general, learning algorithms were executed in a single machine or in multiple machines using cloud/HPC servers. Executing algorithms in cloud machines is well predominantly practiced by several applications. The data, either collected through sensor devices or audio/video gadgets, are apparently diverse and huge. Indeed, transferring a huge volume of diverse data to clouds for inferences is not a viable solution owing to the hefty latency – i.e., a system-level performance issue. Another visible point of disagreement is transferring privacy data to third-party services for attaining global learning. In fact, there exist a few privacy attacks while transferring data to clouds – e.g. malicious client/server attack, multi-organizational computation, device hacks, and so forth. There is a dire need for procedures or solutions to overcome the mounting performance bottlenecks and the privacy-related security challenges. Federated Learning (FL) is an option which most of the researchers have adopted in their works.

FL mechanism [11], in general, utilizes distributed data for inferring information based on decentralized collaborative modeling algorithms – i.e., it promotes a hierarchical learning platform that collaboratively infers information from the local and global learning models. The energy consumption of FL based applications, due to the involvement of federated computing devices that range from battery operated edge nodes to data centers, could lead to significant impacts if unnoticed. The I/O transfer between computing nodes, including wireless communication devices such as IoT Gateways, has direct impacts on the energy consumption of applications. Besides, the data transfer increases the performance overhead of FL mechanisms at large. Most of the FL-enabled applications transfer a large volume of data between the local and global learning models that are housed in different locations. For instance, a tourism planning service of an Intelligent Transportation System, which involves smart city multi-party organizations, could transfer over 1TB data per day between the edge node and computing cloud nodes.

Evidently, there is a dire need to address the energy inefficiency issues of learning algorithms or mechanisms. This paper highlights the classifications of FL mechanisms with an emphasis on the energy efficiency aspects of FL. It stresses on the metrics utilized in the evolving FL frameworks/architectures. In addition, it highlights the energy efficiency mechanisms which could be adopted in FL frameworks or architectures.

The contributions of the paper are listed as follows:

1. it classifies and elaborates the FL mechanisms, metrics, and architectures;
2. it stresses on the need for adopting energy efficiency in FL and a few possible energy reduction mechanisms; and,
3. it discusses on the existing FL applications as case studies.

The rest of the paper is described as follows: Sect. 2 exposes the required basics of FL with a generic architecture; Sect. 3 details on the functioning of different FL mechanisms with distinct classifications; Sect. 4 highlights the energy efficient aspects of FL frameworks or architectures; Sect. 5 centres around the characterization of FL applications; and, finally Sect. 6 conclude the contributions of paper with a few future outlooks.

2 Federated Learning – Generic Architecture

Learning, in general, is termed as the natural process of acquiring new skills or knowledge throughout the lifetime of a human being. It could lead to positive or negative changes in humans owing to the results of their past experiences.

The traditional approach of machine learning approaches often leads to several challenges as described below:

1. *Poor Scalability:* Most of the learning approaches are centralized. This creates a bottleneck in scaling the evolving data. In general, data evolving from IoT devices or sensor nodes are reaching over Terra Bytes per day. For instance, Forbes commented on the IDC report stating that over 175 ZetaBytes would be stored on devices by 2025 [24]. The number of connected devices is also increasing from millions to trillions. In this scenario, the centralized learning models fail to infer realistic information from the data.
2. *Data privacy:* Protecting data leads to a poor sharing model for reaping in learning innovations. In general, knowledge is to serve. However, securing data is equally important in order to protect the data from hackers or intruders. The existing learning mechanism expects the users or clients to submit the entire data to the learning machine.
3. *Reduced Latency:* Owing to the fact that the data needs to be nearer, for quick decisions, the existing learning models fail to address the issue. The emerging higher latency hampers the battery-operated IoT cloud applications at large.
4. *Node Heterogeneity:* Gadgets that are utilized in learning processes might belong to several different manufacturers or organizations. This heterogeneity leads to connectivity issues or delays in processing different protocols. For instance, a ZigBee module device could not be directly connected to WirelessHART devices.

It is a known fact that the learning algorithms are dependent on input data. More the data, the more the accuracy or learning inference. In this scenario, the existing learning models should be replaced with federated learning mechanisms. Federated Learning combined with ML is a newer technology of utilizing decentralized computers along with the other sophisticated learning assistive gadgets. It is a decentralized learning mechanism that includes decentralized data and learning models to reduce high latency and protect data privacy at scale for achieving better learning experiences.

A generic architecture to illustrate the learning process of FL is depicted in Fig. 1. As shown, FL includes multiple decentralized computing platforms in

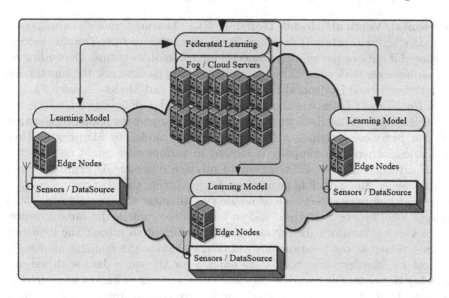

Fig. 1. Federated Learning Architecture – Generic Perspective

addition to the centralized computing platforms. The decentralized computing servers such as edge or mobile nodes are connected to fog or cloud servers. A few learning models are executed on edge nodes and the other portion in clouds. Edge nodes privatize data within their vicinity and submit the inference to the cloud nodes for further learning processes. The FL learning processes are organized in a hierarchical fashion in order to attain its overarching objectives such as latency, scalability, and energy efficiency. A more detailed information about the different procedures of FL learning mechanisms are discussed in Sect. 3. The most commonly applied learning algorithms in FL frameworks are i) Deep Neural Networks (DNN), ii) Federated YOLO, iii) Federated SVM, and iv) Other Federated ML algorithms.

3   Federated Learning – Taxonomy, Metrics, Architectures

This section expresses the taxonomy of FL mechanisms. Besides, the metrics utilized and the computing infrastructures adopted in the learning are studied (see Fig. 2).

3.1   Federated Learning – Taxonomy

Federated Learning (FL) is classified based on how the learning is performed in a federated manner as follows: i) Horizontal/Vertical/Model-Transfer FL, b) Meta-Learning in FL, c) Rewarded FL, and d) Supervised/Semi-Supervised/ Unsupervised FL.

Horizontal/Vertical/Model-Transfer FL. Learning models are mostly dependent on two vectors i) data and ii) modeling parameters. Training models are shared if data or modeling parameters are common in nature. Depending on the commonness noticed in either data or modeling parameters, the functioning of FL differs into i) Horizontal FL, ii) Vertical FL, and Model-Transfer FL.

In *Horizontal FL*, the learning models are applied in different regions consisting of varying training data when the modeling parameters remained constant [18]. For instance, designing a federated learning model for 3D printing IIoT applications where the company is located in various sites could be classified in this category. The applications would produce different 3D printing sensor data. However, the modeling parameters for predicting the 3D printer accuracy using modeling parameters such as nozzle size, filament type, execution time of printing jobs, bed temperature, and so forth would remain the same irrespective of varying locations. In such cases, it is sufficient to submit the modeling parameters across the locations instead of transferring the training models. In *Vertical FL*, the learning models are applied for the same data with varying modeling datasets. For instance, figuring out the *NO2* pollution level or *SO2* pollution level of a smart city would preferably contain the same air quality monitoring dataset. However, the modeling parameter space differs for training models. *Model-Transfer FL* approach transfers the learned findings for one scenario to the other scenario for inferring a deeper knowledge – i.e., the training model obtained for a specific data and the corresponding modeling parameters are shared to the other datasets.

Meta-learning FL. Meta-Learning approach is almost similar to the *Horizontal FL*, where the modeling parameters are shared among the different locations consisting of varying training data, in order to perform the decentralized FL. However, the *Meta-learning FL* is beyond the expectancy of *Horizontal FL*. That is, it shares a meta-representation of algorithms that might initiate federated learning irrespective of training data or modeling parameters. This implies that the *Meta-Learning FL* could be independent of dataset or the accompanying modeling parameters; and, it could be dependent on the shared pseudo/meta-algorithm. [7] and [19] have discussed about the meta-learning FL approach in the context of *Horizontal FL*.

Rewarded FL. FL attains success or failure whenever new algorithms were designed for a given dataset of an application. Rewards may be offered for the algorithms upon attaining success and penalty upon failures. In general, providing rewards for algorithms that are performing using a team of agents could increase the accuracy measure and productivity measure of individual agents. Consequently, the evolving outcome would outperform than any other individual performances.

Supervised/Semi-supervised/Unsupervised FL. *Supervised FL* is a decentralized learning model which assumes that the input and the output are known in advance while training models. However, the learning mechanism attempts to identify a suitable function that clearly maps the input and output variables. *Unsupervised FL* approach assumes that the output variables are not known in advance. Learning functions are applied for any given input and the success or failures are gradually learned over time. Although the approach leads to a hefty time, unsupervised learning is not dependent on input or output data. *Semi-Supervised FL* offers better accuracy when compared to the unsupervised algorithms. In *Semi-Supervised FL*, it is expected that the dataset needs to be labeled for guiding the learning algorithms during the learning processes.

3.2   FL Metrics

The metrics that could improve the performance of FL algorithms are classified into three categories – Performance-oriented, Security oriented, and Algorithm-specific metrics.

Metrics – Performance Oriented. Performance-oriented metrics in FL domains include: i) Reliability, ii) Latency, iii) Cost involved, iv) Energy consumption, v) Scalability, vi) Bandwidth, and vii) Throughput. *Reliability* defines the consistency in providing similar learning results irrespective of the underlying architecture or nodes applied for the federated learning processes. In general, FL environments experience crashes, computation failures, hardware failures, software configurational issues, and so forth; *Latency* metric is well utilized in the FL domain. It deals with the time taken for submitting data to the federated learning models and vice-versa. In [23], Sumudu et al. have proposed an ultra-reliable low latency FL approach for vehicular applications; *Cost* metric is based on the summations of multiple measurable quantities. Typically, the cost involved in FL is dependent on the communications carried out during the entire FL processes. Nicolas et al. [16] have studied the impact of the communication cost over learning accuracy in FL environment; *Energy consumption* metric defines the energy consumption of FL algorithms when executed on computational units such as edge, fog, cloud, or serverless computing instances. This metric is represented in Joules; *Scalability* metric defines the capability of handling varying data sizes from multiple organizations over time for undertaking the FL processes; *Bandwidth* metric studies the network requirement for transferring data or modeling algorithms in order to follow the decentralized FL; *Throughput* determines the number of learning models that are successfully completed within an FL application. It defines the strength of the FL, especially in workflow-based learning models.

Metrics – Security Oriented. Secure transactions are crucial aspects of federated learning as they involve multiple organizations or heterogeneous devices. A few metrics that are considered for availing secure accesses in an FL environment include: *Encryption Level* metric defines the level of encryptions to be adopted during FL. Higher the *Encryption Level*, higher is the security. Higher *Encryption Level* has performance consequences. Homomorphic encryption techniques, which were discussed in a few research works [1,18], have higher *Encryption Level*; *Mean Time to Detect (MTD)* metric is utilized for detecting the time involved in detecting the security breaches of the FL system; *Mean Time to Resolve (MTR)* metric discusses on the time required for solving the security flaws in the federated environments; *Intrusion Level (IL)* metric determines the number of successful intruders for a given period of time. It is a known fact that the security vulnerability of FL environments is high owing to the involvement of several IoT nodes, sometimes un-managed nodes too; *Cross-ref Scripting (CS)* metric is a Boolean indicator that reflects on the false scripts that are functioning on the FL networking systems; *N-Unauthorized Devices* metric illustrates the number of unauthorized devices which submit sensor data or collecting FL algorithms for further processing; *Differential Privacy*, a Boolean metric, defines the privacy of data in remote sites.

Algorithm-Specific Metric. Learning algorithms are tuned based on metrics such as i) accuracy and ii) instruction size. Accuracy of prediction or classification algorithms are represented using squared errors ($R2$) or Mean Squared Errors (MSE); the instruction size of algorithms reflects on the number of instructions for executing FL algorithms in a distributed fashion.

3.3   FL Architectures/Infrastructures

FL mechanisms are implemented in a variety of computing nodes or clusters. The categorization of those environments is detailed below:

Heterogeneous vs. Homogeneous Architectures. FL has to have mechanisms for handling heterogeneity in several aspects – a) data heterogeneity, b) machine heterogeneity, and c) network heterogeneity. Data heterogeneity in FL means that the data has different characteristics for the given domain dataset; Machine heterogeneity relates to different categories of machines, including GPU, for processing the learning algorithms; and, Network heterogeneity discusses the multiple connections involved within the FL environments. For instance, in [3], authors have applied the Federated Averaging algorithm for clustering heterogeneous resources during the FL approach.

Computational Environments. FL architectures or frameworks involve sophisticated computing environments such as mobile, edge, fog, cloud, and so forth. Accordingly, FL is classified as MobileFL, EdgeFL, FogFL, CloudFL, ServerlessFL, or hybridFL – i) MobileFL involves mobile computing devices such as laptops, mobile phones and antenna towers and the other mobile gadgets while transferring data, voice, or video over wireless medium; ii) EdgeFL utilizes edge nodes that are located nearer to the data sources. They are mostly battery

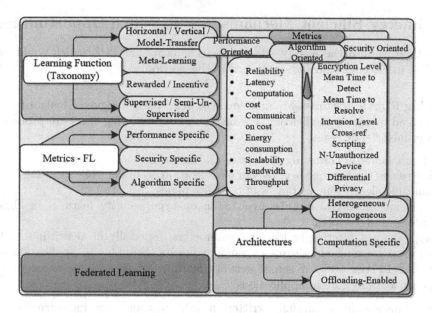

Fig. 2. Federated Learning – Taxonomy, Metrics, Architectures

operated and are sensitive to computations. In EdgeFL the learning algorithms are transferred to the edge nodes. Placing them on appropriate edge nodes is a challenging task while considering various metrics, including energy consumption of learning algorithms; FogFL adopts a large volume of computations when compared to *EdgeFL*; CloudFL involves cloud architectures for processing learning algorithms. In order to enable decentralized FL, private cloud environments could be established nearer to the data sources; *ServerlessFL* avoids continuous powering ON of machines or cloud instances for delivering learning services. In ServerlessFL, learning algorithms are activated in a serverless fashion where the nodes are initially not powered ON; HybridFL combines two or more of the FL approaches such as MobileFL, EdgeFL, FogFL, CloudFL, or ServerlessFL in an elegant manner in order to pursue FL from data sources (e.g., [12], [22]).

Offloading Enabled FL. In general, offloading computational tasks to available resources in the FL environment could improve the performance of applications. The computational units such as edge, fog, cloud, or battery-operated sensor nodes should be efficiently utilized in the FL setting. To do so, computational units should be split into manageable tasks and distributed among the available resources in an elegant manner. A few research works have been undertaken in the past to distribute computations on the freely available computing resources – [10] Jianji et al. have optimized FL environments by offloading tasks on IoT environments.

4   Energy Efficient Mechanisms – Research Opportunities

Investigating into the energy efficiency mechanisms [20] [21], which could be applied in FL environments, is studied in this section.

Tuning FL Algorithms. Malfunctioned or improperly designed FL algorithms could lead to energy inefficiency. For instances, the following cases are prone to energy inefficiency issues:

- circuit faults in clustering or deep neural networks;
- increasing the learning accuracy or classification accuracy while iterating over multiple algorithmic instances of compute nodes;
- inclusion of several `double precision` or `typo` security features in algorithms; and, so forth.
- applying apt filtering or learning parameters, especially in algorithms such as deep learning algorithms or random forests. Notably, an application of `Gabor Filter` assisted neural network learning would increase the convergence learning rate in applications;

Algorithms should be carefully written in order to avoid such inefficiencies. In fact, the most common problem for poor algorithmic solution in FL is due to the non-availability of skilled programmers in the FL domain – the programmers are not aware of the embedded to datacenter level computational architectures.

A few authors have adopted model compression techniques in deep learning algorithms [2]. In fact, incorporating model compression approaches would tremendously reduce the energy consumption of applications and improve the communication speed between the FL computing environments.

Designing Energy-Efficient Languages. System-level languages such as C/C++, Rust, and so forth are energy efficient languages when compared to the interpreting languages, including Python. In fact, most of the machine learning algorithms, including FL, are implemented using interpreting languages such as Python, R, or S. Choosing system-level languages for the entire operation of FL might be incompatible to datacenter level programming languages. In addition, languages could include energy tuning options with the assistance of compilers for the underlying FL architectures.

Tuning Computing Architectures. FL computing infrastructures might get exposed to energy inefficiencies, if unnoticed. Several energy-efficient approaches need to be adopted in FL in order to counteract the energy inefficiency problem. For instances:

1. Offloading computations, considering the energy impact of code movements, would be improve energy efficiencies. FL computing architectures, in such cases, should have a provision to monitor code level energy consumptions. Minghua et al. in [15] have studied the energy efficiency of systems while offloading edge nodes nearer to the communication footprints.

2. Scheduling FL tasks by dividing them into smaller tasks such as authentication tasks, data collection tasks, training tasks, prediction tasks, and so forth, and executing them in parallel improves the energy efficiency. For instances, authors of [14] had developed an energy-aware scheduling mechanism for edge nodes; Authors of [25] had designed scheduling algorithms for a 5G based Unmanned Aerial Vehicles (UAV).
3. Adopting apt load balancing policies in FL environments is another option. A load-balancing algorithm could be employed into the FL architecture such that the lightly loaded nodes could be switched off and the services could be optimally placed on the other nodes.
4. Content caching in FL architectures, indeed, increases the energy efficiency. The latency of FL applications is dependent on caching size involved in the FL nodes. For instance, Ishtiaque et al. [9] and Fu et al. [8] proposed the caching mechanism in IIoT environments to counteract energy inefficiency issues.

Avoiding Security Flaws. Securing devices or algorithmic projections are mandatory tasks in any computing environment, including FL environments. Malfunctioned sensor nodes or FL services are prone to energy inefficiencies. Identifying the apt energy-efficient security policies and encryption algorithms in an FL environment would certainly reduce the energy consumption of FL applications.

Enabling Energy-Efficient Routing/ Networking/ Communications. Minimizing the energy consumption of FL environments or architectures could be impacted by efficiently handling the packets in the underlying FL networks, including wireless networks. For instance, WIFI enabled networks could be replaced with bluetooth4.0 networks if the node vicinity is reachable; or, they could be replaced with mobile networks if possible – WIFI networks could increase the energy consumption of applications due to the increased data transmission rate [5].

5   FL Applications

An exploratory study on seven applications that were implemented by researchers/ practitioners, which utilized FL mechanisms, is disclosed in this section as case studies. The details of these applications include:

Energy Demand Prediction: Predicting energy demand for charging electric vehicles from distributed charging stations using the FL approach is carried out in [27]. Here, a locally available training model updates the globally available training model using the *TensorFlow* tool. The application employed Deep Neural Network (DNN) algorithms for learning the charging demands within a network of HybridFL nodes.

Industrial IoT: Linghe et al. [13] proposed a federated tensor mining framework to collaboratively learn the assembly line features of an automobile industry. The FL application falls under the category of Industrial IoT, or Smart Factory, where the FL approach is dealt with based on transferring secure data among the factory units. The DNN learning algorithm is applied for heterogeneous data sources with homomorphic encryption approaches in the application.

Image Classification: Image classification problem is applied in a typical automotive vehicles using FL approach by DongDong et al. [4]. The authors proposed the application of DNN based FL in this application, where the DNN models are locally trained and the inference of the models are transferred to the global training models. The approach has a selective model aggregation platform to pursue an incentive-based training considering computation cost and the other metrics such as utility and latency of learning algorithms.

Jamming Attack Detection: Jamming attack is a common problem in Unmanned Aerial Vehicles (UAV). Detecting the jamming attacks need to be handled in a collaborative fashion for quick responses in the wireless medium. Nishant et al. [17] studied the application of security-enabled client group prioritization mechanism for suggesting FL in a decentralized fashion using the DNN algorithm. Here, the locally learned models were globally updated for further refining the learning global state of the FL.

Failure Prediction in Aeronautics: FL approach, in collaboration with an Active Learning approach, the semi-supervised learning approach, is applied to predict the failures of aeronautical systems in Nicolas et al. [16]. The authors combined FL and Active learning approaches in order to efficiently handle the computation and communication resources of aeronautical systems during the FL learning phase.

Visual Object Detection: In this application, Yang et al. [26] attempted to apply the FL approach for quickly detecting objects. In fact, video applications could lead to a hefty network bandwidth. This aspect could restrict the utilization of the traditional centralized learning mechanisms. In this application, Federated YOLOv3 and Recurrent-Convolutional Neural Network (R-CNN) learning algorithms were studied in the federated environmental setup.

Mobile Packet Classification: Here, mobile packets were classified using the FL approach so that the unnecessary handoffs or network latency are avoided. Evita et al. [6] implemented the application of Federated SVM classifier and DNN algorithms for classifying mobile packets in the application.

FL Applications – A Comparative Study. Table 1 illustrates the comparison of the use cases. The most important findings from the comparison of these FL applications include:

1. the most of the existing FL applications are based on the *Model-Transfer* FL – i.e., the learning models were transferred between the local and the global computing nodes in an FL environment;

Table 1. Comparison of FL-enabled Applications

FL based Applications	Research Domain	Function Oriented						Architectures		
		Horiz. / Vertical / Model-Transfer	Meta-Learning	Reward	Supervised / Un-Supervised / Semi-Supervised Learning	Metrics	Hetero/ Homo	Computation Specific	Off loading
Energy Demand Prediction for EV	EV vehicles	Model-Transfer	*	*	Un-supervised (CNN)	Latency, RSME	Simulation	*	*
Industrial IoT	Smart Factory	Vertical FL	*	*	DNN	Latency	Hetero Data sources	HybridFL	*
Image Classification	Vehicular Edge	Model-Transfer	*	Incentive	DNN	Comp. cost, Utility, Latency	Simulation	*	*
Jamming Attack Detection	Networking	Model-Transfer	*	*	DNN	Latency	Simulation	*	*
Failure prediction	Aeronautics	Model-Transfer	*	*	Ensemble Trees, Semi-Supervised	Comp. cost, Commn. Cost	Hetero nodes	HybridFL	*
Visual Object Detection	Video Analytics	Horiz. FL	*	*	R-CNN, Federated YOLOv3	Latency	Hetero nodes	HybridFL	*
Mobile Packet Classification	Networking	Model-Transfer	*	*	Federated SVM, DNN	Latency, Cost	Simulation	*	*

2. applications are related to analytics in EVs, factories, networking, including 5G, and so forth.
3. the *Image Classification* application has proposed an incentive mechanism for FL algorithms;
4. the majority of the researchers have applied neural network algorithms or their variants. For instance, applications such as Energy Demand Prediction for EV, Industrial IoT, Image Classification, Jamming Attack, and Mobile Packet Classification have applied DNN or convolutional neural networks or Recurrent Convolutional Neural Network algorithms in a decentralized manner. In fact, there exist several other popular algorithms in the machine learning domains which need to be modified for the Federated Learning domains; and,
5. almost all FL applications have considered the *Latency* based performance metric for evaluating the applications. Notably, none of the applications have studied the impact of energy consumptions of these applications. The research on energy efficiency on FL applications, if conducted, would reap in lots of benefits to the society.

6   Conclusions

The efforts of researchers to broaden the application of innovative computing platforms in machine learning have predominantly reached heights in recent years. The application of FL, a decentralized learning mechanism, has marked a distinct transformation in several evolving applications of various sectors, including biomedical or transportation sectors. Albeit of the benefits of FL in terms of data privacy and latency, what is lacking is a broad and specific energy efficiency-related discussions that elaborate the energy reduction mechanisms of FL frameworks or architectures. This paper disclosed the various possible energy reduction mechanisms for an FL environment; and, it categorized FL mechanisms. In addition, seven FL applications were investigated based on the categorized FL mechanisms.

References

1. Acar, A., Aksu, H., Selcuk Uluagac, A., Conti, M.: A survey on homomorphic encryption schemes: theory and implementation. ACM Comput. Surv. **51**(4), 1–35 (2018). https://doi.org/10.1145/3214303
2. Alvarez, J.M., Salzmann, M.: Compression-aware training of deep networks. In: Proceedings of the 31st International Conference on Neural Information Processing Systems, NIPS 2017, pp 856–867 (2017)
3. Ghosh, A., Hong, J., Yin, D., Ramchandranin, K.: arXiv https://arxiv.org/abs/1906.06629, pp. 1–26 (2019)
4. Ye, D., Rong, Yu., Pan, M., Han, Z.: Federated learning in vehicular edge computing: a selective model aggregation approach. IEEE Access **8**, 23920–23935 (2020). https://doi.org/10.1109/ACCESS.2020.2968399
5. Energy Consumption in WIFI. http://repositorio.uchile.cl/bitstream/handle/2250/132644/Energy-Efficiency-Oriented-Traffic-Offloading-in-wireless-networks.pdf?sequence=1s. Accessed Mar 2020
6. Bakopoulou, E., Tillman, B., Markopoulou, A.: A federated learning approach for mobile packet classification, arXiv https://arxiv.org/abs/1907.13113 (2019)
7. Chen, F., Luo, M., Dong, Z., Li, Z., He, X.: Federated meta-learning with fast convergence and efficient communication, preprint in arXiv https://arxiv.org/abs/1802.07876. Accessed Mar 2020
8. Fu, J., Liu, Y., Chao, H.C., Bhargava, B., Zhag, Z.: Secure data storage and searching for industrial IoT by integrating fog computing and cloud computing. IEEE Trans. Ind. Inform. **14**(10), 4519–4528 (2018)
9. Zahed, M.I.A., Ahmad, I., Habibi, D., Phung, Q.V.: Content caching in industrial IoT: security and energy considerations. IEEE Internet of Things J. **7**, 491–504 (2019)
10. Ren, J., Wang, H., Hou, T., Zheng, S., Tang, C.: Federated learning-based computation offloading optimization in edge computing-supported internet of things. IEEE Access **7**, 69194–69201 (2019). https://doi.org/10.1109/ACCESS.2019.2919736
11. Konecny, J., McMahan, H.B., Yu, F.X., Richtarik, P., Suresh, A.T., Bacon, D.: Federated learning: strategies for improving communication efficiency. In: NIPS Workshop on Private Multi-party Machine Learning (2016)
12. Khan, L.U., et al.: Federated learning for edge networks: resource optimization and incentive mechanism, arXiv https://arxiv.org/pdf/1911.05642.pdf. Accessed Mar 2020
13. Kong, L., Liu, X.-Y., Sheng, H., Zeng, P., Chen, G.: Federated tensor mining for secure industrial internet of things. IEEE Trans. Ind. Inf. **16**(3), 2144–2153 (2020). https://doi.org/10.1109/TII.2019.2937876

14. Munir, Md., Abedin, S., Tran, N., Han, Z., Huh, E., Hong, C.S.: Risk-aware energy scheduling for edge computing with microgrid: a multi-agent deep reinforcement learning approach, arXiv https://arxiv.org/pdf/2003.02157.pdf. Accessed Mar 2020

15. Wang, M., Zhu, L., Yang, L.T., Lin, M., Deng, X., Yi, L.: Offloading assisted energy-balanced IoT edge node relocation for confident information coverage. IEEE Internet of Things 6(3), 4482–4490 (2019)

16. Aussel, N., Chabridon, S., Petetin, Y.: Combining federated and active learning for communication-efficient distributed failure prediction in aeronautics, arXiv preprint https://arxiv.org/pdf/2001.07504.pdf. Accessed Mar 2020

17. Mowla, N.I., Tran, N.H., Doh, I., Chae, K.: Federated learning-based cognitive detection of jamming attack in flying ad-hoc network. IEEE Access 8, 4338–4350 (2019). https://doi.org/10.1109/ACCESS.2019.2962873

18. Yang, Q., Liu, Y., Chen, T., Tong, Y.: Federated machine learning: concept and applications. ACM Trans. Intell. Syst. Technol. 12 (2019). https://doi.org/10.1145/3298981

19. Lin, S., Yang, G., Zhang, J.: A collaborative learning framework via federated meta-learning, preprint arXiv https://arxiv.org/abs/2001.03229 (2020)

20. Benedict, S.: Prediction assisted runtime based energy tuning mechanism for HPC applications. Sustain. Comput. Inform. Syst. 19, 43–51 (2018)

21. Benedict, S.: Threshold acceptance algorithm based energy tuning of scientific applications using EnergyAnalyzer. In: ISEC2014. ACM (2014). https://doi.acm.org/10.1145/2590748.2590759

22. Wang, S.: Adaptive federated learning in resource constrained edge computing systems, arXiv https://arxiv.org/pdf/1804.05271.pdf (2019)

23. Samarakoon, S., Bennis, M., Saad, W., Debbah, M.: Distributed federated learning for ultra-reliable low-latency vehicular communications. IEEE Trans. Commun. (2019). https://doi.org/10.1109/TCOMM.2019.2956472

24. Coughlin, T.: Forbes report on data explosion. https://www.forbes.com/sites/tomcoughlin/2018/11/27/175-zettabytes-by-2025/#7fe3174d5459. Accessed Mar 2020

25. Hesselbach, X., Sanchez-Aguero, V., Valera, F., Vidal, I., Nogales, B.: An NFV-based energy scheduling algorithm for a 5G enabled fleet of programmable unmanned aerial vehicles. Wirel. Commun. Mob. Comput. 2019, 1–20 (2019). https://doi.org/10.1155/2019/4734821

26. Liu, Y., et al.: FedVision: an online visual object detection platform powered by federated learning, arXiv https://arxiv.org/abs/2001.06202. Accessed Mar 2020

27. Saputra, Y., Thai, H.D., Nguyen, D., Dutkiewicz, E., Mueck, M., Srikanteswara, S.: Energy demand prediction with federated learning for electric vehicle networks, arXiv https://arxiv.org/abs/1909.00907. Accessed Mar 2020

Classification of UrbanSound8k: A Study Using Convolutional Neural Network and Multiple Data Augmentation Techniques

Aamer Abdul Rahman[1]($\boxtimes$) (iD) and J. Angel Arul Jothi[2] (iD)

[1] Department of Electrical and Electronics Engineering, Birla Institute of Technology and Science, Pilani, Dubai Campus, Dubai, UAE
ar.aamer@gmail.com
[2] Department of Computer Science, Birla Institute of Technology and Science, Pilani, Dubai Campus, Dubai, UAE
angeljothi@dubai.bits-pilani.ac.in

Abstract. Audio data augmentation methods such as pitch shifting, time stretching and background noise insertion have been proven to improve the performance of deep learning models when it comes to learning discriminative spectro-temporal patterns such as environmental sounds. This work aims to classify the audio samples from the UrbanSound8k dataset using a 5-layer deep convolutional neural network (CNN). The audio samples from the dataset are transformed into their respective mel-spectrogram representation using Short-Time Fourier Transform (STFT). Different audio data augmentation techniques such as pitch shifting, time stretching, background noise and SpecAugment are applied individually and as combinations on the UrbanSound8k dataset and their influence on the performance of the CNN model is studied and compared. 10-fold cross validation is used to ensure the robustness of the results achieved. Results show that the highest accuracy and F1-score of 79.2% and 80.3% respectively is achieved when the CNN model used SpecAugment and time stretching augmented audio data.

Keywords: Environmental sound classification · Deep learning · Data augmentation · Mel-spectrogram · Convolutional neural networks

1 Introduction

As various regions become urbanized and densely populated, the permeation of noises such as cars honking, busses whirring, siren wailing and the mechanical clattering from construction becomes inescapable. It has been shown in various studies that exposure to noise pollution can have a direct impact on the health and wellbeing of the population [1]. As the population continues to grow, noise pollution will continue to expand as a health risk. Understanding these problems better will lead to the creation of new potential solutions. Research in the areas of audio datasets with respect to music and speech is prevalent and continues to grow. Much progress has been made in the last few years in the area of classification of environmental sounds. Classification of urban sounds has a plethora of applications as well, such as, systems that assist those with

© Springer Nature Singapore Pte Ltd. 2021
K. K. Patel et al. (Eds.): icSoftComp 2020, CCIS 1374, pp. 52–64, 2021.
https://doi.org/10.1007/978-981-16-0708-0_5

impaired hearing, predictive maintenance in industrial environments, security and safety in smart homes and multimedia indexing and retrieval [2]. The recognition of these sounds on mobile devices can also lead to new and exciting applications. This paper aims to study the influence of various augmentation methods like the SpecAugment, pitch shifting, time stretching and background noise insertion on the performance of a 5-layer convolutional neural network (CNN) for the classification of environmental sounds from the UrbanSound8k dataset.

The reminder of this paper is organized as follows: Sect. 2 covers the previous research that has been done with respect to the UrbanSound8k dataset and environmental sound classification. Section 3 provides a brief description on the UrbanSound8k dataset. Section 4 details the various augmentation methods used in this work. Section 5 explains the CNN model used. Section 6 elucidates the evaluation metrics and data preparation. The results obtained are given in Sect. 7. The conclusion is given in Sect. 8.

2 Related Work

Salamon et al. presented a taxonomy for urban sounds to enable a common framework for research and introduced a new dataset, UrbanSound8k, consisting of 10 classes of audio that spans 27 h with 18.5 h of annotated event occurrences [2]. The ten classes of sound include the following: "air conditioner, car horn, children playing, dog bark, drilling, engine idling, gun shot, jackhammer, siren, and street music". Piczak implemented an environmental sound classification model with a convolutional neural network (CNN) architecture [3]. The datasets were preprocessed into segmented spectrograms. The CNN architecture consisted of 2 fully connected layers and 2 convolutional layers with max pooling. The proposed model achieved an accuracy of 73%.

The performance of the CNN's on the UrbanSound8k dataset was improved by Salamon et al. using data augmentation [4]. Data augmentation was carried out on raw audio waveform before being transformed into their log-scaled Mel-spectrogram representation. The authors used audio augmentation methods such as time stretching, pitch shifting, dynamic range compression and background noise insertion. Their model achieved 73% accuracy without data augmentation and 79% accuracy with data augmentation. Sang et al. proposed a convolutional recurrent neural network model trained on raw audio waveforms for environmental sound classification [5]. The convolutional layers extracted high level features and the recurrent layers made temporal aggregations of the extracted features. Long short-term networks were used as the recurrent layers. The proposed architecture achieved an accuracy of 79.06%.

Dai et al. proposed a deep CNN architecture for environmental sound classification with 34 weight layers with no addition of fully connected layers [6]. Audio samples were used in their raw waveform as opposed to various feature extraction transformations. The model achieved decent performance and matched the accuracy of some models trained on log-scaled Mel-features. This model scored an accuracy of 71.8%. Zhang et al. used dilated convolutional neural networks and tested the effectiveness of different activation functions such as rectified linear unit (ReLU), LeakyReLU, exponential linear unit (ELU), parametric ReLU (PReLU) and Softplus [7]. The models were tested on the UrbanSound8k, ESC-10 and CICESE datasets. 1D data augmentations were used. The results showed that the LeakyReLU activation function worked better on the UrbanSound8k and ESC-10 datasets whereas the PReLU activation function worked better on the CICESE dataset. The reasoning behind the superior performance of the LeakyReLU activation function being that it trades of network sparsity for more network information leading to better performance by the classifier. The proposed model with the LeakyReLU activation function achieved an accuracy of 81.9% on the urban sound dataset.

Though there are work in the literature that have aimed at classifying the UrbanSound8k dataset, this work is different from the previous research in the following ways: 1) This work uses a 5-layer deep CNN for learning the features and classifying the audio samples from the UrbanSound8k dataset. 2) In this work an in-depth study is conducted to analyze the effect of the SpecAugment augmentation method combined with other augmentation methods such as pitch shifting, time stretching and background noise insertion on the classification of the UrbanSound8k dataset. To the best of our knowledge, there is no previous work in the literature investigating the influence of the SpecAugment augmentation method on the UrbanSound8k dataset.

3 Dataset Description

This work uses the UrbanSound8k dataset introduced by Salamon et al. [2]. The UrbanSound8k consists of 8732 audio tracks belonging to 10 different classes like the air conditioner, car horn, children playing, dog barking, drilling, engine idling, gun shot, jackhammer, siren, and street music. These 10 classes were chosen due to the high frequency of occurrence in the city environments apart from the gun shot class which was added for variety. Each audio track spanned a duration of 4 s. This time length was chosen after testing showed that 4 s are enough for models to classify the dataset with decent accuracy. The sequences which lasted more than 4 s were segmented into slices of 4 s using a sliding window with a hop size of 2s. The total duration of the audio recording for the 8732 audio tracks was 8.7 h. Figure 1 shows the amplitude vs time plot of sample audio tracks from each of the 10 classes of the UrbanSound8k dataset. The matplotlib and librosa python library are used to obtain the plots [13].

4 Data Preprocessing

This section details the various augmentations and transformations used in this study.

1D Data Augmentation. In order to overcome the deficit of samples in the dataset, various data augmentation methods are being used that produce new samples from the existing samples by applying transformations to the samples in the dataset [8]. To produce augmentations to the raw audio dataset, methods such as pitch shifting, time stretching and background noise insertion are used in the literature [4]. The values of pitch shifting and time stretching were chosen based on the results obtain in [4].

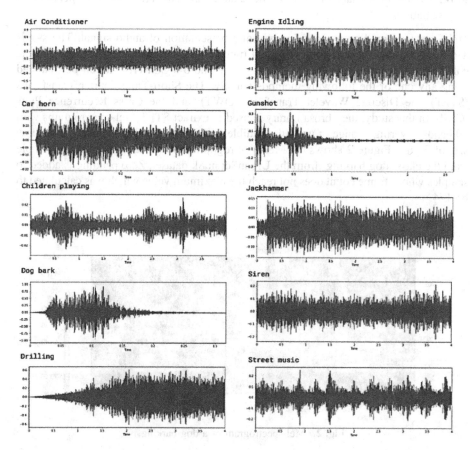

Fig. 1. Amplitude vs time plot of sample audio tracks from each of the 10 class of the UrbanSound8k dataset.

Time Stretching. The audio samples are sped up or slowed down by desired factors. The rates chosen for this study were 0.81 and 1.07.

Pitch Shifting. The pitch of the samples is increased or decreased according to specified values. Previous studies have shown that this augmentation method can improve results obtained by a classifier. The values chosen for this study were −1, −2, 1 and 2.

Background Noise. Noise was generated using the NumPy library and inserted into the audio samples in the dataset.

Audio Transformations. Classification algorithms, especially CNNs, have been shown to work significantly better on audio signals after the signals have been transformed into other representations such as Mel-spectrograms, MFCCs, chroma, tonnetz and spectral contrast. Mel-spectrograms and MFCCs have been found to be the most effective and popular transformations used for audio classification [9]. In this work, the audio signals present in the dataset are converted to Mel-spectrogram representation.

Mel Spectrogram. Spectrogram is a visual representation of audio signal. The x-axis and the y-axis of a spectrogram represent time and the frequency respectively and the colour gradient represents the amplitude of the audio signal [10]. It can be obtained using any one of the following methods namely: The Short-Time Fourier Transforms (STFT), the Discrete Wavelet Transform (DWT), and the Cross Recurrence Plots (CRP). In this study, the librosa library is used to extract STFT Mel-spectrograms with 40 bands covering a range of up to the audible frequency of 22050 Hz using a window size of 93 ms. Figure 2 shows the Mel-spectrogram representation of an audio sample from the class 'dog barking' from the UrbanSound8k dataset. Zero padding is added to samples whose frame count does not reach the maximum value which was calculated to be 174.

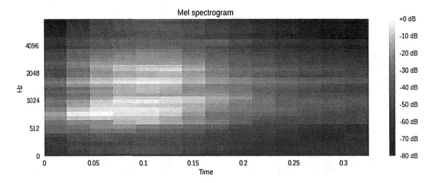

Fig. 2. Mel-spectrogram of a dog barking.

SpecAugment (SA). Traditionally, data augmentation has been applied to audio signals before they were transformed into various visual representations such as spectrograms. Park et al. developed an augmentation method called SpecAugment [11] that can be applied directly to spectrograms by warping it in the time axis and applying blocks of consecutive horizontal (Mel-frequency channels) and vertical masks (time steps). It has been shown that SpecAugment audio signals make the classifier more robust against deformations in the time domain for speech recognition tasks.

5   Methodology

Deep Learning. Deep learning models are able to learn representations of raw data through multiple levels of abstractions due to these models being composed of multiple processing layers. Deep learning models have been able to achieve remarkable levels of performance and accuracy over the years [14, 15]. Recurrent neural networks and convolutional neural networks are the most popular deep learning models prevalent in the literature. Recurrent neural networks work well with sequential data, i.e. text and speech and convolutional neural networks have had tremendous success in processing video, images, speech and audio [12].

Convolutional Neural Network. Convolutional Neural Network is composed of multiple layers that include convolutional, pooling and usually one or more fully connected layers. The convolutional layers consist of kernels or filters that are trained to optimally extract features from an image. The pooling layer reduces the number of parameters by subsampling the feature map output by the convolutional layers. Activation functions are used in order to add non-linearity to the model so that it can perform complex tasks. The ReLU activation function has particularly gained popularity. This is because the ReLU type activation functions overcome the vanishing gradient problem faced by other activation functions such as the sigmoid and tanh activation function. In order to compute and minimize the error of the model, loss functions are used. Cross-entropy and mean squared error are two commonly used loss functions.

Proposed Model. The CNN model used in this study consists of four 2D convolutional layers with batch normalization. Batch normalization stabilizes the learning process and reduces training time by standardizing the inputs of each minibatch to a layer. The audio samples from the UrbanSound8k dataset will first go through various augmentations before being fed into the CNN model for training. The input to the CNN is the Mel-spectrogram representation of an audio signal.

The first convolutional layer (Conv2D) has 32 filters with a filter size of 3 × 3. It receives inputs of dimensions (128,40,174,1), where 128 is the batch size, 40 is the number of Mel-bands and 174 is the frame counts. Its outputs are of dimensions (128,38,172,32) where 32 represents the feature maps created by the filters in the first Conv2D layer. Feature maps are the outputs produced by the filters. The input batch size to the CNN model is set to 128. There is no zero padding and the stride is kept as one.

2D spatial dropout regularization with rates of 0.07 and 0.14 are added to prevent overfitting by regularizing the model by setting random units to zero. Studies by Zhang et al. showed that the leakyReLU activation function worked relatively better on the UrbanSound8k dataset, hence we decided to use the same in this study [7]. The ReLU activation function returns the same value if the input value is positive and returns zero if the input value is negative. The leakyReLU activation function returns small negative values when the input value is less than zero.

The second Conv2D layer has 32 filters with a filter size of 3 × 3 and the output with the dimensions of (128,36,170,32). A max pooling layer of size 2 × 2 was added after the batch normalization of the second Conv2D layer. Max pooling layers down samples the feature maps along the height and the width by choosing the highest values from each patch the layer passes over. The feature map is down sampled by the max pooling layer to the dimensions of (128,18,85,32).

The third Conv2D layer has 64 filters with a filter size of 3 × 3 and the output having dimensions of (128,16,83,64). The fourth Conv2D layer has 64 filters with a filter size of 3 × 3 with the output having dimensions of (128,14,81,64).

A global average pooling layer is added after the batch normalization layer of the fourth 2D convolutional layer without spatial dropout. The global average pooling layer down samples the collection of feature maps into a single value of dimensions (128,64) by taking the average of the values in the feature map.

A fully connected output layer with 10 nodes is added for classification of the data. The final dense layer is followed by the softmax activation function to represent probability distribution over the 10 different classes.

The network is trained using the Adam optimizer to minimize the categorical cross-entropy loss function with early stopping. Figure 3 shows the CNN architecture used in this work. The CNN model is implemented using Keras.

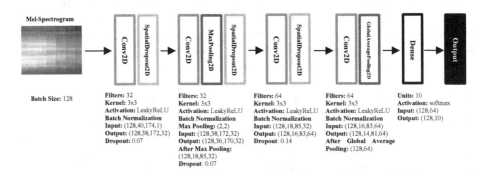

Fig. 3. The proposed CNN Architecture.

6   Evaluation Metrics and Data Preparation

Evaluation Metrics. Accuracy and F1-score are used for comparing and evaluating the results of the CNN model. To be comparable to previous work on the Urban-Sound8k dataset and to ensure robust results, 10-fold cross validation is conducted. For 10-fold cross validation, the dataset is divided into 10-folds. The CNN model is trained on 9 folds and evaluated on the remaining evaluation fold. This process is repeated 10 times. Every time an evaluation fold is chosen such that it had not been chosen previously.

Data Preparation. As mentioned earlier the aim of this work is to explore various audio data augmentation techniques and their combinations in order to identify the individual or combined augmentation technique that yields the best classification accuracy value for the proposed CNN model to classify the given UrbanSound8k dataset. For this purpose, 10 different sets of data are generated using the various augmentation methods mentioned earlier to train and test the CNN model. The 10 different sets of data are denoted as NA, TS, PS, BN, SAxTS, SAxPS, SAxBN, PS+TS +BN, SA and ALL. The way in which these 10 different datasets are obtained is detailed in Table 1.

Table 1. A description of datasets with different combination of augmentations applied.

Dataset	Description
NoAug (NA)	NA is the data containing the original 8732 audio samples from the dataset that is not subjected to any augmentation method
TS	TS data is obtained by applying time stretching data augmentation to the 8732 audio samples to produce 8732 × 2 samples. Consequently, the 8732 NA audio samples are also combined to produce a total of 26,196 audio samples
PS	PS data contains the audio data samples from the dataset that are subjected to pitch shifting data augmentation to produce 8732 × 4 samples. In addition to this the 8732 NA audio samples are also combined to produce a total of 43,660 audio samples
BN	BN data contains the 8732 audio data samples from the dataset that are subjected to background noise insertion data augmentation. In addition to this the 8732 NA audio samples are also combined to produce a total of 17,464 audio samples
SA	SA data contains the 8732 audio data samples from the dataset that are subjected to SpecAugment data augmentation. In addition to this the 8732 NA audio samples are also combined to produce a total of 17,464 audio samples
SAxTS	SAxTS data is obtained by subjecting the 26,196 audio data samples from TS data to SpecAugment data augmentation to produce a total of 26,196 × 2 samples
SAxPS	SAxPS data is obtained by subjecting the 43,660 audio data samples from PS data to SpecAugment data augmentation to produce a total of 43,660 × 2 samples SAxBN: SAxBN data is obtained by subjecting the 17,464 audio data samples from BN data to SpecAugment data augmentation to produce a total of 17,464 × 2 samples
PS+TS +BN	Contains 69,856 data samples from PS, TS, BN and NA data
ALL	ALL data is obtained by subjecting the 69,856 data samples from PS + TS + BN data to SpecAugment to contain 69856 × 2 samples

Figure 4 shows the process pipeline by which the different data are formed. The number of samples and their distribution in the 10 data have been presented in the bar graph in Fig. 5. Pitch shifting, time stretching and background noise insertion augmentations are applied to the audio samples before transforming into the Mel-spectrograms whereas SpecAugment augmentation is applied after the samples are transformed into their corresponding Mel-spectrogram representation. The CNN models trained on the different datasets are then evaluated on the evaluation fold on which no augmentation has been applied.

7 Results and Discussion

The CNN model is trained with 10 different data explained in the previous section. The average accuracy and F1-scores of the different augmentation methods are tabulated in Table 2. It can be observed from Table 2 that applying augmentations to the dataset did indeed improve the performance of the CNN model. The CNN model when trained and tested on the NA data achieved an average accuracy and F1-score of 76.9% and 78.3% respectively while the highest average accuracy and F1-score of 79.2% and 80.3% is obtained when the CNN model is trained using SAxTS data.

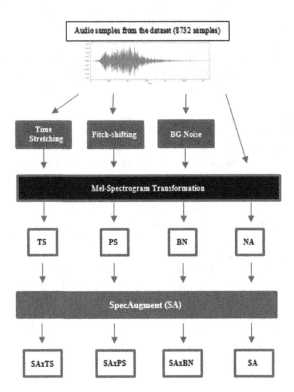

Fig. 4. Process pipeline depicting the formation of the various input data from the UrbanSound8k dataset using various audio data augmentation techniques.

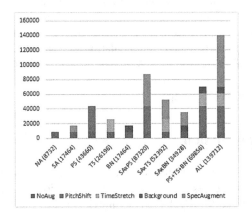

Fig. 5. The number of samples and their distribution in each of the 10 data.

Figure 6 shows the boxplot representation of the accuracy values obtained by 10-fold cross validation of the CNN model using NA and the SAxTS data. It can be observed from the figure that the proposed CNN model using SAxTS data is more robust as the corresponding boxplot covers less area. Also, it can be noted that the CNN model exhibits better accuracy values when it uses SAxTS data. It is worth noting that the performance of the CNN model did not improve as the number of samples in each dataset increased as the model trained on the ALL dataset (139,712 samples) performed worse than the model trained on the SAxTS dataset (52392 samples).

Figure 7 (a) shows the confusion matrix obtained when the CNN model is trained and tested with SAxTS data. Figure 7 (b) shows the difference matrix obtained by computing the difference between the confusion matrices obtained when the CNN model is trained using SAxTS and NA data. Positive values along the diagonal of the difference matrix indicate that the CNN model performs better when trained using SAxTS data. In other words, it shows that the CNN model has better performance when trained using SAxTS data when compared with the NA.

The per-class classification accuracy values of the CNN model when trained and tested with the SAxTS data are 0.98, 0.89, 0.88, 0.87, 0.85, 0.83, 0.78, 0.75, 0.69 and 0.54 for the Gun Shot, Car Horn, Dog bark, Siren, Street Music, Children Playing, Drilling, Engine Idling, Jackhammer, and Air Conditioner classes respectively. Figure 8 shows the per-class accuracy difference values obtained when the CNN model is trained and tested on different data. For computing the accuracy difference, the accuracy value obtained while training the CNN model with the NA data is taken as the base value. It can be seen that for certain classes data augmentation greatly improved the performance of the CNN model. However, it can also be noted that in spite of data augmentation, the CNN model did not achieve good results for certain classes, such as 'air conditioner', 'drilling' and 'jackhammer'.

Table 2. Average accuracy and F1-score of the different augmentation methods.

Data	NA	SA	PS	TS	BN
Accuracy	76.9	78.8	77	77.4	76.8
F1-score	78.3	78.9	78.3	78.8	77.7
Data	PS + TS + BN	SAxPS	SAxTS	SAxBN	ALL
Accuracy	77.1	77.6	**79.2**	78.5	78.6
F1-score	78.2	78.9	**80.3**	79.4	79.6

Table 3. Performance comparison of different classifiers.

Model	Accuracy
PiczacCNN [3]	73
SB-CNN (without data augmentation) [4]	73
SB-CNN (with data augmentation) [4]	79
Dai et al. [6]	71.8
Zhang et al. [7]	81.9
Sang et al. [5]	79.06
SAxTS-CNN (Proposed model)	79.2

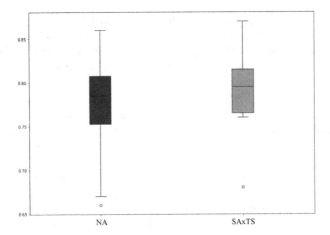

Fig. 6. Boxplot showing the accuracy values obtained by 10-fold cross validation of the CNN model using NA and SAxTS data augmentation methods.

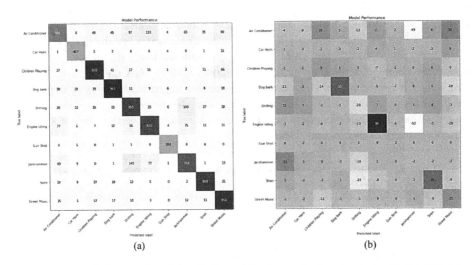

Fig. 7. (a) Confusion matrix of the CNN model when trained and tested with SAxTS data (b) Difference between confusion matrix values of the CNN when trained with SAxTS and NA.

Finally, we compared the performance of our proposed CNN model with other state-of-the-art deep learning models like PiczacCNN [3] and SB-CNN [4] with data augmentation for classifying the audio samples from the UrbanSound8k dataset. The SB-CNN used time stretching, pitch shifting, background noise insertion and dynamic range compression as the data augmentation techniques. It was observed that PiczacCNN without data augmentation produced an average accuracy of 73% and SB-CNN with data augmentation achieved an accuracy of 79%. Further comparisons with other models, as depicted in Table 3, shows that the proposed CNN model along with

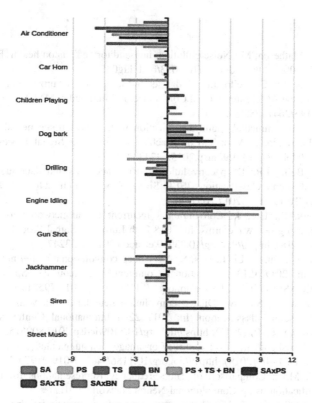

Fig. 8. Per-class accuracy difference values when the CNN model is trained and tested on different data. Note the vertical line corresponding to the value 0 represents the accuracy value of the CNN when trained and tested using the NA data.

SpecAugment and time stretching augmentations is able to achieve performance on par with the state-of-the-art deep models.

8 Conclusion

This paper investigated the effectiveness of various audio data augmentation techniques on the proposed CNN model for classifying the environmental sounds belonging to 10 classes from the Urbansound8k dataset. Several augmentation methods and their combinations were explored in this study. The experiments showed that the proposed CNN model achieved better results when the data was augmented using SpecAugment and time stretching data augmentation techniques. Additionally, the results also support the fact that applying augmentation to the datasets improves the performance of the CNN models.

References

1. Stansfeld, S., Matheson, M.: Noise pollution: non-auditory effects on health. Br. Med. Bull. **68**, 243–257 (2003). https://doi.org/10.1093/bmb/ldg033
2. Salamon, J., Jacoby, C., Bello, J.P.: A dataset and taxonomy for urban sound research. In: Proceedings of the ACM International Conference on Multimedia, MM 2014 (2014). https://doi.org/10.1145/2647868.2655045
3. Piczak, K.J.: Environmental sound classification with convolutional neural networks. In: IEEE 25th International Workshop on Machine Learning for Signal Processing (MLSP) (2015). https://doi.org/10.1109/mlsp.2015.7324337
4. Salamon, J., Bello, J.P.: Deep convolutional neural networks and data augmentation for environmental sound classification. IEEE Signal Process. Lett. **24**(3), 279–283 (2017). https://doi.org/10.1109/lsp.2017.2657381
5. Sang, J., Park, S., Lee, J.: Convolutional recurrent neural networks for urban sound classification using raw waveforms. In: 2018 26th European Signal Processing Conference (EUSIPCO) (2018). https://doi.org/10.23919/eusipco.2018.8553247
6. Dai, W., Dai, C., Qu, S., Li, J., Das, S.: Very deep convolutional neural networks for raw waveforms. In: 2017 IEEE International Conference on Acoustics, Speech and Signal Processing (ICASSP) (2017). https://doi.org/10.1109/icassp.2017.7952190
7. Zhang, X., Zou, Y., Shi, W.: Dilated convolution neural network with LeakyReLU for environmental sound classification. In: 2017 22nd International Conference on Digital Signal Processing (DSP) (2017). https://doi.org/10.1109/icdsp.2017.8096153
8. Shorten, C., Khoshgoftaar, T.M.: A survey on image data augmentation for deep learning. J. Big Data **6**(1), 1–48 (2019). https://doi.org/10.1186/s40537-019-0197-0
9. Md Shahrin, M.H.: Comparison of Time-Frequency Representations for Environmental Sound Classification using Convolutional Neural Networks (2017)
10. Rabiner, L.R., Schafer, R.W.: Theory and Applications of Digital Speech Processing. Pearson (2010)
11. Park, D.S., et al.: SpecAugment: a simple data augmentation method for automatic speech recognition. In: Interspeech 2019 (2019). https://doi.org/10.21437/interspeech.2019-2680
12. Goodfellow, I., Bengio, Y., Courville, A.: Deep Learning. MIT Press (2016)
13. McFee, B., et al.: librosa: audio and music signal analysis in python. In: Proceedings of the 14th Python in Science Conference, pp. 18–25 (2015)
14. Krizhevsky, A., Sutskever, I., Hinton, G.: ImageNet classification with deep convolutional neural networks. In: Neural Information Processing Systems 25 (2012). https://doi.org/10.1145/3065386
15. Simonyan, K., Zisserman, A.: Very Deep Convolutional Networks for Large-Scale Image Recognition. arXiv:1409.1556 (2014)

Quantile Regression Support Vector Machine (QRSVM) Model for Time Series Data Analysis

Dharmendra Patel[✉] [iD]

Smt. Chandaben Mohanbhai Patel Institute of Computer Applications,
CHARUSAT, Changa, Gujarat, India
dharmendrapatel.mca@charusat.ac.in

Abstract. Analysis of time series information is very interesting as it can be used to understand the past and to forecast the future. Mainly, the data models of the time series are based on the normal least square regression (LSR). For handle the outliers, the least square regression is not efficient. Data from the time series contains outliers in a notable quantity that may affect the results of the prediction. The proposed solution will use statistical techniques of quantile regression that robustly gives insights based on different dimensions as well as treats outliers. The advantage of quantile regression is to discover more useful predictive relationships in situations where there is a poor relationship between independent variables. The paper described the statistics of QRSVM model. The paper dealt experiments based on time series data and proved that QRSVM model is superior than LSR model in insights generations and for outlier handling.

Keywords: Least square regression · Quantile regression · Support vector machine · Time series analysis · Quantile regression support vector machine model

1 Introduction

Time series data is very vital for many applications such as economics, medicine, education, social sciences, epidemiology, weather forecasting, physical sciences etc. to derive meaningful insights at different points in time. Conventional statistics methods have several limitations to deal with time series data so specialized methods known as time series analysis requires predominantly in such cases. The simplest and most popular method is linear least square method. Least square method gives the trend line to best fit to a time series data. It exhibits several advantages:

- It is very simple method to understand and derive the prediction
- It is to be applicable for all most all applications
- It gives maximum likelihood solutions if correlate with Markov Conditions.

However, it suffers from several critical limitations:

- Sensitive towards outliers.
- Data needs to be normally distributed for better results.
- It exhibits tendency of outfit data.

© Springer Nature Singapore Pte Ltd. 2021
K. K. Patel et al. (Eds.): icSoftComp 2020, CCIS 1374, pp. 65–74, 2021.
https://doi.org/10.1007/978-981-16-0708-0_6

Quantile Regressing method by utilizing support vector machine approach is an idyllic approach to deal with the limitations of least square regression methods. It has advantages over least square regression. Table 1 describes the comparison between least square and quantile regression.

Table 1. Comparison of least and quantile regression

Parameter	Least square regression	Quantile regression
Prediction	Conditional mean	Condition quantiles
Size of data	Best suit for small data	Requires sufficient data
Distribution of data	Needs normal distributed data	It does not require any assumption in distribution of data. If data is unclear then also it performs well
Preservation	Conditional mean does not preserve under transformation	It preserves under transformation
Computation of data	It does not require rigorous computation so it is cheap	It is computationally rigorous
Response assumption	Constant variance for the response	No constant variance of the response is required

Support vector machine in correlation with quantile regression may produce excellent outcomes for time series analysis. The support vector machine has an ability to solve nonlinear regression estimate problems so it is the prominent candidate for time series data analysis. One more significant feature of SVM is that the learning here is analogous to resolve a problem of linear quadratic optimization. Thus, unlike the other traditional stochastic or neural network methods, the solution obtained by applying the SVM method is always unique and globally optimal.

The Sect. 2 of paper will deal with related work in this field. Section 3 will describe QRSVM model in details. Section 4 will discuss about Experiments and Results of the model. At Last, Paper provides the conclusions of research work carried out.

2 Related Work

Statistical Methods predominantly used for time series data analysis. Autoregressive Integrated Moving Average (ARIMA) model is the most prevalent and commonly used for time series data analysis [6]. Notwithstanding, these sort of models depend on the hypothesis that take into an account that time series must be linear and follows a normal distribution of the data. C. Hamzacebi in 2008 [1] proposed a distinction of ARIMA model called as Seasonal ARIMA (SARIMA). The prototypical produced good results for seasonal time series data, however it required to undertake linear form of associated time series data. The limitations of the linear models could be overcome by non-linear stochastic models [5, 19]. However, the implementation of these kind of models is very complex.

Neural Network based time series models have grown as of late and pulled in expanding considerations [8, 9]. The astounding element of ANNs is their inherent capability of non-linear modeling with no presupposition about the statistical distribution monitored by the annotations. The incredible highlights about ANN based models are self-versatile in nature [28]. There is assortment of ANN models exist in the literature. The Multi-Layer Perceptron (MLP) is the most famous and basic model dependent on ANN [2, 4, 13, 22]. MLPs contain different layers of computational components, unified in a feed-forward way [18].MLPs utilize a variety of learning techniques, the conspicuous is back-propagation [16, 20, 29] where the output esteems are related with the exact response to compute the value of some foreordained error-function. The error is then served back through the network. Utilizing this data, the algorithm controls the degree of each linkage so as to decrease the estimation of the error function by some insignificant quantity. An overall strategy for non-linear optimization called gradient descent [21, 23] is applied to regulate the degrees. Time Lagged Neural Network (TLNN) is another variation of Feed Forward way [15, 26]. In TLNN, the input nodes are the time series values at some specific lags. Likewise, there is a constant input term, which may be expediently taken as 1 and this is linked to every neuron in the hidden and output layer. The presentation of this constant input unit circumvents the need of separately introducing a bias term. In 2007, Pang et al. [17] introduced one model dependent on neural network and efficaciously applied to the simulation in the rainfall. Li et al. [14], In 2008, presented hybrid model based on AR * and generalized regression neural network model (GRNN) and that gave respectable results in the setting to the time series data. Chen and Chang in 2009 [3] came out with an Evolutionary Artificial Neural Network model (EANN) to build automatically the architecture and the connections of the weights of the neural network. Khashei and Bijari in 2010 [11] introduced a new hybrid ANN model, utilizing an ARIMA model to discover predictions more precise than the model of neural networks. Wu and Shahidehpour [27] proposed a fusion model based on an adaptive Wavelet Neural Network (AWNN) and time series models, such as the ARMAX and GARCH, to predict the day by day estimation of electricity in the market. In [7] researchers proposed a regression neural network model to anticipate widespread time series, which is a fusion of diverse algorithms for machine learning. Artificial Neural Network based algorithms are overwhelming for time series data analysis however they show various constraints such as: appropriate network structure is attained through trial and error, sometimes mysterious performance of the network, usually require more data to train the model fittingly, computationally complex and affluent. Support Vector Machine [12, 24, 25] is the vigorous machine learning technique for the pattern generation and classification.

The proposed model will use SVM as it isn't just intended for decent classification yet additionally expected for an improved speculation of the training data. Solutions obtained by SVM is always unique as it depends on linearly constrained quadratic optimization. The model will use the fusion methodology of SVM and Quantile Regression [10]. Quantile Regression methodology permits for comprehension relationships between variables outside of the average of the data, making it valuable in understanding outcomes that are non-normally dispersed and that have nonlinear relationships with predictor variables.

3 Quantile Regression Support Vector Machine (QRSVM) Model

The least square regression model is representing by the Eq. (1).

$$Y = a + b X + \varepsilon \tag{1}$$

Where Y is Dependent Variable whose value is going to be predicted
a is the intercept of Y
b is the slope of line
ε represents an error and s identically, independently, and normally distributed with mean zero and unknown variance σ2.

Least square regression model attempt to define conditional distribution by utilizing the average of a distribution. Another thing is, it assumes that the error term is same across all values of X in which conditional variable (Y/X) to be assumed a constant variance σ2. When this assumption fail, we must change the LSR algorithm to accommodate conditional mean and scale. The new equation based on conditional scale is:

$$Y = a + b X + e^r \varepsilon \tag{2}$$

Where r is the unknown parameter

$$\text{Var}\,(Y/X) = \sigma^2 e^r \tag{3}$$

In this also, conditional scale for dependent variable y is not vary with independent variable X. In order to realize covariate properties in context to dependent variable Quantile Regressing concept is required.

$$Y = a^{(p)} + b^{(p)} X + \varepsilon^{(p)} \tag{4}$$

Where p is the probability and it ranges between 0 and 1.
We specify the pth conditional quantile given X with

$$Q^{(p)}\left(\frac{Y}{X}\right) = a^{(p)} + b^{(p)} X \tag{5}$$

Least square regression having only one conditional mean while Quantile Regression contains numerous conditional quantiles. In the nonlinear quantile regression, the quantile of the dependent variable Y for a given independent attribute X is assumed to be nonlinearly related to the input vector Xi ∈ Rd and represented by nonlinear mapping function φ(…). The new version related to nonlinearity characteristic of quantile function is represented as:

$$QX = W\theta\,\phi(X) \tag{6}$$

Where $\theta \in (0, 1)$,
W_θ is θ^{th} regression quantile.

Absolute deviation loss will occur in quantile regression so SVM with quantile regression plays a vital role. The equation of quantile regression with SVM is represented as:

$$Minimize 12 \|w\theta\|2 + Ci = 1np\theta(Y - W\theta\,\phi(X)) \tag{7}$$

for any $\theta \in (0, 1)$

Equation (7) is considered as QRSVM Model.

4 Experiments and Results

Experiments of proposed study is carried out by considering weather data of Anand District of Gujarat State, India. The sample data is depicted in the Table 1.

Table 2. Sample weather data of Anand district

Temperature(in Celsius)/Month	January	February	March	April	May	June
Avg. temperature	20.5	22.9	27.2	31.1	33.4	32.2
Min. temperature	12	14.1	18.5	22.9	26.4	27.2
Max. temperature	29	31.7	35.9	39.4	40.5	37.3
Rain fall(mm)	1	0	1	0	2	92

Experiment simulation is carried out using R programming language (Figs. 1 and 2).

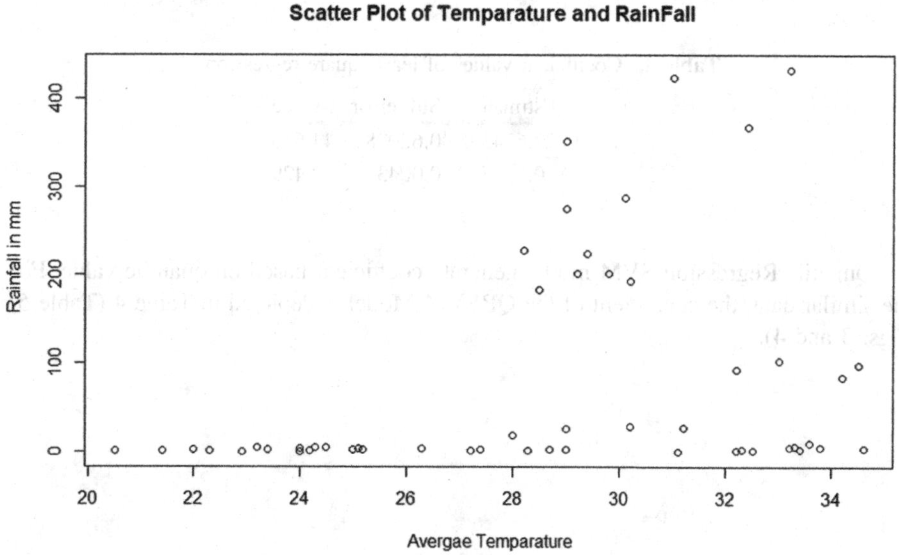

Scatter Plot of Temparature and RainFall

Fig. 1. Scatter plot temperature vs. rainfall

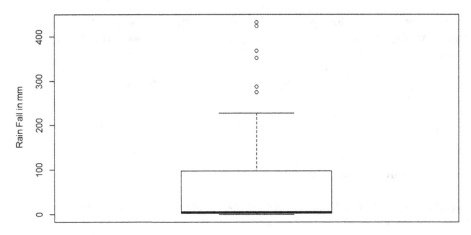

Fig. 2. Box plot for rainfall data

The box plot of rainfall data indicates that several values are outliers. For the accurate prediction of the time series data, outlier values also play an important role.

According to least square regression model, residuals values and Coefficient statistics, are depicted in Table 2 and Table 3 respectively. They having one value based on central tendency value.

Table 3. Residual values of least square regression

Min	First quantile	Median	Third quantile	Max
−7.1849	−2.6955	−0.4849	3.4257	6.8939

Table 4. Coefficient values of least square regression

	Estimate	Std. error	t-value
Intercept	27.674335	0.620280	44.616
X	0.010579	0.004356	2.429

Quantile Regression SVM model generate coefficient based on quantile value. For the similar data, the coefficient of the QRSVM Model is depicted in Table 4 (Table 5, Figs. 3 and 4).

Table 5. Coefficient values of QRSVM model

Quantile to be estimated	Intercept	X
0.05	21.96	0.02
0.1	22.279384	0.020616
0.15	23.125537	0.018616
0.2	23.950000	0.016666
0.25	24.182481	0.017518
0.3	24.433580	0.016605
0.35	24.964210	0.017894
0.4	25.165614	0.017193
0.45	26.259859	0.013380
0.5	27.3810526	0.0094737
0.55	28.2936019	0.0063981
0.6	28.7135135	0.0054054
0.65	29.5286956	0.0034782
0.7	31.1000000	0.0035326
0.75	3.219946e+0	5.449591e$-$04
0.8	32.50027248	$-$0.00027248
0.85	3.320000e+01	$-$1.431147e$-$17
0.9	33.60851063	$-$0.00094562
0.95	34.4413793	$-$0.00287356

Relationship between Quantile and Intercept based on QRSVM Model

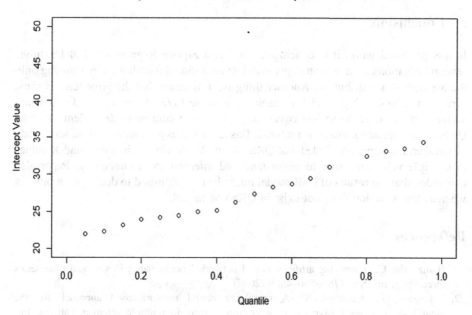

Fig. 3. Scatter plot quantile vs. intercept value in QRSVM

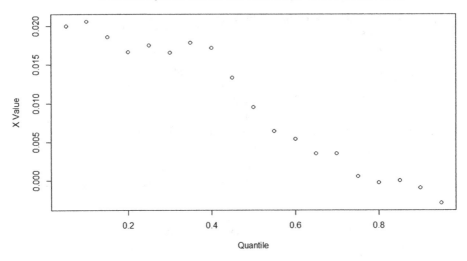

Fig. 4. Scatter plot quantile vs. X in QRSVM

From the results we can see that Least Square regression distributes Intercept and X values on central tendency where as QRSVM model distributes them with multiple values based on the values of percentile so we can understand and explore the insights with multiple dimensions. The other thing is if outlier exist in the data then central tendency value might be compromised whereas this situation will not affect in QRSVM Model.

5   Conclusions

In this proposed work, it is concluded that Least Square Regression Model exhibits several limitations such as it attempts to define conditional distribution by utilizing only the average of a distribution. Another thing is, it assumes that the error term is same across all values of X in which conditional variable (Y/X) to be assumed a constant variance σ^2. In order to realize covariate properties in context to dependent variable, Quantile Regressing concept is required. Based on the experiments of time series data of weather, the paper concluded that QRSVM model distributes Intercept and X values in multiple values in order to understand and interpret them effectively. Paper also concluded that the results of LSR model might be compromised to deal to with outliers whereas this situation does not exist in QRSVM model.

References

1. Hamzacebi, C.: Improving artificial neural networks' performance in seasonal time series forecasting. Inf. Sci. **178**, 4550–4559 (2008)
2. Calcagno, G., Antonino, S.: A multilayer neural network-based approach for the identification of responsiveness to interferon therapy in multiple sclerosis patients. Inf. Sci. **180**(21), 4153–4163 (2010)

3. Chen, Y., Chang, F.-J.: Evolutionary artificial neural networks for hydrological systems forecasting. J. Hydrol. **367**, 125–137 (2009)
4. Wang, D., Liu, D., Zhao, D., Huang, Y., Zhang, D.: A neural-network-based iterative GDHP approach for solving a class of nonlinear optimal control problems with control constraints. Neural Comput. Appl. **22**(2), 219–227 (2013)
5. Zhang, G.P.: A neural network ensemble method with jittered training data for time series forecasting. Inf. Sci. **177**, 5329–5346 (2007)
6. Zhang, G.P.: Time series forecasting using a hybrid ARIMA and neural network model. Neurocomputing **50**, 159–175 (2003)
7. Gheyas, I.A., Smith, L.S.: A novel neural network ensemble architecture for time series forecasting. Neurocomuting **74**, 3855–3864 (2011)
8. Kihoro, J.M., Otieno, R.O., Wafula, C.: Seasonal time series forecasting: a comparative study of ARIMA and ANN models. Afr. J. Sci. Technol. (AJST) Sci. Eng. Ser. **5**(2), 41–49 (2004)
9. Kamruzzaman, J., Begg, R., Sarker, R.: Artificial Neural Networks in Finance and Manufacturing. Idea Group Publishing, USA (2006)
10. Yu, K., Lu, Z., Stander, J.: Quantile regression: applications and current research areas. J. R. Stat. Soc. Ser. D (The Stat.) **52**, 331–350 (2003)
11. Khashei, M., Bijari, M.: An artificial neural network (p,d,q) model for timeseries forecasting. Expert Syst. Appl. **37**(1), 479–489 (2010). https://doi.org/10.1016/j.eswa.2009.05.044
12. Cao, L.J., Tay, F.E.H.: Support vector machine with adaptive parameters in financial time series forecasting. IEEE Trans. Neural Netw. **14**(6), 1506–1518 (2003). https://doi.org/10.1109/TNN.2003.820556
13. Tawfiq, L.N.M.: Design and training artificial neural networksfor solving differential equations. Ph.D. thesis, University of Baghdad, College of Education Ibn-Al-Haitham (2004)
14. Li, W., Luo, Y., Zhu, Q., Liu, J., Le, J.: Applications of AR*-GRNN model for the financial time series forecasting. Neural Comput. Appl. **17**, 441–448 (2008)
15. Moseley, N.: Modeling economic time series using a focused time lagged feed forward neural network. In: Proceedings of Student Research Day, CSIS, Pace University (2003)
16. Nawi, N.M., Ransing, M.R., Ransing, R.S.: An improved conjugate gradient based learning algorithm for back propagation neural networks. J. Comput. Intell. **4**, 46–55 (2007)
17. Pang, B., Guo, S., Xiong, L., Li, C.: A non linear perturbation model based on artificial neural network. J. Hydrol. **333**, 504–516 (2007)
18. Prochazka, A.P.: Feed-forward and recurrent neural networks in signal prediction. In: 4th International Conference on Computational Cybernetics. IEEE (2007)
19. Parrelli, R.: Introduction to ARCH & GARCH models. Optional TA Handouts, Econ 472 Department of Economics, University of Illinois (2001)
20. Rehman, M.Z., Nawi, N.M., Ghazali, M.I.: Noise-induced hearing loss (NIHL) prediction in humans using a modified back propagation neural network. In: 2nd International Conference on Science Engineering and Technology, pp. 185–189 (2011)
21. Ruder, S.: An overview of gradient descent optimization algorithms. https://arxiv.org/pdf/1609.04747.pdf. Accessed 23 Jan 2018
22. Hoda I., S.A., Nagla, H.A.: On neural network methods for mixed boundary value problems. Int. J. Nonlinear Sci. **11**(3), 312–316 (2011)
23. Selvaraju, R.R., Cogswell, M., Das, A., Vedantam, R., Parikh, D., Batra, D.: Grad-CAM: visual explanations from deep networks via gradient-based localization. In: Proceedings of the 2017 IEEE International Conference on Computer Vision (ICCV) (2017). https://doi.org/10.1109/ICCV.2017.74

24. Farooq, T., Guergachi, A., Krishnan, S.: Chaotic time series prediction using knowledge based Green's Kernel and least-squares support vector machines. In: Systems, Man and Cybernetics, pp. 373–378 (2007)
25. Raicharoen, T., Lursinsap, C., Sanguanbhoki, P.: Application of critical support vector machine to time series prediction. In: Proceedings of the 2003 International Symposium on Circuits and Systems, ISCAS 2003, vol. 5, pp. 741–744 (2003)
26. Yolcu, U., Egrioglu, E., Aladag, C.H.: A new linear & nonlinear artificial neural network model for time series forecasting. Decis. Support Syst. **54**(3), 1340–1347 (2013)
27. Lei, W., Shahidehpour, M.: A hybrid model for day-ahead price forecasting. IEEE Trans. Power Syst. **25**(3), 1519–1530 (2010). https://doi.org/10.1109/TPWRS.2009.2039948
28. Wang, X., Meng, M.: A hybrid neural network and ARIMA model for energy consumption forecasting. J. Comput. **7**(5), 1184–1190 (2012)
29. Zweiri, Y., Seneviratne, L., Althoefer, K.: Stability analysis of a three-term backpropagation algorithm. Neural Netw. **18**(10), 1341–1347 (2005). https://doi.org/10.1016/j.neunet.2005.04.007

Selection of Characteristics by Hybrid Method: RFE, Ridge, Lasso, and Bayesian for the Power Forecast for a Photovoltaic System

Jose Cruz[✉][ID], Wilson Mamani[ID], Christian Romero[ID],
and Ferdinand Pineda[ID]

Universidad Nacional del Altiplano, Puno, Peru
{josecruz,cromero,ferpineda}@unap.edu.pe, wmamani@estudiante.unap.edu.pe

Abstract. Currently, the generation of alternative energy from solar radiation with photovoltaic systems is growing, its efficiency depends on internal variables such as powers, voltages, currents; as well as external variables such as temperatures, irradiance, and load. To maximize performance, this research focused on the application of regularization techniques in a multiparametric linear regression model to predict the active power levels of a photovoltaic system from 14 variables that model the system under study. These variables affect the prediction to some degree, but some of them do not have so much preponderance in the final forecast, so it is convenient to eliminate them so that the processing cost and time are reduced. For this, we propose a hybrid selection method: first we apply the elimination of Recursive Feature Elimination (RFE) within the selection of subsets and then to the obtained results we apply the following contraction regularization methods: Lasso, Ridge and Bayesian Ridge; then the results were validated demonstrating linearity, normality of the error terms, without autocorrelation and homoscedasticity. All four prediction models had an accuracy greater than 99.97%. Training time was reduced by 71% and 36% for RFE-Ridge and RFE-OLS respectively. The variables eliminated with RFE were "Energia total", "Energia diaria" e "Irradiancia", while the variable eliminated by Lasso was: "Frequencia". In all cases we see that the root mean square errors were reduced for RFE.Lasso by 0.15% while for RFE-Bayesian Ridge by 0.06%.

Keywords: Regularization Shrinkage · Lasso · Ridge · Bayesian Ridge · RFE · Linear regression · Homoscedasticity

1 Introduction

Due to the increasing use of photovoltaic systems in the generation of alternative energy, it is difficult to obtain mathematical or physical models that result in the efficient use of such systems. Likewise, the tools and algorithms provided

© Springer Nature Singapore Pte Ltd. 2021
K. K. Patel et al. (Eds.): icSoftComp 2020, CCIS 1374, pp. 75–87, 2021.
https://doi.org/10.1007/978-981-16-0708-0_7

by Machine Learning in the use and treatment of data, result in useful tools to model photovoltaic generation systems. Within the field of data-based forecasts we have multiparametric linear regression, which allows forecasts taking into account a set of independent variables that affect the target or dependent variable. These variables affect the prediction to some degree, but some of them do not have so much preponderance in the final forecast, so it is convenient to eliminate them so that the processing cost and time are reduced. Among some of the techniques to exclude irrelevant variables or predictors we have: Subset Selection, Shinkrage Regularization, and Dimension Reduction. Within the first group that identifies and selects among all the available predictors that are most related to the target variable, we have: Bestsubset selection and Stepwiese selection. Within this last group we have: forward, backward, and hybrid. In the backward method we have the elimination of recursive functions (RFE), which is the algorithm used in this paper to model the multiparameter photovoltaic system. RFE is used in various studies such as the selection of attributes in classifiers based on artificial neural networks in the detection of cyberbullying [1]. In conjunction with other techniques such as SVR for feature selection based on twin support vector regression [2]; with SVM and Bayes for categorical classifications [3]. For the modeling of emotions and affective states from EEG, combining RFE with Random Forest (RF), Support Vector Regression (SVR), Tree-based bagging [4]. In identifying features for football game earnings forecast, combining it with were Gradient Boosting and Random Forest [5]. In the prediction of boiler system failures, using the RFE algorithm in combination with the elimination of recursive functions by vector machine (SVM-RFE) [6]. In the phenotyping of high-yield plants [7], to eliminate spectral characteristics, the elimination of vector-machine recursive characteristics (SVM-RFE), LASSO logistic regression and random forest are used. To perform the short-term electricity price and charge forecast using KNN, [8] uses RFE to eliminate redundancy of functions. To perform heart transplant tests, [9] in pig tests use a combination of RFE-SVM to select the parameters for the estimation of V0. In the present work, we perform the combination of RFE with Shinkrage regularization algorithms: Ridge, Lasso, and Bayesian Ridge, establishing a hybrid algorithm for modeling the multiparameter photovoltaic system.

2   Methodology

In regression models, a compromise must be made between the bias and the variance provided by the data to be predicted and the model performed. For this, the theory provides us with the following variable selection methods (feature selection): Subset selection, Shrinkage, and Dimension reduction. The first identifies and selects among all the available predictors those that are most related to the response variable. Shrinkage or Shrinkage fits the model, including all predictors, but including a method that forces the regression coefficient estimates to zero. While Dimension Reduction creates a small number of new variables from combinations of the original variables. Each of them has a subset of techniques such as for subset selection: best subselection and stepwiese selection (forward, backward and hybrid). For Shrinkage: Ridge, Lasso and ElasticNet. For Dimension Reduction we have Principal components, Partial Last Square and tSNE. Subset selection is the task of finding a small subset of the most informative elements in a basic set. In addition to helping reduce computational time and algorithm memory, due to working on a much smaller representative set, he has found numerous applications, including image and video summary, voice and document summary, grouping, feature selection and models, sensor location, social media marketing and product recommendation [10]. The recursive feature removal method (RFE) used works by recursively removing attributes and building a model on the remaining attributes. Use precision metrics to rank the feature based on importance. The RFE method takes the model to be used and the number of characteristics required as input. Then it gives the classification of all the variables, 1 being the most important. It also provides support, True if it is a relevant feature and False if it is an irrelevant feature.

The data was pre-processed by eliminating the null values. Next, the non-multicollinearity between the predictors was determined using a heat diagram. Three hybrid methods of variable selection were performed: RFE-Lasso, RFE-Ridge, RFE-Bayesian Ridge, comparing them with RFE-OLS, it was used as a baseline for our work. Finally, the results were validated under conditions of linearity, normality, no autocorrelation of error terms, and homoscedasticity.

3   Methods

3.1   Recursive Feature Elimination

For RFE we will use the following algorithm:

- 1 Refine/Train the model in the training group using all predictors
- 2 Calculate model performance
- 3 Calculate the importance of variables or classifications
- 4 For (for) each subset size S_i, i = 1...S do (do
  - 4.1 Keep the most important variables of S_i
  - 4.2 Optional: Pre-process the data
  - 4.3 Refine/Train the model in the training group using S_i predictors
  - 4.4 Calculate model performance
  - 4.5 Optional: Recalculate rankings for each predictor
  - 4.6 End (end)
- 5 Calculate the performance profile on S_i
- 6 Determine the appropriate number of predictors
- 7 Use the model corresponding to the optimal S_i

The algorithm fits the model to all predictors, each predictor is classified using its importance for the model. Let S be a sequence of ordered numbers that are candidate values for the number of predictors to retain (S_1,S_2, ...). At each iteration of the feature selection, the highest ranked Si predictors are retained, the model is readjusted, and performance is evaluated. The best performing Si value is determined and the main Si predictors are used to fit the final model. The algorithm has an optional step just at the end of its sequence (8) where the predictor ratings recalculate into the reduced feature set model. For the random forest models, there was a decrease in performance when the rankings were recalculated at each step. However, in other cases when the initial classifications are not good (for example, linear models with highly collinear predictors), the recalculation may slightly improve performance [11].

3.2   Ridge

For Ridge the sum of squared errors for linear regression is defined by Eq. 1:

$$E = \sum_{i=1}^{N} (y_i - \hat{y}_i)^2 \tag{1}$$

Just as the data set we want to use to make machine learning models must follow the Gaussian distribution defined by its mean, μ and variance σ^2 and is represented by $N(\mu, \sigma^2)$, i.e., $X \sim N(\mu, \sigma^2)$ where X is the input matrix.

For any point x_i, the probability of x_i is given by Eq. 2.

$$P(x_i) = \frac{1}{2\pi\sigma^2} e^{-\frac{1}{2}\frac{(x_i-\mu)^2}{\sigma^2}} \tag{2}$$

The occurrence of each x_i is independent of the occurrence of another, the joint probability of each of them is given by Eq. 3:

$$p(x_1, x_2, ...x_N) = \prod_{i=1}^{N} \frac{1}{2\pi\sigma^2} e^{-\frac{1}{2}\frac{(x_i-\mu)^2}{\sigma^2}} \tag{3}$$

Furthermore, linear regression is the solution that gives the maximum likelihood to the line of best fit by Eq. 4:

$$P(X \mid \mu) = p(x_1, x_2, ...x_N) = \prod_{i=1}^{N} \frac{1}{2\pi\sigma^2} e^{-\frac{1}{2}\frac{(x_i-\mu)^2}{\sigma^2}} \tag{4}$$

Linear regression maximizes this function for the sake of finding the line of best fit. For this, we take the natural logarithm of the probability function (likelihood) (L), then differentiate and equal zero by Eq. 5.

$$ln(P(X \mid \mu)) = ln(p(x_1, x_2, ...x_N)) = \tag{5}$$

$$ln \prod_{i=1}^{N} \frac{1}{2\pi\sigma^2} e^{-\frac{1}{2}\frac{(x_i-\mu)^2}{\sigma^2}} = \sum_{i=1}^{N} \ln\left(\frac{1}{2\pi\sigma^2} e^{-\frac{1}{2}\frac{(x_i-\mu)^2}{\sigma^2}}\right) = \tag{6}$$

$$\sum_{i=1}^{N} \ln\left(\frac{1}{2\pi\sigma^2}\right) - \sum_{i=1}^{N} |\frac{1}{2}\frac{(x_i - \mu)^2}{\sigma^2} \tag{7}$$

$$\frac{\partial \ln(P(X \mid \mu))}{\partial \mu} = \frac{\partial \sum_{i=1}^{N} \ln\left(\frac{1}{2\pi\sigma^2}\right)}{\partial \mu} - \frac{\partial \sum_{i=1}^{N} \frac{1}{2}\frac{(x_i-\mu)^2}{\sigma^2}}{\partial \mu} \tag{8}$$

$$= 0 + \sum_{i=1}^{N} \frac{(x_i - \mu)}{\sigma^2} = \sum_{i=1}^{N} \frac{(x_i - \mu)}{\sigma^2} \tag{9}$$

$$\frac{\partial \ln(P(X \mid \mu))}{\partial \mu} = \sum_{i=1}^{N} \frac{(x_i - \mu)}{\sigma^2} = 0 \implies \mu = \frac{\sum_{i=1}^{N} x_i}{N} \tag{10}$$

We take into account here is that maximizing the probability function (likelihood) L is equivalent to minimizing the error function E. Furthermore, and it is Gaussian distributed with mean transposition (w) * X and variance σ^2 is show in Eq. 11.

$$y \sim N(\omega^T X, \sigma^2) \quad o \quad y = \omega^T X + \varepsilon \tag{11}$$

Where $\varepsilon \sim N(0, \sigma^2)$ ε is Gaussian distributed noise with zero mean and variance σ^2. This is equivalent to saying that in linear regression, the errors are Gaussian and the trend is linear. For new or outliers, the prediction would be less accurate for least squares, so we would use the L2 regularization method or Ridge regression. To do this, we modify the cost function and penalize large weights as follows by Eq. 12:

$$J_{RIDGE} = \sum_{i=1}^{N} (y_i - \hat{y}_i)^2 + \lambda |w|^2 \tag{12}$$

Where: $|w|^2 = w^T w = w_1^2 + w_2^2 + \cdots + w_D^2$
We, now have two probabilities:
Posterior:

$$P(Y|X, w) = \prod_{i=1}^{N} \frac{1}{2\pi\sigma^2} exp(-\frac{1}{2\sigma^2}(y_n - w^T x_n)^2) \tag{13}$$

A priori:

$$P(w) = \frac{\lambda}{\sqrt{2\pi}} exp(-\frac{\lambda}{2} w^T w) \tag{14}$$

3.3   Ridge-Bayesian

So, applying Bayes

$$exp(J) = \prod_{n=1}^{N} exp(-(y_n - w^T x_n)^2) exp(\lambda w^T w) \tag{15}$$

Applying Bayes: $J = (Y - Xw)(Y - Xw)^T + \lambda w^T w$

$$= Y^T T - 2Y^T Xw + w^T X^T Xw + \lambda w^T w \tag{16}$$

To minimize J, we use $\frac{\partial J}{\partial w}$ and set its value to 0. Therefore, $-2X^T + 2X^T Xw + 2\lambda w = 0$

So $(X^T X + \lambda I)w = X^T Y$ or $w = (X^T Y)$

This method encourages weights to be small since P (w) is a Gaussian centered around 0. The anterior value of w is called the MAP (maximize posterior) estimate of w.

3.4   Lasso

In the same way for Lasso

$$J_{LASSO} = \sum_{n=1}^{N} (y_i - \hat{y}_i)^2 + \lambda ||w|| \tag{17}$$

Maximizing the likelihood

$$P(Y|X, w) = \prod_{n=1}^{N} \frac{1}{2\pi\sigma^2} exp(-\frac{1}{2\sigma^2}(y_n - w^T x_n)^2) \tag{18}$$

and prior (previous) is given by:

$$P(w) = \frac{\lambda}{2} exp(-\lambda|w|) \tag{19}$$

So that $J = (Y - X_w)^T (Y - X_w) + \lambda|w|$
y $\frac{\partial J}{\partial w} = -2X^T Y + 2X^T Y + 2X^T Xw + \lambda sign(w) = 0$
Where $sign(w) = 1$ If $x > 0$ and -1 if $x < 0$ and 0 if $x = 0$

4   Data Set

4.1   Data Acquisition

The data was collected in the department of Puno whose coordinates are: 15° 29′ 27″ S and 70° 07′ 37″ O. The time period was April and August 2019.

The data to be analyzed were: DC Voltage, AC Voltage, AC Current, Active Power, Apparent Power, Reactive Power, Frequency, Power Factor, Total Energy, Daily Energy, DC Voltage, DC Current, and DC Power. Those that were obtained through the StecaGrid 3010 Inverter. The temperature of the environment and the photovoltaic panel were obtained by the PT1000 sensors that are suitable for temperature-sensitive elements given their special sensitivity, precision and reliability. Irradiance was obtained through a calibrated Atersa brand cell, whose output signal depends exclusively on solar irradiance and not on temperature. The amount of data is reduced from 331157 to 123120 because many of the values obtained are null, for example, the values obtained at night time. Characteristics such as mean, standard deviation, minimum value, maximum value and percentages of the pre-processed data are presented in Table 1 and Table 2. The statistics of the data obtained are shown as median, standard deviation, values: maximums, minimums, and interquartile ranges.

Table 1. Statistic table

Statistic	Tension AC	Corriente AC	Potencia activa	Potencia aparente	Potencia reactiva	Frecuencia	Factor de potencia	Energia total
mean	235.45	6.965	1,621.97	1,643.26	219.883	60.003	0.951	5,233.50
std	2.944	2.931	708.23	696.367	66.593	0.046	0.189	1,013.13
min	223.9	0.58	0	135	−843.9	59.5	−0.99	3,894.30
25	233.5	4.639	1,071.10	1,091.00	196.2	60	0.983	4,184.70
50%	235.4	7.564	1,764.00	1,779.55	228.4	60	0.991	5,910.30
75%	237.6	9.43	2,219.30	2,232.70	256.2	60	0.994	6,175.40
max	247.9	12.416	2,879.20	2,898.00	485.1	60.5	0.998	6,427.60

Table 2. Statistic table

Statistic	Energia diaria	Tension DC	Corriente DC	Potencia DC	Irradiancia	Temp modulo	Temp ambiente
mean	127.683	334.805	5.558	1,831.38	669.007	35.11	16.611
std	86.399	17.334	2.389	737.254	291.94	11.274	3.773
min	0	220.8	0	0	0	2.4	−2
25	56.666	321.9	3.62	1,261.44	432	27.6	14.5
50%	113.423	332.7	5.89	1,973.63	706	37	17.4
75%	190.369	346	7.65	2,450.61	926	44.2	19.4
max	342.906	420.8	10.78	3,142.27	1,522.00	60.3	27.7

5   Results

5.1   Non-multicollinearity Between Predictors - Correlation

The independent variables (predictors) should not be correlated with each other, as they would cause problems in the interpretation of the coefficients, as well as the error provided by each one. To determine this, a correlation heat map was used. Correlation is the basis to eliminate or minimize some variables, this is done by a variable selection algorithm or by the researcher's criteria, of course, advanced methods use an algorithm as will be done later, however, Fig. 1 displays the matrix to validate subsequent results.

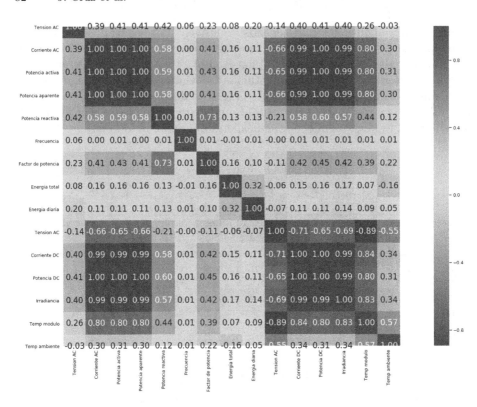

Fig. 1. Correlation matrix.

5.2 Prediction

First the RFE method was applied for the selection of variables, to the obtained results we applied the following Shrinkage regularization methods: Lasso, Ridge and Bayesian Ridge The data set is divided into training data 98496 (80%) and test data set 24624 (20%), for better performance seeds are also used. The best seed is also 8849. The RFE algorithm is applied, the following result is obtained:

['Tension AC', 'Corriente AC', 'Potencia aparente', 'Potencia reactiva', 'Frecuencia', 'Factor de potencia', 'Energia total', 'Energia diaria', 'Tension DC', 'Corriente DC', 'Potencia DC', 'Irradiancia', 'Temp modulo', 'Temp ambiente']

[True, True, True, True, True, True, False, False, True, True, True, False, True, True]

['Tension AC', 'Corriente AC', 'Potencia aparente', 'Potencia reactiva', 'Frecuencia', 'Factor de potencia', 'Tension DC', 'Corriente DC', 'Potencia DC', 'Temp modulo', 'Temp ambiente']

Of the 14 variables evaluated, for RFE the optimal number of characteristic variables was 11 with a score of 0.999768. It is important to mention that RFE discards: "Energia total", "Energia diaria" e "Irradiancia". The hyperparameters are then determined for Ridge an alpha value = 1,538 and for Lasso an alpha value = 0.01. For the models found, we determined R^2 and adjusted R^2, the mean absolute error of R (MAE), the mean square error of R (RMSE) and Score.

Table 3 and Table 4 shows the values obtained for the proposed groups, where the RFE method with OLS is not part of the research proposal, this result is also used to compare the research results. The following RFE methods with Lasso, RFE with Ridge and RFE with Bayesian Ridge; form the proposal of this research.

6   Validation of the Results

To check the results provided by the model, we must check certain assumptions about linear regression. If they are not fulfilled, the interpretation of results will not be valid.

6.1   Linearity

There must be a linear relationship between the actual data and the prediction so that the model does not provide inaccurate predictions. It is checked using a scatter diagram in which the values or points must be on or around the diagonal line of the diagram Fig. 2 shows the linear relationship.

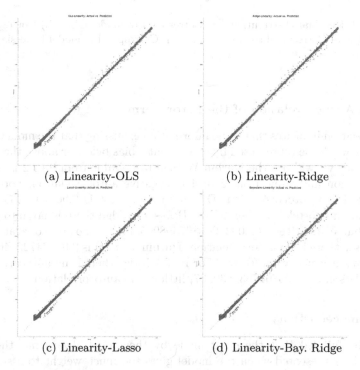

(a) Linearity-OLS   (b) Linearity-Ridge

(c) Linearity-Lasso   (d) Linearity-Bay. Ridge

Fig. 2. RFE-Linearity, (a) Correspond to model OLS, (b) Correspond to model Ridge (c) Correspond to model Lasso, (d) Correspond to model Bayessian Ridge

6.2   Normality of Error Terms

The error terms should be distributed normally. The histogram and the probability graph are shown in Fig. 3.

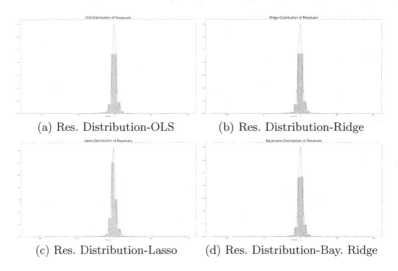

(a) Res. Distribution-OLS   (b) Res. Distribution-Ridge

(c) Res. Distribution-Lasso   (d) Res. Distribution-Bay. Ridge

Fig. 3. RFE-Residual Distribution, (a) Correspond to model OLS, (b) Correspond to model Ridge (c) Correspond to model Lasso, (d) Correspond to model Bayessian Ridge

6.3   No Autocorrelation of the Error Terms

Autocorrelation indicates that some information is missing that the model should capture. It would be represented by a systematic bias below or above the prediction. For this we will use the Durbin-Watson test. Value from 0 to 2 is positive autocorrelation and value from 2 to 4 is negative autocorrelation. For RFE - OLS there is no autocorrelation. Durbin-Watson Test is 2.0037021333412754, little to no autocorrelation. For RFE - Bayesian Ridge there is no autocorrelation. Durbin-Watson Test is 2.0037008807358965, little to no autocorrelation. For RFE - Lasso there is no autocorrelation. Durbin-Watson is 2.0037472224605053, little to no autocorrelation. Have a For RFE - Ridge there is no autocorrelation. Durbin-Watson is 2.0037017639830537, little to no autocorrelation.

6.4   Homocedasticity

It must be fulfilled that the error made by the model always has the same variance. It is presented when the model gives too much weight to a subset of data, particularly where the variance of the error was the greatest: to detect it, residuals are plotted to see if the variance is uniform (Fig. 4).

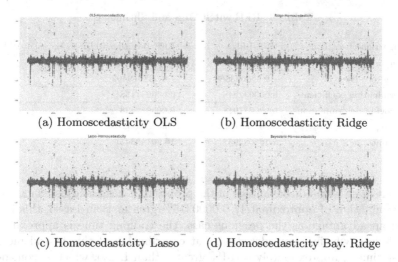

(a) Homoscedasticity OLS   (b) Homoscedasticity Ridge

(c) Homoscedasticity Lasso   (d) Homoscedasticity Bay. Ridge

Fig. 4. RFE-Homocedasticity, (a) Correspond to model OLS, (b) Correspond to model Ridge (c) Correspond to model Lasso, (d) Correspond to model Bayessian Ridge

7 Description and Analysis of the Results

In this article we present three hybrid methods for the selection of variables in the multiparameter regression of photovoltaic systems to predict the levels of the active power of the photovoltaic system with 14 independent variables, these methods are RFE - Lasso, RFE - Ridge and RFE - Bayesian Ridge.

Table 3 and Table 4 shows the method comparison, RFE-OLS, which is not part of our proposal, was compared with OLS to have a benchmark for the following comparisons that are part of the proposal. RFE-Lasso: it has an absolute error of approximately 0.035% greater than Lasso, which is taken as a disadvantage of the proposal, it has a mean squared error of approximately 0.057% less than Lasso, which is a significant result considered as a advantage, it has a coefficient of determination of approximately 0.0000309% higher than Lasso, this is considered greater but almost the same, so it is not considered very advanta-

Table 3. RFE with OLS and Shrinkage

Comparison of methods (%)	RFE-OLS vs OLS	RFE-Lasso vs Lasso
Mean absolute error R	0.003062198	0.034722952
Square root error R^2	−0.068102080	−0.056497772
Determination coefficient	0.000037258	0.000030848
Adj coef of determination	0.000037928	0.000031516
Training time	−37.027209963	−30.903451764
Test time	13.394018205	4.161073826

Table 4. RFE witch OLS and Shrinkage

Comparison of methods (%)	RFE-Ridge vs Ridge	RFE-Bayesian Ridge vs Bayesian Ridge
Mean absolute error R	0.003071248	0.003841610
Square root error R^2	−0.068083868	−0.067919409
Determination coefficient	0.000037248	0.000037158
Adj coef of determination	0.000037918	0.000037828
Training time	−24.017312331	−32.443632788
Test time	2.165087957	16.901408451

geous but in no way a disadvantage of the proposal, it has an adjusted coefficient of determination of approximately 0.0000315% greater than Lasso, this is considered an advantage as the previous case, the training time is approximately 30,904% less, which is considered a great contribution of this hybrid method, the test time is approximately 4,161% greater than Lasso, which is considered a disadvantage of the proposed model. For the following two hybrid RFE-Ridge methods compared to Ridge and RFE-Bayesian Ridge compared to Bayesian Ridge, and shown in Table 3 and Table 4. The description and analysis is similar to RFE-Lasso compared to Lasso.

8 Conclusions

The selection of independent variables of the multi-parameter photovoltaic system allowed us to develop four prediction models with an accuracy greater than 99.97% in all cases. Three RFE proposals are presented, RFE-Ridge, RFE-Lasso, and RFE-Bayesian Ridge; training time was reduced by 71% for RFE-Ridge over Ridge and and 36% RFE-OLS over OLS. The variables eliminated with RFE-Ridge and RFE-Bayesian Ridge were: "Energia total", "Energia diaria" e "Irradiancia", and additionaly the variable eliminated by RFE-Lasso was: "Frequencia". In all cases we see that the root mean square errors were reduced for RFE-Lasso by 0.15% over Lasso while for RFE-Bayesian Ridge by 0.06% over Bayesian Ridge. From all that has been done, we note that the proposed hybrid method, by eliminating variables that are not significant for the system, achieves a decrease in training times, without losing accuracy in predictions. The results can be improved by implementing algorithms in pre-processing stages such as imputation of values; or perform techniques as linear regression such, neural networks or XGBoost.

References

1. Çürük, E., Acı, Ç., Saraç Eşsiz, E.: The effects of attribute selection in artificial neural network based classifiers on cyberbullying detection. In: 2018 3rd International Conference on Computer Science and Engineering (UBMK), Sarajevo, pp. 6–11 (2018). https://doi.org/10.1109/UBMK.2018.8566312

2. Wu, Q., Zhang, H., Jing, R., Li, Y.: Feature selection based on twin support vector regression. In: 2019 IEEE Symposium Series on Computational Intelligence (SSCI), Xiamen, China, pp. 2903–2907 (2019). https://doi.org/10.1109/SSCI44817.2019.9003001

3. Zheng, Z., Cai, Y., Yang, Y., Li, Y.: Sparse weighted Naive Bayes classifier for efficient classification of categorical data. In: IEEE Third International Conference on Data Science in Cyberspace (DSC), Guangzhou, pp. 691–696 (2018). https://doi.org/10.1109/DSC.2018.00110

4. Al-Fahad, R., Yeasin, M., Anam, A.I., Elahian, B.: Selection of stable features for modeling 4-D affective space from EEG recording. In: International Joint Conference on Neural Networks (IJCNN), Anchorage, AK, pp. 1202–1209 (2017). https://doi.org/10.1109/IJCNN.2017.7965989

5. Tanizaka Filho, M.O., Marujo, E.C., dos Santos, T.C.: Identification of features for profit forecasting of soccer matches. In: 8th Brazilian Conference on Intelligent Systems (BRACIS), Salvador, Brazil, pp. 18–23 (2019). https://doi.org/10.1109/BRACIS.2019.00013

6. Qin, H., Yin, S., Gao, T., Luo, H.: A data-driven fault prediction integrated design scheme based on ensemble learning for thermal boiler process. In: 2020 IEEE International Conference on Industrial Technology (ICIT), Buenos Aires, Argentina, pp. 639–644 (2020). https://doi.org/10.1109/ICIT45562.2020.9067216

7. Moghimi, A., Yang, C., Marchetto, P.M.: Ensemble feature selection for plant phenotyping: a journey from hyperspectral to multispectral imaging. IEEE Access 6, 56870–56884 (2018). https://doi.org/10.1109/ACCESS.2018.2872801

8. Ashfaq, T., Javaid, N.: Short-term electricity load and price forecasting using enhanced KNN. In: 2019 International Conference on Frontiers of Information Technology (FIT), Islamabad, Pakistan, pp. 266–2665 (2019). https://doi.org/10.1109/FIT47737.2019.00057

9. Xiao, W., et al.: Single-beat measurement of left ventricular contractility in normothermic ex situ perfused porcine hearts. IEEE Trans. Biomed. Eng. (2020). https://doi.org/10.1109/TBME.2020.2982655

10. Elhamifar, E., De Paolis Kaluza, M.C.: Subset selection and summarization in sequential. In: Guyon, I., et al. (eds.) Advances in Neural Information Processing Systems 30, pp. 1035–1045. Curran Associates Inc. (2017). http://papers.nips.cc/paper/6704-subset-selection-and-summarization-in-sequential-data.pdf

11. Svetnik, V., Liaw, A., Tong, C., Wang, T.: Application of Breiman's random forest to modeling structure-activity relationships of pharmaceutical molecules. In: Roli, F., Kittler, J., Windeatt, T. (eds.) MCS 2004. LNCS, vol. 3077, pp. 334–343. Springer, Heidelberg (2004). https://doi.org/10.1007/978-3-540-25966-4_33

Parameter Optimization of Reaching Law Based Sliding Mode Control by Computational Intelligence Techniques

Vishal Mehra[1,2]([✉]) and Dipesh Shah[3,4]

[1] College of Agriculture Information Technology, Anand Agricultural University, Anand 388001, Gujarat, India
vishal.mehra@nsitonline.in
[2] GTU, Ahmadabad 382424, Gujarat, India
[3] I.C. Department, SVIT, Vasad 388306, Gujarat, India
[4] IIT-Gandhinagar, Gandhinagar 382355, Gujarat, India

Abstract. Sliding Mode Control (SMC) is an efficacious control algorithm for non-linear control system. For a competent implementation of SMC, selection of the gain parameters of SMC is an important task to minimize the chattering, tracking error, disturbances and for the improvement of dynamic response of the system. In this paper, performance of two computational intelligent algorithms such as GA- Genetic Algorithm & PSO - Particle Swarm Optimization are assessed to compute an optimal gain values for reaching based law sliding mode control. The optimal values of the gain are computed for constant-rate, proportional-rate and power-rate reaching laws. The efficacies of the computed optimal gains are validated on spring, mass and damper system using specified reaching laws. The simulation results shows that the gain parameters computed using intelligent techniques for power-rate reaching law outperforms as compared to the other reaching laws (constant-rate and constant plus proportional rate) for SMC in the presence of matched disturbances.

Keywords: Sliding mode control · Genetic algorithm · Particle swarm optimization · Reaching law approaches and Computational intelligence

1 Introduction

Sliding mode control (SMC) is a widely-acknowledged and powerful control method for robust control of nonlinear systems and has some appealing advantageous, such as low sensitive to system parameters changes, robustness, good transient performance and easy implementation [1, 2]. SMC has a wide application ranging from electrical drives to generators, robotics and process control, motion control and networked control system [3]. For illustration, Topalov et al. implemented the SMC for the quadcopter helicopter controlling [4]. Saqib Irfan et al. implemented integral and terminal SMC configuration to the inverted pendulum systems [5].

Apart from mentioned advantages, the performance of SMC is hindered by chattering phenomena which degrade control performance, fatigue of mechanical parts, heat loss and harshness of control forces. In the variable structure control (VSC),

© Springer Nature Singapore Pte Ltd. 2021
K. K. Patel et al. (Eds.): icSoftComp 2020, CCIS 1374, pp. 88–100, 2021.
https://doi.org/10.1007/978-981-16-0708-0_8

Switching function and control law are the two vital parts of the SMC which decides the magnitude of chattering and the control effort. To address the chattering issue two approaches were suggested. In first approach, discontinuous relay type actuator is substituted by a high-gain device with saturation [6] while second approach is design of control signal based on a reaching law [7]. In both cases, selections of gain parameters are critical because performance of the SMC is relied to great extent on gain parameters of the SMC. The improper tuning of SMC gain parameters could lead to poor system response, poor accuracy, higher control energy and even system instability. Traditionally, SMC gain parameters are selected by trial and error method which is very lengthy and tedious procedure. Thus to avoid such scenario, two different heuristic algorithms – G.A. and P.S.O. are used for optimum gain selection [8, 9].

GA is heuristic algorithm based on a biological mechanism of survival of the fittest and basic principle of GA was introduced by Holland [10]. An application of GA includes constrained and unconstrained optimization, parameter and system identification, control, robotics, pattern recognition, training neural network, fault detection, engineering design etc. [11]. Krishnakumar et al. introduced GA technique for aerospace related control system optimization problems [12]. Samantha et al. assess the performance of ANN and SVM classifier with parameter optimization by GA for bearing fault detection [13]. Mehra et al. designed GA based optimal FOPID controller to control the speed of DC motor [14]. Later on, Zhou et al. proposed a GA based optimal sliding mode control for an active suspension system [15].

Particle swarm optimization (PSO) is modern computational intelligence technique developed by Russell Eberhart and James Kennedy based on research of the bird and fish group movement characteristics [16].PSO gained wide popularity due to easy implementation and few parameters – no. of birds, constriction factors $c1$ & $c2$, inertial weight w required for tuning [17]. PSO is applicable to solve lots off optimization problems that include multi-objective optimization, pattern recognition, control optimization, power electronics, biological system modeling, signal processing, robotics, automatic target detection and many more [18]. The optimized gain of PID controller using PSO algorithm for automatic voltage regulator system was investigated in [19]. Zhang et al. blended PSO with back-propagation algorithms to train the ANN [20]. P. Singh et.al optimizes the Type-2 fuzzy model and hybrid fuzzy model by PSO for time series and neutrosophic time series forecasting and implemented for predictions of stock index price and university enrollments predictions [21–24]. Pugh & Martinoli proposed a multi-search algorithm inspired by PSO to develop efficacious techniques that permit a team of robots to work unitedly for determining their objects [25].

Mass-spring-damper-MSD systems are widely used as potent conceptual schemes for modeling purposes in dynamical systems [26]. The concept of MSD system has immense practical applications such as vibration [27], control system [28], vehicle suspension system [15, 29] and Position control system [30]. The position control of MSD system is simple yet challenging problem in control area in the presence of matched disturbances.

The primary aim of this paper is to compute and compare the optimal sliding gains using GA and PSO based approaches for reaching law based SMC in the presence of matched disturbances for MSD system. This paper is shaped in five sections. Section 1 contains introduction about SMC, GA and PSO. In Sect. 2 preliminaries of SMC using reaching law approach and mathematical background of GA and PSO are discussed.

The design of optimal parameters using GA and PSO for SMC is discussed in Sect. 3. In Sect. 4 the efficacy of computed sliding gains are compared through simulation results for MSD system. In Sect. 5 concluding remarks are discussed followed by possible future directions.

2   Preliminaries

2.1   Sliding Mode Control

SMC is a nonlinear control scheme having noteworthy characteristics of robustness, insensitive to parameter variation, accuracy and easy implementation. Designing of an SMC structure consist two phases. In first phase we design sliding surface and in second phase control input is designed.

Sliding surface σ is designed as

$$\sigma(t) = \left(\frac{d}{dt} + C\right)^{n-1} e(t) \tag{1}$$

where, n = relative degree between input and output. C = is the sliding gain, e(t) is an error between output signal y(t) and desired signal $y_{des}(t)$.

For second order dynamical system, sliding surface σ given as

$$\sigma(t) = \left(\frac{d}{dt} + C\right)^{1} e(t) \tag{2}$$

$$\sigma(t) = Ce(t) + \dot{e}(t)$$

$$\sigma(t) = C(y_{des}(t) - y(t)) + (\dot{y}_{des}(t) - \dot{y}(t))$$

$$\dot{\sigma}(t) = C(\dot{y}_{des}(t) - \dot{y}(t)) + (\ddot{y}_{des}(t) - \ddot{y}(t)). \tag{3}$$

Once the sliding surface is decided as in Eq. (3) the next step is to compute the control law by substituting $\sigma(t) = 0$. The control law selected is based on three reaching laws which are discussed as under.

1) Constant rate reaching law.

$$\dot{\sigma}(t) = -\rho sgn(\sigma(t)) \tag{4}$$

2) Constant plus proportional reaching law.

$$\dot{\sigma}(t) = -\rho sgn(\sigma(t)) - K_c \rho \tag{5}$$

3) Power rate reaching law.

$$\dot{\sigma}(t) = -K_c\sigma(t)^\alpha sgn(\sigma(t)) \tag{6}$$

where ρ = switching gain, K_c = controller gain α having the value between 0 and 1. Once the reaching law is selected the control algorithm is derived by taking time derivative of sliding surface such that the system state variables would converge to designed sliding surface at $\sigma(t) = 0$ in the finite time.

2.2 Genetic Algorithm

Genetic Algorithm (GA) is a random variable optimum search process inspired by mechanism of natural phylogeny. Genetic Algorithm initiate without knowledge of results and from its environment and evolution parameters reach to an optimal solution. GA consists of three primary operators namely reproduction, crossover and mutation works with a generation and interchange data from each individual in a population cause GA to uphold a better individual and produce higher fitness generation and enhance the performance.

GA convert the parameter designed into a finite bit string and based on assessment of fitness function it runs repeatedly in a stochastic manner using the reproduction, crossover and mutation operators by copying strings; Interchanging components of strings and altering some bits of strings. For optimization of function with GA one need to define population size, cross over and mutation value.

2.3 Particle Swarm Optimization

Particle swarm optimization is a computational algorithm that tries repeatedly to enhance a candidate solution and find an optimal solution of a problem in line to a given quality parameters. It has members with individual solutions and travels these members in the search-space by mathematical formula based on member's individual position and velocity. It solves a problem by evaluating an objective function at its present location. The movements of each member are regulated by its local as well global best position in the search space. These positions are updated based on improved position searched by former members.

Positions and velocities of individual particle updated as follows:

$$x_{k+1}^i = x_k^i + v_{k+1}^i$$

$$v_{k+1}^i = v_k^i + c_1 r_1 \left(p_k^i - x_k^i\right) + c_2 r_2 \left(p_k^g - x_k^i\right)$$

where $x_k^i, v_k^i, p_k^i, p_k^g$, $c_1 \& c_2$, $r_1 \& r_2$ are member position, velocity, best individual position, Best group position, cognitive and social parameters and random no. Between 0 and 1 respectively.

After movement of all members, next iteration take place and finally members as a whole is likely to go nearer to the optimal value of the objective function.

3 Optimal Reaching Law Based SMC for Mass-Spring-Damper System

Consider a Mass-spring-Damper system described by

$$M\ddot{x}(t) + B\dot{x}(t) + Kx(t) = u(t) + d(t) \tag{7}$$

where M = Mass = 2 kg, B = Damper co-efficient = 5 N/ms^2, K = Spring constant = 2 N/m, u(t) = Control Input and d(t) is a matched disturbance = 2 + 2sin (3t) + sin (5t). The s.s. model of the Eq. (7) is

$$\dot{x}_1(t) = x_2(t) \tag{8}$$

$$\dot{x}_2(t) = -\frac{5}{2}\dot{x}_1(t) - \frac{2}{2}x_1(t) + \frac{u(t)}{2} + \frac{d(t)}{2} \tag{9}$$

The objective is here to follow reference trajectory. In our case we take step signal as reference signal and output y(t) = x_1(t) such that, $\dot{y}(t) = \dot{x}_1(t) = x_2(t), \ddot{y}(t) = \ddot{x}_1(t) = \dot{x}_2(t)(t)$.

Referring Eq. (3), the time derivative of the sliding surface $\sigma(t)$ is

$$\dot{\sigma}(t) = C(-x_2(t)) + (-\dot{x}_2(t)) \tag{10}$$

Using constant-rate reaching law (4), the control algorithm using Eqs. (9) and (10) is defined as

$$-\rho\,sign(\sigma(t)) = C(-x_2(t)) + \frac{5}{2}x_2(t) + \frac{2}{2}x_1(t) - \frac{u(t)}{2} - \frac{d(t)}{2}$$

$$\frac{u(t)}{2} = C(-x_2(t)) + \frac{5}{2}x_2(t) + \frac{2}{2}x_1(t) - \frac{u(t)}{2} - \frac{d(t)}{2} + \rho\,sign(\sigma(t))$$

$$u(t) = (5 - 2 * C)x_2(t) + 2x_1(t) - d(t) + 2\rho\,sign(\sigma(t)) \tag{11}$$

Similarly, the control algorithm derived using constant plus proportional rate reaching law is given as

$$-\rho\,sgn(\sigma(t)) - K_c\rho = C(-x_2(t)) + \frac{5}{2}x_2(t) + \frac{2}{2}x_1(t) - \frac{u(t)}{2} - \frac{d(t)}{2}$$

$$\frac{u(t)}{2} = C(-x_2(t)) + \frac{5}{2}x_2(t) + \frac{2}{2}x_1(t) - \frac{d(t)}{2} + \rho\,sign(\sigma(t)) + K_c\sigma(t)$$

$$u(t) = (5 - 2 * C)x_2(t) + 2x_1(t) - d(t) + 2\rho\,sign(\sigma(t)) + 2K_c\sigma(t). \tag{12}$$

Further, the control algorithm derived using power-rate reaching law (6) using Eqs. (9) and (10) is given as

$$-k_c\sigma(t)^\alpha sgn(\sigma(t)) = C(-x_2(t)) + \frac{5}{2}x_2(t) + \frac{2}{2}x_1(t) - \frac{u(t)}{2} - \frac{d(t)}{2}$$

$$\frac{u(t)}{2} = C(-x_2(t)) + \frac{5}{2}x_2(t) + \frac{2}{2}x_1(t) - \frac{d(t)}{2} + K_c\sigma(t)^\alpha sgn(\sigma(t))$$

$$u(t) = (5 - 2*C)x_2(t) + 2x_1(t) - d(t) + K_c\sigma(t)^\alpha sgn(\sigma(t)) \tag{13}$$

The control signal derived in Eqs. (11), (12) and (13) using reaching laws shows satisfactory response by the proper selection of the constant parameters such as C, ρ, Controller gain K_c and α. Table 1 and Table 3 shows the optimum values using which the sliding gain of SMC is computed using GA and PSO approaches. An integral of absolute of error (IAE) is used as objective function for the computation of parameters. Table 2 and Table 4 describes the value of optimal gain parameters that is computed using GA and PSO respectively. The range for the above unknown parameters is selected as under.

$$C \in [0, 10], \rho \in [0, 10], K_c \in [0, 10], \alpha \in [0, 1]$$

Table 1. Parameter value/Function for GA algorithm.

Parameter	Value/Function
No. of population	20
No. of generations	25
Cross-over fraction	0.9
Creation function	Uniform
Selection function	Stochastic uniform
Cross over function	Arithmetic

Table 2. Reaching law based SMC gain parameters optimized by GA.

Reaching Law	Optimum value C	Optimum value ρ	Optimum Value K_c	Optimum Value α
Constant rate	2.24	2.44	NA	NA
Proportional rate	6.17	0.3199	3.6975	NA
Power rate	5.91	NA	6.08	0.6047

Table 3. Parameter value/Function for PSO algorithm.

Parameter	Value/Function
No. of birds	20
Bird step	25
C1	2.5
C2	1.6

Table 4. Reaching law based SMC gain parameters optimized by PSO.

Reaching Law	Optimum Value C	Optimum Value ρ	Optimum Value K_c	Optimum Value α
Constant rate	2.28	2.48	NA	NA
Proportional rate	5.6267	0.4024	3.5218	NA
Power rate	6.2219	NA	7.3507	0.5049

4 Results and Discussion

In this section, model of Mass-Spring-Damper system with reaching law based SMC control structure was built in MATLAB-SIMULINK to affirm the control performance of the SMC parameter optimized by GA & PSO algorithms.

Figure 1 shows the comparison of step response of MSD system with constant-rate reaching law whose sliding gain parameters are calculated using GA and PSO. It can be noticed in step response that output signal tracks the reference input signal accurately in both times. Moreover, the steady state error of PSO is less to GA. Figure 2 shows the performance of control signal. It can be noticed that the amplitude of the chattering is high due to the presence of sign function in constant-rate reaching law. Figure 3 represents sliding surface response. It can be seen that the state variable slides towards the planned sliding surface $\sigma(t) = 0$ in a finite time in the presence of matched disturbances in both the cases.

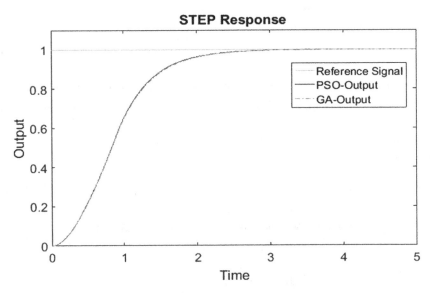

Fig. 1. Comparison of step response of a MSD system for constant rate SMC structure with gain optimization by GA and PSO.

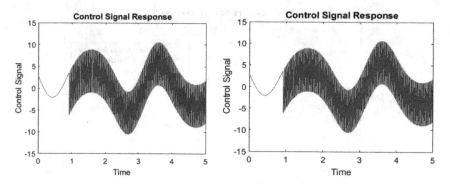

Fig. 2. Control signal response of a MSD system for constant rate SMC structure with gain optimization by GA and PSO.

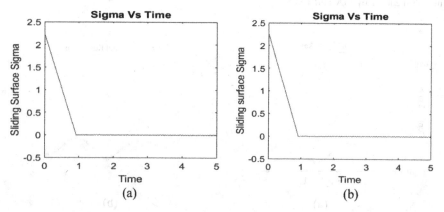

Fig. 3. Sliding Surface response of a MSD system for constant rate SMC structure with gain optimization by (a) GA and (b) PSO.

Figures 4, 5 and 6 show the response of step, control and sliding surface response of the constant plus proportional rate reaching law. Step responses of the system for both the cases shows that the output tracks the reference trajectory with negligible steady state error. Moreover, it can also be noticed that the settling time of the output signal computed using PSO is faster than that of GA. In the case of control response the amplitude level of chattering is less as compared to constant-rate reaching law in both the cases. This indicates that due to less oscillatory behavior of control signal there would be less weir and tier in the actuator which will increases the efficiency and performance of the system. Figure 6 represents the result of sliding surface computed for both the sliding gain parameters shows that for a limited interval of time the state variable slides towards planned sliding surface $\sigma(t) = 0$.

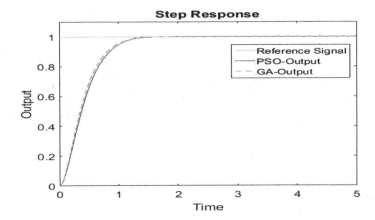

Fig. 4. Comparison of step response of a MSD system for proportional rate SMC structure with gain optimization by GA and PSO.

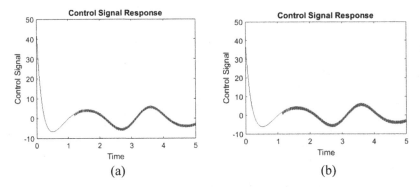

Fig. 5. Control signal response of a MSD system for Proportional rate SMC structure with gain optimization by (a) GA and (b) PSO.

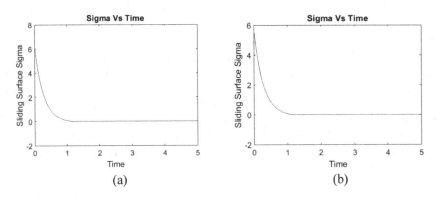

Fig. 6. Sliding surface response of a MSD system for Proportional rate SMC structure with gain optimization by (a) GA and (b) PSO.

Figures 7, 8 and 9 show the step response, control response and sliding surface response for the power-rate reaching law. In both the cases the overall performance of the system in the terms of step response, control signal and sliding surface is satisfactory as compared to previous reaching laws. Moreover, the effect of chattering is also less in the sliding surface which causes the control signal less oscillatory in nature.

Thus from above results, it can be concluded that the sliding gains calculated using GA and PSO for power-rate reaching law is more efficient and robust than other reaching laws as it provides faster convergence and less chattering in the control signal which enhance the overall performance of the system in the presence of matched disturbances. The comparative analysis in the terms of rise time, peak overshoot (%), settling time and steady state error is mentioned in Table 5.

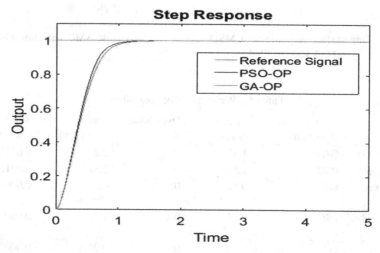

Fig. 7. Comparison of Step response of a MSD system for power- rate SMC structure with gain optimization by GA and PSO.

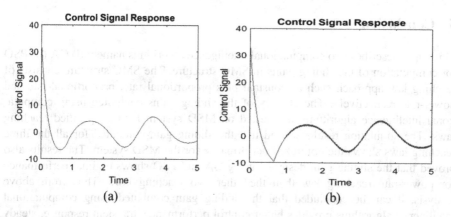

Fig. 8. Control signal response of a MSD system for power rate SMC structure with gain optimization by (a) GA and (b) PSO.

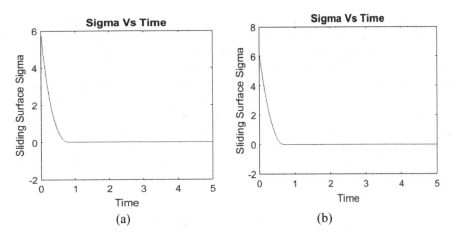

Fig. 9. Sliding surface response of a MSD system for power rate SMC structure with gain optimization by (a) GA and (b) PSO.

Table 5. Performance of controllers

Reaching laws	Optimization algorithm	Rise time (sec.)	Overshoot %	Settling time (sec.)	Steady state error
Constant rate	GA	1.57	0	2.28	0.001
Constant rate	PSO	1.55	0	2.31	0.0012
Proportional rate	GA	0.82	0	1.17	0.00013
Proportional rate	PSO	0.86	0	1.2	0.0002
Power rate	GA	0.74	0	0.95	0.00004
Power rate	PSO	0.68	0	1.02	0.00008

5 Conclusion

This paper describes two computational intelligence algorithms namely (i) GA (ii) PSO for computation of the sliding gains in SMC structure. The SMC structure consists of reaching law approach such as constant plus proportional rate, proportional-rate and power-rate respectively. The efficacy of the sliding gains computed using computational intelligence algorithms was tested on MSD system for the specified reaching laws. The simulation results proved that the sliding gain computed for all the three reaching laws shows the optimized performance for the MSD system. The results also proved that the sliding gain designed using GA and PSO shows optimal performance for power-rate reaching law than the other two reaching laws. Thus from above analysis, it can be concluded that the sliding gain computed using computational intelligence algorithms provides better control performance, transient response, steady state response and minimal chattering as compared to trial and error method available in the literatures [3].In this paper two widely used C.I. algorithms were investigated and currently new C.I. techniques and modified G.A. and P.S.O. techniques are developing so in future modified G.A. and P.S.O. as well new C.I. technique can be investigated for optimal gain tuning for reaching law based SMC.

References

1. Utkin, V.I.: Variable structure systems with sliding modes. IEEE Trans. Autom. Control **22**(2), 212–222 (1977)
2. Young, K.D., Utkin, V.I., Ozguner, U.: A control engineer's guide to sliding mode control. IEEE Trans. Control Syst. Technol. **7**(3), 328–342 (1999)
3. Shah, D.H., Mehta, A.: Discrete-Time Sliding Mode Control for Networked Control System. Springer, Singapore (2018). https://doi.org/10.1007/978-981-10-7536-0
4. Topalov, A.V., Shakev, N.G., Kaynak, O., Kayacan, E.: Neuro-adaptive approach for controlling a quad-rotor helicopter using sliding mode learning algorithm. In: Adaptation and Learning in Control and Signal Processing - ALCOSP, IFAC, Turkey, pp. 94–99 (2010)
5. Irfan, S., Mehmood, A., Razzaq, M.T., Iqbal, J.: Advanced sliding mode control techniques for inverted pendulum: Modeling and simulation. J. Eng. Sci. Technol. **21**(4), 753–759 (2018)
6. Gao, W., Hung, J.C.: Variable structure control of nonlinear systems: a new approach. IEEE Trans. Industr. Electron. **40**(1), 45–55 (1993)
7. Hung, J.Y., Gao, W., Hung, J.C.: Variable structure control: a survey. IEEE Trans. Ind. Electron. **40**(1), 2–2 (1993)
8. Kaynak, O., Erbatur, K., Ertugnrl, M.: The fusion of computationally intelligent methodologies and sliding-mode control-a survey. IEEE Trans. Ind. Electron. **48**(1), 4–17 (2001)
9. Yu, X., Kaynak, O.: Sliding mode control made smarter: a computational intelligence perspective. IEEE Syst. Man Cybern. Mag. **3**(2), 31–34 (2017)
10. Holland, J.H.: Adaptation in Natural and Artificial Systems. MIT Press, Cambridge (1975)
11. Man, K.F., Tang, K.S., Kwong, S.: Genetic algorithms: concepts and applications. IEEE Trans. Ind. Electron. **43**(5), 519–534 (1996)
12. Krishnakumar, K., Goldberg, D.E.: Control system optimization using genetic algorithms. J. Guidan. Control Dyn. **15**(3), 735–740 (1992)
13. Samanta, B., Al-Balushi, K.R., Al-Araimi, S.A.: Artificial neural networks and support vector machines with genetic algorithm for bearing fault detection. Eng. Appl. Artif. Intell. **16**(7–8), 657–665 (2003)
14. Mehra, V., Srivastava, S., Varshney, P.: Fractional-order PID controller design for speed control of DC motor. In: IEEE 3rd International Conference on Emerging Trends in Engineering and Technology-2010, Nagpur, pp. 422–425 (2010).
15. Zhou, C., Liu, X., Chen, W., Xu, F., Cao, B.: Optimal sliding mode control for an active suspension system based on a genetic algorithm. Algorithms **11**(12), 205–220 (2018)
16. Eberhart, R., Kennedy, J.: A new optimizer using particle swarm theory. In: IEEE Proceedings of the Sixth International Symposium on Micro Machine and Human Science, pp. 39–43 (1995)
17. Bai, Q.: Analysis of particle swarm optimization algorithm. Comput. Inf. Sci. **3**(1), 180–184 (2010)

18. Shi, Y.: Particle swarm optimization: developments, applications and resources. In: Proceedings of the 2001 Congress on Evolutionary Computation, pp. 81–86. IEEE Cat. No. 01TH8546 (2001)
19. Gaing, Z.L.: A particle swarm optimization approach for optimum design of PID controller in AVR system. IEEE Trans. Energy Convers. **19**(2), 384–391 (2004)
20. Zhang, J.R., Zhang, J., Lok, T.M., Lyu, M.R.: A hybrid particle swarm optimization–backpropagation algorithm for feed forward neural network training. Appl. Math. Comput. **185**(2), 1026–1037 (2007)
21. Singh, P., Borah, B.: Forecasting stock index price based on M-factors fuzzy time series and particle swarm optimization. Int. J. Approx. Reason. **55**, 812–833 (2014)
22. Singh, P., Dhiman, G.: A hybrid fuzzy time series forecasting model based on granular computing and bio-inspired optimization approaches. J. Comput. Sci. **27**, 370–385 (2018)
23. Singh, P., Huang, Y.P.: A new hybrid time series forecasting model based on the neutrosophic set and quantum optimization. Comput. Ind. **111**, 121–139 (2019)
24. Singh, P.: A novel hybrid time series forecasting model based on neutrosophic-PSO approach. Int. J. Mach. Learn. Cybern. **11**(8), 1643–1658 (2020). https://doi.org/10.1007/s13042-020-01064-z
25. Pugh, J., Martinoli, A.: Inspiring and modeling multi-robot search with particle swarm optimization. In: Swarm Intelligence Symposium, pp. 332–339. IEEE (2007)
26. Kim, S.M.: Lumped element modeling of a flexible manipulator system. IEEE/ASME Trans. Mechatron. **20**(2), 967–974 (2014)
27. Den Hartog, J.P.: Mechanical Vibrations. Courier Corporation (1985)
28. Wang, D., Mu, C.: Adaptive-critic-based robust trajectory tracking of uncertain dynamics and its application to a spring–mass–damper system. IEEE Trans. Ind. Electron. **65**(1), 654–663 (2017)
29. Su, X.: Master–slave control for active suspension systems with hydraulic actuator dynamics. IEEE Access **5**, 3612–3621 (2017)
30. Ayadi, A., Smaoui, M., Aloui, S., Hajji, S., Farza, M.: Adaptive sliding mode control with moving surface: experimental validation for electro pneumatic system. Mech. Syst. Sig. Process. **109**, 27–44 (2018)

Efficiency of Parallelization Using GPU in Discrete Dynamic Models Construction Process

Iryna Strubytska[1]([⊠]) [ID] and Pavlo Strubytskyi[2] [ID]

[1] Separated Subdivision of National University of Life and Environmental Sciences of Ukraine "Berezhany Agrotechnical Institute", Akademichna str., 22, Berezhany 47500, Ukraine
iryna.str@gmail.com
[2] Ternopil National Economic University, Lvivska str., 11, Ternopil 46004, Ukraine
p.r.strubytsky@gmail.com

Abstract. The objectives of this paper are: (i) to estimate parallelization efficiency of discrete dynamic models constructing process using GPU; (ii) to compare the execution time of parallel model depending on the order of model, the number of discrete values, the number of GPU threads and GPU blocks; and (iii) to compare the execution time on CPU and GPU. A parallel model for the prediction of sulfur dioxide emissions into the air of Żywiec city (Poland) based on historical observations is built and researched in this paper. We have obtained a parallelization efficiency of 78.1% while executing the constructed parallel model on GPU Nvidia GTS250. The obtained research results suggest that the constructing discrete dynamical models must include the efficient use of parallel computing resources nowadays.

Keywords: Discrete dynamic models · Optimization methods · Parallel computing · Parallelization · GPU · GPGPU

1 Introduction

Construction methods of discrete dynamic models for different systems are sufficiently developed and widely used. The parametric identification of discrete models was described in articles by L. Ljung [1], L. Zadeh [2] and Ch. Desoer, V. Strejc [3], V. Kuntsevych [4]. In terms of computer simulations, the modeling method, which is based on discrete state equations, is the most promising [5, 6]. In terms of mathematics, this approach is the most formalized and has practical applications in different areas.

The construction of dynamic models of electrical and electronic circuits was made using optimization approach. This approach was used by P. Stakhiv and Y. Kozak [7–9]. This approach makes it possible to build universal models. However, such universalization leads to the appearance of complex optimization problems that are difficult to resolve in a reasonable time, even using modern computer technologies.

© Springer Nature Singapore Pte Ltd. 2021
K. K. Patel et al. (Eds.): icSoftComp 2020, CCIS 1374, pp. 101–110, 2021.
https://doi.org/10.1007/978-981-16-0708-0_9

There is an actual problem to develop such construction methods of models that would be subjected to the implementation on available computer technologies and provide the necessary performance.

Therefore, there is a need to develop sufficiently universal algorithms for construction of discrete dynamical models using parallelization by which you can effectively build the models for ecological, electricity and other complex systems.

Recently, increasingly researchers use GPUs for accelerating results of mathematical modeling. For examples, A. Kłusek, P. Topa, J. Wąs, R. Lubaś [10] use GPU for social distances model, B. Hamilton, C. Webb. [11] for room acoustics modelling, J. Schalkwijk, H. Jonker, A. Siebesma, E. Meijgaard [12] for weather forecast model.

2 Parallelization Method of Optimization Procedures for Constructing of Discrete Dynamical Models

Let's consider the generalized mathematical model in the form of state Eqs. (1):

$$
\begin{cases}
\vec{x}^{(k+1)} = F\vec{x}^{(k)} + G\vec{v}^{(k)} + \overrightarrow{\Phi}\left(\vec{x}^{(k)}, \vec{v}^{(k)}\right), \\
\vec{y}^{(k+1)} = C\vec{x}^{(k+1)} + D\vec{v}^{(k+1)}
\end{cases}
\tag{1}
$$

where $\vec{x}^{(k)}$ – the vector of state variables; $\vec{v}^{(k)}$ – the input vector; $\vec{y}^{(k+1)}$ – the output vector; F, G, C, D – matrixes with unknown coefficients; $\overrightarrow{\Phi}$ – the nonlinear vector-function with many variables.

This form of model (1) is characterized by some vector of unknown parameters $\vec{\lambda}$. This vector for this model consists of the elements of matrixes F, G, C, D and coefficients of the vector-function $\overrightarrow{\Phi}\left(\vec{x}^{(k)}, \vec{v}^{(k)}\right)$.

$Q\left(\vec{\lambda}\right) > 0$ is the criterion for the precision measuring of the model, which determines the deviation of the behavior of the model from the behavior of the simulated object for the known periods of time. The function $Q\left(\vec{\lambda}\right)$ is called the objective function. This function is calculated as a root-mean-square error of model's values:

$$
Q\left(\vec{\lambda}\right) = \sum\left(\vec{y} - \vec{y}^{*}\left(\vec{\lambda}\right)\right)^{2},
\tag{2}
$$

where $\vec{y}$ – known characteristics of modeled object, $\vec{y}^{*}\left(\vec{\lambda}\right)$ – transient response that are calculated using the model.

Therefore, the construction of the model can be reduced to calculation values of the vector $\vec{\lambda}$, when the objective function will be minimal. This problem is solved using the optimization algorithm [13].

The task of finding the minimum point of the nonlinear function $Q\left(\vec{\lambda}\right)$ with many variables is difficult. In discrete dynamic models' construction, the objective function is a "ravine" with many local minima. For the solution of such problems the Rastrigin's method of a director cone has the best characteristics [14]. Purposeful scan of local minima can be done using this approach. It accelerates finding of the global minimum of the objective function. But the computational complexity of this problem is quite huge. Also, the significant number of input data is used for the construction of the qualitative model. Consequently, the execution time of the implementation of optimization procedures is also significant [15].

The time complexity of Rastrigin's optimization algorithm [14] depends linearly on the number of known discrete values from in known function. Accordingly, the computational complexity of the problem will be proportional to the amount of input, not the order of created model. For building a quality model it's necessary to use a large amount of data for calculating the value of the objective function. Therefore, the time spent of calculation the values of functions will also be significant.

The parallelization of this task using SIMD-architecture was proposed in the article [16]. This architecture allows performing the same thread of instructions for many threads of data. Taking into this approach, the objective function for different values of vector $\vec{\lambda}$ is calculate independently. Each objective function will be calculated on a separate core of GPU.

The flowchart diagram of the parallelization algorithm is presented on Fig. 1.

Today the available devices with SIMD-architecture and with better ratio performance/price are the GPUs (Graphics Processing Unit) [17, 18]. Therefore, the proposed algorithm was adapted for these computing accelerators.

In terms of software implementation, the parallelization does not require large expenditures through programming architecture of GPU [19, 20].

According to this proposed algorithm, the selection of each point will be made in a separate thread, which will be executed parallelly. Also, the calculation of the value of the objective function $Q_{i+1}^{(1)}, \ldots, Q_{i+1}^{(m)}$ in m points will also be executing out on separate threads.

Same program code is sent to all threads. The input data for each thread are parameters of the next hypercone, they are the same for all threads. The value of objective function is received in each entrance of thread. This value is calculated in random point of hypercone. This value will be different for each thread. All output data is stored in the shared-memory of threads for further calculation of the minimum [21, 22].

The CUDA (Compute Unified Device Architecture) technology was used for programming implementation of parallelization algorithm [20, 23]. Currently the computing using GPUs and CUDA is an innovative combination of features of new generation of graphics processors NVIDIA, that process thousands of threads with high information loading. These features are available through programming language C [17, 24].

3 Discrete Dynamical Model for Sulfur Dioxide Emission Prediction

Today the problem of environmental protection is becoming one of the most important tasks of science, the development of which is accelerated rapidly by technological progress in all countries of the world. The rapid development of industry and the significant growth of traffic flows contribute to the emergence of an acute problem - the protection of ecological systems. In recent decades, ecological systems have been influenced significantly by anthropogenic factors. Therefore, prediction of character-istics changes in such systems is an actual task.

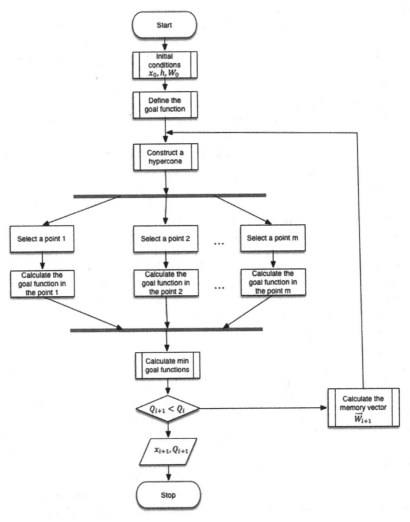

Fig. 1. Flowchart of the parallel algorithm of Rastrigin's director cone [16]

A dangerous environmental situation has already emerged today due to the negative impact of industry in many regions. In particular, pollution of rivers, the air pool, pollution of the landscape, the destruction of forests, vegetation, wildlife, the fertile layer, pollution of groundwater, acoustic, electromagnetic and electrostatic pollution.

For example, the air pool is polluted with gas and aerosol emissions (CO_2, polycyclic aromatic hydrocarbons, CO, NO_x, SO_x, ash, soot and others). Emissions are occurred during the combustion of liquid and solid fuels, which form aerosols when released into the atmosphere. Aerosols can be non-toxic (ash) and toxic ($C_{20}H_{12}$ is a potent carcinogenic compound). Also, gas emissions can be toxic (NO_2, SO_2, NO, CO and others) and non-toxic (CO_2, H_2O). All triatomic gases (H2O, NO_2, SO_2, and especially CO_2) belong to "greenhouse gases". When gas emissions are released into the atmosphere, they have a complex physicochemical and biological effect on living organisms and humans, the level and character of which depend on their concentration in the air.

The combined effects of gas and aerosol emissions from energy objects can lead to various adverse environmental effects, including crises in the biosphere, such as deterioration of atmospheric transparency, rainfall and acid rain, greenhouse effect.

Therefore, it is important to predict the concentrations of harmful emissions into the atmosphere to prevent environmental problems and respond promptly.

Let's build a model for prediction of emissions into the atmosphere. Model inputs are weekly averages values of emissions of SO_2 (sulfur dioxide) into the air in Żywiec (Poland) in 2018 [25]. It is necessary to create a mathematical model that based on this data. This model should be able to predict the emission of SO_2 into the air in 2019.

Let's building the autonomous discrete dynamic model of the third order for testing of the efficiency of the parallel program of calculation of the objective function. This model has the following form:

$$
\begin{cases}
\begin{pmatrix} x_1^{(k+1)} \\ x_2^{(k+1)} \\ x_3^{(k+1)} \end{pmatrix} = \begin{pmatrix} F_{11} & F_{12} & F_{13} \\ F_{21} & F_{22} & F_{22} \\ F_{31} & F_{32} & F_{33} \end{pmatrix} \cdot \begin{pmatrix} x_1^{(k)} \\ x_2^{(k)} \\ x_3^{(k)} \end{pmatrix} \\
\begin{pmatrix} y_1^{(k+1)} \\ y_2^{(k+1)} \\ y_3^{(k+1)} \end{pmatrix} = (C_1 \quad C_2 \quad C_3) \cdot \begin{pmatrix} x_1^{(k+1)} \\ x_2^{(k+1)} \\ x_3^{(k+1)} \end{pmatrix}
\end{cases}
\tag{3}
$$

where $k = 1, \ldots, 52$.

The objective function is:

$$
Q(\vec{\lambda}_i) = \sum_i \left| \begin{pmatrix} y_1 \\ y_2 \\ y_3 \end{pmatrix} - \begin{pmatrix} y_1^* \\ y_2^* \\ y_3^* \end{pmatrix} \right|^2 .
\tag{4}
$$

4   Research of Efficiency of Parallel Model

Let's test the program for calculation of the objective function. The following hardware and system software were used for these tests:

- GPU NVIDIA GeForce GTS250 (16 multiprocessors with 8 cores each);
- RAM 1024 MB;
- CPU Core2Duo E8400, 3 GHz;
- motherboard ASRock G41M-S3.

Let's considering the performance time of the parallel program for calculation of the objective function on 128 GPU cores. The average time (with 100 launches) of parallel computing of the objective function is 2.74 ms.

Then let's research the change of the execution time of the program respecting the change of the model order (see on Fig. 2). Obviously, the execution time of parallel calculation of the objective functions will gradually increase with increase of the order of the constructed model.

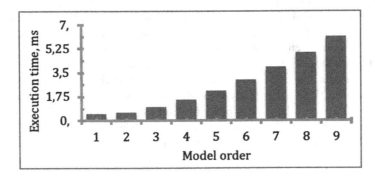

Fig. 2. Dependence of the execution time of the parallel program on the model order

When the number of discrete values will increase, then the execution time of parallel calculation of the objective function will gradually increase (see on Fig. 3).

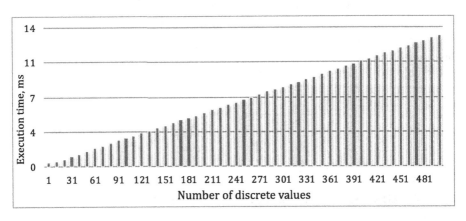

Fig. 3. Dependence of the execution time of the parallel program on the number of discrete values of model

It is also interesting to compare the dependence of the execution time of all the calculations of objective functions on the number of calculations of the objective function. Namely, with different number of threads on GPU. Obviously, such dependence is linear for sequential calculations. This dependence is shown on Fig. 4.

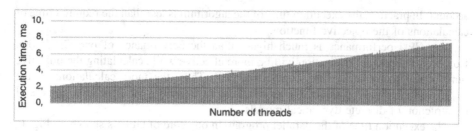

Fig. 4. Dependence of the execution time of the parallel program from the of threads

As it is shown on Fig. 4, this dependence is periodic. Since the execution time was calculated along with the data transfer, then there are constant delays in each cycle of optimization algorithm. If we reject these delays then we will see that the periodicity is repeated every 128 threads. Therefore, it is expedient to use the parallelization when the number of threads is a multiple number of GPU cores. In this case it is 128 cores. Then the parallelization will be the most effective.

Build 3D-graph of the dependence of the execution time of the parallel program on the number of threads and the number of GPU blocks (see on Fig. 5).

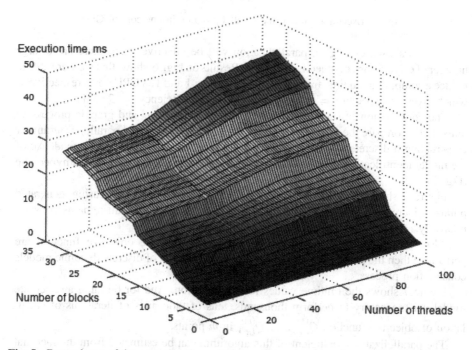

Fig. 5. Dependence of the execution time of the parallel program on the number of threads and the number of blocks

The proposed approach of parallel computing can be used with different optimization algorithms. Therefore, the execution time of the algorithm is not taken into account. In practice, the execution time of the algorithm is less than the required time of calculations of the objective function.

The CPU performance is much higher than the performance of one GPU core. However, the parallel realization will be more effective while calculating the objective function for many sets of the coefficients [20]. Thus, the more calculations of the objective function we conduct, the more efficient will be the parallelization process of construction of discrete dynamical models.

The execution time of the parallel program in one core of GPU is shown on Fig. 6.

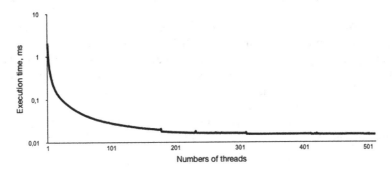

Fig. 6. Execution time of the parallel program in one core of GPU

As it is shown on Fig. 6, parallelization will be effective when there are a large number of calculations of objective function. Results on Fig. 6 show, that we were able to reduce a computational time from 2 ms to 0.02 ms on 1 and 128 GPU cores respectively, which gives us a speedup = 100 and parallelization efficiency = 78.1%.

The construction of such model was performed on central and graphic processing units. Let's compare the execution time of sequential program and parallel program for constructing a discrete dynamic model. To do this, let's determine the dependence of the model identification time on the number of points that generated on the hypercone (Fig. 7).

Figure 7 shows that the time of sequential program with increasing generated points is increasing gradually, and the time of the parallel program remains constant relatively.

Also, Fig. 7 confirms that the more calculations of the objective function are performed then the more efficient will be the parallelization of discrete dynamic models construction process.

Figure 7 shows the runtime values for one iteration. And for building an accurate model it is necessary to perform thousands, tens of thousands of iterations of calculation of objective function $Q_{i+1}^{(1)}, \ldots, Q_{i+1}^{(m)}$ in m points.

The parallelization coefficient of this algorithm can be estimated from the fact that the cost of calculation of the value of the objective function significantly exceeds the computational cost of making decisions according to the optimization algorithm. Since in the parallel implementation of calculation the value of the objective function in different points is performed independently, then the parallelization coefficient is close to the number of processors (provided that the number of calculations of the objective function is multiplied by one step of the optimization procedure).

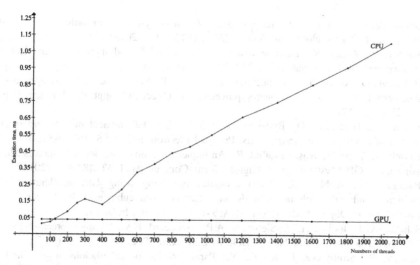

Fig. 7. Execution time on CPU and on GPU

5 Conclusions

A parallel model for the prediction of sulfur dioxide emissions into the air of Żywiec city (Poland) based on historical observations is built and researched in this paper. The construction of this model using traditional sequential algorithm without its parallelization is failed. Because the construction of such model requires tens of thousands of iterations of calculations and computer's RAM is not enough for it. We have obtained a parallelization efficiency of 78.1% while executing the constructed parallel model on GPU Nvidia GTS250. We also conducted the comparison of the execution time of parallel model respecting the model order, the number of discrete values, the number of GPU threads and the number of GPU blocks. The obtained research results suggest that the constructing discrete dynamic models must include the efficient use of parallel computing resources nowadays.

References

1. Ljung, L., Andersson, C., Tiels, K., Schön, T.: Deep learning and system identification. In: Proceedings of the IFAC World Congress, Berlin (2020)
2. Zadeh, L.A., Desoer, C.A.: Linear System Theory: The State Space Approach Dover Civil and Mechanical Engineering Series. Dover Publications, New York (2008)
3. Voicu, M.: Advances in Automatic Control. Springer, New York (2004). https://doi.org/10.1007/978-1-4419-9184-3

4. Kuntsevich, V.M., Gubarev, V.F., Kondratenko, Y.P., Lebedev, D.V., Lysenko, V.P. (eds.): Control Systems: Theory and Applications. Automation Control and Robotics. River Publishers, Gistrup (2018)
5. Hinamoto, T., Lu, W.: Digital Filter Design and Realization. River Publishers, Gistrup (2017)
6. Isidori, A., Marconi, L.: Adaptive regulation for linear systems with multiple zeros at the origin. Int. J. Robust Nonlinear Control 23(9), 1013–1032 (2012)
7. Stakhiv, P., Kozak, Y.: Discrete dynamical macromodels and their usage in electrical engineering. Int. J. Comput. 10(3), 278–284 (2011)
8. Hoholyuk, O., Kozak, Y., Nakonechnyy, T., Stakhiv, P.: Macromodeling as an approach to short-term load forecasting of electric power system objects. Comput. Probl. Electr. Eng. 7 (1), 25–32 (2017)
9. Stakhiv, P., Hoholyuk, O., Byczkowska-Lipinska, L.: Mathematical models and macro-models of electric power transformers. Przeglad Electrotechniczny 5, 163–165 (2011)
10. Kłusek, A., Topa, P., Wąs, J., Lubaś, R.: An implementation of the Social Distances Model using multi–GPU systems. Int. J. High-Perform. Comput. Appl. 32, 482–495 (2016)
11. Hamilton, B., Webb, C.J.: Room acoustics modelling using GPU-accelerated finite difference and finite volume methods on a face-centered cubic grid. In: Proceeding of Conference on Digital Audio Effects (DAFx-13), Maynooth, Ireland (2013)
12. Schalkwijk, J., Jonker, H.J.J., Siebesma, A.P., Meijgaard, E.V.: Weather forecasting using GPU-based large-eddy simulations. Bull. Am. Meteorol. Soc. 96, 715–723 (2015)
13. Stakhiv, P., Strubytska, I., Kozak, Y.: Parallelization of calculations using GPU in optimization approach for macromodels construction. Przegliad Elektrotechniczny 7(9), 7–9 (2012)
14. Kaladze, V.A.: Adaptation of casual search by the method of the directing cone. Vesnik VGTU 8(1), 31–37 (2012)
15. Strubytska, I.: Construction of discrete dynamic model of prediction of particulate matter emission into the air. Comput. Probl. Electr. Eng. 5, 55–59 (2015)
16. Kozak, Y., Stakhiv, P., Strubytska, I.: Parallelizing of algorithm for optimization of parameters of discrete dynamical models on massively-parallel processor. Inf. Extr. Proces. 32(108), 125–130 (2010)
17. Boreskov, A., Kharlamov, A., Markovskyy, N.: Parallel computations on GPU. Architecture and program model CUDA. Publication of Moscow University (2012)
18. Nickolls, J., Dally, W.: The GPU computing era. IEEE Micro 30(2), 56–69 (2010)
19. Kirk, D., Hwu, W.-M.: Programming Massively Parallel Processors: A Hands-on Approach. Morgan Kaufmann, Burlington (2010)
20. Sanders, J., Kandrot, E.: CUDA by Example: An Introduction to General-Purpose GPU Programming. Addison-Wesley Professional, Boston (2010)
21. Strubytska, I.: Research of the parallelization of minimum value algorithm on the GPU. In: Materials of the 1st All-Ukrainian School-Seminar for Young Scientists and Students "Advanced Computer Information Technologies", pp. 104–106 (2011)
22. Stakhiv, P., Strubytska, I.: Parallelization method of parameters identification of discrete dynamic macro models on massively parallel processors. Naukovi notatky 27, 300–305 (2010)
23. Farber, R.: CUDA Application Design and Development. Morgan Kaufmann Publishers, Burlington (2011)
24. Cook, S.: CUDA Programming: A Developer's Guide to Parallel Computing with GPUs. Elsevier Inc., Amsterdam (2013)
25. Air Quality Monitoring System. https://powietrze.katowice.wios.gov.pl/stacje. Accessed 15 Aug 2020

On the Performance Analyses of a Modified Force Field Algorithm for Obstacle Avoidance in Swarm Robotics

Girish Balasubramanian[1(✉)] ,
Senthil Arumugam Muthukumaraswamy[1] , and Xianwen Kong[2]

[1] Heriot-Watt University Dubai Campus, Dubai Knowledge Village,
Dubai, UAE
{gb29,m.senthilarumugam}@hw.ac.uk
[2] Heriot-Watt University, Campus The Avenue, Edinburgh E14 4AS, UK
X.Kong@hw.ac.uk

Abstract. Obstacle avoidance is a major hurdle when implementing mobile robots and swarm robots. Swarm robots work in groups and therefore require an efficient and functional obstacle avoidance algorithm to stay collision free between themselves and their surroundings. This paper reviews previous research in obstacle avoidance implementation using the force field method (FFM), also known as potential field method (PFM). Moreover, this paper aims to execute simulations using a modified and simplified force field algorithm. The obtained results are analysed to identify the performance characteristics and the time taken to perform tasks using a singular mobile robot against a swarm robot environment consisting of four and ten robots, respectively. Simulations showed that the algorithm was successful in navigating obstacles for both single and swarm robot environments. A single robot was found to take up to 340% longer to arrive at the required location compared to the first robot in the experiment.

Keywords: Swarm robotics · Proximity sensor · Obstacle avoidance · Force field algorithm · Performance · Multi robot systems

1 Introduction

Researchers have developed multiple methods in tackling a major hurdle that is obstacle avoidance when it comes to development of various robots. Autonomous robots need to be able to navigate through and around obstacles to be able to carry out tasks efficiently. This can be split into two tasks, path planning and obstacle avoidance [2]. Path planning relies on global information and knowledge of the area that needs to be explored. Obstacle avoidance relies on local information in the present obtained through sensors. While path planning is important to minimize time taken to reach a destination, good obstacle avoidance is critical to ensure the planned path can be carried out with few hindrances.

In this paper, the various methods of procuring and processing the local sensor data to carry out obstacle avoidance are explored. One of the most used algorithms in the

© Springer Nature Singapore Pte Ltd. 2021
K. K. Patel et al. (Eds.): icSoftComp 2020, CCIS 1374, pp. 111–122, 2021.
https://doi.org/10.1007/978-981-16-0708-0_10

real world for obstacle avoidance is the artificial potential field algorithm (APF) [3]. In this algorithm, T represents the target where the robot moves to and O represents the obstacles which the robot avoids. This is like how magnets apply attractive and repulsive forces. A combination of these forces around the object make up the path of the robot to reach its destination. Other algorithms for obstacle avoidance include gap method [4], particle swarm optimization [5], genetic algorithm [6] and fuzzy logic [7].

A modified force field method (also called APF) is evaluated in this paper. In terms of robot application, each proximity sensor is given a weight based on the trajectory at which the robot would face the obstacle on forward movement. The obstacles are given repulsive forces while the target destination is given an attractive force [9]. In the case of no destination, there are only repulsive forces present. The sum of the repulsive forces and the sensor readings aim to provide a sense of direction to the robot.

2   Review of Previous Literature

Seyyed et al. proposed two modified versions of an artificial potential field (APF) algorithm [3]. The first algorithm proposed was called Bug1. In this algorithm, the robot completely bypasses an object and covers it. The weakness of the algorithm is its inefficiency. An example of the Bug1 algorithm pathing can be seen in Fig. 1.

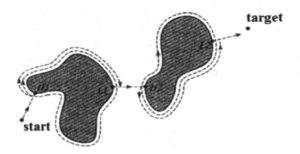

Fig. 1. Bug1 algorithm showcasing pathing of a single robot [3].

Seyyed et. al. Managed to overcome this problem by introducing another modified algorithm called Bug2 [3]. In the Bug2 algorithm, the robot tries to maintain a path directly from start to end while circling any obstacles. When the robot can get back to the line path, the robot continues to move straight to the target location. An example of this pathing can be seen in Fig. 2. One of the major downsides of the APF algorithm includes the inability to handle scenarios in cases where the robot is unable to get back on path or if the robot is surrounded by obstacles. The robot is therefore trapped. The proposed algorithm successfully tackled this problem and they were able to show simulation results for verification.

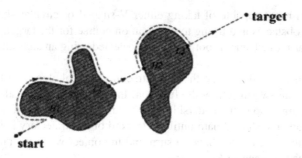

Fig. 2. Bug2 algorithm showcasing direct pathing of a single robot [3].

However, no practical testing was performed to validate the results. Moreover, both algorithms shown did not account for cases in which obstacles are entirely blocking the path to a target and assumes there is a target location to begin with. This algorithm could be further tested in situations where a robot is set to free roam to look for certain objects in applications such as search and rescue. The algorithms shown also did not account for cases in which multiple robots are made to navigate an area at once. These algorithms could be further tested in a swarm robotics environment.

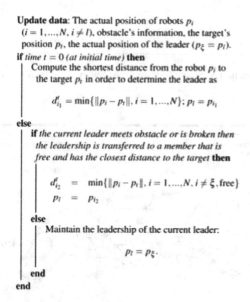

Fig. 3. Leader Selection of Obstacle Avoidance Algorithm to determine target tracking control [12].

Anh et al. proposed a force field method that used rotational force fields and repulsive forces to better avoid more complex shapes [12]. Both clockwise and anti-clockwise forces were analyzed. Simulations were carried out for multiple robots as part of a swarm robot capable of taking either V-shaped or circular shaped positions while avoiding obstacles and trying to maintain on course for the target. They had one robot in the swarm as a leader robot which was selected using an algorithm as shown in Fig. 3.

The leader is set to determine the target tracking control algorithm function while the members of the swarm follow the function. In cases where the leader gets trapped or cannot maintain shape, the leadership role is passed onto the nearest free member. The robots follow a V shaped path until the tracked object trajectory is identified. The robots then assume a circular shape to surround the object while maintaining relative velocity. This can be seen in Fig. 4 and 5.

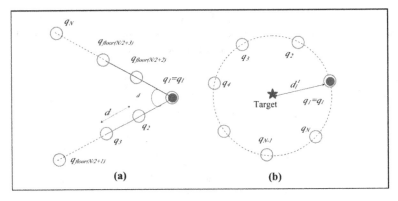

Fig. 4. a) Swarm robots in a V-Shape formation. b) Swarm robots in a circular formation [12].

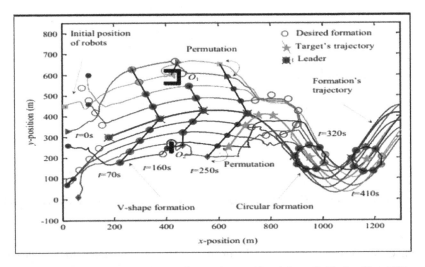

Fig. 5. Path followed by swarm robots using rotational force field algorithm [12].

The algorithm successfully demonstrated the function. However, a few critical areas were missed in the work. The performance of this algorithm was not verified with respect to time. While moving objects were tracked by rotational means, many obstacles were of a static nature and therefore performance of this algorithm in a dynamic environment is unknown. Moreover, the requirement of a leader in the algorithm meant that robots cannot adapt and carry out individual tasks if needed.

3   Experimental Methods

In this paper, the modified force field method of obstacle avoidance was evaluated in a single robot and swarm environments. The number of robots were varied between one, four and ten depending on the experiment. The experiments were all carried out in Simulink using MATLAB and results were recorded in the form of time taken to achieve a certain goal. Each robot was made to have 8 forward infrared proximity sensors. The experiment was carried out using the Robotics Toolbox differential drive algorithm provided by MathWorks [13]. The algorithms were modified to incorporate the modified force field algorithm.

The modified forcefield method assumed simplified weightings as opposed to existing methods. Depending on the expected type of navigation required, each sensor can be assigned a weight. For example, in the case of exploration in an open area with less narrow spaces, weights are assigned uniformly for all sensors. However, if the robots are expected to travel in narrow spaces, less weights can be given to side sensors to reduce oscillation. An example of a single robot with 8 forward sensors is shown in Fig. 6.

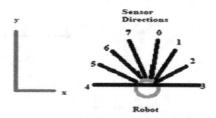

Fig. 6. A swarm robot depiction with 8 forward sensors.

In the case of the proposed force field algorithm, each sensor is given a weight from -1 to 1 for the direction of x and y based on the expected path. For the purposes of both evaluations, the weights were made the same and can be found in Table 1. The theory behind the selection of these weights are not covered in the scope of this paper.

Table 1. Sensor weights chosen for proposed modified force field method.

Sensor directions	0	1	2	3	4	5	6	7
x	− 1	− 0.5	0	0.5	1	0.5	0	− 0.5
y	0	0.5	1	0.5	0	− 0.5	− 1	− 0.5

The sum of the sensor readings multiplied by the contribution is then obtained for both x and y. Using this data, the velocity of the robot is calculated. This is given by,

$$Sum\_x = \sum_{k=0}^{7} |SensorReading(k)| \tag{1}$$

$$Sum\_y = \sum_{k=0}^{7} |SensorReading(k)| \tag{2}$$

A random noise was also added to reduce oscillation in cases where the pathway around obstacles are too tight. This algorithm was designed in MATLAB and incorporated into the robotics toolbox to carry out the test. A flowchart of the algorithm used can be found in Fig. 7.

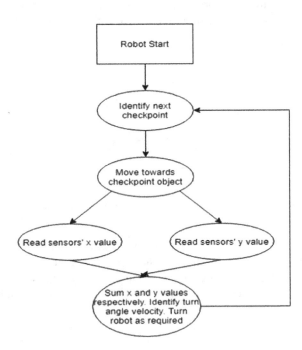

Fig. 7. Algorithm showcasing modified force field algorithm applied robot simulation for the purpose of evaluation 1

For the first evaluation, an open area with multiple target points were selected. A single robot was made to move through the 2-D space until all checkpoints were identified and passed through. The path of the robot was tracked as well to draw other conclusions based on navigation. The purpose of this evaluation was to test the functionality of the tested algorithm and the divergence distance from the object (waypoint in this case). An example of the area used can be seen in Fig. 8.

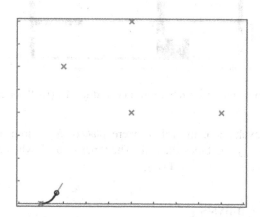

Fig. 8. 2-D environment for robot travel created in MATLAB for evaluation 1.

The map consists of multiple checkpoints and the program records the time taken for the robot to cover all the different checkpoints. The robot is considered successful once all checkpoints are reached.

In the second evaluation, 2-D maps were also used. However, this time, moving objects were introduced into the simulation to act as obstacles along with the robots themselves. The purpose of the second evaluation is to test how the algorithm performs in a dynamic environment in cases where one, four or ten robots are used. The goal was for this experiment was to have a robot leave the map. The tests were also carried about for 500 iterations to normalize the effect of having a robot spawn too close to the exit and to get a more average result. The average reading of the results is then recorded. A 2-D map was created in which these robots were made to maneuver. This test environment can be seen in Fig. 8.

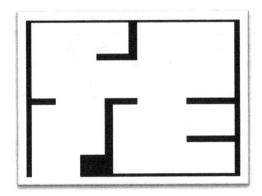

Fig. 9. 2-D environment for robot travel created in MATLAB for evaluation 2.

In this second evaluation, the robots were placed in random areas and moving objects were made to try and block the path. The timer stopped when any one robot was able to cross the exit out of the grid (Fig. 9).

4   Results and Analysis

In the first experiment, the modified force field algorithm was simulated to run in an open area and was tasked with crossing 4 checkpoints. This was performed for 100 iterations to obtain more reliable results. An example of the result for the forcefield method experiment with respect to pathing can be seen in Fig. 12.

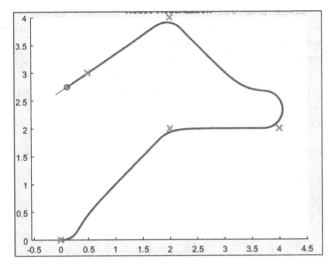

Fig. 10. Pathing of robot using forcefield method in Evaluation 1.

The divergence from each waypoint after the first were recorded to evaluate functionality, this can be seen in Fig. 10.

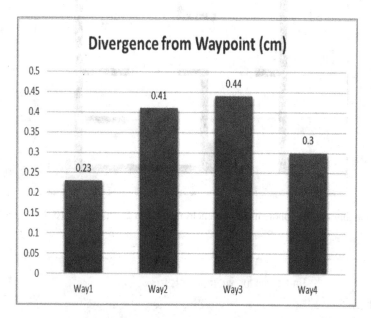

Fig. 11. Average divergence observed from robot to waypoint over 100 iterations

It was observed that the simplified modified forcefield method had a bigger divergence from the waypoint path following a much looser restriction. However, due to this nature of the algorithm, this was expected. Moreover, the robot was successfully able to navigate around the test environment proving the functionality of this algorithm.

In the second experiment, the modified forcefield algorithm was run in an open area with multiple robots and tasked to find the exit. This was done to evaluate how different number of robots perform in a dynamic environment. An example of the simulation results of this experiment being run with four robots can be seen in Fig. 11.

The performance with respect to time taken was also recorded to identify the time taken for every robot to exit via the red goal. This result over 500 iterations was averaged out and recorded in Fig. 12 for three cases where one, four and ten swarm robots were navigating the space.

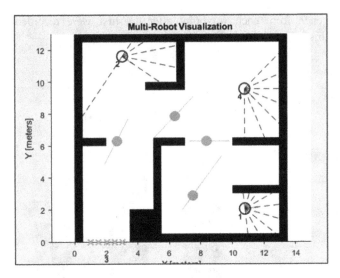

Fig. 12. Pathing of four robots using forcefield method in Evaluation 2. (Color figure online)

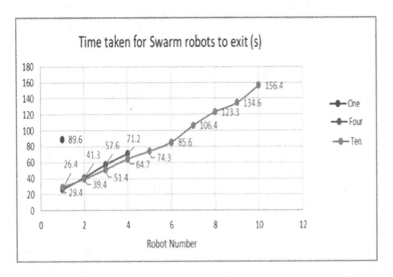

Fig. 13. Average time taken over 500 iterations for each robot to exit space

The red line crossing through the moving objects were added as a guide for clarity to determine the moving path. The red crosses serve as guides for the robots to reach the destination. For example, in Fig. 11, robot 3 can be seen successfully leaving the area.

From analysis of Fig. 12, one swarm robot takes the most time to exit with 89.6s compared to adding multiple robots into the same experiment. This was the expected result since random placements onto the escape grid and lack of robot interaction reduces the ability of the robot to navigate the space. In contrast, the experiment with four and ten swarm robots take 26.4s and 29.4s, respectively. This was again expected as adding more robots provide a multi-robot environment in where the robots can interact with each other and exit the environment. However, in the ten-robot scenario, the initial robot took longer than for four robots which was inconsistent with the expectation. This can be attributed to the size of the experiment space; an observation was made where the correct number of swarm robots need to be selected depending on the available space for the experiment (Fig. 13).

5 Conclusion

In this paper, the performance and functionality of a modified yet simplified forcefield algorithm for obstacle avoidance was analyzed. The experiments and simulations used infrared sensors and tested three scenarios where there were one, four or ten robots present at a given time. The algorithm was successful in navigating an open environment and a dynamic environment in the MATLAB simulation environment.

In open areas, the algorithm with forcefield methods was shown to have a moderate divergence (0.23 cm–0.44 cm) which could be improved with a different sensor type. In more dynamic areas, the infrared algorithm with forcefield methods was shown to be slower by about 340% over 500 iterations with only one robot due to hindrances caused by obstacles and the lack of robots to interact. However, the swarm robotics environments showcased much faster results (26.4–29.4 s) compared to a single robot which was in line with what was expected.

References

1. Mane, S.B., Vhanale, S.: Genetic algorithm approach for obstacle avoidance and path optimization of mobile robot. In: Iyer, B., Nalbalwar, S. , Pathak, N. (eds.) Computing, Communication and Signal Processing. AISC, vol. 810, pp. 649–659. Springer, Singapore (2019). https://doi.org/10.1007/978-981-13-1513-8_66
2. Chan, S.H., Xu, X., Wu, P.T., Chiang, M.L., Fu, L.C.: Real-time obstacle avoidance using supervised recurrent neural network with automatic data collection and labeling. In: 2019 IEEE International Conference on Systems, Man and Cybernetics (SMC), pp. 472–477. IEEE (2019)
3. A.K., Wang, J. and Liu, X. : Obstacle avoidance of mobile robots using modified artificial potential field algorithm. EURASIP J. Wirel. Commun. Netw. **2019**(1), 70. (2019). https://doi.org/10.1186/s13638-019-1396-2
4. Sezer, V., Gokasan, M.: A novel obstacle avoidance algorithm: follow the gap method. Robot. Auton. Syst. **60**(9), 1123–1134 (2012)
5. Chen, X., Li, Y.: Smooth path planning of a mobile robot using stochastic particle swarm optimization. In: Proceedings of the 2006 IEEE International Conference on Mechatronics and Automation, pp. 1722–1727. IEEE (2006)
6. Tu, J., Yang, S.X.: Genetic algorithm based path planning for a mobile robot. In: IEEE International Conference on Robotics and Automation, Proceedings, ICRA 2003, vol. 1, pp. 1221–1226. IEEE (2003)

7. Reignier, P.: Fuzzy logic techniques for mobile robot obstacle avoidance. Robot. Auton. Syst. **12**(3–4), 143–153 (1994)

8. Jiang, Y., Yang, C., Zhaojie, J., Liu, J.: Obstacle avoidance of a redundant robot using virtual force field and null space projection. In: Haibin, Y., Liu, J., Liu, L., Zhaojie, J., Liu, Y., Zhou, D. (eds.) ICIRA 2019. LNCS (LNAI), vol. 11740, pp. 728–739. Springer, Cham (2019). https://doi.org/10.1007/978-3-030-27526-6_64

9. Borenstein, J., Koren, Y.: Real-time obstacle avoidance for fast mobile robots in cluttered environments. In: Proceedings of IEEE International Conference on Robotics and Automation, pp. 572–577. IEEE (1990)

10. Peng, Y., Qu, D., Zhong, Y., Xie, S., Luo, J., Gu, J.: The obstacle detection and obstacle avoidance algorithm based on 2-D LIDAR. In: 2015 IEEE International Conference on Information and Automation, pp. 1648–1653. IEEE (2015)

11. Singh, N.H., Thongam, K.: Neural network-based approaches for mobile robot navigation in static and moving obstacles environments. Intel. Serv. Robot. **12**(1), 55–67 (2018). https://doi.org/10.1007/s11370-018-0260-2

12. Dang, A.D., La, H.M., Nguyen, T., Horn, J.: Formation control for autonomous robots with collision and obstacle avoidance using a rotational and repulsive force–based approach. Int. J. Adv. Rob. Syst. **16**(3), 1729881419847897 (2019)

13. Ghorpade, D., Thakare, A.D., Doiphode, S.: Obstacle detection and avoidance algorithm for autonomous mobile robot using 2D LiDAR. In: 2017 International Conference on Computing, Communication, Control and Automation (ICCUBEA), Pune, pp. 1–6 (2017)

14. Hutabarat, D., Rivai, M., Purwanto, D., Hutomo, H.: Lidar-based obstacle avoidance for the autonomous mobile robot. In: 2019 12th International Conference on Information & Communication Technology and System (ICTS), pp. 197–202. IEEE (2019)

15. Mathworks.com.: Mobile robotics simulation toolbox - file exchange - MATLAB Central (2018). https://www.mathworks.com/matlabcentral/fileexchange/66586-mobile-robotics-simulation-toolbox. Accessed 8 Dec 2018

Rethinking the Limits of Optimization Economic Order Quantity (EOQ) Using Self Generating Training Model by Adaptive-Neuro Fuzzy Inference System

A. Stanley Raj[1]([⊠]) [iD], H. Mary Henrietta[2], K. Kalaiarasi[3], and M. Sumathi[4]

[1] Loyola College, Chennai 600034, Tamilnadu, India
stanleyraj_84@yahoo.co.in
[2] Saveetha Engineering College, Chennai 602105, Tamilnadu, India
[3] Cauvery College for Women (Affiliated to Bharathidasan University), Trichy 620018, Tamilnadu, India
[4] Khadir Mohideen College (Affiliated to Bharathidasan University), Adirampattinam 614701, Tamilnadu, India

Abstract. This paper deals gives an alternate approach to the traditional way of solving an optimization of Economic order quantity (EOQ) by applying self-generating training model in ANFIS. The inventory control for a successful organization has to be sustained with varying parameters such as demand, setup cost and ordering cost. This research work combines the fuzzy inference system and Adaptive neuro-fuzzy inference system to acquire the optimal order quantity with fuzzy logic. The proposed algorithm of self-generating training dataset proclaims the efficient model for predicting EOQ with variable demand. This algorithm is tested with various numbers of datasets and the results are compared with the fuzzified and crisp model. The performance evaluation is done and the results are satisfactory to apply any nonlinear problems.

Keywords: Economic order quantity (EOQ) · ANFIS · Fuzzy logic to EOQ · Optimization of total cost

1 Introduction

It was Zadeh [20] in 1965 introduced the fuzzy sets that refers to vagueness and uncertainty in real life. In the year 1983, Zimmerman [21] observed fuzziness in the study of operational research. Park [12] fuzzified the ordering cost and holding(storage) cost as trapezoidal fuzzy numbers in the traditional EOQ to solve the non-linear programming that resulted in fuzzy EOQ models. Inventory is a part of the major segments in economy which is ambiguous in nature that concentrates on a proper management, by increasing the customers and minimizing the inventory costs. This resulted in an EOQ model introduced by Harris [9] in 1913.Chen [5] was the first person to propose a probabilistic approach to an inventory with imperfect items. In 2007, Wang [18] studied the randomness in fuzzy EOQ model for items with imperfection. Dutta [7] in

K. K. Patel et al. (Eds.): icSoftComp 2020, CCIS 1374, pp. 123–133, 2021.
https://doi.org/10.1007/978-981-16-0708-0_11

the year 2004, fuzzified the inventory parameters demand, holding cost and ordering cost. In inventory management the economic order quantity is the strategy used as a replenishment model that is used to determine the total inventory costs and also manipulates to minimize it. Earlier time demand was assumed to be a constant that resulted as a pitfall in the EOQ model. So, there were models brought with fluctuating demands to face the consistent seasonality in business. To put up with the complications, EOQ can be customized using inventory management software suggesting a well-organized ordering solution. To deal with these limitations it is essential to bring in the artificial intelligence techniques in solving the real problems.

Although many researchers had simulated the artificial intelligence in inventory control for production systems. The study of Artificial intelligence in inventory management was first started off by Jang [10] by combining the fuzzy inference system with adaptive networks. Gupta and Maransa [8] proposed a two-stage stochastic programming uncertainty demand model where in the first, production decisions was considered and supply chain decisions in the second stage.

Fuzzy based study could be convenient for such uncertain situations and works best if combined with artificial neural networks (ANN) in the real business world. When Fuzzy merges with ANN, it results in neuro fuzzy system and fuzzy neural system. The renowned work of Aliev [2] proposed two different design, namely neuro fuzzy systems whose key task is to operate mathematical relations, whereas the fuzzy neural systems is applied to discover the numerical information and knowledge-based data which are represented by fuzzy numbers. In 1991, Pedrycz [14] generated models by its conduct towards unpredictability and characterized the connection between the fuzzy theory and neural networks. Also, Pedrycz [15] extended his study of neurons in pattern classifiers in the year 1992. Further, NFN was defined by a fuzzy structure instructed by an algorithm by a smart model by Jang [11]. Fuzzy neural networks are many distinguished by the connection of their neurons. In 1943, McCulloch [19] developed a mathematical model using a single neuron which established the authenticity of a neuron activation in the brain that was widely accepted in theoretical possibilities. The start of examining the connected nodes to modify the connection weights was carried out by Hebb [6] in the year 1949. It was Rosenblatt [16] brought the perceptron neural model that satisfied the neuron's behavior.

An adaptive neuro-fuzzy logic inventory control system was introduced in the year 2012 by BalazsLenart [4]. Later, Aksoy et al. [1] applied ANFIS in a garment trade with demand prediction. In 2015, Aengchuan and Phruksaphanrat [3] compared the three methods namely fuzzy inference system (FIS), Adaptive Neuro-Fuzzy inference system (ANFIS) and Artificial neural networks with variating membership functions in solving inventory problems. Out of these, the ANFIS along with gaussian membership function resulted with the minimum total cost. In 2015, yet another result that forecasted the advantage of ANFIS over ANN was carried out by Paul, Azeem and Ghosh [13] maintaining the optimum inventory level in the inventory management problem. The economic order quantity equation Kalaiarasi et al. [22] was taken and the adaptive neuro fuzzy inference system is applied to the obtain the desired model.

Many researchers had formulated the hybrid methods of artificial intelligence which had resulted in better results by applying ANFIS in solving complex EOQ problems. ANFIS is a learning tool that is extensively used to get the desired output by applying fuzzy logic with highly interconnected neural network. In this model an inventory management with the advantage of Adaptive neuro-fuzzy inference system (ANFIS) has been developed with modelling done in fuzzy using a given set of data.

2 Inventory Model for EOQ

The input parameters for the corresponding model are.

R - Ordering cost
d - constant demand rate coefficient
α - price-dependent demand rate coefficient
S - selling price
Q - Order size
p - unit purchasing cost
g - constant holding cost coefficient

The total cost [17] per cycle is given by

$$T(Q) = \frac{R(d - \alpha S)}{Q} + p(d - \alpha P) + \frac{gpQ}{2} \tag{1}$$

Partially differentiating w.r.t Q,

$$\frac{\partial T}{\partial Q} = \frac{R(d - \alpha S)}{Q^2} + \frac{gc}{2} \tag{2}$$

Equating $\frac{\partial T}{\partial Q} = 0$ we obtain the economic order quantity in crisp values [22]

$$Q = \sqrt{\frac{2R(d - \alpha S)}{gp}} \tag{3}$$

2.1 ANFIS Model Development

Initially, the data have been subjected to certain degree of membership grade so that at each iterations the firing strength will decide the consequent parameters (Fig. 1).

ANFIS system consists of 5 layers; Output of each layer is symbolized by $O_{1, i}$ with i is a sequence of nodes and 1 is the sequence showing the lining. Here is an explanation for each layer (Jang 1993), namely:

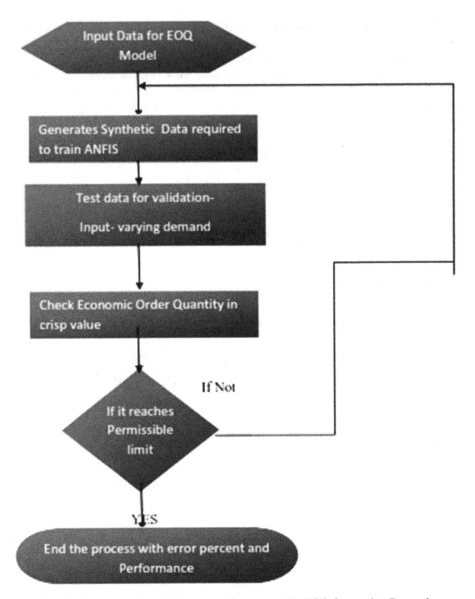

Fig. 1. Flow chart for ANFIS methodology to predict EOQ for varying Demand

Layer 1

Serves to raise the degree of membership and the membership used here is Gaussian membership function.

$$O_{1,i} = \mu_A(x), i = 1, 2 \tag{4}$$

and

$$O_{1,i} = \mu_B(y), i = 1, 2 \tag{5}$$

$$f(x, \sigma; c) = e^{\frac{-(x-c)^2}{2\sigma^2}}$$

by $\{\sigma$ and $c\}$ are the parameters of membership function or called as a parameter premise. σ signifies the cluster bandwidth and, c represents the cluster center.

Layer 2
Serves to evoke *firing-strength* by multiplying each input signal.

$$O_{2,i} = w_i = \mu_A(x) \times \mu_B(y), i = 1, 2. \tag{6}$$

Layer 3
Normalizes the *firing strength*

$$O_{3,i} = \overline{w}_i = \frac{w_i}{w_1 + w_2}, \quad i = 1, 2. \tag{7}$$

Layer 4
Calculates the output based on the parameters of the rule *consequent* $\{p_i, q_i$ and $r_i\}$

$$O_{4,i} = \overline{w}_i f_i = \overline{w}_i (p_i x + q_i y + r_i) \tag{8}$$

Layer 5
Counts the ANFIS output signal by summing all incoming signals will produce

$$\sum_i \overline{w}_i f_i = \frac{\sum_i w_i f_i}{\sum_i w_i.} \tag{9}$$

ANFIS uses the input data scaling by xbounds = [min max] command used in MATLAB software which represents the scaling parameter of the input function varies between minimum to maximum value of the data point. Each data point is scaled for pre-processing of training initially by normalizing it.

2.2   Model Development and Application

Step 1:
The user can import the data for EOQ model. The imported data must be of any form that includes text files, excel spreadsheets, CSV etc.

Step 2:
For ANFIS training is more important. Thus, based on the number of iterations and random permutations of data, ANFIS generates synthetic data. This self-generation of synthetic data will be helpful to evaluate noisy and missed data. Thus, this step is a very important step in this algorithm.

Step 3:

This the key step where the neuro fuzzy algorithm generates synthetic dataset for each data with connection to the adjacent data that controls the noises and errors present in data.

Step 4:

In this step the algorithm calculates the error percentage of the data based on the coefficient of variation.

Step 5:

Every iteration the system generates one synthetic data and a model is generated the based on the number of iterations decided by the user. More the number of synthetic data better performance of the algorithm.

Step 6:

Finally, the EOQ model based on variable demand rate is predicted by the neuro fuzzy algorithm.

2.3   Algorithm Description and Application

This algorithm works on the basis of self-generating training dataset. In self-generating model, the system considers the mean, standard deviation, upper (Maximum value) and lower (minimum value) bounds. After considering all the statistical values from the given input data, the algorithm generates the synthetic data using random permutations. For each iteration, it generates a single synthetic data. For getting a greater number of synthetic data, user has to fix the number of iterations. The consistency may be lost once the user fixes a greater number of iterations than the memory allocated by the system to train the data. The system became unstable after a particular number of epochs.

3   Results and Discussion

ANFIS will test the data using the synthetic training dataset generated by this algorithm. Figure 2 shows the membership function used to train the data (Figs. 3, 4 and 5).

It is very necessary for a company to know the strategy of variable demand with Economic Order Quantity. Thus, using this algorithm, we can easily predict the EOQ for variable demand. This algorithm is proved successful while comparing with crisp and fuzzified model (Fig. 6). Figure 7 represents the three-dimensional model of EOQ for variable demand. In ANFIS training there is a virtual connection between synthetic dataset and output. ANFIS is one of the potential soft computing algorithms integrates neural networks and fuzzy logic. In this EOQ model, Gaussian membership function is applied to guesstimate the output.

Self-generation of data have certain advantages.

1. Errors or noises in the data can be eliminated.

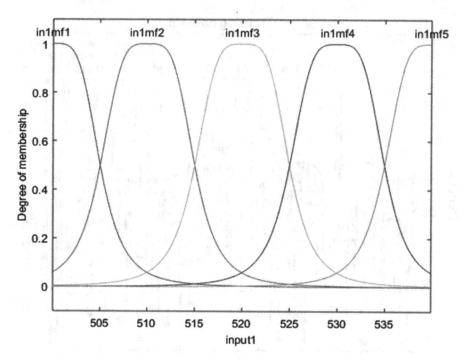

Fig. 2. Represents the Gaussian membership function used for training the data

2. If there is any missing data between two data points, based on the standard deviation and the trend, it can be interpolated. The trend will be maintained.
3. Synthetic training datasets are elastic in nature because the datasets can run between maximum and minimum of the original data and predicts the exact results though the data is nonlinear.
4. Developing synthetic data using this algorithm helps the ANFIS system to decide the output very easily. Fixing the membership functions for a bunch of data, though it consumes time, it will predict the exact result after defuzzification.

Error Estimation [23]
L1-norm error estimation was used to minimize the errors during iteration and this method can be applied in numerous fields due to its robustness compared to L2-norm. L2-norm squares the errors that makes the model more efficient when noisy data are applied.

In this model the over fitting problems which normally occurs in ANFIS were avoided by fixing the allowable error percentage to minimum (10% in this study). To choose the appropriate model parameters during the iteration the permissible error was fixed by the user.

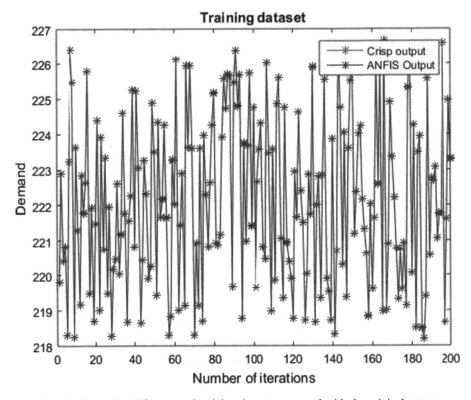

Fig. 3. Shows the self-generated training dataset compared with the original output

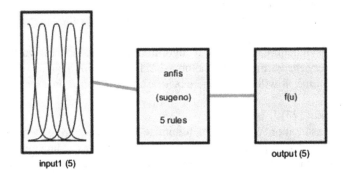

System anfis: 1 inputs, 1 outputs, 5 rules

Fig. 4. ANFIS architecture for EOQ model prediction

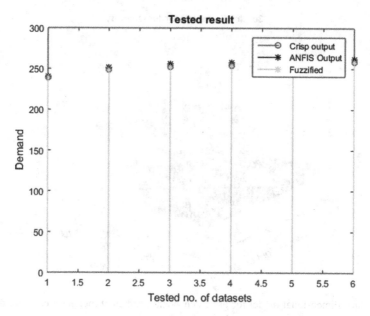

Fig. 5. Represents the tested data using synthetic training dataset by self-generating algorithm

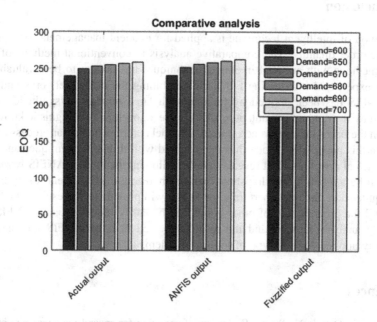

Fig. 6. Comparative analysis of ANFIS output with crisp and fuzzified model.

3d plot-Economic Order Quantity

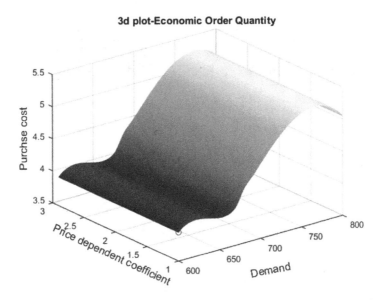

Fig. 7. Three-dimensional model for price dependent coefficient, purchase cost and demand

4   Conclusion

This method of intelligent technique is applied for efficient management for acquiring economic order quantity. The comparative analysis in conventional methods of linear solving methods with artificial intelligent techniques has proven to be a valuable and logically expert tool is assessing EOQ. On combining the neural networks and fuzzy logic, ANFIS has been applied by training with large number of synthetic datasets generated by the random permutations of software algorithm. The linguistic knowledge present in the fuzzy logic approach is used to model complex nonlinear process of EOQ model. In this paper EOQ model has been solved with different techniques and tested with the actual crisp model. It reveals that the following method of ANFIS works well and it can be applied in any logistic expert to analyze the EOQ. Neurofuzzy training time is quite short and the expert training dataset will provide exact results. The flow of goods and the procurement of other goods can be easily modeled using ANFIS. The sensitivity analysis is done and the results revealed that the ANFIS tool has been universally applied for any type of logistic problem.

References

1. Aksoy, A., Ozturk, N., Sucky, E.: Demand forecasting for apparel manufacturers by using neuro-fuzzy techniques. J. Model. Manag. **9**(1), 18–35 (2014)
2. Aliev, R.A., Guirimov, B., Fazlohhahi, R., Aliev, R.: Evolutionary algorithm-based learning o fuzzy neural networks. Fuzzy Sets Syst. **160**(17), 2553–2566 (2009)

3. Aengchuan, P., Phruksaphanrat, B.: Comparison of fuzzy inference system (FIS), FIS with artificial neural networks (FIS +ANN) and FIS with adaptive neuro-fuzzy inference system (FIS+ANFIS) for inventory control. J. Intell. Manuf. **29**, 905–923 (2015)
4. Lénárt, B., Grzybowska, K., Cimer, M.: Adaptive inventory control in production systems. In: Corchado, E., Snášel, V., Abraham, A., Woźniak, M., Graña, M., Cho, S.-B. (eds.) HAIS 2012. LNCS (LNAI), vol. 7209, pp. 222–228. Springer, Heidelberg (2012). https://doi.org/10.1007/978-3-642-28931-6_21
5. Chen, C.Y.: A probabilistic approach for traditional EOQ model. J. Inf. Optim. Sci. **24**, 249–253 (2003)
6. Hebb, D.O.: The Organization of Behavior. Wiley, London (1949)
7. Dutta, D., Kumar, P.: Optimal policy for an inventory model without shortages considering fuzziness in demand, holding cost and ordering cost. Int. J. Adv. Innov. Res. **2**(3), 320–325 (2004)
8. Gupta, A., Maransa, C.D.: Managing demand uncertainty in supply chain planning. Comput. Chem. Eng. **27**, 1219–1227 (2003)
9. Harris, F.: Operations and Cost. AW Shaw Co., Chicago (1913)
10. Jang, J.R.: ANFIS: adaptive-network-based fuzzy inference system. IEEE Trans. Syst. Man Cybern. **23**(3), 665–685 (1993)
11. Jang, J.-S.R., Sun, C.-T., Mizutani, E.: Neuro-Fuzzy and Soft Computing-A Computational Approach to Learning and Machine Intelligence. Prentice Hall, New York (1997)
12. Park, K.S.: Fuzzy set theoretical interpretation of economic order quantity. IEEE Trans. Syst. Man Cybern. SMC **17**, 1082–1084 (1987)
13. Paul, S.K., Azeem, A., Ghosh, A.K.: Application of adaptive neuro-fuzzy inference system and artificial neural network in inventory level forecasting. Int. J. Bus. Inf. Syst. **18**(3), 268–284 (2015)
14. Pedrycz, W.: Neurocomputations in relational systems. IEEE Trans. Pattern Anal. Mach. Intell. **13**(3), 289–297 (1991)
15. Pedrycz, W.: Fuzzy neural networks with reference neurons as pattern classifiers. IEEE Trans. Neural Networks **3**(5), 770–775 (1992)
16. Rosenblatt, F.: The perceptron: a probabilistic model for information storage and organization in the brain. Psychol. Rev. **65**(6), 386–408 (1958)
17. Garai, T., Chakraborty, D., Roy, T.K.: Fully fuzzy inventory model with price-dependent demand and time varying holding cost under fuzzy decision variables. J. Intell. Fuzzy Syst. **36**, 3725–3738 (2019)
18. Wang, X., Tang, W., Zaho, R.: Random fuzzy EOQ model with imperfect quality items. Fuzzy Optim. Decis. Mak. **6**, 139–153 (2007)
19. McCulloch, W., Pitts, W.: A logical calculus of the ideas immanent in nervous activity. Bull. Math. Biophys. **5**(4), 115–133 (1943). https://doi.org/10.1007/BF02478259
20. Zadeh, L.A.: Fuzzy sets. Inf. Control **8**, 338–353 (1965)
21. Zimmerman, H.J.: Using fuzzy sets in operational research. Eur. J. Oper. Res. **13**, 201–206 (1983)
22. Kalaiarasi, K., Sumathi, M., Mary Henrietta, H., Stanley, R.A.: Determining the efficiency of fuzzy logic EOQ inventory model with varying demand in comparison with Lagrangian and Kuhn-tucker method through sensitivity analysis. J. Model Based Res. **1**(3), 1–2 (2020)
23. Stanley Raj, A., Srinivas, Y., Damodharan, R., Hudson Oliver, D., Viswanath, J.: Presentation of neurofuzzy optimally weighted sampling model for geoelectrical data inversion. Modell. Earth Syst. Environ. (2020). https://doi.org/10.1007/s40808-020-00935-2

Hybrid POS Tagger for Gujarati Text

Chetana Tailor[✉] and Bankim Patel

Shrimad Rajachandra Institute of Management and Computer Application,
Uka Tarsadia University, Bardoli-Mahuva Road, Surat, Gujarat, India
chetana.tailor@gmail.com, bankim.patel@srimca.edu.in

Abstract. POS tagger is one of the most essential steps in Natural Language Processing applications to analyze the text. We perform a comparative study of POS taggers available for Gujarati language. Comparative study is based on evaluation criteria namely Precision, Recall, and F1 score for each tag and overall accuracy of the POS tagger. A hybrid approach for improving the accuracy of POS tagger has been proposed for Gujarati Language which comprises the LSTM based POS tagging and Computational Linguistic Rules. We found that accuracy of the statistical taggers is improved by applying language specific rules.

Keywords: Natural Language Processing · POS tagger · Deep learning · Gujarati language

1 Introduction

Part-of-Speech tagging is one of the essential steps in Natural Language Processing (NLP) that attaches the appropriate tag from the given tag set to each word of the sentence. POS tagger helps not only in solving NLP problems such as Text Chunking, Syntactic parsing, Semantic role labeling, and Semantic parsing but also helps in NLP applications, including Information extraction, Question answering, and Machine Translation [19]. As compare to foreign languages like English, very less amount of work has been carried out for Indian languages [6, 10].

Three different approaches are used to develop POS tagger for Indian languages: Rule based, Machine learning based and Hybrid approach. Pure rule based system development is difficult as Indian languages are morphologically rich and a word may have multiple contextual meaning. Therefore, Machine learning approach in which tagging is done based on the variety of words and features covered in training data set including the context of the word is used. Machine learning based approach has advantage of tagging unknown words by using the probabilities and features. Annotated data, domain of the data and feature selection play an important role in Machine learning approach [14]. In Machine learning based approach, the perfect feature selection incorporating language characteristics affects the accuracy as there is no flexibility and control in assigning weights to the selected features [14]. Therefore, Hybrid approach is better.

Linguistically, Gujarati is a free word order language [20] as well as partially agglutinative. Words in Gujarati have multiple senses according to the context in the

© Springer Nature Singapore Pte Ltd. 2021
K. K. Patel et al. (Eds.): icSoftComp 2020, CCIS 1374, pp. 134–144, 2021.
https://doi.org/10.1007/978-981-16-0708-0_12

sentence where the tags for different senses are different. e.g. "હે દી"-"deʋī" can be used as a common noun– "Goddess", proper noun –as "Devi", Auxilary: Participle Noun for the verb "to give", or as verb "to give".

In the following section, study of the existing taggers for Indian languages w.r.t. accuracy, data set and approach used to build the POS tagger has been carried out. The objective of this study is to develop the POS tagger for Gujarati language with good accuracy. State-of-the-art techniques for POS taggers for Gujarati Language and other Indian languages have been studied in Sect. 2. Comparative study to select the statistical POS taggers for Gujarati language has been conducted in Sect. 3. Design the Gujarati language specific rules for improving the accuracy of statistical POS tagger in Sect. 4. In Sect. 5, experimental analysis and conclusion have been discussed.

2 Literature Survey

Oldest POS tagger was part of the parser developed by Zelling Harris under the Transformations and Discourse Analysis Project developed using 14 handwritten rules [24]. Current trend is shifted towards the Machine learning based approach [10] for which featureset, techniques, and dataset play a key role in developing POS tagger for any language.

Lot of work has been carried out for English and other foreign languages and state-of-art-accuracy is achieved. But very less work has been carried out for Indian languages. POS tagger for the Indian languages have been developed by using Rule based approach, Hybrid approach, and Machine learning approach consisting Decision Tree, HMM, Maximum entropy, SVM and CRF techniques as stated in the survey [12] but among all Hybrid approach outperforms rest of the other approaches for Indian languages. Comparison is based on the accuracy, method and data set. According to the survey analysis, Machine learning approach has given good result only when corpus is having more than 25,000 words [12]. In this section, focus is given to study the state-of-the-art techniques in the field of POS tagging for Indian languages to find the best POS tagging techniques and features to improve the accuracy of Gujarati Statistical POS taggers. Attention of this study is approach, technique, featureset and domain of the corpus used for improving accuracy of POS tagger.

POS taggers are available for Indian Languages namely Hindi, Bengali, Punjabi, Dravidian, Malayalam, Marathi, Tamil, Sindhi, Telugu, and Gujarati [4, 6, 7, 12, 13, 15, 17]. Approaches used for Indian Languages other than Gujarati language are CRF [13], HMM [7], Maximum Entropy [7], SVM [7], Trigram model [15], Bidirectional LSTM [17].

From the above study conducted for other than Gujarati language, Machine learning approach is giving good result only when corpus contains enough annotated quality data and language specific features are provided. After studying other Indian Languages, study of approaches used for Gujarati language has been carried out.

Kapadia & Desai, (2017) have developed a POS tagger by adopting Rule based approach for Gujarati language using suffix list as well as list of nouns [11]. They have manually created the corpus containing 500 sentences with 2514 words for the testing purpose. Accuracy of this system is 87.48%. If current word suffix is not matched with any of rule made up of suffix, system fails to assign appropriate tag.

Hala & Virani, (2015) have used the Hybrid approach to improve the accuracy of POS tagging for Gujarati language [9]. They have tagged data using HMM model. Linguistic rules are applied to improve the accuracy of POS tagger. Two rules are discussed. One of them is about verb identification: if sentence has the structure in which unknown word is followed by Noun followed by Pronoun, then it has to be a verb. This rule is not suitable for complex sentence structure.

Table 1. Frequency of the POS tags in percentage

POS tag	Percentage
NN	27.33
PUNC	12.68
VAUX	8.78
VM	8.16
JJ	8.09
VAUX_VNP	6.27
PSP	4.53
RPD	3.16
DMD	2.96
NNP	2.91
PRP	2.85
CCD	2.54
NST	1.83
NEG	1.62
QTC	1.46
QTF	1.06

Consider the sentence "તેઓનું_PRP સ્કૂટર_NN જયને_NNP વેચાઈ_VM ગયું_VAUX ._PUNC" [ṯeonu ṣkuṭər dʒəjəne ʋetʃəjə gəjuõ.] [Their scooter has been sold out to Jay.] This example is contradiction to the rule defined for tagging verb.

Patel & Gali, (2008) have developed a POS tagger for Gujarati language using semi supervised machine learning approach [1]. They have used CRF with 600 manually tagged sentences and 5,000 untagged sentences. Testing corpus contains 5,000 words. Few of the features used in this work are suffixes, prefixes, and number. Achieved accuracy for this POS tagger is 91.47%. Major.errors are found in tagging nouns.

Garg et al., (2013) have developed a POS tagger for Gujarati language using CRF to improve the accuracy of Named entity recognition [8]. For training, they have used the corpus available at TDIL website which contains 25 documents each containing 1000 sentences. A feature set is made up of 18 features comprises of suffix and prefix of word with length 3, word length, previous and last two words, current word, and word combination up-to context window size five. Similarly, POS tagger for Gujarati language by Knowledge Based Computer Systems Division of CDAC Mumbai [3] is developed using the Stanford library of Maximum Entropy model. They have not published its accuracy as well as training and testing dataset details.

From the above study, we infer that language dependent features are important for developing and improving the accuracy of POS tagger using Machine learning based POS tagger. It can be further increased by adding language specific rules. In addition, the domain and size of corpus also affect the accuracy of POS tagger.

3   Comparative Study of Statistical POS Taggers

As we are working for Anaphora Resolution for Gujarati text, we have developed Gujarati Sentence Tokenizer, Chunker, Context based Gender and Number Identification of a noun phrase for Gujarati Text where POS tagger is important component of the system Anaphora Resolution. As it is used as key feature not only for Anaphora Resolution but also for developing other components namely Chunker, Context based Gender and Number Identification of a noun phrase for Gujarati Text. Therefore, in this section, our main focus is to identify the best statistical Gujarati POS tagger in terms of accuracy, precision (P), recall (R), and F1 score (F1).

Gujarati monolingual TDIL corpus [21] is used to measure the accuracy of Statistical POS taggers. This corpus consists of multiple domains namely Art and Culture, Economy, Entertainment, Religion, Sports, Science and Technology. There are total 30,000 sentences with 3,50,298 tokens in this corpus. We have found around 1200 words were annotated with the wrong tags which were corrected. Tags which are corrected are: NN, NNP, QTC, QTF, and NEG.

By exploring the Gujarati text of TDIL corpus, we analyze that most frequent tags used in Gujarati Language listed in Table 1. It also shows that if nouns are accurately identified then accuracy of POS tagger increases as its contribution as compare to other tags are more in Gujarati corpus.

There are five existing POS taggers for Gujarati language as discussed in previous section. Among all, we have studied POS taggers developed by Knowledge Based Computer Systems Division of CDAC Mumbai using Max-Entropy technique and Garg et al., (2013) developed at IR Lab Gandhinagar using Conditional Random Fields (CRF). As these two taggers are developed by covering multiple domain dataset and publicly available. Rest of the three taggers out of five is not available publicly for the further study. Accuracy of CRF based Gujarati tagger is available but Max-Entropy based Gujarati tagger's accuracy is not available. These both taggers CRF based tagger and Max-Entropy tagger are tested on TDIL corpus and result the accuracy 67.27% and 77.54% respectively that is below the state-of-art accuracy found in literature which is shown in Table 2.

As Bidirectional LSTM POS tagger outperforms the existing tagger for Tamil language [17], we have developed and added Bidirectional Recurrent Neural Network with LSTM based POS tagger for Gujarati Language which supports long term dependency of the words in the sentence. At LSTM layer, output vector dimension is 256 and activation function is tanh as to provide non-linearity and tanh performs better as compare to sigmoid [25]. By evaluating activation functions Relu and tanh for Gujarati POS Tagging, tanh has performed 1% more accurately than Relu. Adam Optimizer is used with optimized parameters' value provided in [17]. Adam Optimizer with Sparse categorical cross entropy optimization function as a loss function performs better as POS tagging is multi-labeling problem where data is not encoded using one-hot encoding [26]. 128 number of samples per gradient update and 5 epochs are used for generating the model during the training. Corpus is divided into 80%, 20% for training and testing dataset. 20% of training dataset is used for validation purpose. Accuracy of this tagger is listed in Table 2.

Table 2. Accuracy of statistical Gujarati POS taggers

POS tag	Max-entropy tagger			CRF based tagger			RNN with bidirectional LSTM		
	P	R	F1	P	R	F1	P	R	F1
Cardinals Quantifiers (QTC)	0.93	0.93	0.93	0.89	0.74	0.81	0.97	0.84	0.90
General Quantifiers (QTF)	0.76	0.83	0.79	0.99	0.57	0.72	0.98	0.97	**0.98**
Ordinals Quantifiers (QTO)	0.49	0.74	0.59	0.61	0.18	0.28	0.79	0.74	**0.76**
Adjective (JJ)	0.83	0.62	0.71	0.72	0.46	0.56	0.86	0.81	**0.83**
Common Noun (NN)	0.84	0.89	0.86	0.65	0.76	0.70	0.86	0.94	**0.90**
Proper Noun (NNP)	0.37	0.63	0.47	0.15	0.68	0.24	0.76	0.62	**0.68**
Nloc Noun (NST)	0.60	0.88	0.71	0.58	0.82	0.68	0.92	0.90	**0.91**
Postposition (PSP)	0.86	0.44	0.59	0.86	0.34	0.49	0.94	0.94	**0.94**
Personal Pronoun (PRP)	0.74	0.81	0.77	0.83	0.45	0.59	0.86	0.87	**0.87**
Reflexive Pronoun (PRF)	0.99	0.88	0.93	0.96	0.90	0.93	0.96	0.96	**0.96**
Relative Pronoun (PRL)	0.24	0.94	0.39	0.19	0.90	0.32	0.94	0.90	**0.92**
Reciprocal Pronoun (PRC)	0.76	0.79	0.77	1.00	0.01	0.03	1.00	0.83	**0.91**
Wh-word Pronoun (PRQ)	0.94	0.84	0.89	0.98	0.38	0.54	0.94	0.96	**0.95**
Indefinite Pronoun (PRI)	0.10	0.05	0.07	0.00	0.00	0.00	0.61	0.60	**0.60**
Deictic Demonstrative (DMD)	0.93	0.49	0.64	0.89	0.57	0.69	0.87	0.88	**0.87**
Indefinite Pronoun (DMI)	0.69	0.68	0.68	0.67	0.61	0.64	0.87	0.85	**0.86**
Adverb (RB)	0.41	0.47	0.44	0.61	0.20	0.31	0.87	0.68	**0.76**
Main Verb (VM)	0.57	0.88	0.69	0.66	0.61	0.63	0.87	0.85	**0.86**
Auxiliary Verb (VAUX)	0.88	0.86	0.87	0.88	0.87	0.87	0.97	0.96	**0.96**
Auxilary: Participle Noun (VAUX_VNP)	0.95	0.31	0.46	0.95	0.20	0.34	0.91	0.77	**0.83**
	0.68	0.60	0.63	0.83	0.61	0.70	0.89	0.93	**0.91**

(*continued*)

Table 2. (*continued*)

POS tag	Max-entropy tagger			CRF based tagger			RNN with bidirectional LSTM		
	P	R	F1	P	R	F1	P	R	F1
Conjunction Coordinator (CCD)									
Conjunction Subordinator (CCS)	0.65	0.34	0.45	0.71	0.67	0.69	0.97	0.99	**0.98**
Conjunction Subordinator: Quotative CCS_UT	0.00	0.00	0.00	0.00	0.00	0.00	0.92	0.86	**0.89**
Default Particles (RPD)	0.58	0.88	0.70	0.82	0.83	0.83	0.94	0.90	**0.92**
Classifier Particles (CL)	0.00	0.00	0.00	0.00	0.00	0.00	0.00	0.00	0.00
Interjection Particles (INJ)	0.93	0.18	0.30	0.00	0.00	0.00	0.82	0.49	**0.61**
Intensifier particles (INTF)	0.00	0.00	0.00	0.00	0.00	0.00	0.00	0.00	0.00
Negation particles (NEG)	0.99	0.67	0.80	1.00	0.66	0.79	0.99	0.99	**0.99**
Foreign word (RDF)	0.94	0.35	0.51	0.04	0.04	0.04	0.73	0.21	0.32
Symbol (SYM)	0.97	0.94	0.96	1.00	0.92	0.96	1.00	0.99	**1.00**
Punctuation (PUNC)	1.00	0.99	1.00	1.00	0.94	0.97	1.00	1.00	**1.00**

From the Table 2, we have observed that accuracy of Max-Entropy tagger developed by Knowledge Based Computer Systems Division of CDAC Mumbai for tags namely QTC, QTF, JJ, NN, NNP, NST, PSP, PRP, PRL, PRC, PRQ, DMI, VAUX, VAUX_VNP, INJ, NEG, RDF, and PUNC is better as compared to CRF based tagger developed by Garg et al. (2013) at IR-lab Gandhinagar. Both taggers are having equal accuracy for the tags: PRF, DMR, DRQ, CCS_UT, and ECH. For rest of the POS tags, accuracy of the tagger developed by Garg et al. (2013) at IR-lab Gandhinagar is better as compared to tagger developed at CDAC- Mumbai. But RNN with bidirectional LSTM outperforms both the taggers in each of the POS tags except only for the POS tags RDF and QTC. Overall accuracy of tagger developed at IR-lab Gandhinagar, CDAC-Mumbai and RNN with bidirectional LSTM is 67.27%, 77.54% and 90.83% respectively. In the next section, we have designed Gujarati language specific rules to improve the accuracy of the Gujarati POS tagger.

4 Gujarati Language Rules with Lookup Table for Improving the Accuracy of Statistical POS Taggers

For applications like Anaphora Resolution, Text Summarization and Information Retrieval, personal pronouns (PRP), and nouns including both common nouns (NN) and proper nouns (NNP) play an important role which indicates the needs of accurate identification of POS tags [23]. POS tags namely Nouns (NN/NNP) and adjective (JJ) are important for lexical and syntactic analysis like Shallow Parsing, Gender identification for Gujarati language [22]. These kinds of POS tagger usage lead to the need of POS tagger with high-quality. Therefore, to improve the accuracy of Statistical Gujarati POS taggers, linguistic rules and individual look up tables are designed after analyzing the errors found after statistical tagging.

As discussed in previous section and from Table 2, it is clear that RNN with bidirectional LSTM outperforms among all three statistical POS taggers but still there is a scope to improve the overall accuracy of the POS taggers. As per the corpus analysis shown in Table 1, in Gujarati most frequent words are common noun, proper noun, auxiliary verb, participle noun, and adjective, as well as by considering the accuracy of each tag in Table 2, Gujarati language specific rules are designed and implemented with the individual lookup tables according to the lexical categories. Overall architecture is given in the Fig. 1.

Accuracy of system components are as follows: Gujarati Text is tokenized using Gujarati sentence tokenizer of 99.34% accuracy [16]. Gujarati statistical POS taggers with accuracy 90.83%, 77.54% and 67.27% are selected for further study. After analyzing the accuracy of each POS tag listed in Table 2 of the statistical POS tagger, major errors occur due to adjective, adverb, and noun as shown in Table 2. Another key point affecting the accuracy is loan words from English and Hindi transliterated words. Therefore, we have created lookup table and added rules to improve the accuracy of proper noun, noun, noun indicating time and space, quantifiers, adjective, adverb, pronoun, and postpositions. Tagwise size of the lookup table is listed in Table 3. Gender, Number and Case markers

Table 3. Lookup table for POS tags

Tag	Size of the lookup table (words)
QTO	527
NNP	426 names of villages, cities, states 38 names of week-days and months
QTC	145
PRP	61
NST	51
INJ	37 prefix
PSP	33
NEG	23
VAUX	20
PRF	11
CCS_UT	9
CCD	8
DMD	8
PRC	8
PRL	7
CCS	6
PRF (with or without any case markers)	6

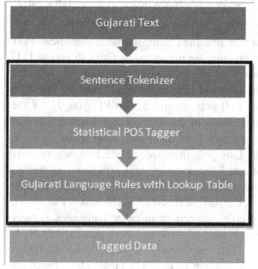

Fig. 1. Hybrid Gujarati POS tagger system

are not attached with the words in the lookup table. Followings are the few highlighted rules out of 37 rules including lookup table designed for improving accuracy of Gujarati POS tagger:

- If the current word ends with any one of the suffix "પૂર્વક", "પણે", "ભેર", "હીન", or "યુક્ત" and next word is verb then current token is adverb.
- If the current word ends with the suffix "નીય", "વાદી", "શાળી", or "ગ્રસ્ત", but word is not "કોઈનીય" then word is considered as adjective.
- If the current word ends with the suffix any one of "પૂર્વક", "પણે", "ભેર", "હીન", or "યુક્ત" with or without any one of the case markers "નુ", "નું", "ના", "નાં", or "ની" and next word is not of verb, then current token is adjective.

- If the current word is made up of Gujarati or English digits with any one of the suffix "મું", "મી", or "મો", then the current word is assigned the tag QTO.
- If the current word is only made up of Gujarati or English digits with or without decimal point ".", ",", or "-", then the current word is assigned the tag QTC.
- If the current word is made up of English or Gujarati name initial, then the current word is assigned the tag "NNP".
- If the current word has any one of 54 the suffixes with or without any one of the case markers: "ને", "નું", "નાં", "ની", "માં", "માંથી", "થી", then current word is assigned the tag "NNP".
- If any one of the suffixes among "નારી", "નાર", "નારૂં", "ચેલું", "ચેલી", "ચેલાં", or "ચેલા" is found at the end of the word, then the current word is assigned the tag VAUX_VNP.
- If the current word ends with suffix "વવા" with or without any one of the case markers "નુ", "નું", "ના", "નાં", and "ની", then current word is assigned the tag "VAUX_VNP".
- If the current word is matched with any of the 5000 nouns with or without suffixes for honor: "જી","શ્રી", plural markers: "ો", "ઓ" and case markers: "ે", "એ", "ને", "નું", "ના", "નાં", "ની", "નો", "માં", "માંથી", "થી", "માંની", "માંના", "માંનો", "એથી", then current word is assigned the tag NN.

else if noun from the lookup table has suffix "ું" or "ો", then this suffix is removed and plural markers markers ("ોા" or "ોઃ") and ("ો" or "ઓ") are added to the noun, **if** the current word is matched with updated common noun with or without any one of case markers: "ઇ", "એ", "ને", "નું", "ના", "નાં", "ની", "નો", "માં", "માંથી", "થી",, "માંની", "માંના", "માંનો", "એેથી", then current word is assigned the tag "NN".

Accuracy of the Gujarati Hybrid tagger designed using Gujarati statistical POS taggers and designed rules including lookup table are measured on Gujarati corpus [21] and Table 4 contains the tag-wise accuracy of the POS tags after applying rules. In Table 4, F1 score of POS tags in bold font indicate the improvement in the tags. Accuracy of POS tag QTF has decrease as it gets confused with POS tag JJ for the word like "બીજી" [bidʒi] [Second/other]. Rests of the tags are not much affected in case of Max-Entropy POS tagger developed by CDAC-Mumbai. After applying rules, accuracy of the tagger developed at IR-Lab gets improved to 75.16% where only adverb and main verb tags are slightly affected and accuracy of it gets down. In case of RNN, we have not applied all the rules but we have only applied rules for the POS tags: QTC, QTO, PRF, PRC, VAUX_VNP, CCS_UT, INJ, NEG, RDF and SYM which increases the accuracy upto 91.10%. Words adopted from other languages namely Hindi and English are increasing the error in case of NNP tag. POS tags namely NST, PRQ, PRI are confused with PSP, DMQ, DMI respectively. If semantic knowledge is added, then accuracy can be improved. Dimension of the POS tagset also affects the accuracy of the POS tagger. Domain of training data as well as testing data plays an important role in the accuracy of POS tagger.

Table 4. Accuracy after applying rules

POS tag	RNN with bidirectional LSTM			Max-entropy tagger			CRF tagger		
	P	R	F1	P	R	F1	P	R	F1
QTC	0.93	0.93	0.93	0.95	0.97	**0.96**	0.94	0.89	0.92
QTF	0.96	0.97	**0.97**	0.75	0.71	0.73	0.99	0.56	0.72
QTO	0.57	0.83	0.67	0.52	0.86	0.65	0.60	0.83	**0.70**
JJ	0.92	0.79	**0.85**	0.87	0.59	0.70	0.81	0.44	0.57
NN	0.86	0.96	**0.91**	0.83	0.91	0.87	0.70	0.87	0.78
NNP	0.73	0.57	**0.64**	0.4	0.6	0.48	0.20	0.64	0.31
NST	0.93	0.89	**0.91**	0.75	0.92	0.83	0.76	0.90	0.82
PSP	0.96	0.94	**0.95**	0.98	0.7	0.81	0.97	0.68	0.80
PRP	0.89	0.86	**0.88**	0.8	0.82	0.81	0.80	0.74	0.77
PRF	0.98	0.97	0.98	0.99	1	**0.99**	0.98	1.00	**0.99**
PRL	0.94	0.79	**0.86**	0.32	0.93	0.48	0.32	0.90	0.48
PRC	1.00	0.96	**0.98**	0.94	0.99	0.96	0.97	0.99	0.98
PRQ	0.82	0.97	**0.89**	0.94	0.84	0.89	0.98	0.38	0.55
PRI	1.00	0.01	0.02	0.1	0.05	**0.07**	0.00	0.00	0.00
DMD	0.86	0.92	**0.89**	0.85	0.68	0.75	0.83	0.69	0.75
DMI	0.77	0.95	**0.85**	0.69	0.68	0.69	0.67	0.61	0.64
RB	0.89	0.53	**0.66**	0.48	0.4	0.43	0.62	0.16	0.26
VM	0.89	0.87	**0.88**	0.61	0.79	0.69	0.71	0.55	0.62
VAUX	0.97	0.96	**0.96**	0.94	0.93	0.93	0.91	0.91	0.91

(continued)

Table 4. (*continued*)

POS tag	RNN with bidirectional LSTM			Max-entropy tagger			CRF tagger		
	P	R	F1	P	R	F1	P	R	F1
VAUX_VNP	0.96	0.79	**0.87**	0.96	0.34	0.51	0.96	0.27	0.42
CCD	0.93	0.93	**0.93**	0.94	0.7	0.8	0.94	0.70	0.80
CCS	0.99	0.96	**0.98**	0.94	0.99	0.96	0.80	1.00	0.89
CCS_UT	0.95	0.97	0.96	0.99	0.99	**0.99**	0.99	0.99	**0.99**
RPD	0.94	0.93	**0.94**	0.64	0.94	0.76	0.83	0.91	0.87
INJ	0.79	0.58	**0.67**	0.43	0.59	0.5	0.77	0.60	**0.67**
NEG	0.99	1.00	**0.99**	0.99	0.99	**0.99**	0.99	0.99	**0.99**
RDF	0.95	0.97	**0.96**	0.97	0.92	0.94	0.59	0.91	0.72
SYM	0.98	0.97	**0.97**	1	0.94	**0.97**	1.00	0.93	0.96
PUNC	1.00	1.00	**1.00**	1	1	**1**	1.00	0.96	0.98
Accuracy	**91.10%**			81.36%			75.16%		

5 Conclusion

We have deduced that corpus size and domain have major effect on the performance of the POS tagger. For any language, Hybrid approach for developing POS tagger is promising as compare to purely Rule based and Machine learning based approach. If linguistic rules are added to Machine learning based tagger with lookup table for closed class and open class words with proper suffix list, performance of the tagger is improved. Even though different taggers are available for Gujarati language, Hybrid approach using RNN with Bidirectional LSTM combined with language specific Rules outperforms CRF and Max-entropy tagger. Out of vocabulary words are correctly tagged with the help of contextual features of the words. The proposed method can also be applied to various language processing applications like Shallow Parser, Named Entity, etc. We are working to improve the accuracy of Hybrid tagger developed using RNN with bidirectional LSTM and Rules.

References

1. En.wikipedia.org, August 2018. https://en.wikipedia.org/wiki/Bengali_language
2. Gujarati-English Learner's Dictionary, June 2003. https://ccat.sas.upenn.edu/plc/gujarati/gujengdictionary
3. Knowledge Based Computer Systems Division of CDAC Mumbai. https://kbcs.in/tools.html
4. Antony, P.J., Soman, K.P.: Parts of speech tagging for Indian languages: a literature survey. Int. J. Comput. Appl. **34**(30), 1–8 (2011)
5. Antony, P.J., Mohan, S.P., Soman, K.P.: SVM based part of speech tagger for Malayalam. In: International Conference on Recent Trends in Information, Telecommunication and Computing, pp. 339–341 (2010)

6. Bharati, A., Mannem, P.: Introduction to the Shallow Parsing Contest for South Asian Languages, Hyderabad, pp. 1–8 (2007)
7. Ekbal, A., Bandyopadhyay, S.: Part of speech tagging in Bengali using support vector machine. In: Proceedings of the 2008 International Conference on Information Technology, Bhubaneswar, pp. 106–111 (2008)
8. Garg, V., Saraf, N., Majumder, P.: Named entity recognition for Gujarati: a CRF based approach. In: Prasath, R., Kathirvalavakumar, T. (eds.) MIKE 2013. LNCS (LNAI), vol. 8284, pp. 761–768. Springer, Cham (2013). https://doi.org/10.1007/978-3-319-03844-5_74
9. Hala, S., Virani, S.: Improve accuracy of part of speech tagger for Gujarati language. Int. J. Adv. Eng. Res. Dev. **2**(5), 187–192 (2015)
10. Horsmann, T., Erbs, N., Zesch, T.: Fast or accurate? – A comparative evaluation of PoS tagging models. In: International Conference of the German Society for Computational Linguistics and Language Technology, pp. 22–30 (2015)
11. Kapadia, U., Desai, A.: Rule based Gujarati morphological analyzer. Int. J. Comput. Sci. Issues **14**(2), 30–35 (2017)
12. Mehta, D., Desai, N.: A survey on part-of-speech tagging of Indian languages. In: 1st International Conference on Computing, Communication, Electrical, Electronics, Devices & Signal Processing, March 2015
13. Motlani, R., Lalwani, H., Shrivastava, M., Sharma, D.M.: Developing part-of-speech tagger for a resource poor language: Sindhi. In: Proceedings of the 7th Language and Technology Conference (2015)
14. Patel, C., Gali, K.: Part-of-speech tagging for Gujarati using conditional random fields. In: Proceedings of the IJCNLP-08 Workshop on NLP for Less Privileged Languages, Hyderabad, pp. 117–122 (2008)
15. Singh, J., Joshi, N., Mathur, I.: Part of speech tagging of Marathi text using trigram method. Int. J. Adv. Inf. Technol. 35–41 (2013)
16. Tailor, C., Patel, B.: Sentence tokenization using statistical unsupervised machine learning and rule base approach for running text in Gujarati language. In: International Conference on Emerging Trends in Expert Applications & Security, Jaipur (2018)
17. Gokul Krishnan, K.S., Pooja, A., Anand Kumar, M., Soman, K.P.: Character based bidirectional LSTM for disambiguating tamil part of speech categories. IJCTA **10**(3), 229–235 (2017)
18. Kingma, D., Ba, J.: Adam: a method for stochastic optimization. In: Proceeding ICLR 2015, pp. 1–15, January 2017
19. Bach, N.X., Linh, N.D., Phuong, T.M.: An empirical study on POS tagging for Vietnamese social media text. Comput. Speech Lang. **50**, 1–15 (2018)
20. Sheth, J., Patel, B.: Saaraansh: Gujarati text summarization system. IRACST **3**(7), 46–53 (2017)
21. Gujarati Monolingual Text Corpus ILCI-II, Tdil-dc.in (2017). 1?option=com_download &task=showresourceDetails&toolid=1882&lang=en. Accessed 05 May 2018
22. Tailor, C., Patel, B.: Context based gender identification of noun phrase for Gujarati text. Presented at National Conference on Emerging Technologies in IT, Surat (2019)
23. Dakwale, P., Mujadia, V., Sharma, D.M.: A hybrid approach for anaphora resolution in Hindi. In: International Joint Conference on Natural Language Processing, pp. 977–981 (2013)
24. Harris, Z.S.: String Analysis of Sentence Structure. Mouton, The Hague (1962)
25. Goodfellow, I., Bengio, Y., Courville, A.: Deep Learning. The MIT Press, London (2017)
26. Wei, L.: October 2018. https://cwiki.apache.org/confluence/display/MXNET/Multi-hot +Sparse+Categorical+Cross-entropy

Optimization of ICT Street Infrastructure in Smart Cities

Gayatri Doctor[1]($\boxtimes$) (iD), Shamik Joshi[2], and Axay Gandhi[1]

[1] Faculty of Management, CEPT University, Ahmedabad, India
gayatri.doctor@cept.ac.in, axay.gandhi11@gmail.com
[2] Products and Technology, Amnex, Ahmedabad, India
shamik@amnex.com

Abstract. Technology solutions are now helping the urban local bodies in Indian Smart Cities to make smart and effective decisions. With these technologies coming up there IoT devices can be seen making its place on urban streets. This paper focuses on the overall view of the ICT (Information and Communication Technology) components and its placement in the city at various locations on the streets. The research for ICT street infrastructure when deployed for upcoming smart cities would help in optimization of ICT street infrastructure and bring down the total life cycle cost in terms of the cost of ownership and the recurring expense for operation and maintenance, for the deployment in upcoming cities.

Keywords: Smart city · IoT · ICT · Street infrastructure · Optimization

1 Introduction

1.1 Smart City

There is no universally accepted definition for Smart City, Smart City has different meanings for different people in different countries. On a broader level, Smart Cities are the urban areas that utilize electronic data collection sensors to give and transfer information in order to manage the assets and resources efficiently in order to give better services to the citizens of the city [1]. Technology solutions are now helping the urban local bodies in Indian Smart Cities to make smart and effective decisions. Smart systems have become the key for providing citizen-centric services like traffic, health, safety, transit, etc.

Smart City projects are further divided into pan-city and area-based development projects. The research is focused on the Pan city ICT (Information and Communication Technology) projects in a smart city. All Pan city IT and ICT projects have two components; Hardware (Field devices, sensors, IoT devices and its supporting components) and software. Smart cities in India usually include following hardware components, CCTV, ANPR (Automatic Number Plate Recognition), RLVD (Red Light Violation Detection), ECB (Emergency Call Box), PA (Public Address), ATCS (Automatic traffic Control System), VMD (Virtual Messaging Display), Environmental Sensors, Smart Lights, PIS (Passenger information Screen) at City Bus stops,

K. K. Patel et al. (Eds.): icSoftComp 2020, CCIS 1374, pp. 145–156, 2021.
https://doi.org/10.1007/978-981-16-0708-0_13

Supporting Infrastructure such as Junction Box, OFC (Optical Fibre Cable), Electric Meters, Poles, etc. All these hardware components form the basic components of the street infrastructure. They are installed on streets, which usually have just 12% to 18% of the land of the city.

"Smartness" doesn't come from installing smart devices on traditional infrastructure. It is using technology to analyse the data gathered, to facilitate decisions and help improving citizen services to enhance quality of life. Quality comes up with many dimensions, it includes everything from the air that citizens breathe to how they feel on the streets. There are dozens of smart sensors/devices installed on the streets, to sense & communicate the same to the command centres [2].

This paper focuses on the overall view of the ICT (Information and Communication Technology) components and its placement in the city at various locations. This shows the complexity due to the haphazard and unplanned ICT street infrastructure. It was noticed that the most advance cities need to improve a lot for its fundamental street infrastructure for all smart devices to function and achieve the larger goal of city operations.

2 Methodology

Research commenced with the background research, which helped derive the problem statement and research questions. This was followed by a literature review, a study of street design guidelines for different cities to understand the placement of ICT Street Infrastructure in cities. Case studies of various cities having different street infrastructure with IoT and ICT components were also studied. (Chicago, New York, Colombia & Pune). This was followed by primary data collection which involved site visits to various locations in the city. Interactions with various stakeholders were done to understand the complexity in implementation of ICT street infrastructure. Based on the data available from primary and secondary data collection, analysis was done of the ICT street infrastructure in the city. An in-depth study and analysis of current infrastructure was done to find the root cause analysis for its high CAPEX and OPEX costs. Based on this research, a modular pole was designed, and a pilot study was conducted at one junction in City A.

2.1 Problem Statement

The City Government (Urban Local Body) is investing huge quantum in ICT Street Infrastructure; however, this infrastructure becomes an integral part of day-to-day operations. Despite this aspect being so important in daily life, it is not organized and placed haphazardly. Hence it is important to manage the street infrastructure for better operations and cost-effectiveness.

2.2   Research Objective

- Understanding the Different ICT Infrastructure on Streets and Junctions
- Studying the implementation procedure for the street infrastructure in a smart city.
- Optimizing the ICT Street Infrastructure for O&M and cost-effectiveness.

3   Literature Review

The concept of Smart Cities can be looked upon as a framework for implementing a vision to help achieve the benefits of modern urbanization. The inclination to adopt the Smart City model is driven by the need to surpass the challenges posed by traditional cities, as well as, overcoming them in a systematic manner [3]. It is crucial for cities therefore to explore a shift towards adopting sustainable city development measures amongst all stakeholders, namely - Citizens, Businesses and the Government. City-level interventions to support the development of urban environments that enhance economic growth and enhance overall quality of life are more vital than ever, but need to be tailored to the historical, spatial, political, socio-economic and technological context of cities at different stages of urbanization [4].

As part of literature review, street design guidelines of Pune, New-York & Colombia were referred. It was found that most of the Indian cities don't have street design guidelines. Better Streets, Better Cities by ITDP (Institute for Transportation and Development Policy) & EPC (Environmental Planning Collaborative) helped to understand the principles of street infrastructure [3]. Streetlight policy and design guidelines by the Department of Transportation, District of Columbia helped to understand Methodology for change in street infrastructure [4]. Pre-Standardization study report, Unified, secure and resilient ICT infrastructure by Bureau of Indian Standards helped understand the standardization procedure adopted for the services [5].

AoT (Array of Things) in Chicago has essentially served as a "fitness tracker" for the city, measuring factors that impact livability in cities such as climate, air quality and noise. The node is created which contains all sensors and it can be mounted on a traffic pole or wall whichever is feasible. Department of Transport Chicago is currently installing it on Light pole and data is hosted on open data portal for private companies and students to do research [6].

For all cities, the task was to fix all the elements to the street template so that it defines a unique street, based on the requirement, size, location and demand. Principles for the street design guideline were Public Safety, Environment, Design and Aesthetics. Cities like New York have a street design guideline describing all different elements that can come to a street [7].

"How to design and maintain a city is critical to creating a sustainable ecosystem— one that provides not only for today's needs but for the needs of future generations, and one that takes not only humans into account but all life. To achieve this goal, cities must end the 'business as usual' approach and become caretakers for both the people they serve and the environment in which they live" [8].

4 Analysis of ICT Street Infrastructure

4.1 Different ICT Infrastructure on Streets and Junctions

Smart cities in India usually include following hardware components, CCTV, ANPR (Automatic Number Plate Recognition), RLVD (Red Light Violation Detection), ECB (Emergency Call Box), PA (Public Address), ATCS (Automatic traffic Control System), VMD (Virtual Messaging Display), Environmental Sensors, Smart Lights, PIS (Passenger information Screen) at City Bus stops, Supporting Infrastructure such as Junction Box, OFC (Optical Fibre Cable), Electric Meters, Poles, etc. All these hardware components form the basic components of the streets in the city. The data collected by these components is collected at the Integrated Command and Control Centre (ICCC) of the city. At ICCC this data is analysed and based on the data further actions are decided by ULB (Urban Local Body).

4.2 Comparative Analysis of Street Infrastructure in Five Different Smart Cities

A study of the street infrastructure across the different smart cities in India was done based on the smart city proposals submitted by the respective cities. It was observed that City A had the maximum street infrastructure, as seen in Table 1. To understand in-depth the ICT street infrastructure in city a detailed case study was done for the infrastructure installed in the City A [11].

Table 1. Comparative analysis of street infrastructure in smart cities

Street infrastructure	City A	City B	City C	City D	City E
Optical fiber	Yes	–	–	Yes	Yes
CCTV	Yes	Yes	Yes	Yes	Yes
ANPR	Yes	Yes	Yes	Yes	Yes
PA system	Yes	Yes	Yes	Yes	Yes
ECB	Yes	Yes	Yes	Yes	Yes
Env. sensors	Yes	Yes	Yes	Yes	Yes
ATCS	Yes	Yes	Yes	Yes	Yes
VMD	Yes	Yes	Yes	Yes	Yes
Smart light	Yes	Yes	Yes	–	–
Smart roads	Yes	Yes	Yes	Yes	Yes
Smart POLES	Yes	–	Yes	–	Yes

4.3 A Study of Street Infrastructure at Two Locations in City A

After site visits to various locations in City A, it was found that at different junctions there were different infrastructures as shown in Fig. 1. There are three different poles installed in a row for three different purposes, namely, streetlight, traffic signal and CCTV pole. The streetlight was installed first at the junction and the traffic light followed later. Another image in Fig. 1 shows the location where traffic light and Street light pole are installed adjacent to each other.

Ideally, this should be optimized so that there can be a cut of expenses on the infrastructure with all the solutions being implemented in the city and utilize it for other projects. Here this can be optimized by keeping both on the same pole and utilizing the existing street infrastructure to its optimum level.

Legend

☐ Street light Pole   ☐ Traffic light   ☐ CCTV pole

Fig. 1. Image on left shows the junction A where there are three different poles installed for different purpose. The figure on right shows Junction B where there are two different poles installed for different purpose.

4.4   Design Principles for ICT Street Infrastructure

Literature study indicated that there were design guidelines for streets in various cities (Pune, New York, Colombia & Chicago), but there was no clarity about guidelines for ICT infrastructure coming up in the city as a part of smart city mission projects. This results in street infrastructure being placed haphazardly throughout the smart city. So, how should this infrastructure be placed? Where should it be placed on the street? These were questions that needed to be answered.

A detailed study was conducted, and data was collected from various locations in City A. This data included placement of street infrastructure, type of street infrastructure, total count of devices installed and its locations, Operations and management plan for this infrastructure, stakeholders etc. Also based on the data available a detailed study was done for the cost and the bill of material for all locations.

Various stakeholders involved in the street infrastructure were identified. Group discussions were held with members of Special Purpose Vehicle (SPV) of City A, Consultants and System integrators of various ICT projects. As part of stakeholder consultation, it was derived that the design principles for ICT street infrastructure should have a Façade, be Scalable, Safe, Cost-Effective, Sustainable, and Resilient as shown in Fig. 2.

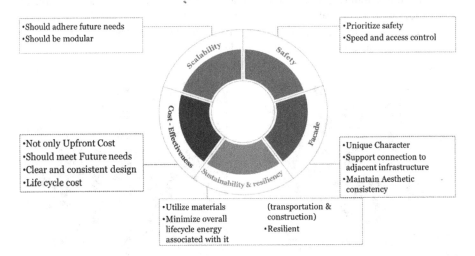

Fig. 2. Design principles for street infrastructure

5   Implementation Phases of ICT Street Infrastructure

All ICT street infrastructures to be placed, go through three phases, namely, Pre-implementation phase, Implementation phase & Post-implementation phase.

5.1   Pre-implementation Phase

The pre-implementation phase includes the design and planning of the street infrastructure for its entire life cycle. The design component includes the design of street infrastructure, which can adhere to the requirement for the present, and the future. The planning component includes the deployment of street infrastructure taking into consideration the location, feasibility and future scalability.

In the existing scenario, there are multiple vendors for multiple infrastructures placed on the streets. Multiple infrastructure increases the complexity of the operation and maintenance of the field devices. As different vendors lay different infrastructure for different IoT components, there are complications in project operations.

For the projects in smart city mission, there is a need to have smart components/sensors/devices on the street which can help to collate data for increasing efficiency and customer satisfaction for the services. Considering the need for infrastructure a design needs to be prepared for the infrastructure and its implementation in such a way that that multiple infrastructure at the same locations can be avoided.

In the proposed optimized street infrastructure, there can be a common shared street infrastructure solution and a single vendor for the street infrastructure. The vendor would do the implementation of civil infrastructure for the smart city. This would help have common, unique, durable and aesthetic infrastructure in streets of the city. This would allow new ICT Infrastructure coming up in the future installed on the common infrastructure available. This makes the scope of both vendors clear for operation and maintenance of the field devices or infrastructure.

5.2 Implementation Phase

Implementation of street infrastructure involves three areas, namely, Civil Infrastructure, Supporting Infrastructure like Electricity box, Junction Box, network connectivity, etc. and the Underground Infrastructure.

Civil infrastructure includes poles/gantry that supports the IT/IoT devices on the street. This infrastructure houses all IoT devices on the street. The existing scenario was understood by the site visits and mapping all civil infrastructure at all locations. The observations at these locations showed that the civil infrastructure for all IoT components was different and this infrastructure was laid adjacent to each other. Duplication of civil infrastructure at all locations increases the CAPEX cost for the project as well as the operation and maintenance costs. It was clear that, to optimize the civil infrastructure a single modular structure where all the current IoT devices can be connected and the devices or sensors that would come in future also can be housed on this structure. A Modular Pole should be so compact that it can stand on the space available at divider on roads. Also, this pole should mount the existing streetlight. Along with streetlight there should be a space available at different heights say 3.5 mts, 4 mts, 4.5 mts & 5 mts to mount devices and sensors coming to that location. So, no additional cost is levied for the civil infrastructure. This makes work easier for all agencies working at the same locations. It also increases the efficiency of the civil infrastructure that is placed in the city as a part of smart city mission projects. Figure 3 shows the sample modular pole installed on the divider as part of the pilot study. It also shows the current layout and the layout after placement of modular poles on road junctions/interactions.

The supporting infrastructure includes electricity box, junction box, network box, etc., this houses all supporting infrastructure for the IoT devices to function; a UPS, switch for OFC, power supply point, network for communication, etc. In the existing scenario, this infrastructure is located at the corner of the junctions. It is then connected to the civil infrastructure laid in the centre of the street by underground connectivity. As the civil infrastructure for all IoT devices is different, so the supporting infrastructure is also different. Thus, multiple junction boxes & electrical boxes can be observed. There is a need to optimize these also. It was possible to integrate the junction box and electrical box to the modular pole, thereby saving space and making it easier for electrical and networking work. So, the junction box and electrical box are integrated into one common box in the modular pole. Also, the IoT was installed on the modular pole. The Modular pole which was installed is seen in Fig. 4.

Underground infrastructure includes electrical line, network line, earthing, etc. that are laid under the ground for the working of the IoT devices. In the existing scenario, it was observed that, the junction box/electrical box are in the corner of the junctions and civil infrastructure is at the centre of the road, thus all their electrical lines and network lines are laid underground. As the IOT components are different, their Junction boxes

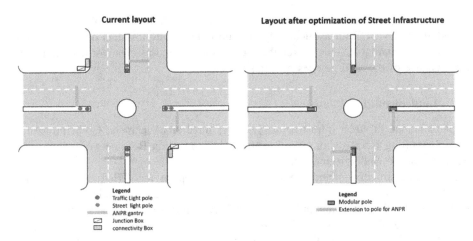

Fig. 3. Placement of modular poles on road junctions/interactions

Fig. 4. Modular infrastructure installed in the city

and electrical boxes are also different. This causes duplicity of lines under the ground. Earthing for each is also different. This results in damage of the road during any maintenance activity and increases the costs of maintenance. The maintenance of different devices at different timings means frequent damage to the road. In order to stop this, a simple procedure can be developed in the city.

All the modular poles need to be connected with each other. A common duct for electrical and network lines is to be laid as a part of connectivity for the poles. The current layout and the optimized layout of common underground infrastructure on road junctions/interactions can be observed in Fig. 5.

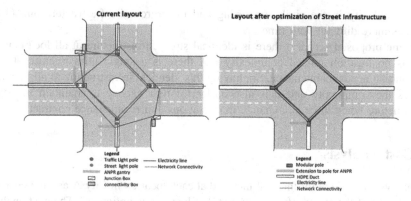

Fig. 5. Placement of common underground infrastructure on road junctions/interactions

Maintenance would involve only a simple trenching to open the duct, thus minimizing the damage to the road. This activity need not be repeated for all devices as they all are connected to the same line at one location. This would remove the duplicity in work, decreasing the operation and maintenance activity, and change the CAPEX and OPEX costs.

5.3 Post-implementation Phase

The post-implementation phase includes operations and maintenance of the street infrastructure installed. The operations and maintenance depend on how the infrastructure was procured and installed, and the type of contract agreed with the vendor and the owner. In some cases, if only the infrastructure is procured and there is no operations and maintenance contract agreed at time of contract, then the municipal corporation itself manages the street infrastructure or it can have new infrastructure maintenance contract after go-live of the infrastructure. In some cases, if the operation and maintenance contract is agreed for a certain period at the time of procurement of the infrastructure then vendor itself operates and maintains the infrastructure for that time period. Post completion of operations and maintenance contract can be renewed or transferred to another party or Municipal Corporation can itself manage the infrastructure.

Operations and maintenance is the most critical period of the street infrastructure, as in that period it facilitates the service operations and it is the period when the municipal corporation can get the payback from the street infrastructure procured. This payback can be monetary or can be citizen service facilitation and satisfaction. This operations and maintenance decide how efficiently the street infrastructure can be used.

In the existing scenario, the street infrastructure procured as a part of a smart city mission is to be operated and maintained by the installing agency for certain years from the go-live of it. But the installation is haphazard on street, and the installing agency knows the installation details and its technical and functional diagrams. The street infrastructure for all different devices/service is different and so any location there is large complexity in the civil, supporting and underground infrastructure and O&M becomes more difficult with time.

In the proposed scenario there is identical street infrastructure at all locations, so there is no location related complexity and there is a single infrastructure at each location that needs maintenance. So, having this identical infrastructure at all locations reduces the complexity and it is also easier for new agency to maintain the street infrastructure when there is a change in operations and maintenance contract.

6 Cost Analysis

The analysis was done for the cost incurred at each location in City A and the cost that can be saved if the street infrastructure at that location is optimized. The cost analysis was done based on the commercial information available of the current system integrator and the quote that came up for new optimized street infrastructure. Based on the site visits the draft BoQ (Bill of Quantity) was filled with the quantities at each location. Then it was analyzed that if all quantities are changed as per the proposed solution of optimization, there can be a calculated percentage difference that can be achieved. Figure 6 shows the analysis done for the field infrastructure utilized in City A with the infrastructure that would be saved if field infrastructure is optimized. Based on this analysis it was observed that there can be a further decrease of 15%–20% in quantity if field infrastructure was optimized.

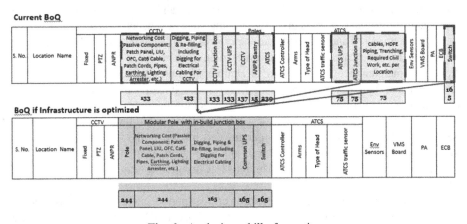

Fig. 6. Analysis on bill of quantity

Based on this BOQ calculation as shown in Fig. 6, cost analysis was done for 10 junctions in the city A. This can be seen in Fig. 7. This helped understand the cost differences arising due to the installation of modular infrastructure at junctions in the city.

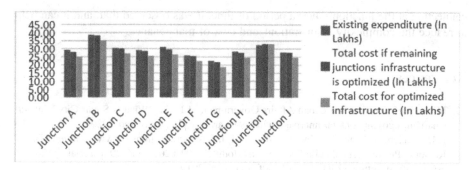

Fig. 7. Cost analysis for junctions in City A

7 Conclusion

Building resilience comes with taking the investment designs wisely and prioritize the efficiency and utilization of the resource allocated. Higher the standardization of the infrastructure and the processes, higher is the resilience of the city. There is a need to understand the urban project and its process of operation and maintenance in the city to contribute to the resilience of the city.

With the change in street infrastructure, there are certain direct benefits that ULB (Urban Local Body) can have and there are some benefits that can be observed with time.

- Sharing of the resources for different ICT systems.
- As all devices are using the same infrastructure and supporting devices, thus, removing the duplicate infrastructure at same location and decreasing the cost incurred for the same.
- Improvement in financials by decrease in the lifecycle cost of asset (by decreasing upfront cost and operations and management cost for the asset installed).
- Providing identical infrastructure throughout the city results in the unique character of infrastructure in the city and helps to maintain the aesthetic consistency.
- Building city resilience to withstand the changes and adopt future technologies.
- Increasing the sustainability by decreasing the street infrastructure and increasing the efficiency of the infrastructure procured.

The aim of this research was to study the current ICT infrastructure in smart cities and the ways available to optimize the infrastructure. The simplest way identified was to have modular poles, that can house the current and upcoming IoT's, also there can be a different research itself to develop a single device which can carry out work of multiple IoT's as it was done in developing Array of Things in Chicago.

Based on the pilot study at a junction in City A, it was found that having a modular pole helped to reduce the components of street infrastructure in the city. It would help to reduce the cost of installation for the additional IoT that will be coming at the junction. Also, the aesthetics of the junction looked unique and similar on all roads' connection at the junction. Over a period of time, it was observed that, and it can help to reduce the complexity of operations and cost of maintenance.

References

1. Ministry of Housing and Urban Affairs Government of India, "What is Smart City". https://smartcities.gov.in/content/innerpage/what-is-smart-city.php. Accessed 2020
2. ITU Academy: Smart Sustainable Cities ICT Infrastructure. https://www.itu.int/en/ITU-D/Regional-Presence/AsiaPacific/Documents/Module%202%20Smart%20Sustainable%20Cities%20Infrastructure%20Draft%20H.pdf. Accessed 2019
3. World Econimic forum & PwC: Circular Economy in Cities Evolving the model for a sustainable Urban Future (2018). https://www3.weforum.org/docs/White_paper_Circular_Economy_in_Cities_report_2018.pdf. Accessed 02 2019
4. Price waterhouse Coopers: Creating the smart cities of the future (2018)
5. ITDP (Institute for Transportation and Development Policy) & EPC (Environmental Planning Collaborative): Better Streets, Better Cities. https://www.itdp.in/wp-content/uploads/2014/04/07.-Better-Streets-Better-Cities-EN.pdf. Accessed 2020
6. District of Columbia: Street Light policy and Design Guidelines. https://comp.ddot.dc.gov/Documents/Streetlight%20Policy%20and%20Design%20Guidelines.pdf. Accessed 2019
7. Bureau of Indian Standards: Pre Standardisation Study Report: Unified, Secure and Resilient ICT framework for Smart Infrastructure. https://smartnet.niua.org/content/f85221e9-4f9b-4b9d-a3e5-85ee63478b1d. Accessed 2019
8. Department of Transport, Chicago: Array of Things (AOT). https://arrayofthings.github.io/. Accessed 2019
9. Department of Transport New York: Street Design Manual. https://www.nycstreetdesign.info/. Accessed 2019
10. World Economic Forum: Inspiring Future Cities & urban services shaping the future of Urban development & services initiative, April 2016. https://www3.weforum.org/docs/WEF_Urban-Services.pdf. Accessed 2019
11. NIUA (National Institute for Urban Affairs): Smart Net. https://smartnet.niua.org/. Accessed 2019
12. World Economic Forum: Reforms to Accelerate the development of India's Smart Cities Shaping the Future of Urban Development & Services, April 2016. https://www.weforum.org/reports/reforms-to-accelerate-the-development-of-india-s-smart-cities-shaping-the-future-of-urban-development-services. Accessed 2019
13. Pune Municipal Corporation: Urban Street Design Guidelines. https://www.itdp.in/wp-content/uploads/2016/07/Urban-street-design-guidelines.pdf. Accessed 2019
14. Ministry of Housing and Urban Affairs, Government of India: Mission Statement and Guidelines. https://smartcities.gov.in/upload/uploadfiles/files/SmartCityGuidelines(1).pdf. Accessed 2020

Transfer Learning-Based Image Tagging Using Word Embedding Technique for Image Retrieval Applications

M. Poonkodi$^{(\boxtimes)}$, J. Arunnehru, and K. S. Anand

Department of Computer Science and Engineering,
SRM Institute of Science and Technology, Vadapalani, Chennai, Tamilnadu, India
poonkodm@srmist.edu.in, arunnehru.aucse@gmail.com

Abstract. In recent days, social media plays a vital role in day to day life which increases the number of images that are being shared and uploaded daily in public and private networks, it is essential to find an efficient way to tag the images for the purpose of effective image retrieval and maintenance. Existing methods utilize feature extraction techniques such as histograms, SIFT, Local Binary Patterns (LBP) which are limited by their inability to represent images in a better way. We propose to overcome this problem by leveraging the rich features that can be extracted from convolutional neural network (CNN) that have been trained on million images. The features are then fed into an Artificial Neural Net, which is trained on the image features and multi-label tags. The tags predicted by the neural net for an image is mapped on to a word embedding plane from which the most similar words for the given tag is retrieved. Along with this ANN, we include an Object detection neural net, which provides additional tags for the image. The usage of an additional neural net and a word vector model adds to the aspect of Zero-shot tagging i.e., the ability of the tagger to assign tags to images outside its own training class examples. The dataset utilized here is the Flickr-25k dataset.

Keywords: Image tagging · Retrieval · Transfer learning · Neural networks · Convolutional neural network

1 Introduction

With the incredible outreach of the internet and the explosive growth of the smartphone market millions of images are uploaded to internet daily. Therefore, it is important to have an efficient way of tagging and keeping the images for efficient retrieval. It has been already found that using text as a way of indexing the images, so finding and efficient and effective way of tagging images is important. Tag is a piece of text that describes the content of an image or any digital media. Figure 1 illustrates the image tagging process of assigning images tags based on the content of the image. The need for automated image tagging

© Springer Nature Singapore Pte Ltd. 2021
K. K. Patel et al. (Eds.): icSoftComp 2020, CCIS 1374, pp. 157–168, 2021.
https://doi.org/10.1007/978-981-16-0708-0_14

is due to spamming of same tags again and again and assigning useless tags to media content. Therefore, for effective retrieval of images it is important to have tags that reflect on the content of the image perfectly. The process of image tagging can be divided into identifying the content in the image and assigning the tags properly. The usage of natural language processing in image processing [1–4] promises better results than the existing models.

Fig. 1. An example of Image tagging

In general, the content of image is generally identified by using features extracted from them. Earlier, the features used were color histograms, histogram of gradients (HoG), texture of the images, Scale-Invariant-Feature-Transformation (SIFT) etc., they lack the representational ability. Due to recent advances in the field of deep learning, and the increase in the computational ability, high level features can be extracted easily from pre-trained neural nets. The neural net that can be utilized for this purpose is generally trained on millions of images. By leveraging this pre-trained neural net, we can extract high level features from these nets that can be leveraged for better training accuracy.

This method of extracting features from a neural net is called as transfer learning, shown in Fig. 2. By utilizing transfer learning training time of a neural net is reduced, without compromising the accuracy of the model. Deep learning paradigm is the ability of the neural network to learn from the images directly, without the usage of hand-crafted image features. In this paper we look on the work carried out previously and propose a new method of image tagging based on transfer learning.

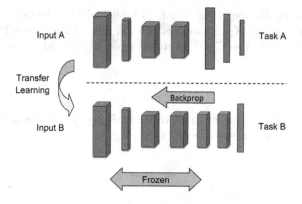

Fig. 2. Transfer learning architecture

1.1 Challenges

As mentioned earlier, the existing systems utilize features extracted from images such as histograms, color histograms and Scale invariant feature transformation, which are ineffective at modelling the image contents. This leads to poor performance while trying to predict the tags/contents of the image. Moreover, the time spent in training a system to assign tags to the images based on these features is very high. For the above specified reasons, we propose to utilize transfer learning to model the image better as well as reducing the training time of the system. By using transfer learning, we extract the best features from the images, which ultimately leads to better performance when compared to the existing systems.

2 Related Works

The previous proposed models proposed use the concept of transfer learning, but are mainly an extension of multi-label multi-class classification. Jianlong Fu and Yong Rui [5] on their proposal mentioned two ways of tagging images. One of them, was based on neighbor voting to tag images and the other one was to use a CNN which employs multi label multi class classification to tag the images based on the training set. Although both of these methods had a good mean Average Precision (mAP) score, they lacked the ability to assigning tags that the neural net hasn't been trained on.

2.1 Word Embedding

Word embedding or word vectorization is the process of converting word into numbers/vectors for the usage in classification and clustering tasks. We propose to utilize GloVe [6] model to convert words into vectors. GloVe is an unsupervised algorithm developed by Stanford researchers, which is used to obtain word embedding for word. Figure 3 shows the GloVe vector based co-occurrence of the words. This co-occurrence of the words is modelled by a co-occurrence matrix X, where each element X_{ij}, tabulates the number of times word i appears in the context of word j. The GloVe vector is generally modelled by the following Eq. 1.

$$F(w_i, w_j, w_k) = \frac{P_{ik}}{P_{jk}} \tag{1}$$

where w_i, w_j, w_k are the word vectors and $P_{ij} = \frac{X_{ij}}{X_i}$ be the probability that word j appear in the context of word i.

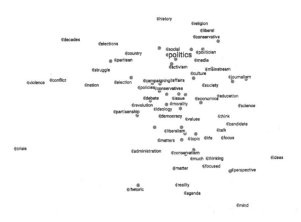

Fig. 3. Representation of word embedding in Vector space

2.2   Zero-Shot Tagging

Zhang et al. [7] on their paper, proposed a method of zero shot tagging based on associating an image to a tag and principal direction on a word vector plane. But the word vector plane and the unseen tag set used by them is limited. They assign tags to the images based on the principal direction of the image features and rank the words in that direction. This is illustrated in the following Eq. 2.

$$f(X_m) \approx W_m \tag{2}$$

Where $f(X_m)$ is the principal direction, X_m is the set of visual features and W_m is the word along the principal direction ranked linearly. By approximating this function f, zero shot tagging is achieved. Zero shot taggers learn from the training classes but ultimately it tries to classify test images into unseen classes [8–10]. This is made possible by the usage of word embeddings, which ultimately help in zero shot tagging. Our proposed method uses a glove vector model to provide the word embeddings and based on the tags assigned by the neural net to assign unseen tags to the images. So, the problem is reduced to training a neural network to tag the images and a word vector model to assign unseen tags to them.

3   Proposed Methodology

The previous models-built lack the capacity to assign totally unseen tag sets to images and to overcome this problem, we propose to utilize *"aa"* word vector model combined with a pre-trained CNN and a neural network to assign tags that are unseen by the neural network classifier.

3.1   Architecture of the Proposed System

The architecture of our proposed model is illustrated in the Fig. 4. The tagger we propose consists of 3 parts namely, TaggerNet, Object Detection Net, and a GloVe model.The important part of the model is the TagNet which does the initial tagging, after which the Object Detection Net and GloVe net augments the tags given by TagNet.

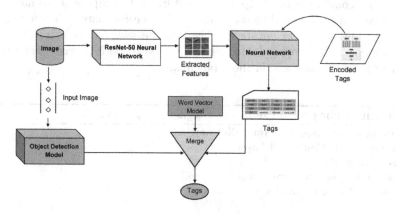

Fig. 4. Architecture of the proposed system

TaggerNet. The TaggerNet is the first component which is a collection of pre-trained CNN combined with a neural network to assign tags to images. The pre-trained neural net used here is the ResNet-50 which is trained on the ImageNet dataset. ResNet-50 is used to extract features from the training as well as testing images, which is then fed into the neural network that is trained on these features and corresponding tags. Essentially TaggerNet can be thought of as a Multi-label Multi-class classifier that tags images based on its training experiences. The main work of TaggerNet is to assign initial tags to a given image. The Eq. 3 illustrates the working of the TaggerNet.

$$f(V_i) = \{T_i\} \tag{3}$$

TaggerNet is used to find the mapping function f which maps image features V_i to a set of tags T_i.

Object Detection Net. Object detection net is a neural net that has been trained on the MSCOCO dataset [11] which detects the objects in the given image. We utilize only the top 3 objects detected by the neural net to augment the tags already predicted by TaggerNet. We remove any duplicate tags if any assigned by the object detection neural net.

GloVe Net. We use the GloVe model to generate word embeddings which are then used to predict similar words. The GloVe model follows the TaggerNet i.e., GloVe model works on the output provided by TaggerNet. The tags returned by TaggerNet is converted into vectors using GloVe model after which all of the vectors included in the GloVe model is compared with the vector of tags returned by the TaggerNet model to find most similar tags. We use cosine similarity as the measure to compare similarity. In this way, two most similar tags are returned for each tag that is assigned by the TagNet.

Thus, by combining the output returned by each component we have a set of tags that can be assigned to each image based on its content. These tags can be indexed and stored in database which can be used in image retrieval and search systems. The proposed Algorithm 1 is used to perform zero-shot tagging /augmenting the basic tags on the input image.

Algorithm 1. For perform zero-shot tagging / augmenting

Initialize : Resnet-50 with ImageNet weights
Remove : Fully Connected Layer
image = resize(Image)
image_array = img_to_array(image)
features = Resnet-50.predict(image_array)

Initialize : TaggerNet with trained-weights
Tags = TaggerNet.predict(Features)
for tag in Tags: **do**
    vector_tag = vectorize(tag)
    similar_tag = most_similar(vector_tag)
end for

Initialize : ObjectDetectionNet
Top_tags = ObjectDetectionNet.predict(Image)
Total_tags=[]
Total_tags.append(Tags)
Total_tags.append(similar_tag)
Total_tags.append(Top_tags)
Return: Total_tags

3.2   Training

The learning process of the proposed tagger consists of three different stages that are dependent on each other. The first stage is the training of the TaggerNet and the second stage is the training of the word embedding model and the last stage is the finding out the neighbor tags in the word embedding model to the tags assigned by the TaggerNet in the first step.

As mentioned earlier in the architecture of the TaggerNet, we initialize a ResNet-50 neural net with image net weights for feature extraction. After the features are extracted, a neural net is created to learn the tags from the image features. The neural net utilizes an Adam optimizer [12] with a learning rate of 0.001.

$$W_t = W_{t-1} - \eta \frac{m_t}{\sqrt{v_t + \varepsilon}} \tag{4}$$

The changing of weights by the Adam optimizer is carried out based on the formula given in Eq. 4, where W_t is the weight of the current step, W_{t-1} is the weight of previous step, η is the step size, m_t and v_t are bias corrected first and second moment values. The structure of the neural net is depicted in Fig. 5.

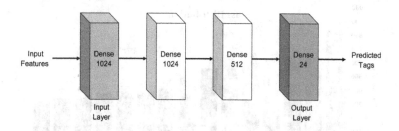

Fig. 5. Structure of the neural network

The Second stage involves training a word embedding model. The model is trained on large corpus of data (Brown corpus). The pre-processing steps involved in training the model includes, removal of stop words, lemmatization of the words. Then, we train the model for set number of iterations, with a fixed embedding size and the context window size.

After the TaggerNet is trained, the tags returned by it is vectorized using the word embedding model to find two nearest neighbor words to each tag. The nearest word to a given tag is calculated using the cosine distance between the tag vector and a potential similar word vector. By, this way we extract the two most similar words to each given tag.

$$D = \frac{T.E}{||T||.||E||} \tag{5}$$

The above Eq. 5 specifies the cosine distance D where, T is the vector of tag returned by TaggerNet and E is the vector of a potentially similar word in the vector space. We find vector E, which increases the value of D, which in turns means that the two vectors are more similar to each other. Given a set of tags T_i we find set of tags W_i that consists of most similar words returned by the model utilizing the cosine distance specified in Eq. 6.

$$\{W_i\} = similar(T_i) \tag{6}$$

4   Experimental Analysis

The dataset used to build the tagger is the MIRFLICKR-25000 dataset [13] which consists of 25000 images with their corresponding tags and ground truth tags. There are 24 ground truth classes and 1386 tags. The tags have semantic overlapping i.e., an image of tree will be tagged as (tree, plant life). The distribution of each tag is shown in Fig. 6.

The neural net is trained for 15 epochs with the 20000 image data with a train and validation split of 80 and 20 respectively. After the neural net is trained, it is tested on the remaining 5000 images.

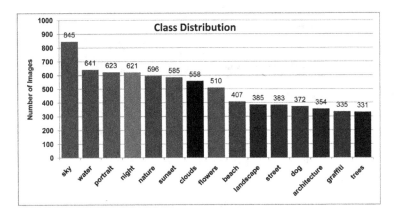

Fig. 6. Distribution of number of images per class in MIRFLICKR dataset

4.1   Results

We compare our neural network model's mean average precision (mAP) score with pre-existing works in Table 1 which shows that our model outperforms them. The Area Under Curve (AUC) of the precision recall curve of each of the 24 classes of MIR-FLICKR 25k dataset is specified in Table 2. The micro-averaged precision over all the classes is found out to be 0.81. The graph in Fig. 7 represents the precision-recall curve of each of the 24 ground truth classes of the MIR-FLFICKR 25k dataset. As, we treat tagging as a form of multi-label

Table 1. Comparison of results of TaggerNet with existing works

MODEL	mAP SCORE
BoW + KNN [14]	0.34
BoW + Tagprop [15]	0.33
Bow + TagVoting [16]	0.34
CNN + KNN [14]	0.63
CNN + TagProp [16]	0.65
TaggerNet	**0.72**

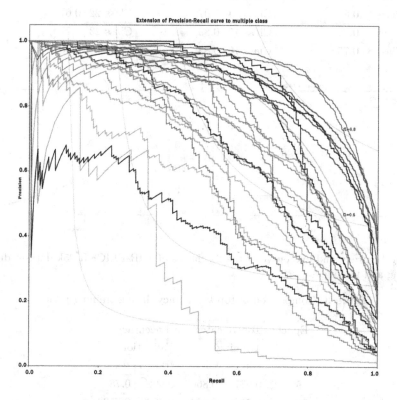

Fig. 7. Precision – Recall curve of the 24 classes of MIR-FLICKR 25k dataset

classification we use cross entropy as the loss function coupled with sigmoid function as the activation function. The variation of the loss and accuracy during each epoch is shown in the Fig. 8.

Top k accuracy is a performance evaluation metric used especially for multi-label classification models. The general idea behind this metric is that, it takes into account the number of guesses that is taken by the model to correctly classify an image into a set of classes. Top k accuracy scientifically means that the correct class is in the Top-k predicted probabilities by the model for it to

Table 2. Area under curve (AUC) of Precision-recall graph of the classes in FLICKR-25k dataset.

Class	Precision - Recall Value	Class	Precision - Recall Value	Class	Precision - Recall Value
Class 1	0.81	Class 9	0.69	Class 17	0.49
Class 2	0.32	Class 10	0.83	Class 18	0.75
Class 3	0.64	Class 11	0.37	Class 19	0.91
Class 4	0.61	Class 12	0.66	Class 20	0.88
Class 5	0.83	Class 13	0.61	Class 21	0.65
Class 6	0.85	Class 14	0.91	Class 22	0.67
Class 7	0.75	Class 15	0.89	Class 23	0.77
Class 8	0.75	Class 16	0.83	Class 24	0.80

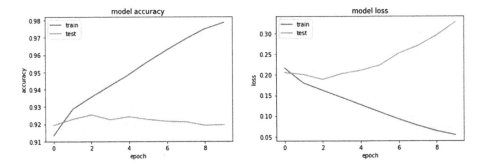

Fig. 8. Accuracy and loss curve of the 24 classes of MIR-FLICKR 25k dataset during training and testing

Table 3. Comparison of top k accuracy during training period

Epochs	Top K categorical accuracy			
	Training		Validation	
	@k = 3	@k = 5	@k = 3	@k = 5
5	0.6779	0.8667	0.6021	0.78
10	0.7529	0.9248	0.6028	0.7723
15	0.7635	0.9297	0.5856	0.7631

count as correct. The top-k categorical accuracy of the TaggerNet during various stages of training period is summarized in the Table 3.

From, the Table 3 it is evident that the top k validation accuracy increases till five epochs, after which it starts reducing, indicating that the neural network is starting to over-fit. Hence, the training is stopped at five epochs.

Fig. 9. Results obtained by the proposed image tagger method (Color figure online)

As mentioned earlier, if we compare the results yielded by the neural net augmented with the GloVe and Object detection model, we find that the augmented model identifies more content in the image than the TaggerNet, and is more effective in describing and tagging the images. The tags in green indicate the tags that are added by the GloVe model and tags in yellow indicate tags that are added by the Object Detection model (Fig. 9).

5   Conclusion

In this paper, we propose a model to perform Image tagging based on multi-label multi-class classification approach. The tagging can be improved by adding a GloVe model and object detection neural net which helps the tagger to tag the images on unseen tags also. To, test the performance of TaggerNet, we evaluated it on a set of 5000 images, which shows that out neural net performs well amongst the existing systems. Moreover, by adding the extra layers of word vectors Zero-shot tagging is incorporated into the system, which augments the tags to describe the content of the given image effectively.

References

1. Mikolov, T., Chen, K., Corrado, G., Dean, J.: Efficient estimation of word representations in vector space. arXiv preprint arXiv:1301.3781 (2013)

2. Mikolov, T., Sutskever, I., Chen, K., Corrado, G., Dean, J.: Distributed representations of words and phrases and their compositionality. In: Advances in Neural Information Processing Systems, pp. 3111–3119 (2013)
3. Socher, R., Bauer, J., Manning, C.D., Ng, A.Y.: Parsing with compositional vector grammars. In: Proceedings of the 51st Annual Meeting of the Association for Computational Linguistics (vol. 1: Long Papers), pp. 455–465 (2013)
4. Tellex, S., Katz, B., Lin, J., Fernandes, A., Marton, G.: Quantitative evaluation of passage retrieval algorithms for question answering. In Proceedings of the 26th Annual International ACM SIGIR Conference on Research and Development in Information Retrieval, pp. 41–47. ACM (2003)
5. Fu, J., Rui, Y.: Advances in deep learning approaches for image tagging. APSIPA Trans. Signal Inf. Process. 6 (2017)
6. Pennington, J., Socher, R., Manning, C.D.: Glove: global vectors for word representation. In: Proceedings of the 2014 Conference on Empirical Methods in Natural Language Processing (EMNLP), pp. 1532–1543 (2014)
7. Zhang, Y., Gong, B., Shah, M.: Fast zero-shot image tagging. In: 2016 IEEE Conference on Computer Vision and Pattern Recognition (CVPR), pp. 5985–5994. IEEE (2016)
8. Frome, A., et al.: Devise: a deep visual-semantic embedding model. In: Advances in Neural Information Processing Systems, pp. 2121–2129 (2013)
9. Akata, Z., Perronnin, F., Harchaoui, Z., Schmid, C.: Label-embedding for attribute-based classification. In: Proceedings of the IEEE Conference on Computer Vision and Pattern Recognition, pp. 819–826 (2013)
10. Gong, Y., Jia, Y., Leung, T., Toshev, A., Ioffe, S.: Deep convolutional ranking for multilabel image annotation. arXiv preprint arXiv:1312.4894 (2013)
11. Lin, T.-Y., et al.: Microsoft COCO: common objects in context. In: Fleet, D., Pajdla, T., Schiele, B., Tuytelaars, T. (eds.) ECCV 2014. LNCS, vol. 8693, pp. 740–755. Springer, Cham (2014). https://doi.org/10.1007/978-3-319-10602-1_48
12. Kingma, D.P., Ba, J.: Adam: a method for stochastic optimization. arXiv preprint arXiv:1412.6980 (2014)
13. Huiskes, M.J., Lew, M.S.: The mir flickr retrieval evaluation. In: Proceedings of the 1st ACM International Conference on Multimedia Information Retrieval, pp. 39–43. ACM (2008)
14. Makadia, A., Pavlovic, V., Kumar, S.: Baselines for image annotation. Int. J. Comput. Vis. 90(1), 88–105 (2010). https://doi.org/10.1007/s11263-010-0338-6
15. Li, X., Snoek, C.G., Worring, M.: Learning tag relevance by neighbor voting for social image retrieval. In: Proceedings of the 1st ACM International Conference on Multimedia Information Retrieval, pp. 180–187. ACM (2008)
16. Branson, S., Van Horn, G., Belongie, S., Perona, P.: Bird species categorization using pose normalized deep convolutional nets. arXiv preprint arXiv:1406.2952 (2014)

Comparison of Deep Learning Models for Cancer Metastases Detection: An Experimental Study

Vijaya Gajanan Buddhavarapu[(✉)] and J. Angel Arul Jothi[iD]

Department of Computer Science, Birla Institute of Technology and Science Pilani,
Dubai Campus, Dubai, UAE
{f20160062,angeljothi}@dubai.bits-pilani.ac.in

Abstract. Deep Learning (DL) models have shown to achieve remarkable results for classification, segmentation and detection tasks in medical image analysis. In this study, we experiment on Autoencoders (AEs), a Deep Learning model that aims to encode features from the input images into a sparse representation by reconstructing the input images. We experiment whether the sparse features from an Autoencoder be effectively used for the detection of metastases from breast histopathology patches when compared with a Convolutional Neural Network (CNN) for the same task. Two Autoencoder models are explored in this study. In order to make fair comparison, the architecture of the CNN is made similar to the encoder part of the AE models. All the models are trained using the breast cancer lymph node histopathology patches from the PatchCamelyon dataset. The features extracted from the AEs are passed to a Random Forest classifier. Experimental results show that for the given task, the CNN has an edge over extracting the features from the autoencoder and classifying it through the Random Forest classifier.

Keywords: Deep learning · Histopathology · Autoencoders ·
Convolutional Neural Networks (CNN) · Random forest

1 Introduction

Cancer is one of the leading causes of death in the world. Breast Cancer (BC) is the second most common type of cancer in women worldwide. According to a report from WHO, 627,000 women died from BC in 2018. Studies have shown that the incidence of BC is increasing globally [1]. Early detection, diagnosis and treatment of BC leads to decline in mortality related to the disease [2,4]. Effective treatment of BC is attributed by determining the cancer stage. One of the indicators to determine the BC stage involves pathological examination of lymph node samples for the evidence of metastases [17]. However, the study of the samples by professional pathologists takes a considerable amount of time. There is also variability in the diagnostic results of the same sample between different pathologists and by the same pathologist at different point in time.

© Springer Nature Singapore Pte Ltd. 2021
K. K. Patel et al. (Eds.): icSoftComp 2020, CCIS 1374, pp. 169–181, 2021.
https://doi.org/10.1007/978-981-16-0708-0_15

Automated diagnostics systems aim to assist pathologists by annotating and segmenting important structures such as nuclei, by predicting the number of mitotic cells, and by classifying samples to be cancerous or non-cancerous. These systems do not aim to replace licensed medical professionals. However, they intend to make the diagnostic process much more streamlined and efficient.

Traditional Machine Learning (ML) techniques have been used for decades to build computer assisted systems for medical image classification and segmentation using handcrafted features [13]. ML models need data to be sufficiently pre-processed before the learning step which could result in added complexity. A newer approach, gaining significant interest over the recent decade, is Deep Learning (DL). DL models consist of several layers of interconnected neurons that can perform feature extraction and learning automatically from the input data [6]. Training of Deep Learning models require lots of data and physical resources such as GPU cores. However, in the recent times this is no longer an issue due to the widespread availability and affordability of resources such as datacenters, GPUs and cloud platforms.

Among the DL models, the Convolutional Neural Networks (CNNs) is well suited for image classification. It is a supervised learning model. The CNNs can learn both global and local features effectively from 2D or 3D images and are widely used for medical image classification and segmentation tasks. Autoencoders (AEs), is another type of an unsupervised deep neural network that aims to capture salient features of the input in a 'Bottleneck' with the output being the reconstructed image. Thus, the network learns to effectively encode the input image in a sparse and unsupervised manner. Autoencoders (AEs) are used for different applications such as reconstruction and denoising. The sparse features learnt from an AE can be passed to a classifier for prediction.

The objective of this study is to develop deep learning models to automatically detect breast cancer lymph node metastases from histopathology images. Specifically, we intend to experimentally determine how effective autoencoder features are in comparison to CNN features for classification of breast cancer lymph node histopathology images into two classes namely positive (indicating metastases) or negative (indicating absence of metastases). For this purpose we, experiment on two autoencoder models namely the Fully Convolutional Autoencoder (FCAE) and the Convolutional Autoencoder with dense Bottleneck (CAEB). These models are compared against an Encoder CNN (ECNN) which is a CNN.

The rest of this paper is organized as follows: Sect. 2 discusses related work. Section 3 describes the dataset. The deep neural architectures are detailed in Sect. 4. Implementation details and evaluation metrics are given in Sect. 5. Section 6 presents the results of the experiments. It also discusses and compares the performance of the experimented models. Section 7 concludes the paper.

2   Related Work

Convolutional Neural Networks (CNN) have experimentally been shown to be effective at classification and segmentation tasks for histopathology image analysis. Common tasks include classification of patches or whole slide images (WSIs) into cancerous or non-cancerous or sub-types of cancer, segmentation of structures such as tumor and detection of nuclei [9].

Xu et al. proposed stack sparse autoencoder (SSAE) for nuclei detection [22]. The proposed method was able to outperform 9 other strategies for nuclei detection. The authors also proposed method of using SSAE with softmax (SM) for classification of nuclei patches [21]. The method of SSAE+SM performed better than Principal Component Analysis PCA+SM, SM and SAE+SM with AUC of 0.8992.

Feng et al. proposed a method for classification of nuclei from breast cancer histopathology images using stacked denoising autoenoder (SDAE) with softmax [5]. The method outperformed other strategies with benign and malignant accuracies of 98.27% and 90.54% respectively. It was also able to outperform other architectures even with randomized pixel errors introduced into the data.

Hou et al. proposed a convolutional autoencoder (CAE) with cross sparsity for the tasks for detection, classification and segmentation of nuclei [7]. The crosswise sparsity enables feature representation of the background and foreground. The model performed well against other state of the art methods using different datasets such as MICCAI and TCGA.

The dataset used in the study, PatchCamelyon, is derived from the Camelyon16 challenge. The challenge involved the classification of WSIs based on the presence of metastatic tissue. It has been used as a bench-marking dataset for many studies in Deep Learning [11,12,15,16,20].

The contribution of this study is the application of unsupervised features extracted using Autoencoders for the classification of histopathology patches.

3 Dataset

In this work, we use the PatchCamelyon (PCam) dataset [18]. The PCam dataset contains 327,680 hematoxylin and eosin (H&E) stained patches of sentinal lymph node sections. The size of each patch is 96×96. Each patch in the PCam dataset is associated with a binary label (positive or negative) indicating the presence or absence of metastatic tissue in the patch. Thus, this dataset translates the task of metastatic detection to a two-class image classification problem. If the center of a patch contains at least one pixel of tumor tissue then the patch is assigned a positive label otherwise it is assigned a negative label. The dataset is split into train, validation and test sets in the ratio of 80:10:10 respectively. The patches of the PCam dataset are derived from the Camelyon16 challenge dataset that contains 400 H&E-stained whole slide images (WSIs) of sentinal lymph node sections of breast cancer patients [3]. Table 1 shows the breakdown of the PCam dataset into training, validation and testing sets. Figure 1 shows sample patches from the dataset belonging to the two classes.

Table 1. Breakdown of PCam dataset into training, validation and testing sets.

PatchCamelyon Dataset	
Training Set	262,144 patches
Validation Set	32,768 patches
Testing Set	32,768 patches
Total	327,680 patches

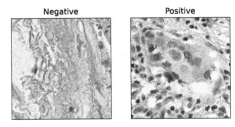

Fig. 1. Sample images from the PCam dataset belonging to the two classes.

4   Methodology

4.1   Convolutional Neural Networks

Convolutional Neural Networks (CNNs) consists of an input layer, output layer and several hidden layers of Convolutional layers, Pooling layers, Fully-Connected layers and optionally Batch Normalization layers. The input layer is generally the image data represented by $N \times W \times H \times D$, where N is the number of images, W, H and D are the width, height and depth of the image respectively. For a 2-D image, D represents the number of channels. For grayscale images $D = 1$ and for RGB images $D = 3$. One common application of CNNs are for classification of image data. In such a case, the output O is the set of nodes that represent the labels.

The Convolutional layer takes input feature map (image if previous layer is the input layer) of dimensions $W \times H \times D$ and transforms it to output feature map of dimensions $N_f \times W_f \times H_f \times D_f$, where N_f is the number of feature maps. The dimensions of the output feature map depend upon the filter size $k \times k$. Common filter sizes include 1×1, 2×2, 3×3, 5×5 and 7×7. After the convolution, the output feature maps are passed to an activation function in order to eliminate any linearity. One commonly used activation function is the Rectified Linear Unit (ReLu) given as $f(x) = \max(0, x)$ where x is the input to the ReLu unit.

The output of the convolution is then passed to a Pooling layer. The role of the Pooling layer is to reduce the dimensions of the data. The degree of reduction is given by the pooling size $p \times p$. Additionally, there are different types of pooling. The two most commonly used pooling layers are Max Pooling

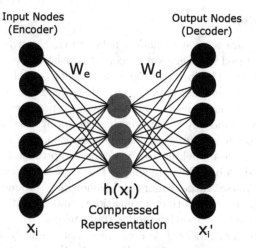

Fig. 2. Basic structure of autoencoder.

and Average Pooling that compute the max and average of each pooling size cluster (commonly 2 × 2) respectively.

Optionally, a Batch Normalization layer is used after the Convolutional layer. Batch Normalization is a technique that is used to improve the stability and performance of the CNN by re-scaling and re-centering the inputs [8].

Typically, a CNN consists of multiple Convolutional blocks that consist of Convolutional, Pooling and Batch Normalization layers. At the end of the final Convolutional block, the multi-dimensional output is flattened to a linear set of neurons. The neurons are then fully-connected (every input neuron is connected to every output neuron) with another set of neurons. This layer is called the Fully-Connected layer. Finally, the output of the Fully-Connected layer is connected to a set of neurons that represent the labels of the classification task. If the classification task is binary-classification, then the sigmoid function is used. Otherwise, multi-classification tasks use the softmax function. Equation (1) shows the formula for sigmoid activation function where x is the input value. Equation (2) shows the formula for softmax activation function where $x_i \in X$ and X is a set of logit scores.

$$\text{Sigmoid(x)} = \sigma(x) = \frac{1}{1 + e^{-x}} \tag{1}$$

$$\text{Softmax}(x_i) = \frac{\exp(x_i)}{\sum_j \exp(x_j)} \tag{2}$$

4.2   Autoencoders

Autoencoders [14] are a type of neural network that can learn sparse encodings in an unsupervised manner. Autoencoders consist of two separate networks: Encoder and Decoder. The input to the Autoencoder is at the Encoder side, and the output of the Autoencoder is at the Decoder side. The Encoder and Decoder are connected via the Bottleneck where the sparse representation is located. The model is generally trained by reconstructing the input data at the output side. The training, like other feed-forward neural networks, is performed through backpropogation. Thus, the model learns to encode a representation that is close to the original input data but sparse in shape. There are numerous types of Autoencoders including Sparse Autoencoders and Denoising Autoencoders [19] that are utilized in learned representation applications, and Variational Autoencoders [10] that are utilized in generative model applications.

Figure 2 depicts a generalized Autoencoder. Let X and X′ be the set of input nodes and output nodes respectively. If $x_i \in X$, then $h(x_i) = \sigma(W_e \times x_i + b)$ where σ is the sigmoid function, W_e is the weight matrix and b is the bias. If $x_i' \in X'$, then the reconstructed output is given by $x_i' = \sigma(W_d \times h(x_i) + b')$. The weights and biases are updated during backpropogation. Ideally, the input data and the reconstructed data are identical: $X \approx X'$.

4.3   Architectures Used

There are 3 architectures used in this study: Fully Convolutional Autoencoder (FCAE), Convolutional Autoencoder with Bottleneck (CAEB) and Encoder Convolutional Neural Network (ECNN). Among these the FCAE and CAEB are AEs and the ECNN is a CNN.

Fully Convolutional Autoencoder (FCAE). FCAE network is divided into the Encoder network and Decoder network consisting only of Convolutional, Pooling and Batch Normalization layers. Figure 3 shows the architecture of the FCAE network used in this work.

At the Encoder side, the network takes $96 \times 96 \times 3$ image at the input layer. The image is then passed to the first Convolutional block that consists of three sets of Convolution - Batch Normalization - Max Pooling layers. The Convolution layer transforms the input into 32 feature maps with filter size 3×3 and activation function ReLu. After this transformation, the output is passed into a Batch Normalization layer. After Batch Normalization, it is finally passed through a Max Pooling layer with pooling size of 2×2. The output feature maps from the first Convolution block are then passed into the second Convolution block.

The second Convolutional block consists of two sets of Convolution - Batch Normalization - Max Pooling layers. The Convolution layer in this block transforms the input into 64 feature maps with filter size 3×3 and activation function ReLu. After this transformation, the output is passed into a Batch Normalization layer. After Batch Normalization, it is then passed through a Max Pooling layer with pooling size 2×2. The output feature maps of the second Convolution

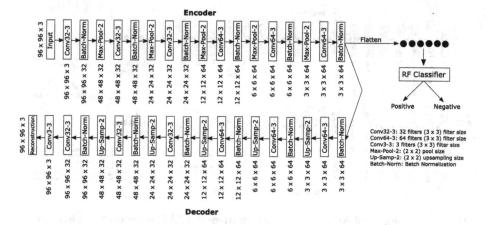

Fig. 3. Fully Convolutional Autoencoder (FCAE) network architecture.

block are then passed to a set of Convolution - Batch Normalization layers. The Convolution layer is the same as the previous block with 64 filters and filter size 3×3. The output feature maps are then sent to the Decoder network.

The Decoder network follows the same order of layers as described in the Encoder network but reversed. After the input of the Decoder passes through a set of Convolution - Batch Normalization layers, it enters the first Convolutional block. The first Convolutional block of the Decoder network uses the same layers as described in the second Convolutional block of the Encoder network. However, the Max Pooling layer is replaced by an Up Sampling layer that will increase the dimensionality of the input in contrast to the Max Pooling layer. The output of the first Convolution block then proceeds to the second Convolutional block. The second Convolutional block of the Decoder network uses the same layers as described in the first Convolutional block of the Encoder network. Finally, the output of the second Convolutional block is passed through one set of Convolution - Batch Normalization. The Convolutional layer has 3 filters and filter size 3×3. The output of this set is the reconstructed image of dimensions $96 \times 96 \times 3$.

The FCAE network is trained on the train set of the PCam dataset. After training the FCAE network, the output encoded feature maps of the Encoder are flattened and these flattened features are then used to train a Random Forest classifier for classifying an image into positive (metastatic) or negative (non-metastatic) class.

Convolutional Autoencoder with Bottleneck (CAEB). In CAEB, the structure of the Encoder network and the Decoder network are the same as the FCAE network but the difference is in how the output of the Encoder is transformed before being sent to the input of the Decoder. After passing through

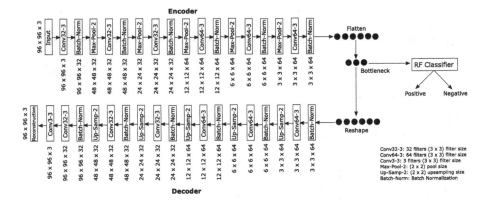

Fig. 4. Convolutional Autoencoder with Bottleneck (CAEB) network architecture.

the Encoder network, the feature maps are flattened into a linear set of neurons. The linear set of neurons are then connected to a Fully-Connected Layer of 100 neurons. These neurons constitute the 'bottleneck'. After passing through the bottleneck. The neurons are then connected to a layer of 576 neurons. These neurons are then reshaped back to a 3-dimensional array as input to the Decoder network. Figure 4 shows the network architecture of the CAEB network.

The CAEB network is trained on the train set of the PCam dataset. After training the CAEB network, the output features of the bottleneck layer are used to train a Random Forest classifier for classifying an image into positive (metastatic) or negative (non-metastatic) class.

Encoder Convolutional Neural Network (ECNN). In order to benchmark the performance of FCAE and CAEB, a CNN called Encoder CNN is used. It is termed Encoder CNN because the structure of the CNN is the same as the Encoder network of FCAE and CAEB. After the final Convolution layer, the feature maps are flattened and the linear set of neurons is then connected to a set of 576 neurons. These neurons are then connected to an output node with Sigmoid activation. Figure 5 shows the network architecture of the ECNN network. The ECNN network is trained on the train set of the PCam dataset for classifying an image into positive (metastatic) or negative (non-metastatic) class.

5 Implementation Details

Experiments are conducted in order to verify if the features extracted from the Autoencoder networks FCAE and CAEB are better than training the CNN network ECNN from the scratch. For this, as mentioned earlier, all the three models FCAE, CAEB and ECNN are initially trained and validated using the train and validation images of the PCam dataset. After training the FCAE and CAEB networks, the features are extracted from them and the extracted features are used to train a Random Forest classifier. Let the trained random forest classifier be denoted as FCAE+RF and CAEB+RF where FCAE+RF represents the RF classifier trained using features from the FCAE and CAEB+RF represents the RF classifier trained using features from the CAEB. The Random Forest classifier use 128 estimators. After this, the FCAE+RF, CAEB+RF classifiers and the trained ECNN model are tested using the test images from the PCam dataset.

All the models in this work are written using Python 3.6 with Tensorflow 1.x deep learning library and Keras as the API. The hardware and software environment consist of 2 Nvidia Tesla V100 GPUs with 32 GB dedicated memory and Ubuntu 18.04 Operating System respectively. All the three models are trained for 500 epochs and a batch size of 512 with early stopping callback. The callback is used as a precautionary measure to prevent overfitting.

All the models used the Adam optimizer. The Mean Squared Error (MSE) loss function is used to train the FCAE and the CAEB models whereas the Binary Cross-entropy (BCE) loss function is used to train the ECNN model. Equation (3) shows the formula for MSE loss function where y is the actual value and y′ is the predicted value. Equation (4) shows the formula for BCE loss function where y is the actual value and y′ is the predicted value. In ECNN, there is a Dropout regularizer layer of rate 0.5 after the fully connected layer of 576 neurons and before the sigmoid classification layer.

$$\text{MSE} = \frac{1}{N} \sum_{i=1}^{N} (y_i - y_i')^2 \tag{3}$$

$$\text{BCE} = -(y \log y' + (1 - y) \log (1 - y')) \tag{4}$$

5.1   Evaluation Metrics

Let positive class represent a patch having metastatic tissue and negative class represent a patch not having metastatic tissue. The general confusion matrix showing True Positive (TP), False Positive (FP), False Negative (FN) and True Negative (TN) is shown in Fig. 6. The performance of the classification models

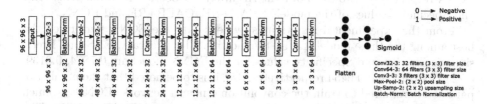

Fig. 5. Encoder Convolutional Neural Network (ECNN) network architecture.

is evaluated using metrics like Accuracy, Precision, Sensitivity, Specificity and F1-Score as given by Eqs. (5)–(9).

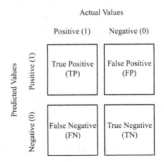

Fig. 6. General Confusion Matrix showing TP, TN, FP and FN.

$$\text{Accuracy} = \frac{\text{TP} + \text{TN}}{\text{TP} + \text{FP} + \text{TN} + \text{FN}} \tag{5}$$

$$\text{Precision} = \frac{\text{TP}}{\text{TP} + \text{FP}} \tag{6}$$

$$\text{Sensitivity/Recall} = \frac{\text{TP}}{\text{TP} + \text{FN}} \tag{7}$$

$$\text{Specificity} = \frac{\text{TN}}{\text{TN} + \text{FP}} \tag{8}$$

$$\text{F1-Score} = 2 \times \frac{\text{Precision} \times \text{Recall}}{\text{Precision} + \text{Recall}} \tag{9}$$

6   Results and Discussions

The classification results of the various models are presented in this section. Table 2, Table 3, and Table 4 shows the classification results in the form of confusion matrices for the three models namely FCAE+RF, CAEB+RF and ECNN respectively. Table 5 shows the Accuracy, F1-Score, Precision, Sensitivity and Specificity values of the models FCAE+RF, CAEB+RF and ECNN.

From the experimental results it is evident that the ECNN performed the best among the three models for all the metrics. The Accuracy, F1-Score, Precision, Sensitivity, and Specificity values for the ECNN model are 0.7874, 0.8139, 0.7240, 0.9292, and 0.6454 respectively. Also, it is to be noted that the number of parameters required to train the convolutional neural network (ECNN) is much less when compared to both the autoencoder architectures (FCAE, CAEB). The number of parameters that need to be trained (excluding classifier) in FCAE, CAEB and ECNN are 261,507, 377,583 and 112,897 respectively. So, with less

Table 2. Confusion matrix of FCAE+RF.

Predicted labels	True labels		
	Positive	Negative	Total
Positive	14199	7373	21572
Negative	2192	9004	11196
Total	16391	16377	32768

Table 3. Confusion matrix of CAEB+RF.

Predicted labels	True labels		
	Positive	Negative	Total
Positive	13714	9346	23060
Negative	2677	7031	9708
Total	16391	16377	32768

Table 4. Confusion matrix of ECNN.

Predicted labels	True labels		
	Positive	Negative	Total
Positive	15231	5807	21038
Negative	1160	10570	11730
Total	16391	16377	32768

Table 5. Classification results of all models.

Method	Accuracy	F1-Score	Precision	Sensitivity	Specificity
FCAE+RF	0.7081	0.7480	0.6582	0.8663	0.5498
CAEB+RF	0.6385	0.6953	0.5947	0.8367	0.4460
ECNN	0.7874	0.8139	0.7240	0.9292	0.6454

training time, ECNN is able to generalize the dataset much faster. However, it must be noted that ECNN extracts features in a supervised manner while the feature extraction in both FCAE and CAEB networks is unsupervised. Thus, there is an increase in the number of parameters to be learnt and the training time for the FCAE and CAEB networks.

Between the autoencoder models, though CAEB encoded the features much more sparsely when compared to FCAE, experimental results show that it do not improve the performance of the classification. From Table 5 it can be noted that FCAE performed much better compared to CAEB. Both the FCAE and the CAEB networks have not given satisfactory results when compared with ECNN model. Thus, it can be noted that a CNN model is more preferable if we have large labelled training data whereas during lack of labelled data autoencoders are useful. The classification performance of the features learned in an unsupervised manner are less when compared with those of the features learned in a supervised manner. The ECNN model can be further tuned with careful network design to improve the classification accuracy to be considered for computer assisted metastases detection system from breast cancer lymph node histopathology images.

7   Conclusion

In this study, deep neural network models like autoencoders and convolutional neural networks are explored for the task of automatic metastases detection from histopathology images. Experimental results showed that CNNs are superior then autoencoders for the given task. The results also showed that autoencoders can be used for unsupervised feature extraction of sparse features that can be utilized for semi-supervised classification task of histopathology images. This would allow for training of classifiers even with limited labeled training data. Future work includes optimization of parameters and architecture for better performance.

References

1. Breast cancer. https://www.who.int/cancer/prevention/diagnosis-screening/breast-cancer/en/. Accessed 02 Dec 2019
2. Cancer statistics. https://www.cancer.gov/about-cancer/understanding/statistics. Accessed 02 Dec 2019
3. Bejnordi, B.E., et al.: Diagnostic assessment of deep learning algorithms for detection of lymph node metastases in women with breast cancer. JAMA **318**(22), 2199–2210 (2017)
4. DeSantis, C.E., et al.: Breast cancer statistics, 2019. CA: Cancer J. Clin. **69**(6), 438–451 (2019)
5. Feng, Y., Zhang, L., Yi, Z.: Breast cancer cell nuclei classification in histopathology images using deep neural networks. Int. J. Comput. Assist. Radiol. Surg. **13**(2), 179–191 (2018). https://doi.org/10.1007/s11548-017-1663-9
6. Goodfellow, I., Bengio, Y., Courville, A.: Deep Learning. MIT Press, Cambridge (2016)
7. Hou, L., et al.: Sparse autoencoder for unsupervised nucleus detection and representation in histopathology images. Pattern Recogn. **86**, 188–200 (2019)
8. Ioffe, S., Szegedy, C.: Batch normalization: accelerating deep network training by reducing internal covariate shift. arXiv preprint arXiv:1502.03167 (2015)
9. Janowczyk, A., Madabhushi, A.: Deep learning for digital pathology image analysis: a comprehensive tutorial with selected use cases. J. Pathol. Inform. **7**, 29 (2016)
10. Kingma, D.P., Welling, M.: An introduction to variational autoencoders. arXiv preprint arXiv:1906.02691 (2019)
11. Kong, B., Sun, S., Wang, X., Song, Q., Zhang, S.: Invasive cancer detection utilizing compressed convolutional neural network and transfer learning. In: Frangi, A.F., Schnabel, J.A., Davatzikos, C., Alberola-López, C., Fichtinger, G. (eds.) MICCAI 2018. LNCS, vol. 11071, pp. 156–164. Springer, Cham (2018). https://doi.org/10.1007/978-3-030-00934-2_18

12. Koohbanani, N.A., Qaisar, T., Shaban, M., Gamper, J., Rajpoot, N.: Significance of hyperparameter optimization for metastasis detection in breast histology images. In: Stoyanov, D., et al. (eds.) OMIA/COMPAY -2018. LNCS, vol. 11039, pp. 139–147. Springer, Cham (2018). https://doi.org/10.1007/978-3-030-00949-6_17

13. Kourou, K., Exarchos, T.P., Exarchos, K.P., Karamouzis, M.V., Fotiadis, D.I.: Machine learning applications in cancer prognosis and prediction. Comput. Struct. Biotechnol. J. **13**, 8–17 (2015)

14. Kramer, M.A.: Nonlinear principal component analysis using autoassociative neural networks. AIChE J. **37**(2), 233–243 (1991)

15. Li, Y., Ping, W.: Cancer metastasis detection with neural conditional random field. arXiv preprint arXiv:1806.07064 (2018)

16. Liu, Y., et al.: Detecting cancer metastases on gigapixel pathology images. arXiv preprint arXiv:1703.02442 (2017)

17. Liu, Y., et al.: Detecting cancer metastases on gigapixel pathology images. CoRR abs/1703.02442 (2017). http://arxiv.org/abs/1703.02442

18. Veeling, B.S., Linmans, J., Winkens, J., Cohen, T., Welling, M.: Rotation equivariant CNNs for digital pathology. In: Frangi, A.F., Schnabel, J.A., Davatzikos, C., Alberola-López, C., Fichtinger, G. (eds.) MICCAI 2018. LNCS, vol. 11071, pp. 210–218. Springer, Cham (2018). https://doi.org/10.1007/978-3-030-00934-2_24

19. Vincent, P., Larochelle, H., Lajoie, I., Bengio, Y., Manzagol, P.A., Bottou, L.: Stacked denoising autoencoders: Learning useful representations in a deep network with a local denoising criterion. J. Mach. Learn. Res. **11**(12), 3371–3408 (2010)

20. Wang, D., Khosla, A., Gargeya, R., Irshad, H., Beck, A.H.: Deep learning for identifying metastatic breast cancer. arXiv preprint arXiv:1606.05718 (2016)

21. Xu, J., Xiang, L., Hang, R., Wu, J.: Stacked sparse autoencoder (SSAE) based framework for nuclei patch classification on breast cancer histopathology. In: 2014 IEEE 11th International Symposium on Biomedical Imaging (ISBI), pp. 999–1002. IEEE (2014)

22. Xu, J., et al.: Stacked sparse autoencoder (SSAE) for nuclei detection on breast cancer histopathology images. IEEE Trans. Med. Imaging **35**(1), 119–130 (2015)

A Lightweight Hybrid Majority Vote Classifier Using Top-k Dataset

Moses L. Gadebe[1]($\boxtimes$) ⓘ and Okuthe P. Kogeda[2] ⓘ

[1] Tshwane University of Technology, Pretoria, Private Bag X680,
Pretoria 0001, South Africa
gadebeml@tut.ac.za
[2] University of the Free State, P. O. Box 339, Bloemfontein 9300, South Africa

Abstract. Human activity recognition on resource constrained device such as Smartphone is possible using small dataset. In this paper, we present our unique Split-then-join strategy to combine two data hungry algorithms (KNN and Naives Bayes) into Lightweight Hybrid Majority Vote algorithm for Smartphone using little compressed dataset. We simulated our proposed classier and compare it with state of the art classification algorithms (C4.5, K Nearest Neighbor, Support Vector Machine and Naïve Bayes, Random Forest) in R for machine learning with Caret, Rweka and e1071 packages using our top-k personalized dataset collected from 13 randomly selected subjects. The result our experimentation demonstrate the superiority of our algorithm over its predecessor Naive Bayes and KNN. Moreover it is comparative with Tree-Oriented and ensembles algorithms such as C4.5, Boosted Trees and Random Forest with accuracy and precision above 85% in all static and most complex human activities.

1 Introduction

Human activity aims to capture the state of a subject and his/her environment using different sensors attached on their bodies and within a closed location which enables computing-aware application. Thus permits continuous monitoring of individual numerical physiological behavior to provide personalized healthcare to improve individuals' well-being [1]. The effort of identification of human activity is automatically derived using supervised learning and classification algorithms in Human Activity Recognition (HAR) to predict and improve human behavior within their environment [1, 2]. Monitoring is achievable through Smartphone which is carried by its owners 24 h a day. Notwithstanding, its resource constraints including: (a) computational power, (b) storage space, (c) memory allocation, (d) small screens and (e) battery life span. Most Smartphones are equipped with sensor such as accelerometer, gyroscope, GPS, Bluetooth, Light sensor, which unlocked context-aware computing [3]. Most researchers in HAR use in-expensive accelerometer sensor to train and classify Human Activities (HAs) such as sitting, standing, laying, walking, running, jumping, and cycling, etc. in real time using Smartphone [1–6].

The supervised algorithms such as KNN, Naïve Bayes, Support Vector Machine, C4.5 with largest training dataset can produce reliable classifier at expense of limited

© Springer Nature Singapore Pte Ltd. 2021
K. K. Patel et al. (Eds.): icSoftComp 2020, CCIS 1374, pp. 182–196, 2021.
https://doi.org/10.1007/978-981-16-0708-0_16

resources of Smartphone [1–3, 7]. Recently, researchers in personalized HAR employed ensemble algorithms based on voting schemes using tree-based algorithm, because they [8–12] found tree-oriented algorithms to per-form optimally with smallest dataset. Most of techniques in [9–11, 13] uses Chan & Stolfo [14] three integration strategies (combiner, arbiter and hybrid strategies) to combine multiple classification algorithms of different architectural structures to boost prediction accuracy.

In this study, we proposed our unique Split-Then-Vote combiner strategy to combine two heavy duty algorithms (KNN and Naïve Bayes) to use compressed little dataset to increase classification accuracy and precision. We simulated our proposed supervised lightweight voting algorithm in R programming language using our top-k personalized dataset collected from 13 randomly selected subjects in comparison to other R tree-oriented and ensemble algorithms. The remainder of this paper is organized as follows: In Sect. 2 we present Related Work. The Methodology and Experimentation are discussed in Sects. 3 and Sect. 4, respectively. Conclusion and Future work are presented in Sect. 5.

2 Related Work

In this section we review related work of tree-oriented and ensemble algorithms. Researchers in [9] proposed HAR model for Android running on Nexus One, HTC Hero and Motorola Backflip. Their test subjects were required to slide-in Smartphones inside front pants pockets while performing human activities. They [9] transformed raw accelerometer sensor data into smaller 10-s segments from 200 readings and extracted time domain features. Where "time between the peaks" were used to accurately identify repetitive activities such walking and jogging. They [9] trained and tested C4.5/J48, logistic regression, multilayer Perceptron and Straw on WEKA. The overall accuracy increased above 90%.

Based on the study of [9], researchers in [10] proposed another HAR using ensemble techniques based on the concept of voting classifier. The voting classifier employed three classification algorithms on Wireless Sensor Data Mining (WSDM) training dataset collected by [9], and used 10-fold cross validation approach similar to their predecessors [9]. Their results of voting ensemble model showed a sharp increase in accuracy to 91% compared to 85%, 77% and 88% of J48, Logistic regression and Multi-Layer Perceptron respectively.

Similar to [9, 10] researchers in [11] they built their ensemble model combining C4.5 decision tree and AdaBoost Meta classifier using personalized WSDM dataset in WEKA. They were motivated with their findings that AdaBoost enhances performance of classifier when used in combination with other classification algorithms. Also 10-fold cross validation and confusion matrix were employed for each activity. Their results indicated an improved performance as compared to [9] and [10].

In [12] they used different classification algorithms to recognize human activity using dataset collected from 20 subjects with ASUS ZenFone 5 Smartphone. Subjects were required to slide-in Smartphone their jeans pockets while performing supervised human activities. The Smartphone recorded the forces applied along the X, Y, Z axes per m/s^2 for each activity at frequency rate of 0.5 s, collecting 120 samples per minute. Similar to the work of [9], time domain features were extracted and used to train and test the AdaBoost, J48, Support vector Machines and Random forest in WEKA. They [12] reported the accuracy rate of 98%, 96%, 95% and 93% for each models in the order given. Most ensemble techniques in HAR combines tree-oriented algorithms, because they are effective with smallest personalized dataset and achieved accuracy of 98% [15–19].

Contrarily to tree-oriented ensemble algorithm, the technique proposed by [20] combines a bunch of data hungry Naïve Bayes classifier as expert algorithms using weighted majority voting rule similar to [14]. The technique observes both experts and true class for each sample of training set in order to compute conditional probability, where once conditional probability is learned from training data, the combiner classifies each unknown sample using weighted voting strategy. The overall rationale of their [20] technique is to jointly analyst expert responses to capture collective behavior to classify a sample. Thus, their [20] decision classifier, is based on all expert responses without considering the performance of single classifiers. The technique was evaluated using three dataset (MFeat, Optodigit and Pendigit) against bagging and boosting algorithms, and found a slight increase in accuracy averaging to 97% in all datasets. Another similar technique using data hungry algorithms (Naïve Bayes Tree, KNN and third C4.5) was proposed by [13] based on [14] combiner strategy. Their technique averages the probability voting rules used to combine three hypothesis (h1, h2 and h3) of each leaners. Thus, each output class, a posteriori probabilities are generated by individual learners, a class with maximum posteriori average is selected to be voting hypothesis (h*). They [13] performed experiments using 10 fold cross validation on 28 datasets on WEKA, and found that their proposed voting models perform better than individual classifier (Naïve Bayes Tree and KNN) in exception to C4.5.

In this article we propose a new ensemble algorithms to integrate Gaussian Naïve Bayes (GNB) and KNN based on our split-then-vote strategy. Our technique combines GNB and KNN into joint marriage of convenience based on integral conditionality to address minor features problem presented in [7, 21] and [22] using a little compressed dataset meant for resource constraint Smartphone. Since both algorithms performs far better with higher dimensional space dataset. We found that GNB algorithm postpones data processing until classification arises similar to KNN. Because GNB depends on computation of standard deviation for new instance data point relative to mean average of training input predicators per class. Moreover, the KNN is prone to minor-feature miss-classification problem that cause two similar attributes to be recognized far apart from each other due to limited [21–24]. Lastly, KNN uses constant K value to control number of nearest neighbors to determine majority class to classify new instance data point, see Fig. 1.

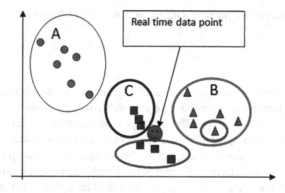

Fig. 1. K Value of closet neighbors of KNN [21]

3 Methodology

In this paper we propose a reliable and effective lightweight algorithm suitable for small personalized dataset and constraint Smartphone. A combination of Gaussian Naïve Bayes (GNB) with KNN as hybrid algorithm for little dataset is rare, because both algorithms heavily depends on largest dataset. We combine both algorithms based on joint majority vote probability function to include data points in each class as potential neighbors to resolve minor feature miss-classification indicated in Fig. 1. Our proposed split-then-vote combiner strategy in Fig. 2 is presented in three steps to reduce, split and combine GBN and KNN into Lightweight Hybrid Majority Vote (LHMV).

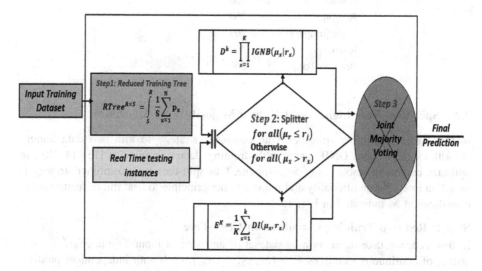

Fig. 2. Split-then-vote Lightweight Hybrid Majority Vote architecture

In the next Section we present data collection method followed to collect personalized dataset.

3.1 Data Collection

We followed convenience sampling to randomly select 13 participants to collect personalized dataset under the supervision of researcher using our prototype presented in [21]. We installed our user-friendly prototype on Samsung Galaxy Grand Prime +Smartphone. Each participant performs a selected activity to collect human activity features until the stop sound is triggered after 2 min. Then our prototype in [21] prompts for next human activity. The researcher would select next human activity until all the pre-loaded human activities are exhausted. Thereafter, all generated features with labels are automatically written locally on Smartphone SD card (see top-k dataset sample in Appendix A). All 13 collected top-k datasets files were merged and transferred from Smartphone using USB cable to researcher's personal computer. A total of 2860 rows of top-k personalized were collected as listed in Table 1.

Table 1. Real-time top-k personalized dataset

Human activity	Total human activities
Laying	260
Standing	260
Sitting	260
Walking slowly	260
Walking downstairs	260
Walking upstairs	260
Normal walking pace	260
Jogging	260
Rope jumping	260
Running	260
Brisk walking	260

3.2 Split-then-Vote Lightweight Hybrid Majority Vote Algorithm

In this paper we follow split-then-vote combiner strategy to join two data hungry algorithms (KNN and GNB) using little training dataset similar to [13, 14, 20], to optimize constraint resources of Smartphone. Our split-then-vote combiner strategy is based on integral conditionality and majority vote principle to heal minor feature missclassification as indicated in Fig. 1.

Step 1: Reduced Training Classification Class-Tree
In this step, we take input training dataset of any size as input $TrainingSet^{N \times M}$ consisting of continuous examples $E = \{e_1, e_2, \ldots, e_m\}$, each with independent predicators $P = \{p_1, p_2, \ldots, p_n\}$ belonging to a class category in a set $C = \{c_1, c_2 \ldots, c_m\}$. Therefore, we reduce input training dataset dimension by compressing a series

numerical values in each predicators p_n into R segments groupings of mean μ averages. We used our improved bottom-up segmentation technique defined by Eq. (1) to select best classification features similar to [22, 23, 24].

$$reducedTrainingTree^{R \times S} = \int_S^R \frac{1}{S} \sum_{x=1}^N p_x \qquad (1)$$

Where R is upper limit of transformation reductions to divide and segment N rows of input training dataset $TrainingSet^{N \times M}$ into a reduced subgroup of size S defined by Eq. (2).

$$S = \left| \frac{N}{R} \right| \qquad (2)$$

N is the number of rows from original input $TrainingSet^{N \times M}$ transformed and reduced to subgroups R, each with class category c_m consisting of S rows of best mean averages $\phi = \{\mu_1, \mu_2, ..., \mu_r\}$ of reduced predicators p_x. That is if R equal to 5, the input training dataset is divided into 5 segments of N rows reduced to S rows of best classification predicators. The resulted $reducedTrainingTree^{R \times S}$ is lightweight classification features to train our lightweight classifier.

Step 2: Data Segmentation Splitter Technique
In this step of our split-then-vote combiner strategy, we split input $reducedTrainingTree^{R \times S}$, into first and second classifiers based on integral functions $f(\mu_r \le r_j)$ and $f(\mu_r > r_j)$. We implemented $SpliterData(\mu_r, r_j)$ function, to split best mean averages $\phi = \{\mu_1, \mu_2, ..., \mu_r\}$ in relation to new instance r in each class category c_r as proper distribution function to satisfy first and second integral function defined by Eq. (3):

$$SpliterData(\mu_r, r_j) = \int_\mu^r p(\mu|r) \qquad (3)$$

Expanded to Eq. (4)

$$SpliterData(\mu_r, r_j) = \left\{ \begin{array}{l} 1 : \mu_r \le r_j \\ 0 : \mu_r > r_j \end{array} \right\} \qquad (4)$$

Provided that $SpliterData(\mu_r, r_j)$ function is a Cumulative Distribution Function (CDF). Therefore, we used predicators μ_r under area of CDF within first integral function $f(\mu_r \le r_j)$ to train our first classifier, otherwise all predicators in $f(\mu_r > r_j)$ are used to train supplementary classifier. Then, we combined first and second classifiers results as voting lists D^k and E^k into union of convenience to join GNB and KNN into LHMV in step 3 [7, 22].

Step 3: Majority Vote Classification

In this step, we introduce joint majority vote to address minor-feature miss-classification due to smaller training dataset [7, 22]. We implemented GNB as first classifier, because it relies on a normally distributed data features [25, 28], by including integral $f(\mu_r \leq r_j)$ function such that all mean μ_r under area of CDF are used to train our Integrated Gaussian Naïve Bayes (IGNB) defined by Eq. (5).

$$IGNB = \int_{\mu_r}^{r} \frac{1}{\sqrt{2\pi\sigma^2}} e^{-\frac{(r-\mu_r)^2}{2\sigma^2}} \tag{5}$$

That is, for all mean averages ordered as $\{\mu_1 \leq \mu_2 \leq \mu_3 \leq \ldots \leq \mu_r\}$ under area of CDF, are normally distributed within integral conditional function $f(\mu_r \leq r_j)$ relative to real time instances $RT = \{r_1, r_2, r_3, r_j\}$. Therefore, we compute standard deviation σ using Eq. (6), for all mean averages μ_r for each class c_m category in relation to real-time data point r_j

$$\sigma = \sqrt{\frac{1}{k-1} \sum_{x=1}^{k} (r_x - \mu_x)^2} \tag{6}$$

All computed σ are accumulated as product probabilities into vote list D^k using Bayes Theorem Eq. (7), used to classify real-time instance.

$$D^k = \prod_{x=1}^{K} IGNB(\mu_x | r_x) \tag{7}$$

Secondly, we implemented our improved KNN as supplementary classifier to accommodate all potential neighbors not within first classifier function $f(\mu_r \leq r_j)$ based on Euclidean Distance defined by Eq. (8):

$$E^K = \frac{1}{K} \sum_{x=1}^{k} DI(\mu_x, r_x) \tag{8}$$

Where DI is a computed Euclidean distance between all mean μ_x averages and real-time data points r_x within integral conditional $f(\mu_x > r_x)$ function. All computed smallest distances are accumulated into voting list E^K using Eq. (8) and (9):

$$DI(\mu > r_i) = \sqrt{\sum_{x=1}^{k} \int_{r_x}^{\mu_x} (\mu_x - r_x)^2} \tag{9}$$

Lastly voting list D^K and E^K of IGNB and KNN are joined into union of convenience $D^K \cup E^K$ as joint majority voting and thus increases classification features as potential neighbors within K neighborhood. The joint majority vote probability is based on existing principle of KNN, where D^K and E^K are called Joint Voting (JV) as our LHMV defined by Eq. (10):

$$JV = \frac{argmax}{v} \sum_{(D_k \cup E_k) \in V_K} \frac{(D_k \cup D_k)}{K},\tag{10}$$

Where K is a number of potential neighborhood majority in D_k and E_k voting lists, corresponding to predicted class label in vote list V_K for each class $C = \{c_1, c_2, ..., c_m\}$ in $reducedTrainingTree^{R \times N}$. Equation (10) determines a majority class by comparing D_k and E_k for the most appearing class category in both majority votes lists. Where D_k is maximum probability of IGNB ranked in descending order due to the maximum probability Gaussian Naïve Bayes algorithm, whereas a vector E_k of KNN is sorted in ascending order, therefore top K neighbours are matched, a class category that appears the most in both sorted vectors is taken as majority class and is assigned to new instance as class label.

4   Experimentation

Our experiments aim at answering the question "Will the integration of two simpler algorithms KNN and Naïve Bayes improves the accuracy and precision of human activities using compressed personalized dataset?". We simulated our Split-Then-Vote LHMV in R programming language and compare it with R existing algorithms (C4.5, Boosted Tree, Naïve Bayes, SVM, and Random Forest) [25–27]. As input, we partitioned our collected top-k Personalized Dataset of 2860 rows into 0.7:0.3 ratio as 70% training and 30% test datasets respectively. Afterward, the partitioned training dataset is further normalized and transformed 70% training dataset to 60 compressed groups of best mean averages per human activity similar to [7, 22]. Consequently, we used our transformed and reduced class-tree as input to train our LHMV algorithm.

The remaining 0.3 dataset is used for testing. We selected the neighborhood K to 1, 3 and 5 as majority voting [22, 28]. We repeated the experiments 5 times to determine the consistence of each run. The results are given in confusion matrix, which include True Positive (TP), False Positive (FP), False Negatives (FN), Precision and Accuracy. We also compared our results with R existing algorithms (C4.5, Boosted Tree, Naïve Bayes, SVM, and Random Forest) using default settings [25, 26, 28]. The results of our implemented LHMV algorithm using different K (1, 3 and 5) neighbors are presented in confusion Table 2, Table 3 and Table 4 respectively.

The results presented in Table 2, Table 3 and Table 4 reveal consistent overlap of similar postural human activities with highest accuracy and precision irrespective of the

Table 2. LHMV Confusion matrix with K nearest equal to 3.

	Walking slowly	Brisk walking	Jogging	Laying	Normal walking pace	Rope jumping	Running	Sitting	Standing	Walking downstairs	Walking upstairs	Total	TP	TN	FP	FN	Accuracy	Precision
Walking slowly	11	3	0	0	13	0	1	0	0	0	8	36	11	24	1	0	97	92
Brisk walking	4	20	7	0	7	0	6	0	0	10	6	60	20	27	13	0	78	61
Jogging	0	5	21	0	0	4	16	8	0	3	2	59	21	16	22	0	63	49
Laying	0	0	0	9	1	0	0	0	48	0	2	60	9	48	3	0	95	75
Normal walking pace	8	6	1	0	12	0	0	0	0	24	7	58	12	45	1	0	98	92
Rope jumping	1	7	4	0	0	39	8	0	0	1	0	60	39	0	21	0	65	65
Running	0	8	13	0	1	2	34	0	0	2	0	60	34	0	1	0	57	97
Sitting	5	0	3	0	3	0	0	16	4	29	0	60	16	0	44	0	27	27
Standing	2	0	0	24	2	0	0	10	20	1	1	60	20	34	6	0	90	77
Walking downstairs	9	6	1	0	10	1	0	0	0	23	7	57	23	32	2	0	96	92
Walking upstairs	6	5	2	0	19	0	0	0	0	10	12	54	12	40	2	0	96	86

Table 3. LHMV Confusion matrix with K nearest equal to 3

	Walking slowly	Brisk walking	Jogging	Laying	Normal walking pace	Rope jumping	Running	Sitting	Standing	Walking downstairs	Walking upstairs	Total	TP	TN	FP	FN	Accuracy	Precision
Walking slowly	15	3	0	0	8	0	1	0	0	0	6	33	15	17	1	0	97	94
Brisk walking	4	20	6	0	5	1	7	0	0	11	6	60	20	26	14	0	77	59
Jogging	0	3	22	0	0	4	17	8	0	4	1	59	22	17	20	0	66	52
Laying	0	0	0	9	1	0	0	0	48	0	2	60	9	48	3	0	95	75
Normal walking pace	9	5	1	0	13	0	0	0	0	25	5	58	13	44	1	0	98	93
Rope jumping	0	2	4	0	0	51	2	0	0	1	0	60	51	0	9	0	85	85
Running	0	2	11	0	0	2	43	0	0	2	0	60	43	0	1	0	72	98
Sitting	2	0	3	0	2	0	0	41	1	11	0	60	41	0	19	0	68	68
Standing	2	0	0	7	0	0	0	10	39	1	1	60	39	17	4	0	93	91
Walking downstairs	6	7	2	0	10	1	0	1	0	29	3	59	29	26	4	0	93	88
Walking upstairs	6	5	1	0	17	1	0	0	0	15	10	55	10	43	2	0	96	83

Table 4. LHMV Confusion matrix with K nearest equal to 5

	Walking slowly	Brisk walking	Jogging	Laying	Normal walking pace	Rope jumping	Running	Sitting	Standing	Walking downstairs	Walking upstairs	Total	TP	TN	FP	FN	Accuracy	Precision
Walking slowly	14	2	0	0	13	0	1	0	0	19	6	55	14	40	1	0	98	93
Brisk walking	3	25	5	0	4	0	6	0	0	13	4	60	25	24	11	0	82	69
Jogging	0	3	20	0	0	4	19	8	0	4	1	59	20	19	20	0	66	50
Laying	0	0	0	12	1	0	0	0	45	0	2	60	12	45	3	0	95	80
Normal walking pace	6	6	2	0	11	0	0	0	0	29	4	58	11	45	2	0	97	85
Rope jumping	0	3	4	0	0	50	2	0	0	1	0	60	50	0	10	0	83	83
Running	0	1	12	0	0	2	44	0	3	1	0	60	44	0	1	0	73	98
Sitting	1	0	3	0	0	0	0	42	3	11	0	60	42	0	18	0	70	70
Standing	2	0	0	3	0	0	0	10	44	1	0	60	44	13	3	0	95	94
Walking downstairs	3	6	1	0	13	1	0	1	0	31	3	59	31	25	3	0	95	91
Walking upstairs	5	4	1	0	21	1	0	0	0	13	10	55	10	43	2	0	96	83

value of *K* neighbors. There is a balanced accuracy and precision of 95% and 83% respectively across similar walking activities (walking slow, normal walking, and brisk walking and walking upstairs and downstairs). This accuracy is attributed to majority of TN than TP due to existing resemblance among walking activities owing to human legs strides and transitions which was captured using harmonic motion discussed in [21]. In all Table 2, Table 3 and Table 4 there is a constant accuracy of 66% in presence of overlapping similar human activities such as jogging and running activities; in comparison to higher accuracy bracket of 83% and 85%, and precision range of 83% and 85% for rope jumping activities. The results also indicate steady accuracy and precision of 95% on static human activities. However, the presented results showed and proved that our LHMV algorithm with small personalized dataset achieves higher classification accuracy and precision in presence of TN majority than TP on complex human activities. The results presented in Table 2, Table 3 and Table 4 are summarized and compared with R existing C4.5, Boosted Tree, Naïve Bayes, SVM, and Random Forest results presented in accuracy and precision in Fig. 3 and Fig. 4.

The comparison results show that our LHMV comes third after tree-oriented classifiers (Random Forest and C4.5) and above Boosted Tree in most complex and static human activities with accuracy above 80% and 90%. Hence, we can confidently

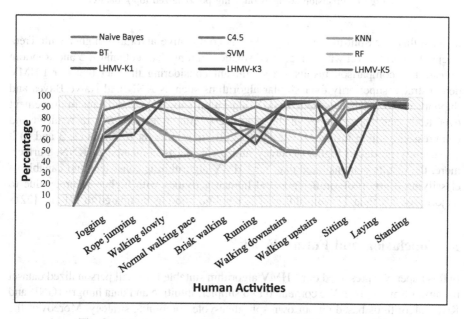

Fig. 3. Accuracy comparison using personalized top-k dataset.

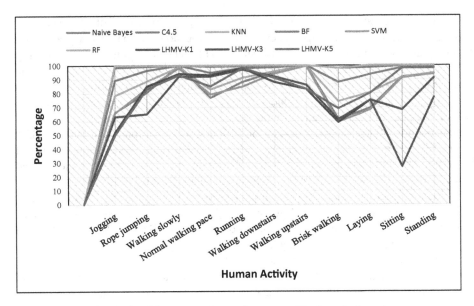

Fig. 4. Precision comparison using personalized top-k dataset.

indicate that our Split-then-vote algorithm is competitive and ranks higher with Tree-oriented algorithm yet with compressed smaller training dataset than C4.5 and Random Forest. The comparison results are significant considering the fact that our LHMV demonstrated superiority over similar algorithms such as KNN and Naive Bayes and Support Vector Machines. Our LHMV algorithm showed a significant improvement over KNN and Naïve Bayes in the presence of minor features due to reduced and compressed training instances; yet again in all three different K values (1, 3 and 5) it consistently produced higher accuracy and precision as compared to KNN. Furthermore, the results demonstrated that our LHMV algorithm is consistent and capable of classifying a group of similar postural human activities with higher accuracy due to majority of TN than TP with different K neighborhood as compared to [7] and [22].

5   Conclusion and Future Work

In this paper, we presented our LHMV algorithm suitable for small personalized dataset meant for Smartphone. We combined two simpler, intuitive and data hungry (GNB and KNN) algorithms based on our own split-then-vote combining strategy. Moreover, the training dataset is compressed to select best features similar to C4.5 algorithm based on best mean average of input predicators. The compressed dataset reduces the training time of lazy classifier, yet improves classification accuracy and precision with higher TN than TP, than its predecessor KNN and Naïve Bayes. We can conclude that our LHMV as union of convenience of KNN and Naïve Bayes improved classification accuracy and precision of data hungry algorithms using smallest personalized dataset. In future we intend to implement and evaluated using different datasets.

References

1. Anguita, D, Ghio, A., Oneto, L., Parra, X., Reyes-Ortiz, J.L.: A public domain dataset for human activity recognition using smartphones. In: ESANN, pp. 437–442 (2013)
2. Zhang, M., Sawchuk, A.A.: USC-HAD: a daily activity dataset for ubiquitous activity recognition using wearable sensors. In: Proceedings of the 2012 ACM Conference on Ubiquitous Computing, 5 September, pp. 1036–1043. ACM (2012)
3. Parkka, J., Ermes, M., Korpipaa, P., Mantyjarvi, J., Peltola, J., Korhonen, I.: Activity classification using realistic data from wearable sensors. IEEE Trans. Inf Technol. Biomed. 10(1), 119–128 (2006)
4. Reiss, A., Stricker, D.: Introducing a new benchmarked dataset for activity monitoring. In: 2012 16th International Symposium on Wearable Computers (ISWC), June 18, pp. 108–109. IEEE (2012)
5. Su, X., Tong, H., Ji, P.: Activity recognition with smartphone sensors. Tsinghua Sci. Technol. 19(3), 235–249 (2014)
6. Mannini, A., Intille, S.S., Rosenberger, M., Sabatini, A.M., Haskell, W.: Activity recognition using a single accelerometer placed at the wrist or ankle. Med. Sci. Sports Exerc. 45(11), 2193 (2013)
7. Kaghyan, S., Sarukhanyan, H.: Activity recognition using K-nearest neighbor algorithm on smartphone with tri-axial accelerometer. Int. J. Inform. Models Anal. (IJIMA) 1, 146–156 (2012)
8. Breiman, L.: Random forests. Mach. Learn. 45(1), 5–32 (2001)
9. Kwapisz, J.R., Weiss, G.M., Moore, S.A.: Activity recognition using cell phone accelerometers. ACM SIGKDD Explor. Newslett. 12(2), 74–82 (2011)
10. Catal, C., Tufekci, S., Pirmit, E., Kocabag, G.: On the use of ensemble of classifiers for accelerometer-based activity recognition. Appl. Soft Comput. 31(37), 1018–1022 (2015)
11. Daghistani, T., Alshammari, R.: Improving accelerometer-based activity recognition by using ensemble of classifiers. Int. J. Adv. Comput. Sci. Appl. 7(5), 128–133 (2016)
12. Gupta, S., Kumar, A.: Human activity recognition through smartphone's tri-axial accelerometer using time domain wave analysis and machine learning. Int. J. Comput. Appl. 127(18), 22–26 (2015)
13. Gandhi, I., Pandey, M.: Hybrid ensemble of classifiers using voting. In: 2015 International Conference on Green Computing and Internet of Things (ICGCIoT), pp. 399–404. IEEE, October 2015
14. Chan, P.K., Stolfo, S.J.: Experiments on multistrategy learning by meta-learning. In: Proceedings of the Second International Conference on Information and Knowledge Management, pp. 314–323, December 1993
15. Reiss, A., Hendeby, G., Stricker, D.: A competitive approach for human activity recognition on smartphones. In: European Symposium on Artificial Neural Networks, Computational Intelligence and Machine Learning, ESANN 2013, Bruges, Belgium, pp. 455–460, 24–26 April 2013. ESANN (2013)
16. Reiss, A.: Personalized mobile physical activity monitoring for everyday life. PHD thesis in Computer Science, Technical University of Kaiserslautern (2014)
17. Bao, L., Intille, S.: Activity recognition from user-annotated acceleration data. Pervasive Comput. 1–7 (2004)
18. Ravi, N., Dandekar, N., Mysore, P., Littman, M.L.: Activity recognition from accelerometer data. In: AAAI 2005, vol. 5, no. 2005, pp. 1541–1546, 9 July 2005
19. Lockhart, J.W., Weiss, G.M.: Limitations with activity recognition methodology & data sets. In: Proceedings of the 2014 ACM International Joint Conference on Pervasive and

Ubiquitous Computing: Adjunct Publication, 13 September 2014, pp. 747–756. ACM (2014)

20. De Stefano, C., Fontanella, F., Di Freca, A.S.: A novel Naive Bayes voting strategy for combining classifiers. In: 2012 International Conference on Frontiers in Handwriting Recognition, pp. 467–472. IEEE, September 2012

21. Gadebe, M.L., Kogeda, O.P., Ojo, S.O.: Personalized real time human activity recognition. In: 2018 5th International Conference on Soft Computing & Machine Intelligence (ISCMI), pp. 147–154. IEEE, November 2018

22. Kose, M., Incel, O.D., Ersoy, C.: Online human activity recognition on smart phones. In: Workshop on Mobile Sensing: From Smartphones and Wearables to Big Data, 16 April 2012, vol. 16, no. 2012, pp. 11–15 (2012)

23. Ruggieri, S.: Efficient C4. 5 [classification algorithm]. IEEE Trans. Knowl. Data Eng. **14**(2), 438–444 (2002)

24. Arlot, S., Celisse, A.: A survey of cross-validation procedures for model selection. Stat. Surv. **4**, 40–79 (2010)

25. Slim, S.O., Atia, A., Elfattah, M.M., Mostafa, M.S.M.: Survey on human activity recognition based on acceleration data. Int. J. Adv. Comput. Sci. Appl. (IJACSA) **10**(3), 84–98 (2019)

26. Kuhn, M.: Building predictive models in R using the caret package. J. Stat. Softw. **28**(5), 1–26 (2008)

27. Kuhkan, M.: A method to improve the accuracy of k-nearest neighbor algorithm. Int. J. Comput. Eng. Inf. Technol. **8**(6), 90 (2016)

28. Gadebe, M.L., Kogeda, O.P., Ojo, S.O.: Smartphone Naïve Bayes human activity recognition using personalized datasets. J. Adv. Comput. Intell. Inform. **24**(5), 685–702 (2020)

Systems and Applications

Twitter Emotion Analysis for Brand Comparison Using Naive Bayes Classifier

Siva Shanmugam[1]([⊠])[iD] and Isha Padmanaban[2][iD]

[1] Loyola Institute of Business Administration, Mahalingapuram, Nungambakkam,
Chennai 600034, India
sivashanmugam008@gmail.com
[2] College of Engineering, Anna University, Guindy, Chennai 600025, India

Abstract. Every brand created by the company plays a vital role in its recognition, differentiation and sustaining loyal customer base. These brands are analysed at different stages of their life cycle to understand their personality, sentiments and emotions that are perceived and expressed by their customers, thereby helping the companies to achieve a positive brand image. Real time experience data about brands are available in abundance in the form of short texts on Twitter. In this paper, based on Plutchik's wheel of eight primary emotions-joy, sadness, trust, fear, surprise, disgust, anger and anticipation, we have proposed a brand comparison tool which carries out emotion analysis on the tweets with the help of Synonym based Naive Bayes retry approach, thus quantifying emotions from tweets about the brands. The tool has achieved an overall accuracy of about 82.5%. This brand comparison tool helps companies to understand their strengths and shortcomings among their competitors. The feedback from this tool can be used to realign the marketing strategies and goals of the companies.

Keywords: Plutchik's emotion theory · Twitter · Naive Bayes classifier

1 Introduction

There is an enormous amount of data available in Social Media about various products, services, brands and their companies. From unboxing a product to reviewing its performance, registering complaints by directly tagging the specific company profiles, and resolving customer issues are some of the activities happening in Social media like Twitter, Facebook, and Instagram. Thus they have become a place for customers to express their satisfaction or dissatisfaction and for companies to promote their products, engage customers and maintain brand image. These opinions hugely influence the company's brand image, decision making of other potential customers and loyalty of existing customers who own those products.

K. K. Patel et al. (Eds.): icSoftComp 2020, CCIS 1374, pp. 199–211, 2021.
https://doi.org/10.1007/978-981-16-0708-0_17

Consumers provide their opinions about products and services in the form of videos, photos, or texts. Among them, textual data provide a wider scope to easily analyse their emotions and sentiments. Twitter has evolved as a giant information sharing platform over the years. It provides specific features of retrieving the tweets with keyword or hashtag for a specific period of time. As per Brand-Watch report in January 2020, Twitter has around 330 Million monthly active users, 145 Million daily active users contributing to 6,000 tweets every second, accounting to 500 million tweets every day.

Artificial Intelligence is gaining profound importance in Brand Management. Naive Bayes, Maximum Entropy and Support Vector Machines are some of the Machine Learning approaches used for classification. Of this, Naive Bayes classifier proved to be one of the most accurate text classification techniques for sentiment and emotion analysis. In addition, we are implementing a Synonym based Naive Bayes retry approach in our tool to minimise the impact of data scarcity and assumption of a generic probability value for classifying tweets. Maintaining the brand image is significant for any company to survive in this competitive world. Positive brand image has a direct correlation to the profitability of the company [5]. Hence, companies are investing in AI based technologies for understanding the current positioning of their brands.

Till now, sentiment analysis is given prime importance in classifying customer views. Sentiment analysis only categorises the opinions as positive, neutral and negative feedback. The current scenario demands in-depth understanding about customers perceptions about the brand. This is possible through classifying their feelings with the help of emotion analysis. This, in turn, helps to get in line with the impulse and motives of the end users towards the brand. Hence we attempt to create a brand comparison tool that uses the above to identify the gap between a company's expectations of the brand and how it is recognised by the consumers. This tool assists the brand managers and marketers to devise a strategic plan for brand management.

The paper is organized as follows: Sect. 2 gives a brief explanation of related work in the research area of sentiment and emotion analysis. Section 3 explains the proposed approach to pre-process tweet data for effective categorization and the enhanced implementation of a supervised classifier for emotion analysis. Section 4 gives a brief overview of the performance evaluation metrics carried out for the tool and the inferences derived from the outcomes of the tool. Section 5 concludes with discussing the potential works that can be carried out in the future as an extension of this research work.

2   Related Works

In a technology driven world, customers' opinions posted in digital format have gained much importance like word of mouth. [1] speaks about the huge value of Twitter and other social media to gauge public perception. Brand comparison can be done at various levels such as equity [9], personality [11], emotion [10], and sentiment [13]. It is found that most of the research has been carried out

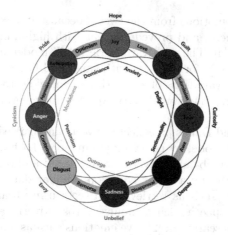

Fig. 1. Plutchik's wheel of eight primary emotions and twenty four secondary feelings

with Sentiment analysis. In [1], a tool called Geo-location specific Public Perception Visualizer was designed where tweets were mined, manually annotated, and classified into positive, negative or neutral sentiments using the Maximum Entropy model. [13] focuses on understanding the opinions of people from Twitter to compare top colleges in India using Sentiment Analysis. These tweets of various colleges are widely classified into positive, negative ad neutral opinions and are plotted in a graph. This paper focuses on effective data cleaning processes including removal of URLs and elimination of duplicate tweets to avoid spam reviews which we have also incorporated in our work.

Emotions are "preconscious social expressions of feelings and affect influenced by culture" [7]. Sentiments are explained as "partly social constructs of emotions that develop over time and are enduring". Opinions and Emotions together form information which are the result of personal interpretation. Since feelings are expressed in majority as text in Social Media impulsively at a raw emotional level than sentimental level, analyzing the emotions provides vital outcomes. According to [3], data was extracted using Twitter API and processed with Stanford NLP to rate the tweets using sentistrength method. At last each tweet was classified under five categories based on the overall score of the tweet such as worst, bad, neutral, decent and wonderful. The Sentistrength method focuses on categorising an emotion using a range of values based on its intensity. This research was aimed at finding the sentiment of a product, iphone6. While this paper concentrated on analyzing a specific brand, our project analyzes various emotions of brands.

Text emotion classification is carried out majorly by Naive Bayes, Maximum Entropy and Support Vector Machine (SVM) under Supervised Learning techniques. Naive Bayes and SVM are very accurate in sentiment analysis [8]. However, the performance and rate of the Naive Bayes model is higher and more accurate than the Maximum Entropy model, K-nearest neighbor classifier, Decision Tree classifier in text classification [14]. Our tool uses the Naive Bayes method to compute emotions from the tweets because it is comparatively easier and faster to implement, and proved efficient with high-dimensional data such as text classification [4]. The multivariate Bernoulli model and the multinomial model which are suitable for datasets with small and large vocabularies respectively are some of the variations of Naive Bayes. Since our tool analyzes a brand which is described using huge vocabulary, we are implementing a Synonym based Naive Bayes model.

Kumar, Dogra, and Dabas [2] collected tweets and carried out emotion analysis using a heuristic model by receiving a name or a hashtag as an input from the user. Adjectives, verbs and adverbs were filtered and overall score for each emotion was calculated by a linear equation. Similar data collection and pre-processing techniques such as retrieval of tweets using brand name, selection of weighted parts of speech such as nouns, verbs, adverbs and adjectives were implemented in our research. In [2], five emotions such as happiness, anger, sadness, fear and disgust were evaluated. The Plutchik wheel [6] of emotions is used as a primary base for emotional categorisation from text, hence it has a great impact on the affective computing field. Our project focuses on examining tweets based on Plutchik's eight primary emotions such as joy, sadness, trust, fear, surprise, disgust, anger and anticipation resulting in twenty four combinations of feelings from the tweet data. This wider examination of various emotions results in better realization of the consumers' opinions about the brands.

The outcome of emotion analysis of tweets acts as a measurement for brand comparison and it can be used in Customer Relationship Management as well. These metrics play a vital role in impacting customer awareness, maintaining customer engagement and retention which has a direct influence on profitability [5]. The presence of such tools provide a competitive advantage for businesses.

3   Our Approach

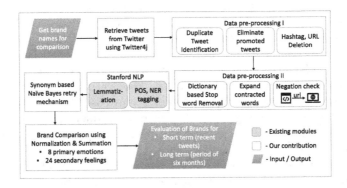

Fig. 2. Flow chart of Twitter Emotion Analysis based on Plutchik's wheel of emotions for Brand Comparison using Synonym based Naive Bayes retry mechanism

3.1 Training a Classification Model

A learning dataset of nearly 4000 tweets were retrieved and preprocessed widely as explained in Sect. 3.3. They are manually categorized into the following emotions - joy, sadness, disgust, anger, fear, surprise, anticipation and trust for training our multi-class classification model as shown in Table 1. The model was trained on 3200 tweets and tested on 800 tweets, yielding a successful classification of around 660 tweets across multiple emotions. The overall accuracy of the model was found to be 82.5%.

Table 1. Sample training dataset for root words across eight primary emotions

Words	Joy	Sadness	Anger	Disgust	Surprise	Fear	Anticipation	Trust
Able	0.004504	0.004219	0.000176	0.0017	0.00183	0.00186	0.001096	0.000987
Abuse	0.01595	0.005241	0.037363	0.040532	0.0177	0.02659	0.0961593	0.0852
Academy	0.092857	0.004111	0.007143	0.027143	0.021429	0.035714	0.08164604	0.072746
Accept	0.054812	0.022797	0.028872	0.028271	0.006767	0.038346	0.01360092	0.014701
Account	0.089286	0.057571	0.017857	0.037857	0.017857	0.017857	0.07807461	0.079175
Accuracy	0.065714	0.039714	0.035714	0.005571	0.010714	0.035714	0.0445013	0.045603
Achieve	0.012212	0.010912	0.005069	0.037857	0.004147	0.005069	0.11090871	0.112009

3.2 Data Collection

The brands which need to be compared extensively based on emotions are obtained as input from the user as shown in Fig. 3. Those brand names are globally searched on Twitter. Figure 4 displays some of the Tweets of the brands in English language which are retrieved with the help of Twitter4j. Twitter4j is an open source Java library used for accessing the Twitter API after getting OAuth authorization which includes access tokens and consumer keys. Once this authorization is obtained, the Twitter developer account can be accessed without entering credentials like user id or password. Minimum of thousand recent tweets for each brand is fetched by our tool. Retweets are excluded in our search explicitly to avoid duplicate reviews.

3.3 Data Pre-processing

In this step, data is filtered in the following sequences. Duplicate tweets are identified by string comparison. Repeated tweets are ignored for further processing to enhance the output of the tool. Promoted tweets are identified and removed based on their Twitter account names containing the brand name. The retrieved tweets are then filtered to remove hashtag symbols, urls, and special characters using pattern matching with regular expressions. Contracted words are expanded for better performance. For example - words like "can't", "'re" are replaced as "can not", "are" respectively. Stop words from the collected tweets whose information is trivial for emotion analysis are eliminated by comparing them with the pre-constructed dictionary of existing stop words. Then, negative phrases are replaced

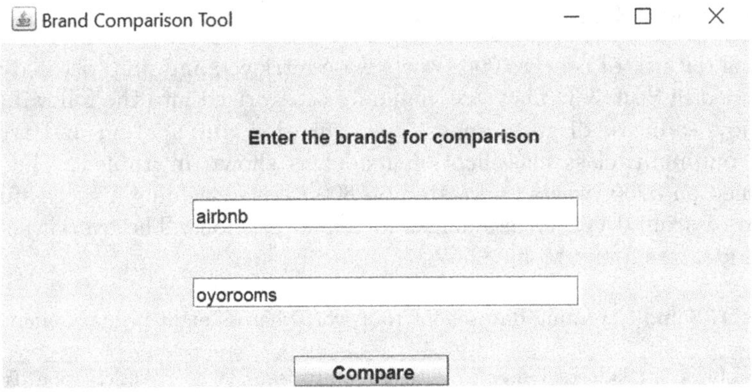

Fig. 3. Get brand names as input for comprehensive brand comparison

with a single negative word for example - "not happy" is replaced as "sad" which is almost equal in emotion. This is achieved by identifying the appropriate word following the negative identifier ("not") till the next following punctuation, and fetching the antonym of the word from the online thesaurus finder website by establishing a url connection to the site. The antonym is retrieved by crawling and parsing the website. These filtering steps help in better classification of data based on emotion and improve the accuracy of the tool.

Original Tweet: @73colleens said: I went on airbnb last night and the price of the place I wanted to go has doubled, I am not convinced and can't stay there now because there's so much uncertainty around how the second lap of this pandemic is going to unfold!!! #covid19 #priced http://www.airbnb.com/rooms

After checking for duplicate/promoted tweets & removing URL, hashtags, punctuations, expansion of contracted words: I went on airbnb last night and the price of the place I wanted to go has doubled I am not convinced and can not stay there now because there is so much uncertainty around how the second lap of this pandemic is going to unfold covid19 priced

After removing stop words and processing negative phrases: went airbnb last night price place wanted go doubled unconvinced leave now much uncertainty second lap pandemic going unfold covid19 priced

Fig. 4. Output of a pre-processed tweet from an original tweet

3.4   Stanford NLP

Figure 5 displays how the filtered tweets are then processed by Stanford CoreNLP which is comparatively faster and more accurate than other similar NLP tools. As an output of this process, every word of the filtered tweets undergoes lemmatization thereby giving a root form of the word tagged with its appropriate Part-Of-Speech (POS) and Named Entity Recognition(NER) labels. This is done so as to eliminate the words containing insignificant information like location, duration, any other organization name, and other miscellaneous words. Then, we get the most important forms of words like nouns, verbs, adjectives, and adverbs for tweet emotion analysis. As a result of this process, unnecessary words are eliminated and the effectiveness of this tool is improved to get better results. The brand and its reviews in the form of a series of root words are inserted in a multimap with the brand name as a key for further processing.

```
Print: word:  [good] pos: [JJ] ne: [O]
Print: word:  [customer] pos: [NN] ne: [O]
Print: word:  [service] pos: [NN] ne: [O]
Print: word:  [cost] pos: [NNS] ne: [O]
Print: word:  [time] pos: [NN] ne: [O]
Print: word:  [money] pos: [NN] ne: [O]
```

Fig. 5. Stanford CoreNLP output with root words and their corresponding POS and NER tags

3.5   Enhanced Implementation of Naive Bayes

In this step, based on Plutchik's wheel of emotions as referenced in Fig. 1, a list of primary emotions - joy, sadness, disgust, anger, fear, surprise, anticipation, trust is chosen as a measure to analyze the brands. The probability of the emotion for each tweet is calculated for every brand using Naive Bayes approach. This approach follows a supervised classification technique that helps in predicting output by learning from training data. One of the limitations of Naive Bayes models is the possibility of data scarcity. When the word for which the probability to be calculated is unavailable in the training dataset, a likelihood value is generally assumed [4]. Sometimes, this assumption may not be efficient and may lead to incorrect classification. To address this scenario, an enhanced implementation of Naive Bayes approach like Synonym based Naive Bayes counter retry mechanism is proposed in our model. If the word for which the probability to be found out is not present in the training dataset, then instead of assuming a generic value, synonyms of the word are retrieved from an online thesaurus website and looked up for its probability value in the training dataset for every emotion. The use of counters to limit the number of synonyms for every absent word kept the execution time of the tool in check. For every word of the pre-processed tweet, a probability value across all emotions is calculated using conditional probability formula mentioned in Eq. 1,

$$P(A|B) = \frac{P(B|A)P(A)}{P(B)} \tag{1}$$

where A is each word of pre-processed tweet and B is the emotion. Each tweet of the brand is classified to an emotion that has the highest cumulative probability, compared to other emotions. This probability value is stored in a multi key map which has brand and emotion as a key and the probability of emotion as a value. Finally, the cumulative emotion values for each brand are normalised and represented graphically for visualisation and better understanding of the emotions exhibited by people towards the brand in the form of tweets.

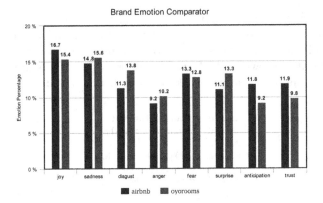

Fig. 6. Comparison of brands with recent customer review tweets across eight primary emotions

3.6   Brand Comparison

Once the tweets are analyzed and emotional value for both the brands are computed, the outputs are described in the form of Pie charts and Bar charts as shown in Fig. 6, 7, 10 and 11. The pie chart of the particular brand quantifies the emotional impact the brand has over its consumers that are expressed in the form of tweet data. The bar chart shows the comparison of various emotional responses of consumers between brands. Based on the eight primary emotions calculated for a brand, the corresponding twenty four secondary feelings have been derived according to Plutchik's wheel of emotions. This level of in-depth classification of emotions and feelings will help marketers in better understanding of the existing position of the brand in the minds of consumers. For example, optimism (feeling) is a secondary dyad which is obtained by the combination of primary emotions - anticipation and joy.

3.7   Extended Brand Comparison

Tweets of the brands for the past six months are also retrieved for in-depth analysis and understanding of the change in consumer emotions across time periods. These tweets are pre-processed and go through emotion analysis as discussed in the above steps. Figure 8 and 9 gives a sample output of the effect of brand resonance over a period of six months. This helps marketers to understand how the marketing campaigns and engagement programmes by the brands influence the consumers. Based on this analysis, they can understand whether the strategies undertaken by companies across the past months have created a satisfactory influence on customers or not.

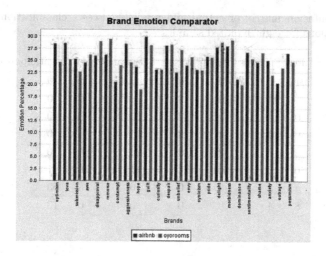

Fig. 7. Comparison of brands with recent customer review tweets across twenty four secondary feelings

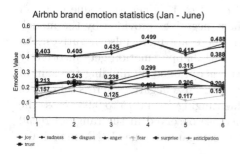

Fig. 8. Emotion Analysis of Airbnb with consumer reviews from Twitter for a period of six months

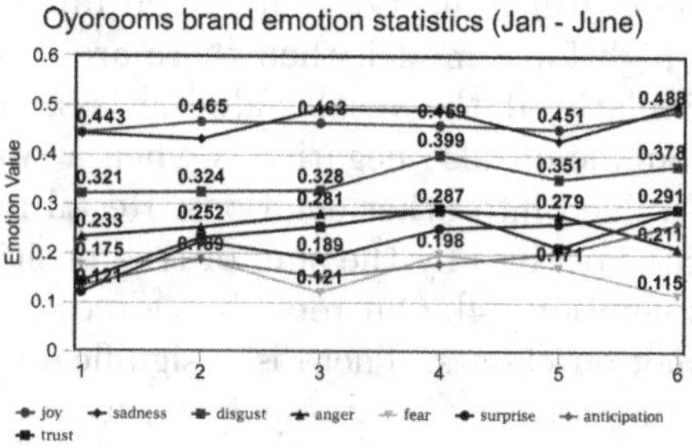

Fig. 9. Emotion Analysis of OYO Rooms with consumer reviews from Twitter for a period of six months

4   Experiments and Evaluations

4.1   Experiments

We collected around eight hundred tweet reviews expressing varied emotions and fed them to our tool for evaluation. We matched every tweet to their respective emotion using our brand comparison tool. Our dataset collected for performance evaluation has an equal number of tweet reviews in various emotions - joy, sad, angry, disgust, surprise, fear, anticipation and trust. After analyzing the output from our tool, we found the values of the various performance metrics such as recall, precision, F1 score and accuracy as displayed in Table 3. Firstly, we constructed a confusion matrix as shown in Table 2 which represents the actual and predicted classifications executed by our tool. Then, from that confusion matrix, the performance metrics were calculated using respective formulas.

Table 2. Confusion matrix of actual and predicted tweets classification into eight primary emotions for eight hundred samples

Emotions	Joy	Sadness	Anger	Disgust	Surprise	Fear	Anticipation	Trust
Joy	91	2	0	0	3	0	0	4
Sadness	4	93	0	3	0	0	0	0
Anger	0	4	81	12	0	0	0	3
Disgust	0	9	0	78	13	0	0	0
Surprise	2	0	2	0	83	8	0	5
Fear	0	0	0	6	11	76	7	0
Anticipation	4	0	0	0	0	8	83	5
Trust	8	4	0	0	0	0	13	75

4.2   Evaluations

Recall. Recall as a metric is used to calculate the completeness of a classifier model using the Eq. 2. Its value ranges from 0 to 1. When the value of recall is high for a model, then there are less false negatives provided by the model. Similarly, if the recall value is less, then there are more false negatives. An example of false negative is when a tweet with happy emotion gets incorrectly classified into other emotions. Recall metric is obtained by dividing the sum of true positives by the sum of true positives and false negatives across all classes of emotions [4]. Our tool gives a recall value ranging from 0.75 to 0.93 across the emotion classes. There is a significant increase observed in the range of recall values for various emotions in our model as compared to the GRNN model [6].

$$recall = \frac{\sum_{l=1}^{L} TP_l}{\sum_{l=1}^{L} TP_l + FN_l} \qquad (2)$$

Precision. Precision metric computes the exactness of a classifier model. With higher precision value, the model is said to have less false positives, whereas with lower value, there are more false positives as outcome. Precision is calculated by dividing the sum of true positives by the sum of true positives and false positives across all classes of emotions [4] as shown in Eq. 3. We have received a precision value ranging from 0.75 to 0.98 for our multi-class model.

$$precision = \frac{\sum_{l=1}^{L} TP_l}{\sum_{l=1}^{L} TP_l + FP_l} \qquad (3)$$

F1-Score. F1-Score measures the accuracy of a model with the combined results of Precision and Recall to give an harmonic mean value as result with the help of Eq. 4. This metric provides more insight towards how our tool is performing accurately. The F1 score for all emotion classes computed from our tool ranges from 0.78 to 0.89.

$$F1 - Score = \frac{\sum\limits_{l=1}^{L} 2TP_l}{\sum\limits_{l=1}^{L} 2TP_l + FP_l + FN_l} \tag{4}$$

Accuracy. Accuracy is attributed to the number of correct predictions achieved by the tool. It is calculated by dividing the number of correct predictions with the total number of predictions as shown in Eq. 5. The overall accuracy of our model is reported as 82.5% whereas accuracy of individual classes of emotions vary from 94.5% to 96.38%. This proves that our tool is performing as good as the other existing classifier tools [6, 12].

$$accuracy = \frac{TP + TN}{TP + FP + FN + TN} \tag{5}$$

Table 3. Output of performance evaluation metrics for our Brand Comparison tool

Emotions	n(truth)	n(classified)	Accuracy	Precision	Recall	F1 Score
Joy	100	109	93.63%	0.83	0.91	0.87
Sadness	100	112	96.75%	0.83	0.93	0.88
Anger	100	83	97.38%	0.98	0.81	0.89
Disgust	100	99	94.63%	0.79	0.78	0.78
Surprise	100	110	94.5%	0.75	0.83	0.79
Fear	100	92	95%	0.83	0.76	0.79
Anticipation	100	103	95.28%	0.81	0.83	0.82
Trust	100	92	94.75%	0.82	0.75	0.78

4.3   Findings

We chose the hospitality industry for brand comparison wherein the top brands like OYO Rooms and Airbnb are chosen. For each brand, 2000 recent tweet reviews are extracted and processed with the brand comparator. From the output it is inferred that OYO Rooms has sadness as the top emotion with 15.6% among its customers who expressed their views on twitter. Similarly, Airbnb has joy as the top emotion with 16.7%. Two of the extreme primary emotions- joy and sadness are obtained as output in this scenario. With respect to feelings, guilt which is a combination of joy and fear is the highest feeling received for Airbnb. Remorse is the most incurred feeling for OYO Rooms which is a combination of sadness and disgust. Extended brand comparison is carried out for a period of six months. It can be deduced from Fig. 8 and 9 that the top two emotions - joy and sadness remain the same for Airbnb and OYO Rooms, wherein we could see a direct relationship between the two emotions in Airbnb but there is a huge fluctuation observed in the above two emotions for OYO Rooms.

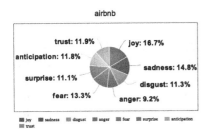

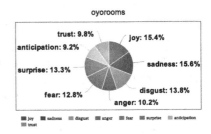

Fig. 10. Emotion Analysis of twitter reviews for Airbnb

Fig. 11. Emotion Analysis of twitter reviews for OYO Rooms

5   Conclusion and Future Scope

5.1   Conclusion

We have devised a brand comparison tool based on Plutchik's wheel of eight primary emotions and twenty four secondary feelings to capture the impact of marketing campaigns, and advertisements of brands among its consumers. Further, an enhanced implementation in the form of Synonym based Naive Bayes Machine Learning approach along with detailed data pre-processing techniques is used in this tool that significantly increased the accuracy of the classifier model. Based on the outcome of this tool, reaction from customers towards specific advertisements, campaigns and engagement programmes can be estimated. In addition to the metrics designed to measure physical engagement parameters like turnout ratio, these types of tools measure engagement at emotional level. From the feedback obtained from the tool, a new way of communication can be created to align the target customer's emotions with the company's vision.

5.2   Future Scope

This module can be attached to existing sentiment analysis tools to gain better insights at emotional level. A multi brand comparison tool can be developed as an extension of this project with an approach that has improved accuracy.

In addition to the tweet as an input, demographic data such as age, gender and location of the consumers will result in better analysis and visualisation of customer segments on the basis of their expressed emotions. We have included customer responses in English language only. There is an opportunity to use regional languages as well thereby understanding the emotions of customers better.

References

1. Aggarwal, A., Singh, A.K.: Geo-localized public perception visualization using GLOPP for social media. In: 8th IEEE Annual Information Technology, Electronics and Mobile Communication Conference (IEMCON), pp. 439–445 (2017)
2. Kumar, A., Dogra, P., Dabas, V.: Emotion analysis of Twitter using opinion mining. In: 2015 8th International Conference on Contemporary Computing (IC3), pp. 285–290 (2015)
3. Geetha, R., Rekha, P., Karthika, S.: Twitter opinion mining and boosting using sentiment analysis. In: International Conference on Computer, Communication, and Signal Processing (ICCCSP), pp. 1–4 (2018)
4. Kowsari, K., Jafari Meimandi, K., Heidarysafa, M., Mendu, S., Barnes, L., Brown, D.: Text classification algorithms: a survey. Information 10(4), 150 (2019)
5. Thomas, H., Sondoh Jr, S., Mojolou, D., Tanakinjal, G.: Customer relationship management (CRM) as a predictor to organization's profitability: empirical study in telecommunication company in Sabah (2018)
6. Abdul-Mageed, M., Ungar, L.: EmoNet: fine-grained emotion detection with gated recurrent neural networks. In: Proceedings of the 55th Annual Meeting of the Association for Computational Linguistics (vol. 1: Long papers), pp. 718–728 (2017)
7. Munezero, M., Montero, C.S., Sutinen, E., Pajunen, J.: Are they different? affect, feeling, emotion, sentiment, and opinion detection in text. IEEE Trans. Affect. Comput. 5(2), 101–111 (2014)
8. Yu, B.: An evaluation of text classification methods for literary study. Literary Linguist. Comput. 23(3), 327–343 (2008)
9. Stocchi, L., Fuller, R.: A comparison of brand equity strength across consumer segments and markets. J. Prod. Brand Manag. (2017)
10. Becheur, I., Bayarassou, O., Ghrib, H.: Beyond brand personality: building consumer–brand emotional relationship. Glob. Bus. Rev. 18, S128–S144 (2017)
11. Srivastava, K., Sharma, N.K.: Consumer perception of brand personality: an empirical evidence from India. Glob. Bus. Rev. 17(2), 375–388 (2016)
12. Le, B., Nguyen, H.: Twitter sentiment analysis using machine learning techniques. In: Le Thi, H.A., Nguyen, N.T., Do, T.V. (eds.) Advanced Computational Methods for Knowledge Engineering. AISC, vol. 358, pp. 279–289. Springer, Cham (2015). https://doi.org/10.1007/978-3-319-17996-4_25
13. Mamgain, N., Mehta, E., Mittal, A., Bhatt G.: Sentiment analysis of top colleges in India using Twitter data. In International Conference on Computational Techniques in Information and Communication Technologies (ICCTICT), pp. 525–530 (2016)
14. Wang, Y., Fu, W., Sui, A., Ding, Y.: Comparison of four text classifiers on movie reviews. In 3rd International Conference on Applied Computing and Information Technology/2nd International Conference on Computational Science and Intelligence, pp. 495–498 (2015)

A Smart Card Based Lightweight Multi Server Encryption Scheme

Pranav Vyas$^{(\boxtimes)}$ (iD)

Smt. Chandaben Mohanbhai Patel Institute of Computer Applications,
Charotar University of Science and Technology, Changa, India
Pranavvyas.mca@charusat.ac.in

Abstract. Due to advancements in connectivity and networking, the Internet has become integral part of our lives. Today, the Internet is used in all spheres of life from health and medicine to finances, education and entertainment. In order to get services from various Internet based platforms users need to prove their identity. A single smart card can be used to prove identity of users to avail services offered by various platforms. This benefit is also a vulnerability of the system. We propose a smart token based scheme for mutual authentication between the user and the service provider. We apply modified Diffie-Hellman protocol to keep the proposed solution lightweight for use over variety of devices.

Keywords: Multi server encryption · Smart card · Smart token

1 Introduction

These days the world is increasingly becoming app oriented. The apps are used for different purposes, starting from purchasing groceries and electronics to financial transactions to health and fitness. While using these apps, users share large amount of personal information that is sensitive in nature. The users receive many services over the internet in response of payment. Currently in India one of the preferred modes of payment for online transactions is by debit card. The usage of debit card for payment serves multiple purposes: 1) from the perspective of issuing authority it is also easier as giving a single card to customer reduces cost of production 2) it keeps your actual account number hidden 3) a single card can be used on multiple platforms for payment towards variety of services 4) since it is just a single card, managing its information is much easier for the user.

A debit card is associated with a single pin. This feature of a single pin makes it very suitable to use for multiple services. A user can use the debit card to pay towards a number of services provided by various platforms on the internet. However, if a user wishes to subscribe to new service, he/she must register with the new platform and provide identity details to the new platform. A debit card can effectively be used in instances such as online grocery shopping, reservation or ticket booking and payment for variety of utilities. A malicious user can keep a close watch on the activities of the user and gather information that can be used to reveal debit card details or such similar confidential information. This can result in misuse of cards or even identity theft. This scenario highlights a major drawback of using a single set of information (debit card details) on multiple platforms. This issue can be addressed with remote authentication.

© Springer Nature Singapore Pte Ltd. 2021
K. K. Patel et al. (Eds.): icSoftComp 2020, CCIS 1374, pp. 212–223, 2021.
https://doi.org/10.1007/978-981-16-0708-0_18

A remote authentication is possible in two ways: 1) single server authentication 2) multi-server authentication. The single server authentication was the first concept that was introduced in the field of remote authentication. This concept is widely researched with a large amount of literature available. It was Lamport who first proposed password based remote authentication method with use of cryptographic hash function [1]. After that, large number of researchers have contributed to the field of single server authentication by proposing novel and innovative solutions [2–10].

The multi-server authentication schemes were introduced due to drawback of single server authentication scheme of user having to remember large number of PINs or pass phrases. In their paper Lee et al. proposed the first multi-server authentication protocol [11]. According to this scheme, when the user wants to use the service for the first time, the user needs to register with the registration server. This is a onetime process. Once, the user is successfully authenticated by the registration server, all the services are made available to the user from the remote server. Multiple researchers have proposed a variety of solutions of the problem of multi-server authentication using different techniques [12–19].

Most protocols proposed by the researchers for multi-server authentication are having static ID. This technique is not secure as it is possible to capture the static ID by performing imitation type of attack. To prevent this drawback we need a dynamic ID based scheme. One such scheme is proposed by Biswas and Roy [18]. This scheme is able to thwart man-in-the-middle and imitation type of attacks. However, it falls short when it is exploited with spoofing, masquerade or insider types of attacks. Sahoo et al. [20] have proposed a multi-server authentication scheme, which is a smart card, based system with low computation cost making it extremely suitable for distributed network. However this scheme cannot thwart backward reply attacks. In order to solve problem of mutual authentication faced by the client and server, Chen, Hsiang and Shih [21] have proposed a scheme. However, their scheme is also vulnerable to reply type of attacks and insider attacks. According to Lee et al. [22], Chen's scheme is also vulnerable to masquerade and spoofing type of attacks as well. To thwart issues mentioned by them, Lee et al. proposed a new scheme. The scheme proposed by Lee et al. is vulnerable to password guessing type of attacks. Few notable dynamic ID based protocols are by [13, 23]. These protocols do not suffer from vulnerabilities like Lee et al.'s protocol on the other hand they have computational complexity resulting in higher load on the device.

In this paper, we present a new authentication scheme that thwarts attacks mentioned above. We add a novel service layer with support of smart tokens. The tokens are generated and allocated by the authentication server. The tokens are used to bridge the trust gap between the user and the web server. This results in reduction of initial key exchange stage and simplifying the overall communication process. We believe that it is an effective multi-server authentication scheme due to following reasons:

- Provides secure communication link over an insecure network with help of an authentication server.
- Stores passwords in card in hashed format increasing the security of passwords.
- Smart tokens aid in authentication in multi-server environment and bridge the trust gap.
- Resistance to spoofing attack in absence of verification table, resulting in light load on processor and communication.

- A modified Diffie-Hellman algorithm for key exchange and an innovative block cipher algorithm for encryption and decryption process. As a result, we achieve higher efficiency and security standards.

Our paper is organized in four sections. Section 1 introduces the topic of paper. Section 2 presents detailed background on various concepts referred to in the paper. In Sect. 3 we present our multi-server authentication scheme. In Sect. 4, we present our conclusion.

2   Background

In this section we present an in depth analysis of concepts used in designing of the authentication protocol. We begin our analysis with a study of different attacks possible in multi-server authentication setting and then move to analyze the concept of smart token service and modified Diffie-Hellman protocol.

2.1   Attacks on Multi-server Setting

Here we are studying threats from an attacker's point of view. Our study of threats is based on the goal of the attacker. Following are possible attacks in multi-server authentication environment:

Lost Smart Card Attack: Attack is possible in case of lost or stolen smart card. Attacker can use password-guessing techniques once getting physical access to the card.

Impersonation Attack: The attacker monitors message exchange between two parties to gather identification information. This information is later utilized to impersonate one of the parties.

Stolen Verifier Attack: Attacker is able to steal a verification table containing hashed passwords, which he/she later utilizes to for impersonation.

Reply Attack: Attacker captures data and sends the message later posing it as a duplicate message.

Dictionary Attack: Attacker captures packets with password information and tries to predict password.

Denial of Service Attack: Attacker is able to modify password information stored in smart card rendering it unusable. The attacker can also send a large number of packets to the authentication server, diminishing its ability to process the genuine messages.

Man-in-the-Middle Attack: Attacker works as an intermediator capturing and forwarding messages to and from both sides enabling attacker to read all messages exchanged between both parties.

Forward Secrecy Attack: Attacker is able to access past session keys enabling him/her to guess the future keys.

Spoofing Attack: Attacker acts as a genuine server gathering the genuine user's data.

2.2   Smart Token Service

The concept of using token for security comes from project Athena at MIT. This project resulted in Kerberos system [1]. Kerberos enables users to authenticate themselves in a multi-server environment using tokens issued by the authentication server. The system also supports SAML and client based authentication. It also features time synchronization between different servers.

The Kerberos system is based on assumption that each time the user is trying to authenticate from a server, he/she is doing it from an untrusted host and over an insecure network. The system's security is compromised if a malicious user gets access to ticketing server. One way to overcome this problem is with help of token service.

A web based smart token service can issue security tokens over the internet to its clients. The clients use these tokens to authenticate themselves with different servers. Here the token issuing service acts as a broker issuing tokens to the clients based on their identity. This service provides flexibility in authorization, authentication and exchange of session keys in heterogeneous environment. The services usually applies to four entities: the client, the server, the broker and the issuer. However, this system is vulnerable if client becomes a victim of a successful insider attack.

By removing the issuer and enabling the broker to issue the tokens, we can thwart the insider attack. We introduce the token-based authentication scheme with three entities: client, issuer and server. Here, the client is the user wishing to authenticate him/herself. The issuer is responsible for issuing tokens based on client's identity. Issuer also validates identity of the client and server where the client is attempting to authenticate him/herself. The server is an entity that requires user to authenticate him/herself before providing services.

2.3   The Modified Diffie-Hellman Key Exchange Protocol

The original Diffie-Hellman protocol is the first key exchange protocol enabling secure key exchange over insecure network. However, the original Diffie-Hellman protocol does not support user authentication. Therefore, it is possible for the attacker to modification, injection or interpretation types of attacks. The Diffie-Hellman protocol is most vulnerable by the man-in-the-middle type of attack. We propose using modified Diffie-Hellman proposed by Phan to overcome this vulnerability [2].

2.4   Symmetric Encryption Technique

There are two major symmetric encryption techniques, block cipher and stream cipher. Some of the well-known block cipher techniques are AES and DES. We propose a block cipher technique based on matrix rotation, XOR operations and swapping for high security. The major features of this technique are functions for message expansion, rounds and swapping. The expansion function will expand each 64-bit message into a 128-bit message block. Each round of the algorithm consists of arranging each block into an 8×8 matrix. The matrix is then rotated based on value of bit in bottom right corner for horizontal rotation and top left bit for vertical rotation. 16 rounds are carried out to strengthen the encryption. Lastly swapping is performed to further reinforce the encryption. The Fig. 1 shows rotation of matrix for scrambling of the bits. Message expansion is shown in Fig. 2 and finally Fig. 3 shows overall encryption technique.

Assuming that the original message is: 11111111 10100001 11111111 10001110 11111111 11001111 11111111 10111100.

1	1	1	1	1	1	1	1
0	1	0	0	0	0	1	1
1	1	1	1	1	1	1	0
1	0	0	0	1	1	1	0
1	1	1	1	1	1	1	1
1	0	0	1	1	0	1	1
1	1	1	1	1	1	1	1
1	0	1	1	1	1	0	0

No shift as bottom right is zero →

1	1	1	1	1	1	1	1
0	1	0	0	0	0	1	1
1	1	1	1	1	1	1	0
1	0	0	0	1	1	1	0
1	1	1	1	1	1	1	1
1	0	0	1	1	0	1	1
1	1	1	1	1	1	1	1
1	0	1	1	1	1	0	0

Rotation in row 2 and 6 →

1	1	1	1	1	1	1	1
1	0	1	0	0	0	0	1
1	1	1	1	1	1	1	0
1	0	0	0	1	1	1	0
1	1	1	1	1	1	1	1
1	1	0	0	1	1	1	1
1	1	1	1	1	1	1	1
1	0	1	1	1	1	0	0

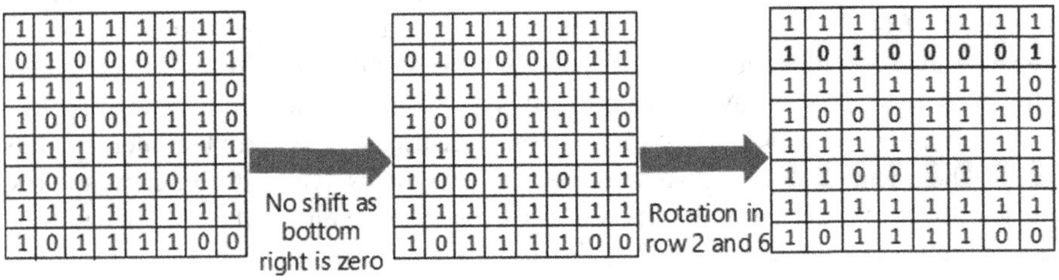

Fig. 1. Matrix rotation

We describe the steps for matrix based block-cipher encryption technique as follows:

Step 1. We divide a 512-bit input block into eight blocks (B1...B8) of 64-bits each. We transform each 64-bit block into an 8 × 8 matrix.

Step 2. We perform two matrix rotations: one vertical and one horizontal. If the bottom right bit of matrix contains value 1, the columns 3 and 5 are rotated. The bits are rotated circularly by one place in vertical direction. No vertical rotation is performed if the value is 0. Similarly, we look at the value of top left bit for horizontal rotation. If it is found to be holding value of 1, we rotate rows 2 and 6. The bits are rotated circularly by one place in horizontal direction. No horizontal rotation is performed if value is 0. Matrix rotation is described in Fig. 1.

Step 3. We run each 64-bit block through expansion function to receive a 128 bit expanded block. Expansion process is described in Fig. 2.

Step 4. We perform XOR operation among following blocks: B1 ⊕ B2, B3 ⊕ B4, B5 ⊕ B6 and B7 ⊕ B8. This operation results in 4 blocks of 128-bits each.

Step 5. We divide our round key of 512-bits into 4 blocks of 128-bits each (K1...K4).

Step 6. We perform another XOR operation Bi ⊕ Ki. This results in four cipher text blocks of 128 bits each. From round 1 to 15 these are put together to form a 512-bit cipher text corresponding to the round.

Step 7. This step is performed only once at the last round, here instead of putting the blocks in normal order, C1's place is swapped with C3 and C2 is swapped with C4. For decryption process, we follow the steps in reverse order from step 7 to 1.

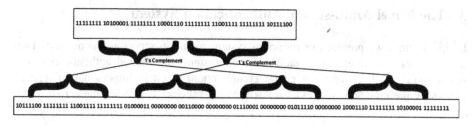

Fig. 2. Message expansion

2.5 Round Key Generation

In each round, we generate a single 512-bit key. We use it to generate a of round cipher text. We divide it into two 128-bit blocks. In second round, we perform swapping and joining of two blocks to produce the final key. To produce key for next round, we perform right shift by shifting 8 bits in circular manner. We again divide it into four blocks of 128-bits and use it in next round to generate cipher text. We repeat this process for each round to generate four keys.

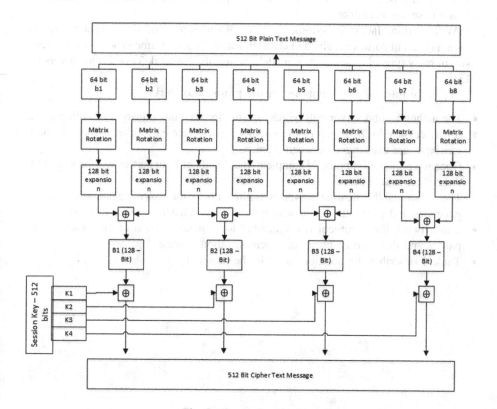

Fig. 3. Encryption process

3   The Novel Multi-server Authentication System

In this section, we present our proposed system for multi-server authentication. Two major issues with multi-server authentication systems are mutual authentication and non-repudiation. Lack of these characteristics could result in impersonation type of attacks by the malicious user. Our authentication scheme overcomes these issues.

3.1   The System Model

Our proposed system is designed with keeping in mind N clients communicating with O number of servers. In our model, if a user Ni wants to access the services of server Oi, we refer to Oi as Service Provider Server (SPS). We also have a server that provides authentication service to the users, we refer to it as Authentication Service Provider (ASP). In our model the ASP is based on PKI and used PKIX standard developed by IETF for certificate management. In order to receive the services provided by SPS the user needs to authenticate himself/herself to ASP. Initially, during the registration phase, both SPS and the user need to authenticate themselves with ASP. The ASP will provide both SPS and the user with the token. The token can be used by both ASP and the user to generate the secret key through Phan's modified Diffie-Hellman protocol. Thereafter, the data can be encrypted by our proposed algorithm before pushing it through unsecure networks.

An important factor in symmetric key distribution is of time synchronization between different parties involved in communication. Lack of time synchronization can result in reply type of attack. In our model, we use the Network Time Protocol version 4 [3].

We make following assumptions for our protocol to work:

- The authentication server will be responsible for the authentication of both parties.
- It is necessary for both parties to mutually authenticate each other before the main messages are exchanged between them.
- Once the registration phase is complete, the details of both parties will be stored by the authentication server.
- The role of authentication server is limited up to the token generation. Once it generates and shares the token with both parties, it has no further role to play.
- The network time protocol is responsible for synchronization of clocks of all the parties and there are no errors in synchronization process.
- Table 1 describes the notations used in the protocol.

Table 1. Protocol notations with description

Notation	Description
T1, T2	Timestamps for user and server
W, X, Y, Z	Round sub keys
ASP	Authentication server
UID	User's unique ID
SID	Server's unique ID
SIDASP	Authentication server's unique ID
H()	Hash function
$\oplus$	XOR operation
$\parallel$	Concatenation Operation
T	Security token
PU, PS	Secret numbers used to generate keys of user and server respectively
PKU	User's public key
PKS	Server's public key
SKU	User's secret key
SKS	Server's secret key
KAB	User's secret key for messaging SPS
KBA	Server's secret key for user
TΔ	Delay in transmission
TS	Session Time
SPS	Service provider server
PK	Shared secret key between the user and SPS
NU, NS	Nonce for user and server respectively

3.2 Registration Process

This process is carried out when the user or a service provider wishes to register with the authentication server.

The following steps are performed by the user to register with the authentication server:

1. The user begins registration process by submitting an online form with exclusive UID and a secret number (PU) along with necessary information. The authentication server will send an email containing a link to the email address provided by the user to authenticate the user. The link has an expiry time after which it will not be usable anymore. The link can only be used one time. Once it is used the authentication server will mark it as used and this will render the link unusable. When the user clicks on the link first time user is taken to a page to setup a password (PWD).
2. The authentication server will generate the user's identity key by generating hash of UID $P = H (UID \parallel PU)$ and performing XOR operation between identity key and hash of the password set by the user $N = P \oplus H (PWD)$. The values of P and N are stored in the card and that card is issued to the user.

The SPS has to follow following steps for registration:

1. The SPS will submit a unique ID SID and a secret number (PS) along with other necessary information to the ASP.
2. The ASP will compute M = H (SID || PS), it will share the newly calculated M with the SPS.

3.3   Login Process

Once the registration of the user and SPS is done by the ASP, the user will initiate the process when it requires service of the SPS. The user will begin by logging into the system. The steps for the login are given below:

1. To login to the system and get a token, the user will insert the card into the card reader. The card reader will extract the values of P and N from the card. The authentication system will ask the user for the UID and PWD. The authentication system will compute P' by $N \oplus H$ (PWD). It will authenticate user if the $P' = P$. The authenticated user will now generate the message for the ASP. The user will generate $M_1 = H (P || N_U)$. The encrypted message to ASP is $(M_1||SID||UID||N_U) EN_{ASP}$.
2. On receiving the message from the user the ASP will decrypt the message and extract the values of M_1, SID, UID and N_U. It will compute $M_1' = H (H (UID||P_U) || N_U)$. It will verify authenticity of the message by comparing values of $M_1 = M_1'$. If the user is authenticated the ASP will send message to the SPS asking to validate the login request. This message will contain following details: $(UID || SID_{ASP}) EN_M$.
3. After receiving the message the SPS will decrypt the message and compute values $M2 = H (M||N_S)$. The SPS will send message to ASP. This message will contain following details $(C2 ||NS) E_{PS}$.

3.4   Token Generation Process

Before generating the token, the ASP will need to authenticate the SPS. Once authentication is successful, it will generate the token and share it to the user and SPS respectively. The process for generating token is described below:

1. The ASP will generate $C2'$ where $C2' = H (H (SID ||P_S) || N_S)$. If the value of $C2' = C2$ then the SPS is authenticated. In case of successful authentication the ASP will generate two ephemeral keys X and Y. The keys will be generated from following information: $X = H (Z || N_U || N_S)$ and $Y = H (R ||N_U || N_S)$.
2. Based on the ephemeral keys the ASP will also generate C3 and C4 where $C3 = X \oplus Y$ and $C4 = H (X || Y)$. Next, the ASP will generate two tokens T1 and T2, one each for the user and the SPS respectively, where $T1 = (C3||C4)$ and $T2 = (C3||C4)$. The ASP will also generate the $C = NS \oplus NU$ and the shared secret key. Here, the ASP will send two identical messages to SPS and the user. The message will contain following information: $(T1 || C || PK) EPU$ and $(T2|| C || PK) EPS$. Here the PK comes from the modified Diffie-Hellman protocol [2] discussed earlier in the paper.

3.5 Mutual Authentication Process

The user and the SPS will first verify the token received from the ASP and then perform following steps to mutually authenticate each other:

1. The genuine user will be able to compute X' and Y' from the information available for him/her. X' = C3 $\oplus$ Y' and Y' = H (H (UID $\|P_U\|$) $\|$ N$_U$ $\|$ N$_S$). This is possible after extraction of N$_S$ from C. Now, the user will compute C4' = H (X' $\|$ Y'). The user will compare C4 with the C4', if the match is found then the token is validated. The SPS will also authenticate the token received from ASP by calculating X' = H (H (SID $\|$ P$_S$) $\|$N$_U$ $\|$N$_S$) and Y' = C4 $\oplus$ X'. This will be computed after extracting N$_U$ from C. The SPS will also compute C4' = H (X'$\|$Y'). The SPS will also verify the token by comparing values of C4' and C4.
2. Once the token is authenticated from the user's side, the user will prepare the following message for the SPS beginning the mutual authentication process: C5 = H (UID$\|$SID) $\oplus$ N$_U$. This message is then sent to the SPS with following information: [(C5 $\|$ T1 $\|$ N1) $\|$PU$_A$) PK$_S$. Here, N1 is the nonce generated by the user.
3. After receiving the message the SPS will compute C5' where C5' = H (UID $\|$ SID) $\oplus$ N$_U$. It compares C5' with C5 to authenticate the user. In case of successful authentication the user's public key is accepted by the SPS. Before accepting the public key the delay T Δ with the timestamp present in the message from the user. The SPS will generate the challenge nonce N2 and secret keys K$_{AB}$ and K$_{BA}$ using the integrated Diffie-Hellman key exchange protocol [2].
4. Next, the ASP computes C6 where C6 = H (UID$\|$SID) $\oplus$ NS. The ASP will send message with following information to authenticate the user: [(C6$\|$T2$\|$N2) $\|$PU$_B$] PK$_U$.
5. On receiving the message from the SPS the user computes C6', where C6' = H (UID$\|$SID) $\oplus$ N$_S$. The user will compare C6' with C6 to and will also check the timestamp with delay T Δ before finally validating the message. The user will also generate the public and private keys K$_{AB}$ and K$_{BA}$ using integrated Diffie-Hellman key exchange protocol. Finally the user will send the following message to confirm the mutual authentication process: (H (N2)) PK$_S$.

4 Conclusion

The major vulnerability of multi-server authentication schemes is repeated use of same identity for authenticating with different services. In our protocol we propose a security token based authentication service. The absence of verification table also enhances security of the proposed protocol. Our protocol can resist major attacks described in this paper.

References

1. Lamport, L.: Password authentication with insecure communication. Commun. ACM **24** (11), 770–772 (1981)
2. Chan, C.-K., Cheng, L.-M.: Cryptanalysis of a remote user authentication scheme using smart cards. IEEE Trans. Consum. Electron. **46**(4), 992–993 (2000)
3. Mitchell, C.: Limitations of challenge-response entity authentication. Electron. Lett. **25**(17), 1995–1996 (1989)
4. Awasthi, A.K., Lal, S.: An enhanced remote user authentication scheme using smart cards. IEEE Trans. Consum. Electron. **50**(2), 583–586 (2004)
5. Chang, C., Hwang, K.: Some forgery attacks on a remote user authentication scheme using smart cards. Informatica **14**(3), 289–294 (2003)
6. Shen, J.-J., Lin, C.-W., Hwang, M.-S.: A modified remote user authentication scheme using smart cards. IEEE Trans. Consum. Electron. **49**(2), 414–416 (2003)
7. Radhakrishnan, N., Karuppiah, M.: An efficient and secure remote user mutual authentication scheme using smart cards for Telecare medical information systems. Inform. Med. Unlocked **16**, 1–11 (2019)
8. Banerjee, S., Chunka, C., Sen, S., Goswami, R.S.: An enhanced and secure biometric based user authentication scheme in wireless sensor networks using smart cards. Wirel. Pers. Commun. **107**(1), 243–270 (2019)
9. Kumar, S., Singh, V., Sharma, V., Singh, V.P.: Advance remote user authentication scheme using smart card. Telecommun. Radio Eng. **78**(11), 957–971 (2019)
10. Pan, H.-T., Yang, H.-W., Hwang, M.-S.: An enhanced secure smart card-based password authentication scheme. IJ Netw. Secur. **22**(2), 358–363 (2020)
11. Lee, W.-B., Chang, C.-C.: User identification and key distribution maintaining anonymity for distributed computer networks. Comput Syst Sci Eng **15**(4), 211–214 (2000)
12. Chang, C., Cheng, T., Hsueh, W.: A robust and efficient dynamic identity-based multi-server authentication scheme using smart cards. Int. J. Commun Syst **29**(2), 290–306 (2016)
13. Jangirala, S., Mukhopadhyay, S., Das, A.K.: A multi-server environment with secure and efficient remote user authentication scheme based on dynamic ID using smart cards. Wirel. Pers. Commun. **95**(3), 2735–2767 (2017)
14. Chiou, S.-F., Pan, H.-T., Cahyadi, E.F., Hwang, M.-S.: Cryptanalysis of the mutual authentication and key agreement protocol with smart cards for wireless communications. IJ Netw. Secur. **21**(1), 100–104 (2019)
15. Chang, C.-C., Hsueh, W.-Y., Cheng, T.-F.: An Advanced anonymous and biometrics-based multi-server authentication scheme using smart cards. IJ Netw. Secur. **18**(6), 1010–1021 (2016)
16. Lwamo, N.M., Zhu, L., Xu, C., Sharif, K., Liu, X., Zhang, C.: SUAA: a secure user authentication scheme with anonymity for the single & multi-server environments. Inf. Sci. **477**, 369–385 (2019)
17. Xu, D., Chen, J., Liu, Q.: Provably secure anonymous three-factor authentication scheme for multi-server environments. J. Ambient Intell. Humaniz. Comput. **10**(2), 611–627 (2018). https://doi.org/10.1007/s12652-018-0710-x
18. Biswas, A., Roy, A.: A study on dynamic ID based user authentication system using smart card. Asian J. Converg. Technol. **5**(2), 1–7 (2019)
19. Barman, S., Chaudhuri, A., Chatterjee, A., Ramiz Raza, M.: An elliptic curve cryptography-based multi-server authentication scheme using cancelable biometrics. In: Bhateja, V., Satapathy, S.C., Zhang, Y.-D., Aradhya, V.N.M. (eds.) ICICC 2019. AISC, vol. 1034, pp. 153–163. Springer, Singapore (2020). https://doi.org/10.1007/978-981-15-1084-7_16

20. Sahoo, S.S., Mohanty, S., Sunny, S.K.M.B.: An improved remote user authentication scheme for multiserver environment using smart cards. In: Recent Findings in Intelligent Computing Techniques, pp. 217–224 (2019)
21. Chen, T.-H., Hsiang, H.-C., Shih, W.-K.: Security enhancement on an improvement on two remote user authentication schemes using smart cards. Future Gener. Comput. Syst. 27(4), 377–380 (2011)
22. Lee, C.-C., Lin, T.-H., Chang, R.-X.: A secure dynamic ID based remote user authentication scheme for multi-server environment using smart cards. Expert Syst. Appl. 38(11), 13863–13870 (2011)
23. Li, S., Wu, X., Zhao, D., Li, A., Tian, Z., Yang, X.: An efficient dynamic ID-based remote user authentication scheme using self-certified public keys for multi-server environments. PLoS ONE 13(10), 1–19 (2018)

Firmware Attack Detection on Gadgets Using Ridge Regression (FAD-RR)

E. Arul[1](✉) [ID] and A. Punidha[2] [ID]

[1] Department of Information Technology, Coimbatore Institute of Technology, Coimbatore, Tamilnadu, India
arulcitit@gmail.com
[2] Department of Computer Science and Engineering, Coimbatore Institute of Technology, Coimbatore, Tamilnadu, India
punitulip@gmail.com

Abstract. Firmware is workstation equipment optimized running software. This is a vulnerable threat field that hackers use with a networking footprint an unverifiable Internet of things node is basically an unblocked main gate which enables hackers to switch through the public network outwards as long as they bring around a Smart home system. The suggested Software Ridge Regression (RR) to characterize such a software assault on gadgets. From knowledge from a non-regular source area of malicious file, the firmware RR can select a set of better characteristics to estimate the inherent diffusion of malicious API Calls. Firmware Ridge Regression is a method for the analysis of multi-linear regression results various malicious firmware attack. If multi-country linearity develops on pool of API extracted from various files, the least square results are impartial data, however their deviations are wide and they might not be valid. The round map shows the differences in the input density: the area of reference from which measured training parts are derived corresponds to the broader trouble spots and is better than experiment field areas by means of which test measurements with lower percentages are extracted. The rough map reflects shifts in the source volume data. The analysis reveals that 98.57 percentile is unfavorable, and 0.01 percentile is favorable for the adware attack.

Keywords: Gadgets · Backdoors · Firmware · API calls · Classification · Ridge Regression · Software · Adware

1 Introduction

Firmware security is fairly weak; threats aren't seen as much as vulnerabilities that threaten certain industries [22]. Seeing as the exploitation of firmware by altering it is not easy; the targeted program is more quickly and effectively utilized for traditional malevolent operations like breaching PII. The firmware also has a modified application installed on a specific number of computers and is therefore a somewhat wider hit-rate than that of the vulnerability attacking hardware operating systems such as Windows, or software that is widely used on machines [23].

Software bugs enable unauthorized parties with keys to their systems—often unseen. This is how the manipulation of software exploits a computer until it ever boots

© Springer Nature Singapore Pte Ltd. 2021
K. K. Patel et al. (Eds.): icSoftComp 2020, CCIS 1374, pp. 224–233, 2021.
https://doi.org/10.1007/978-981-16-0708-0_19

[17]. It is achieved by inserting malware into the bottom layer framework that manages the devices during the controller's start-up. When the unauthorized script has reached the device, it's able to change the hardware, hack the OS objective, penetrate devices, and much more. Multiple modes of assault will come from basic BIOS and modern UEF IT devices. Spam, key packs and kernel sets both are common portals for distribution [18].

There would be bugs, like in other technology deployments. If the array of applications has been ignored over time, which is since exposed vulnerabilities can also be used for assaults [21]. Deep rooted vulnerabilities are likely to be discovered. UEFI serves a crucial part safely in loading applications, and it presents hackers with a captivating assault surface [19]. Formerly considered only by nation states to be abused, recent work and attacks also modified assumptions regarding the flaws of the cpu firmware. For UEFI protection the main aim is to remove and fix the good kick-a-mole strategy. The industrial sector will insure that such entry obstacles for hackers stay high only through its sustained developments in aggressive technology and best activities, creation of advanced digital innovations and improved cooperation with partners' communities [20].

For hardware it is always the device software including BIOS and its quite recent substitute, UEFI, which becomes very main component to be considered [25]. This machine firmware is fairly strong, but neither one of tens of modules in consumer machines dependent on firmware and capable of performing important functions in an assault. Such essential firmware can be the first application to operate while the interface is in action which can be changed by modifying the startup configuration, updating the OS framework which jeopardizing hypervisors and also the compute nodes as well [29]. Device software could be used to distribute harmful software to other machine modules.

Use CPU loopholes to access details including codes that usually stay in restricted storage, which will stay secure. The capacity of the cpu bugs to be centrally abused often increases the harm. In fact, the limitations of CPUs are caused by every device or kernel as there are no other program exploitable vulnerabilities then all OS security rates have been activated. In addition, the deployment of firmware fixes, processor opcodes bug fixes, OS security patches, VMM patches, and application bug fixes will present problems with fixing processors [28].

The PCIe bridge links to a vast range of essential devices, including GPUs, communication adapters among far others [10]. Code and hence the infrastructure will affect either the hardware of PCIe chips and Bios-connected computers. If infected, destructive breaches will contribute to machine memory being read and written and unauthorized code being run inside the framework of the victim's kernel [12].

The firmware strategy is also close to conventional malicious attacks. "Application offline" The first solution may be by spoofing, push-by-downloads, or online media [13]. The intruder may target the weaknesses of compromised software involved in order to distribute an exploit or use more resources, such as sensitive drivers for increased rights and software control if required [9]. Both alternatives for an intruder are rather simple. Firstly, the easy usage of a loophole, and secondly, it reflects the traditional Key logger/Dispenser pattern used during decades by hackers.

Threats on firmware provide a collection of modules and methods which are not commonly used in conventional threats on devices. During this article we will demonstrate some of the key firmware elements in a system, whether they can be exploited as major aspect of an assault, and how attackers utilize tactics and technologies. The portion is not comprehensive or authoritative, but is meant to address core firmware assaults paradigms [15].

2 Related Work

Roy research done on the society has developed to a level where contact through communications or links among computers and individuals becomes difficult to conceive [1]. The emergence and development of integrated machines and 'stuff' was the result of the fifth industrialization. The Foreign New technology (IoT) is now the basis of connectivity for computers and men. The older products on the market, the more software needs to be upgraded in order to combat attacks on technology. Each system must be upgraded to the new firmware to retain stable and efficiently function; this article suggests a safe software upgrade framework in a centralized faith-based Smart home platform repository.

Kumar did research on the mobile systems the cloud services/new software operates daily. Updates are received via the Web on IoT gadgets Throughout the Cloud (OTA) [2]. OTA upgrade functionality can be exploited in the lack of appropriate protection steps. The challenges to protection such as the decoding of the software and the installation of illegitimate code on compromised networks would result in the theft, device copying and packet sniffing assault. Throughout this article, we suggest a protection architecture for the stable OTA hotfix phase by the logic analyzer/SoC users. The comprehensive approach suggested promotes JTAG protection, preserves IP privileges of OEMs and stable OTA updates. The safety mechanism is planned to resolve all safety risks associated with the OTA system software-software upgrade, not handled in previous techniques, by means of correct routing protocols and configuration controls.

Thakur analysis the conventionally, intermittent system output disruptions and degrades almost sometimes culminated in a centralized update of the computer firmware [3]. Programmers needed to be at the ground to reintroduce the system from their machine, update or fix the latest code to place the product back in the field. Nonetheless, for companies this entire method is very difficult and un-scalable. However, Off - the-Air software upgrade is actually a popular way to upgrade smart devices without interruption. The document is intended to demonstrate the research that we are doing in this field by creating a system for updating the firmware of diverse IoT gadgets from a distance [5].

Dhobi deals throughout this report, we suggest using Safe Software Update for integrated equipment that uses technologies from TrustZone to install new software in a stable way [4]. TrustZone offers the software to be installed in the system with its reliability and protection. It tests the validity, reliability and protection of the framework using a trustworthy application together with the host program. The authentication of a firmware, which can be safely done in TrustZone setting, is checked using a unique identifier method [15].

3 Delineation Firmware Attack Detection on Gadgets Using Ridge Regression (F-RR)

Ridge Regression is a multi-linear analysis methodology for least squares results. If tri-collinearity exists, the minimum round figures are not statistical, yet the differences were wide and so away from the real meaning. If the regression results contain a degree of truth, a ridge approximation eliminates typical deviations [16]. The overall result is expected to have more accurate forecasts. Regularization is a means of preventing overpowering by fining strongly regarded correlations of regression. Simply speaking, they reduce (simplify) prototype variables and narrows. A simpler, more common-sensical approach would generally conduct well in forecasts. Regularization places limitations on more complicated models, and instead sets alternative models from fewer overfits to larger; the smallest overfit method generally allows the better option for predictive value [11].

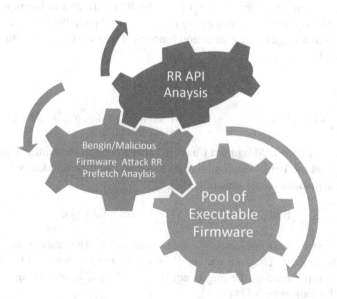

Fig. 1. Flow diagram of Firmware Attack Detection on Gadgets Using Ridge Regression (F-RR)

Regularization is required while techniques of regression with fewer frames may be unreliable, with minimization of the remaining round number. This is extremely valid if the framework is multi-linear. The pure process of framework matching, though, has a significant downside: every data collection can be tailored to a specification although it is incredibly complicated [29].

Through biasing data for other values (such as tiny values similar to zero), legislative analysis functions. A parameters function is applied for supporting certain values. The L1 configuration imposes an L1 restriction proportional to the actual sum of the scale of the coefficients [27]. It restricts the scale of the coefficients, in other words. L1 may yield scattered models; certain coefficients can be zero and removed. L1 may yield models of very certain correlations. This approach is used for the regression of Lasso [6].

Ridge regression refers to a family of L2 reconstruction software. The other method of convolution, L1, reduces the sum of the coefficients by applying a penalty of L1, which is equivalent to the exponential function of the factor degree. Often, certain factors are entirely omitted, which may generate fuzzy prototypes [7]. The regulated L2 system provides an L2 points deduction, which is equal to the square of coefficient scale. The same component shrinks all coefficients (so no element is removed). L2 does not contribute to fragmented templates without L1 convolution.

For the calculation of parameters OLS regression uses a similar formula:

$$\hat{B} = (X2\ X) - 1Y \tag{1}$$

The Cross Product Mats (X'X) becomes nearly unique because the X vectors are strongly connected while the X matrix becomes oriented and measured. Ridge progression adds a new sequence (X'X + kI), of the ID multiverse to the bridge-product matrix [8]. This is considered the ridge regression, even though the vertex of one would be represented as a ridge in the connection function. To locate the factors, the following method is used:

$$\hat{B} = (X'X + kI) - 1X'Y \tag{2}$$

$$\sum [yi - yi] = \sum [yi - (\beta 0 + \beta 1\ x1 + \beta 2\ x1 + \cdots \ldots + \beta 2\ x1)]2 \tag{3}$$

argmin here implies "Maximum Case" in order to obtain the minimal goal. It finds the β throughout the light, which minimizes the RSS. So therefore know how to make β out of the equations of the equation [17].

$$B20 + \beta 21\ x1 + \beta 22\ x1 + \cdots \ldots + \beta 2p \leq C2 \tag{4}$$

Also, a type of least squares is the ridge correlation. The latter word is the OLS exponent's ridge limit. They are searching for the β, and yet they will fulfill the latter limit. The circumference of the ring is equal to the C, and it will be right on the rim throughout the loop region [24].

$$\|B\|2 = \sqrt{B0 + \beta 1\ x1 + \beta 2\ x1 + \cdots \ldots + \beta p} \tag{5}$$

They need the matrix equivalent to take a course, which is little more than the next description.

The explanation is the shortest, but always the just like with everything were addressed. Note that in the preceding expression the next term is actually OLS, so the next phrase is the variance of the slope. The phrase lambda is sometimes referred to as "Foul," although it raises RSS. They place those parameters on the lambda then calculate the function with the aid of a 'Mean Square Error' calculation [19]. The lambda meaning decreasing MSE will then be used as the final standard. In fact, this device regression model is stronger than the quantitative OLS method. Should be seen in the following figure, the β range varies with the lambda and is identical to OLS β, unless the lambda is close to zero (no penalty) [20].

The lambda probably ends up going with the denominator by applying the matrix rule used before. This implies that the β ridge will reduce if we growing the lambda value. Yet β's can't be negative irrespective of the scale of the lambda number. This implies that ridge regression provides weights to the features specific value but does not decrease irrelevant aspects [10].

$$\left(\ldots\ldots\ldots + \frac{1}{\lambda} + \ldots\ldots\right) x^T \, y \tag{6}$$

4 Experimental Results and Comparison

Ridge regression is a multivariate regression variant. It is basically a formalized form of linear regression. The β parameter is also a scalar and can be discovered by means of a process named cross-validation [26]. Another very significant thing we have to note is that it allows the β coefficients smaller, but it does not render them zero depicted in Fig. 1. This ensures that the unnecessary characteristics are not omitted but that their effect on the learned model is minimized [21].

Lasso is yet another branch, but with a minor variation based on a computationally efficient linear correlation. Lasso's failure function is as follows:

$$L = \sum (\hat{Y}i - Yi)2 + \lambda \sum |\beta| \tag{7}$$

Only other variation between Ridge reconstructions is the independent variable of the regularization concept in Fig. 2. However, this disparity has an immense effect on our previous debate depicted in Fig. 3. Lasso solves the drawback of Ridge's analysis by eliminating also large values of β coefficients, but also limiting them to 0. It will then wind up with features less than you began in design plan, which is an immense benefit in Table 1 [17] (Fig. 4).

- Any problem of machine learning is fundamentally a problem of optimization. In other terms, any feature will be minimized (or maximised).
- Each dataset is composed of (X) and (Y) characteristics. In this case-the main function is the ExportRVA, the IATRVA is the mark
- It choose to reduce the polynomial loss in least squares questions, and that is the number of deviations between projections and the real value (ground truth).
- Then it really must run an incremental method to reduce the depletion factor and determine the strongest β correlations.
- So it still can use the qualified model to forecast a new building's architecture (IATRVA) centered on its scale in Table 1 (Table 2).

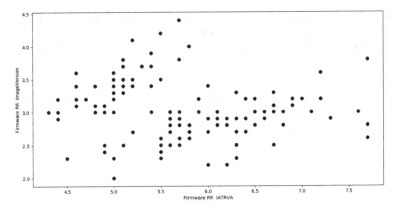

Fig. 2. The proposed Firmware – LAR Finding with IATRVA component against the malware image version

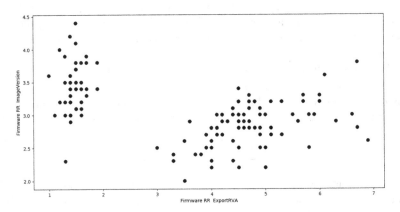

Fig. 3. The proposed Firmware – LAR Finding with ExportRVA component against the malware image version

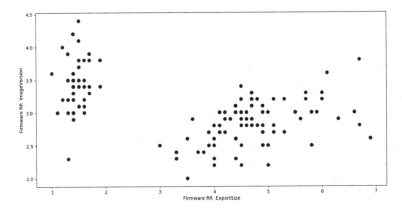

Fig. 4. The proposed Firmware – LAR Finding with ExportSize component against the malware image version

Table 1. Compared Lasso and RR with malware methods of the proposed Firmware - LAR

FirmwareEXE	Lasso		Ridge Regressor	
IATRVA	Alpha	Best Score	Alpha	Best Score
	1e−15	−0.103634	1e−15	−0.1024663
	1e−10	−0.103634	1e−10	−0.103634
	1e−08	−0.103634	1e−08	−0.103634
	1	−0.726114	1	−0.103234
	5	−0.688257	5	−0.102466
	10	−0.661110	10	−0.102840
	20	−0.657820	20	−0.105992

Table 2. Compared with existing malware methods of the proposed Firmware - LAR

Methods	Number of Malware are Detected	TP Ratio (%)	FP Detected	FP Ratio (%)
Yohan	1095	97.50	28	0.02
Xie	1035	92.16	88	0.06
Proposed Firmware-LAR	1107	98.57	16	0.01
Test Scale of Malware: 1123		Collection of Harmless Samples: 1322		

5   Conclusion and Future Work

Even if an Smart home system is hacked, it could be utilized for the purposes of stealing information, breaching data privacy and undertaking such attacks which may lead to loss of profits, considerable expense to resolve the issue, possible corporate governance expenses and potential financial damages. This paper is neither final nor accurate, but aims to lay forth the main guidelines for firmware attacks. Firmware Ridge regression, which does not have a particular approach, is by far the most commonly employed form of regularization for untouched issues. Regularizations essentially offer extra details to select the "right" remedy for a problem. Regression from Ridge and Lasso is effective approaches widely used to build prosaic frameworks of 'big' characteristics. There, "high" would usually mean one of two things: big enough to boost the propensity of an over-powered model (so small as 10 variables will trigger overpower). It could occur for millions or even billions of characteristics in advanced systems The outcome is a real 98.57% positive score and an incorrect positive score of 0.01% on the different firmware apps. In the future, this is to be replicated by other APIs, which enable malicious network operations to be performed.

References

1. Roy, G., Britto Ramesh Kumar, S.: An Architecture to Enable Secure Firmware Updates on a Distributed-Trust IoT Network Using Blockchain. In: Smys, S., Bestak, R., Chen, J.I.-Z. , Kotuliak, I. (eds.) International Conference on Computer Networks and Communication Technologies. LNDECT, vol. 15, pp. 671–679. Springer, Singapore (2019). https://doi.org/10.1007/978-981-10-8681-6_61

2. Kumar, S.K., Sahoo, S., Kiran, K., Swain, A.K., Mahapatra, K.K.: A novel holistic security framework for in-field firmware updates. In: 2018 IEEE International Symposium on Smart Electronic Systems (iSES) (Formerly iNiS), Hyderabad, India, pp. 261–264 (2018)

3. Thakur, P., Bodade, V., Achary, A., Addagatla, M., Kumar, N., Pingle, Y.: Universal firmware upgrade over-the-air for IoT devices with security. In: 2019 6th International Conference on Computing for Sustainable Global Development (INDIACom), New Delhi, India, pp. 27–30 (2019)

4. Dhobi, R., Gajjar, S., Parmar, D., Vaghela, T.: Secure firmware update over the air using TrustZone. In: 2019 Innovations in Power and Advanced Computing Technologies (i-PACT), Vellore, India, pp. 1–4 (2019)

5. Islam, M.N., Kundu, S.: IoT security, privacy and trust in home-sharing economy via blockchain. In: Choo, K.-K., Dehghantanha, A., Parizi, R.M. (eds.) Blockchain Cybersecurity, Trust and Privacy. AIS, vol. 79, pp. 33–50. Springer, Cham (2020). https://doi.org/10.1007/978-3-030-38181-3_3

6. Parizi, R., Dehghantanha, A., Azmoodeh, A., Choo, K.-K.R.: Blockchain in cybersecurity realm: an overview. In: Choo, K.-K.R., Dehghantanha, A., Parizi, R.M. (eds.) Blockchain Cybersecurity, Trust and Privacy. AIS, vol. 79, pp. 1–5. Springer, Cham (2020). https://doi.org/10.1007/978-3-030-38181-3_1

7. Solangi, Z.A., Solangi, Y.A., Chandio, S., bin Hamzah, M.S., Shah, A.: The future of data privacy and security concerns in Internet of Things. In: 2018 IEEE International Conference on Innovative Research and Development (ICIRD), Bangkok, pp. 1–4 (2018)

8. Wazid, M., Das, A.K., Rodrigues, J.J.P.C., Shetty, S., Park, Y.: IoMT malware detection approaches: analysis and research challenges. IEEE Access 7, 182459–182476 (2019)

9. Makhdoom, I., Abolhasan, M., Lipman, J., Liu, R.P., Ni, W.: Anatomy of threats to the internet of things. IEEE Commun. Surv. Tutor. 21(2), 1636–1675 (2019)

10. Darabian, H., et al.: A multiview learning method for malware threat hunting: windows, IoT and android as case studies. World Wide Web 23(2), 1241–1260 (2020). https://doi.org/10.1007/s11280-019-00755-0

11. Du, M., Wang, K., Chen, Y., Wang, X., Sun, Y.: Big data privacy preserving in multi-access edge computing for heterogeneous internet of things. IEEE Commun. Mag. 56(8), 62–67 (2018)

12. Ahmed, A., Latif, R., Latif, S., Abbas, H., Khan, F.A.: Malicious insiders attack in IoT based Multi-Cloud e-Healthcare environment: a Systematic Literature Review. Multimed. Tools Appl. 77(17), 21947–21965 (2018). https://doi.org/10.1007/s11042-017-5540-x

13. Ntantogian, C., Poulios, G., Karopoulos, G., Xenakis, C.: Transforming malicious code to ROP gadgets for antivirus evasion. IET Inf. Secur. 13(6), 570–578 (2019). https://doi.org/10.1049/iet-ifs.2018.5386

14. Patel, Z.D.: Malware detection in android operating system. In: 2018 International Conference on Advances in Computing, Communication Control and Networking (ICACCCN), Greater Noida (UP), India, pp. 366–370 (2018)

15. Yoon, S., Jeon, Y.: Security threats analysis for android based mobile device. In: 2014 International Conference on Information and Communication Technology Convergence (ICTC), Busan, pp. 775–776 (2014)
16. Erdődi, L.: Finding dispatcher gadgets for jump oriented programming code reuse attacks. In: 2013 IEEE 8th International Symposium on Applied Computational Intelligence and Informatics (SACI), Timisoara, pp. 321–325 (2013)
17. https://securityboulevard.com/2019/12/anatomy-of-a-firmware-attack/
18. https://www.thesslstore.com/blog/firmware-attacks-what-they-are-how-i-can-protect-myself/
19. https://www.refirmlabs.com/centrifuge-platform/
20. https://uefi.org/sites/default/files/resources/Getting%20a%20Handle%20on%20Firmware%20Security%2011.11.17%20Final.pdf
21. https://www.helpnetsecurity.com/2019/07/17/hardening-firmware-security/
22. https://www.statisticshowto.datasciencecentral.com/regularization/
23. https://towardsdatascience.com/ridge-regression-for-better-usage-2f19b3a202db
24. https://ncss-wpengine.netdna-ssl.com/wp-content/themes/ncss/pdf/Procedures/NCSS/Ridge_Regression.pdf
25. https://towardsdatascience.com/how-to-perform-lasso-and-ridge-regression-in-python-3b3b75541ad8
26. https://hackernoon.com/practical-machine-learning-ridge-regression-vs-lasso-a00326371ece
27. https://www.analyticsvidhya.com/blog/2016/01/ridge-lasso-regression-python-complete-tutorial/
28. https://solidsystemsllc.com/firmware-security/

Automatic Text Extraction from Digital Brochures: Achieving Competitiveness for Mauritius Supermarkets

Yasser Chuttur$^{(\boxtimes)}$ (iD), Yusuf Fauzel, and Sandy Ramasawmy

University of Mauritius, Reduit 80837, Mauritius
y.chuttur@uom.ac.mu, {muhammad.fauzel,
sandy.ramasawmy3}@umail.uom.ac.mu

Abstract. In recent years, it has been observed that there is a growing number of supermarket stores coming into operation in Mauritius. Being a small country, Mauritius has got a limited customer base, and developing marketing strategies to stay in the market has become a priority for supermarket owners. A common marketing strategy is for decision makers to frequently offer sales on items in stock. These sales are advertised using brochures that are distributed to customers as soft copies (PDF digital brochures online) or hard copies within the supermarket premise. To ensure competitiveness of sales prices, decision makers must consult their competitor's brochures. Given that each competitor's brochure must be manually checked, the process can be costly, time consuming and labor intensive. To address this problem, we present the components of a system suitable for automatically collecting and aggregating information on items on sale in each supermarket by extracting useful information from digital brochures published online. The proposed system has been implemented on a pilot scale and tested in the local context. The results obtained indicate that our proposal can be effectively used to help local supermarkets easily keep track of market trends in order to remain competitive and attract customers.

Keywords: Text extraction · Business competitiveness · Digital information processing

1 Introduction

Today, companies rely on data for their day-to-day activities and for the development of a long-term strategy [1–4]. Decision makers' measures are also vital to the business on the ground that these choices will bring the company either benefit or loss. In Mauritius, which is a small island, the number of operating supermarkets has undergone an increase over the past years. To survive and gain competitive advantage in the highly competitive marketplace of Mauritius, local supermarkets regularly offer sales on their products. Items on sales are listed in brochures and distributed to customers as hard copies within the supermarket store or soft copies as online brochures. In parallel to the current marketing strategy in place, decision makers of supermarkets have adopted an alternative approach to decide on the next marketing or sales strategy:

© Springer Nature Singapore Pte Ltd. 2021
K. K. Patel et al. (Eds.): icSoftComp 2020, CCIS 1374, pp. 234–248, 2021.
https://doi.org/10.1007/978-981-16-0708-0_20

Competitor's brochures are often analyzed and future sales strategies to achieve competitiveness are then formulated.

However, the process of analyzing competitor's brochures to get an overview on which products are on sale remains a costly, tedious and time-consuming task, as the whole task is conducted manually. A physical visit to each competitor's store is required to collect the physical brochures or online brochures for each competitor must be individually and manually downloaded. Decision-makers must then go through each competitor's catalogue and take note for each item price to obtain enough information prior to coming up with necessary sales strategies that can maintain or boost up transactions in their respective supermarkets.

Consequently, automating the process of extracting useful information from brochures is desired. Such an approach will not only help in quickly obtaining useful information in a cost-effective manner, but it may also serve to build a database of sales data for later analysis. By creating a repository of sales data from multiple competitors over a given period of time, data processing techniques such as data mining may be used to discover marketing trends otherwise hidden from simple analysis [5].

In this paper, therefore, we present the design and implementation of a system along with the required components that should be able to automatically and regularly fetch digital brochures from online sources to be then subjected to further processing. The outcome of the processing would be an aggregate of information extracted from PDF files such as product name, description and price from each competitor's brochure. We expect that such a system would allow decision makers to have quick access to information that can be used to better formulate marketing and sales strategies. It is to be noted that there are already several approaches to extract data from PDF files. However, those methods 1) usually employ complex algorithms, which are not necessarily essential to extract information required from PDF supermarkets brochures and 2) have not been applied to the problem domain addressed in this work. In this work, we instead adopt a simplified approach involving format conversion to extract only essential information that would help in identifying product items and their corresponding prices.

The rest of the paper is organized as follows: A description of the common methods used by supermarket for advertisement is provided followed by an overview of related work on text extraction. Then the components for the proposed system for data extraction from digital brochures are presented. Each underlying component of the proposed tool is then explained along with brief implementation details. Testing result of the implemented prototype is provided, and its effectiveness is discussed. We finally offer some conclusions based on the results obtained.

2 Advertising and Marketing by Supermarkets

Supermarkets assume a significant function in the distribution of a wide assortment of products to customers. To attract customers, a large sum of money is invested on advertisements and marketing campaigns. In general, supermarkets create marketing campaigns around each end of the month or regular festivities such as Easter, Mother's Day, end of the year, etc. [6].

Popular advertising mediums include billboards, TV commercials and radio announcements [7]. Recently, the use of social media such as Facebook and YouTube are also being used for marketing purposes [8]. In addition, supermarkets maintain their own websites to provide information on latest updates on products and services offered. Very often, banner space in highly visited websites are also rented to display store names and brands. By doing so, supermarkets can reach out several customers and mark their presence on the market [9]. However, such forms of advertisements and marketing do not necessarily make an impact on direct sales. This is because, customers may not necessarily obtain all information regarding a complete list of products on sale at a given store and are therefore unable to decide whether visiting a certain store will have any added benefits. For that purpose, brochures become handy.

Brochures has become a very popular method employed by supermarkets to regularly advertise and market the list of their products on sale. As shown in Fig. 1, brochures offer a concise approach for a supermarket to display all of its products on sale listed under different categories that a customer can quickly browse through.

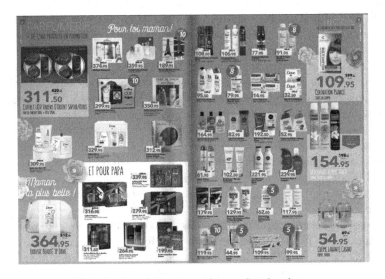

Fig. 1. A typical supermarket product brochure

The brochure takes the form and size of a newspaper, which is published by the end of each month or near the period of a festive season. Brochures can be collected as prints in stores or they can be accessed, viewed and downloaded as PDF file from a store website. Brochures, thus, not only serve as a guide to customers to know which products are on sale in a given supermarket, but it also serves as a means for competitors to quickly learn about trending price on the marketplace.

In this study, the goal is to eliminate the need for manual intervention when extracting information from online brochures and instead come up with the components of a system to automatically aggregate information from various brochures for the same sales period. As noted in Fig. 1, brochures, however, do not necessarily have a standard approach to present items and their details (price, quantity, image, etc.). Texts and images are presented as random blocks and different brochures may follow a different approach to present their data making the task of extracting and aggregating information from digital brochures a challenging task.

3   Text Extraction from PDF Documents

The Portable Document Format (PDF) is the file format used for digital brochures online. It is a popular format due to its lightweight characteristics and being portable across systems. In PDF files, text data is stored as a series of string objects. These objects can vary in font style, font size, orientation, and line spacing. Hence, when extracting text data from different PDF documents, special attention must be paid to any variation in data presentation within the processed document. As summarized in [32], the main steps involved in the extraction of text from a PDF document are: *Layout analysis, Segmentation, Character/Symbol recognition, Structure recognition* and *Text extraction*. Brief notes on each step are provided further.

3.1   Layout Analysis

In Layout analysis, the document is broken down into a hierarchy of similar regions (Fig. 2.). In general, layout analysis helps in capturing document contents, conversion into electronic formats, data retrieval and optical character recognition (OCR).

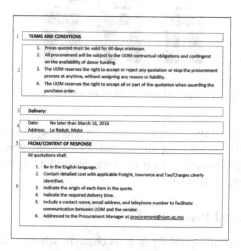

Fig. 2. Homogeneous regions identified by Layout Analysis.

Several statistical algorithms and methods have been used for conducting layout analysis [10]. Based on the underlying method, layout analysis algorithms are often divided primarily into either bottom-up or top-down algorithm. In bottom-up algorithm, layout analysis starts within the smallest components in a text (pixels or linked components), afterward these components are grouped into a larger region. In contrast, in top-down algorithm, layout analysis begins with the document as a whole and repeatedly divides the complete document to shape smaller regions. Each technique described has its own advantages and must be carefully selected to fit specific situations. Furthermore, a hybrid strategy which make use of a fusion of top-down and bottom-up strategies has also been proposed in [11, 12].

3.2 Segmentation

In storage and retrieval systems, segmentation is considered a simple task in which underlying algorithms manipulate complex document formats and backgrounds [13]. Besides, segmentation is a labeling method, the latter involves the process where same label is assigned to spatially aligned units (such as pixels, linked components or characteristic points) as shown in Fig. 3.

Fig. 3. Segmentation applied to a document [33].

Similar to layout analysis, algorithms used for page segmentation fall under three categories that are: bottom-up, top-down and hybrid algorithms. Furthermore, the choice of a technique for segmentation must be carefully chosen as it will depend on the document structure complexity.

3.3 Character/Symbol Recognition

Optical character recognition (OCR) is a mechanism where a machine searches for pattern in an image to recognize text data. OCR technology is particularly important in recognizing characters from Portable Document Format (PDF) documents where text, otherwise inaccessible in the document, are identified and converted into editable and searchable format. Without PDF character recognition, there are many disadvantages to PDF documents, which hinder their use in tasks involving text extraction [14, 15].

3.4 Structure Recognition

The interpretation of the structure deals with conceptual explanations of regions instead of their physical attributes [16]. Mapping from the physical regions in a document to their corresponding logical labels is considered as the logical structure of a document. Furthermore, document structure analysis is the method which is used to allocate logical labels during layout analysis to physical regions detected. Title, sub-title, abstract, paragraph, words, header, sentence, footer, caption, page number and others are all considered logical labels.

4 Related Works

Over the past three decades, systematic studies as evidenced in [17–24] have been carried out in text extraction for different types of documents. We summarize some of the relevant studies here. Anewierden [25], for instance, documented his findings using PDF file where his work is based on restoring the logical structure of technical manuals. He developed a system called AIDAS that takes a PDF file, extracts the logical structure, then in this logical structure assigns indexes to each part. Indexes refer to two things, firstly the content of the element and secondly, how the element can be included in the instruction. Once extraction has been completed, indexes can be used to query the database, an instructor can then retrieve suitable training content. The first step taken by AIDAS is to describe a document's overall layout. During this stage footers, columns, headers, and the dominant font are defined. By statistical analysis, all of these are calculated and can be overridden by the user. AIDAS subsequently divides each page into segments. Compared with few text elements, drawings are recognized though several graphical elements. Furthermore, tables are recognized by a texts labeled as floating and the remaining segments are considered as the segments of the document.

Another method for extracting structures from PDF documents called Xed has been developed by Hadjar et al. [26]. Xed is a software with main features transforming original PDF files into canonical XML form. This process consists of two key steps, first, it transforms PDF documents into an internal Java tree, normalizes the original document's primitives, and considers all types of embedded tools. Second, to recover the physical structures and their representation in the canonical format, Xed proceeds by analyzing Internal Java tree text.

Chao et al. [27] have also worked on methods for segmenting logical structure regions in a PDF document. The page is firstly divided into three layers namely text, image and vector graphic layer. This is done to reduce the possible logical component overlay and the interference between different logical components. Through this layering process, each layer is transformed into a PDF of its own, then the PDF document is transformed into bitmap images which is used to define the logical structural component blocks in each layer. Document image segmentation is then performed. A polygon outline is obtained for each component as well as the component's style values and content. Text components, shapes of the images are extracted for processing. Moreover, for vector graphic components, a SVG file has been created for every component defined.

Ramakrishnan et al. [28] worked on a tool to extract text blocks using research papers as raw data. Text blocks were grouped using rules that characterize sections, called LA-PDFText. The LA-PDF Text scheme involves mainly on the text component of the research documents. The tool can be used as an inspiration for more sophisticated techniques that does not only involve text. The system goes through three stages: identifying contiguous text blocks, categorizing text blocks into metaphorical categories using a rule-based approach, and linking categorized text blocks together by correctly arranging them, resulting in extracting text from section-wise grouped text.

Gao et al. [29] implemented another method, SEB, that uses PDF format book documents as input data. The extraction process involves the main physical and logical structures of a book. The authors suggest a series of new methods in the scope of PDF-based books to enhance traditional image-based methods by using the two characteristics of PDF files and books. These characteristics are firstly page component (SCC) style consistency and secondly natural rendering order local reliability. Bipartite graph plays an important to decide the reading order as well as extracting metadata from title pages.

Tkaczyk et al. [30] further launched CERMINE, an open source framework for the extraction of born-digital metadata and parsed bibliographic references using scientific papers as input. This framework made use of supervised and unsupervised machine learning techniques. A workflow is used that consist of three steps. First a TrueViz format [31] document is generated using the PDF file as input. Secondly the Metadata Extraction path analyzes parts of the geometric hierarchical structure of metadata and extracts from them a rich collection of record metadata. Thirdly the extraction path for references analyzes parts of the framework classified as references.

Singh et al. [32] proposed an open-source system for a variety of scholarly paper knowledge extraction tasks, including metadata (title, name of author, affiliation and e-mail), structure (headings of section and body text, headings of table and figure, URLs and footnotes), and bibliography (citation instances and references). The system accepts a PDF article, (1) convert the PDF file to an XML format, (2) process the XML file to extract useful information, and (3) export the output to TEI-encoded structured documents. With rich metadata, namely x and y coordinates, font size, font weight, font style etc., each token in the PDF file is annotated. For the extraction mission, machine learning models, handwritten rules/heuristics and the rich knowledge found in the XML files were used.

It can seen from the techniques described above that, the underlying process of extracting information from PDF files is based on the extraction of multiple components making the PDF documents such as images, texts, colors, etc. In the case of supermarket brochures, the main goal is to extract text data containing product name, price, quantity, etc. such that the underlying techniques presented in this section may be overrated for the problem at hand. Alternatively, we propose that to speed up processing time without compromising on the set objective of extracting essential text data from PDF brochures, the focus should be on block of texts alone. We posit that once texts blocks are extracted from brochures, the rest of the work would simply require the accurately alignment of appropriate labels (price, name quantity, etc.) to the corresponding values listed in the brochures. We present our proposed approach to extract brochure data in the next section.

5 Automating Extraction of Text Contents

In this paper, we seek to automatically access and extract useful information from PDF brochures published online for supermarkets in Mauritius. The goal is to provide decision makers with products details from competitors for strategic planning. The architecture for our proposed system is shown in Fig. 4.

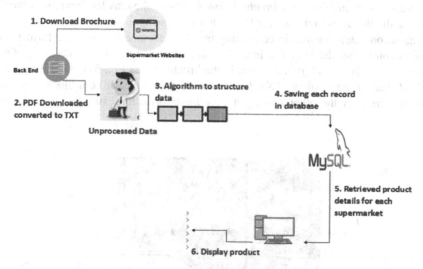

Fig. 4. Components of proposed system to extract text from supermarket brochures

The main components are: 1) A crawler, 2) A PDF to Text Converter, 3) A customized Text Extraction Algorithm, 4) A Data Storage function and 4) A Retrieve and Display Function. Each of those components was implemented and tested separately and then integrated for evaluation. Brochures data available from supermarket stores in Mauritius were used for the overall evaluation of the proposal. Namely two supermarkets were targeted for this study: Jumbo and Monoprix (now Winner's). For each supermarket, the corresponding online brochures for a period of 3 months were obtained from their websites https://catalogue.jumbo.mu/14012 and https://www.winners.mu/. The dataset consisted of about 3000 product items to be extracted from the downloaded brochures. Details of implementation on each component and test results are presented in the next section.

6 Implementation, Testing and Results

The task of the crawler is to regularly visit supermarket websites and download their respective brochures. The crawler is implemented in Java and we make use of the Jsoup[1] library to obtain the HTML home page of the two supermarkets used in this

---

[1] https://jsoup.org/.

study (i.e., jumbo and monoprix). Because brochures link are dynamic and cannot be hard coded in our program, we designed our crawler in such as a way that it extracts all links available on the home page of the supermarket and it specifically looks for any link that contains a PDF extension with the domain name of the supermarket's. It must be pointed out that based on our observation, at the time of conducting this study, Jumbo and Monoprix would offer their latest brochures in PDF format for downloads on their websites. No other documents with the PDF extension were accessible on each supermarket website. Once the brochure link is found, the crawler downloads the file and save the document on a server for further processing.

The second step consists in converting the PDF documents into TXT format. The result of converting the brochure into TXT format turned out to be interesting. Once converted, details of each product item in the brochure (see Fig. 5) could be seen as a block of data in the resultant TXT file. Block of data for each item block is aligned vertically one after the other making it easy for information extraction one line at a time.

Fig. 5. Different Blocks of Items and resultant TXT contents file

Once conversion from PDF to TXT is completed, the next step consists in reading each block of data from the TXT file one by one for later storage in a database. The main challenge for this part lies in accurately identifying details of the item blocks for later storage and retrieval in the database. For instance, the TXT files provided us with block of texts that contained information presented in a linear but randomized and unstructured format. We had to identify, which part of the block of data referred to the any of product description, price (old and promotional), details (colour, quantity, dimensions, etc.) and supermarket information (jumbo or winners).

To add to the complexity of the task, blocks of data identified did not always follow the same format within the same brochures or in brochures from same store on different dates or even in brochures from different stores. The diversity in the way information was presented in a brochure did not allow us to apply techniques already adopted in previous studies. Instead, we proceeded in devising our own algorithms based on manual analysis of the brochures downloaded from the supermarket's websites.

Following document analysis, it was found that although blocks of data from a sample of brochures could appear randomly, the underlying contents made it relatively easy to determine the semantics of each part of the text for each block. As an example of block variation, it was found that given two brochures, one brochure may present block of items in the order of name, description, old price, and promotion price while in the other brochure, block of data would present information in the order of name and promotion price only. To accurately identify and classify blocks of items accurately, therefore, we had to devise our own algorithm for information extraction as shown in Figs. 6, 7 and 8.

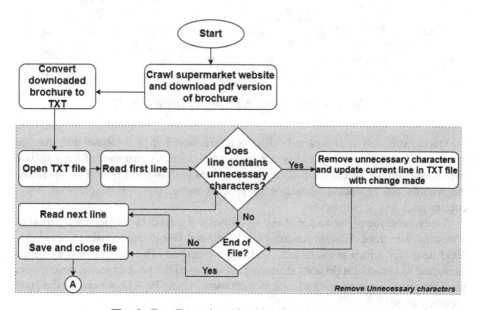

Fig. 6. Text Extraction Algorithm flowchart (part 1)

At the core of the algorithm, once unwanted characters are removed from the TXT files, we posit that any piece of text, which contains numbers followed by a period '.' and two digits such as '135.00', would be price values, with the larger value being the current price and the smaller value being the promotional price. We also created our corpus of data, which acted as a data dictionary to identify product name and description. Supermarket product vocabularies are more or less standardized such that once a line of text is matched with our dictionary; we were, thus, able to identify whether the text referred to the product name or product description.

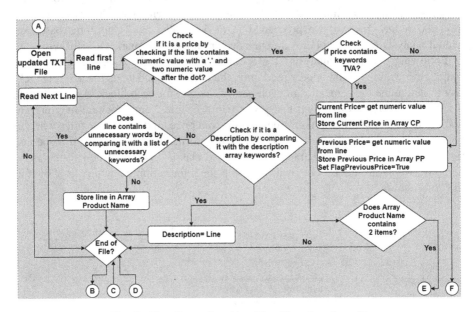

Fig. 7. Text Extraction Algorithm Flowchart (part 2)

Once extraction is completed, all details are stored in a database that may be accessed either via a web portal or a mobile application. A snapshot of the database populated from data extracted from tested brochures is shown in Fig. 9. For this study, the records are organized according to product name, description, previous price, current price and supermarkets.

To evaluate the performance of our algorithm, we used data crawled for a period of 3 months from three different supermarkets brochures. Our dataset consisted of roughly 3000 items for which relevant texts had to be extracted. The total records extracted amounted to around 15000 texts structured according to the product name, description, previous price, current price and supermarket name. Using Eq. (1), we obtained a good accuracy of 85%.

$$Accuracy = \frac{No.\ of\ Items\ Correctly\ Extracted}{Total\ No.\ of\ Items\ in\ Brochures} \tag{1}$$

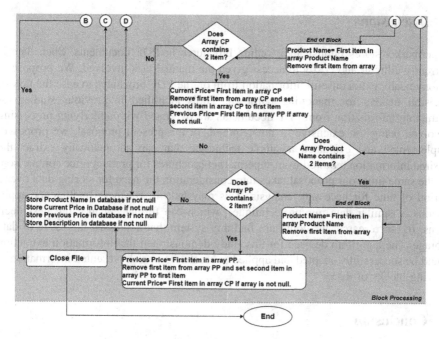

Fig. 8. Text Extraction Algorithm flowchart (part 3)

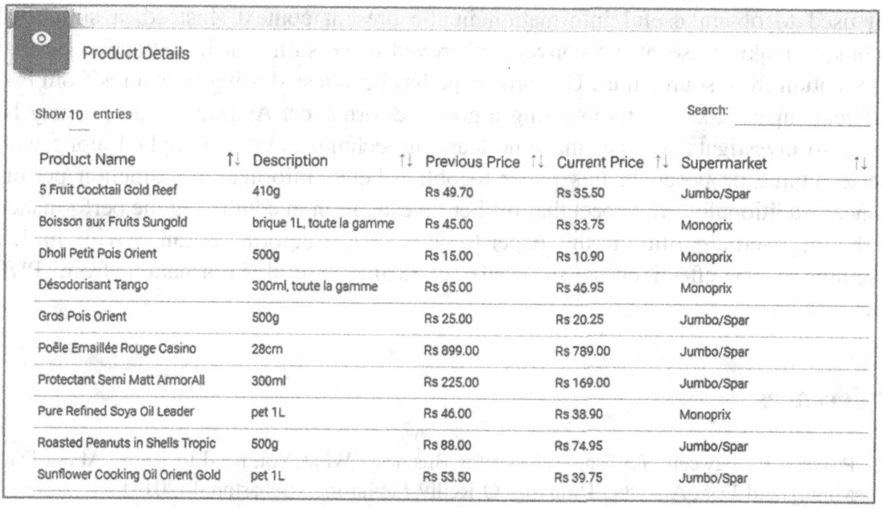

Product Details				

Show 10 entries   Search:

Product Name ↑↓	Description ↑↓	Previous Price ↑↓	Current Price ↑↓	Supermarket ↑↓
5 Fruit Cocktail Gold Reef	410g	Rs 49.70	Rs 35.50	Jumbo/Spar
Boisson aux Fruits Sungold	brique 1L, toute la gamme	Rs 45.00	Rs 33.75	Monoprix
Dholl Petit Pois Orient	500g	Rs 15.00	Rs 10.90	Monoprix
Désodorisant Tango	300ml, toute la gamme	Rs 65.00	Rs 46.95	Monoprix
Gros Pois Orient	500g	Rs 25.00	Rs 20.25	Jumbo/Spar
Poêle Emaillée Rouge Casino	28cm	Rs 899.00	Rs 789.00	Jumbo/Spar
Protectant Semi Matt ArmorAll	300ml	Rs 225.00	Rs 169.00	Jumbo/Spar
Pure Refined Soya Oil Leader	pet 1L	Rs 46.00	Rs 38.90	Monoprix
Roasted Peanuts in Shells Tropic	500g	Rs 88.00	Rs 74.95	Jumbo/Spar
Sunflower Cooking Oil Orient Gold	pet 1L	Rs 53.50	Rs 39.75	Jumbo/Spar

Fig. 9. Database contents displaying extracted product details

7 Discussions

Supermarket stores publish their online brochures in PDF documents. Such data is currently difficult and costly to access given the manual task involved. We propose to automatically extract useful information from online PDF brochures to ease the task of decision makers for marketing purposes. Tools identified in previous studies for extracting information from PDF documents are overrated with underlying processing involved being too extensive or not required. In the present proposal, we proposed, implemented and evaluated a simple technique that can automatically extract the desired information required from supermarket brochures for product price comparison. At the same time, our proposal takes into consideration the need for storing data over a period of time for necessary analysis. This may help in Business Intelligence applications or similar data mining techniques, which can further enhance business decisions. In our research, we could not find any system that addressed this issue of data storage. The algorithm devised for this study demonstrated that information extraction could be successfully adapted and applied to brochures, which presented information in varying blocks of data.

8 Conclusion

In this paper, we present a system that can be used to extract useful information from online PDF files. The techniques used in our proposal contrast with those used in previous studies in that complex natural language or image processing techniques are not used to obtain useful information in the present context. Instead, a simplified technique making use of file conversion proved to be sufficient in extracting desired information from source files. Our prototype has been tested using brochures from two different supermarkets demonstrating a good performance. As future work, it may be useful to investigate whether machine learning techniques can be applied along with the technique proposed in this paper to obtain better information extraction performance. Additionally, we expect that further investigation in comparing the performance of the proposed algorithm in this paper to other similar algorithms can provide further insights on its effectiveness in easily extracting useful information from PDF documents.

References

1. Provost, F., Fawcett, T.: Data Science for Business: What You need to Know About Data Mining and Data-Analytic Thinking. O'Reilly Media Inc., Sebastopol (2013)
2. Amankwah-Amoah, J., Adomako, S.: Big data analytics and business failures in data-Rich environments: an organizing framework. Comput. Ind. **105**, 204–212 (2019)
3. Bal, H.Ç., Erkan, Ç.: Industry 4.0 and competitiveness. Procedia Comput. Sci. **158**, 625–631 (2019)

4. Nyanga, C., Pansiri, J., Chatibura, D.: Enhancing competitiveness in the tourism industry through the use of business intelligence: a literature review. J. Tour. Futures **6**, 139–151 (2019)

5. Pustulka, E., Hanne, T.: Text mining innovation for business. In: Dornberger, R. (ed.) New Trends in Business Information Systems and Technology. SSDC, vol. 294, pp. 49–61. Springer, Cham (2021). https://doi.org/10.1007/978-3-030-48332-6_4

6. Cohen, M.C., Perakis, G.: Optimizing promotions for multiple items in supermarkets. In: Ray, S., Yin, S. (eds.) Channel Strategies and Marketing Mix in a Connected World. SSSCM, vol. 9, pp. 71–97. Springer, Cham (2020). https://doi.org/10.1007/978-3-030-31733-1_4

7. MasKhanam, M., Ali, A.: Impact of advertising: end user perspective. J. Soc. Sci. Humanit. **58**(1), 179–189 (2019)

8. Wiese, M., Martínez-Climent, C., Botella-Carrubi, D.: A framework for Facebook advertising effectiveness: a behavioral perspective. J. Bus. Res. **109**, 76–87 (2020)

9. Knezevic, B., Davidaviciene, V., Skrobot, P.: Implementation of social networks as a digital communication tool in social supermarkets. Int. J. Mod. Res. Eng. Manag. (IJMREM) **1**(6), 41 (2018)

10. Binmakhashen, G.M., Mahmoud, S.A.: Document layout analysis: a comprehensive survey. ACM Comput. Surv. (CSUR) **52**(6), 1–36 (2019)

11. BinMakhashen, G.M., Mahmoud, S.A.: Historical document layout analysis using anisotropic diffusion and geometric features. Int. J. Digit. Libr. **21**(3), 329–342 (2020). https://doi.org/10.1007/s00799-020-00280-w

12. Hassan, T.: Object-level document analysis of PDF files. In: Proceedings of the 9th ACM Symposium on Document Engineering, Munich, Germany. Association for Computing Machinery (2009)

13. Sesh Kumar, K.S., Namboodiri, A.M., Jawahar, C.V.: Learning segmentation of documents with complex scripts. In: Kalra, P.K., Peleg, S. (eds.) ICVGIP 2006. LNCS, vol. 4338, pp. 749–760. Springer, Heidelberg (2006). https://doi.org/10.1007/11949619_67

14. Lovegrove, W.S., Brailsford, D.F.: Document analysis of PDF files: methods, results and implications. Electron. Publ.-Orig. Dissem. Des. **8**(3) (1995)

15. Audithan, S., Chandrasekaran, R.M.: Document text extraction from document images using haar discrete wavelet transform. Eur. J. Sci. Res. **36**(4), 502–512 (2009)

16. Mao, S., Rosenfeld, A., Kanungo, T.: Document structure analysis algorithms: a literature survey. In: Document Recognition and Retrieval X, vol. 5010, pp. 197–207. International Society for Optics and Photonics, January 2003

17. Nagy, G., Seth, S., Viswanathan, M.: A prototype document image analysis system for technical journals. Computer **25**(7), 10–22 (1992)

18. Dengel, A.: Initial learning of document structure. In: Proceedings of 2nd International Conference on Document Analysis and Recognition (ICDAR 1993), pp. 86–90. IEEE (1993)

19. Dengel, A., Dubiel, F.: Clustering and classification of document structure-a machine learning approach. In: Proceedings of 3rd International Conference on Document Analysis and Recognition, 14–16 August 1995, vol. 2, pp. 587–591 (1995)

20. Jain, A.K., Bin, Y.: Document representation and its system to page decomposition. IEEE Trans. Pattern Anal. Mach. Intell. **20**, 294–308 (1998)

21. Alpizar-Chacon, I., Sosnovsky, S.: Order out of chaos: construction of knowledge models from PDF textbooks. In: Proceedings of the ACM Symposium on Document Engineering 2020, p. 10, September 2020

22. Jensen, Z., et al.: A machine learning approach to zeolite synthesis enabled by automatic literature data extraction. ACS Central Sci. **5**(5), 892–899 (2019)

23. Payak, A., Rai, S., Shrivastava, K., Gulwani, R.: Automatic text summarization and keyword extraction using natural language processing. In: 2020 International Conference on Electronics and Sustainable Communication Systems (ICESC), pp. 98–103. IEEE, July 2020

24. Khatavkar, V., Kulkarni, P.: Trends in document analysis. In: Balas, V.E., Sharma, N., Chakrabarti, A. (eds.) Data Management, Analytics and Innovation. AISC, vol. 808, pp. 249–262. Springer, Singapore (2019). https://doi.org/10.1007/978-981-13-1402-5_19

25. Anjewierden, A.: AIDAS: incremental logical structure discovery in PDF documents. In: Proceedings of Sixth International Conference on Document Analysis and Recognition, 13–13 September 2001, pp. 374–378 (2001)

26. Hadjar, K., Rigamonti, M., Lalanne, D., Ingold, R.: Xed: a new tool for extracting hidden structures from electronic documents. In: 2004 Proceedings of the First International Workshop on Document Image Analysis for Libraries, 23–24 January 2004, pp. 212–224 (2004)

27. Chao, H., Fan, J.: Layout and content extraction for pdf documents. In: Marinai, S., Dengel, A.R. (eds.) DAS 2004. LNCS, vol. 3163, pp. 213–224. Springer, Heidelberg (2004). https://doi.org/10.1007/978-3-540-28640-0_20

28. Ramakrishnan, C., Patnia, A., Hovy, E., Burns, G.A.P.C.: Layout-aware text extraction from full-text PDF of scientific articles. Source Code Biol. Med. **7**, 7 (2012). https://doi.org/10.1186/1751-0473-7-7

29. Gao, L., Tang, Z., Lin, X., Liu, Y., Qiu, R., Wang, Y.: Structure extraction from PDF-based book documents. In: Proceedings of the 11th Annual International ACM/IEEE Joint Conference on Digital Libraries, Ottawa, Ontario, Canada. Association for Computing Machinery (2011)

30. Tkaczyk, D., Szostek, P., Dendek, P.J., Fedoryszak, M., Bolikowski, L.: Cermine–automatic extraction of metadata and references from scientific literature. In: 2014 11th IAPR International Workshop on Document Analysis Systems, pp. 217–221. IEEE, April 2014

31. Lee, C., Kanungo, T.: The architecture of TrueViz: A groundTRUth/metadata editing and VIsualiZing ToolKit. Pattern Recogn. **36**(3), 811–825 (2003)

32. Singh, M., et al.: OCR++: a robust framework for information extraction from scholarly articles. In: Proceedings of COLING 2016, the 26th International Conference on Computational Linguistics: Technical Papers, Osaka, Japan, 11–17 December 2016, pp. 3390–3400 (2016)

33. Sasirekha, D., Chandra, E.: Text extraction from PDF document. In: IJCA Proceedings on Amrita International Conference of Women in Computing. AICWIC, pp. 17–19 (2013)

Improved Predictive System for Soil Test Fertility Performance Using Fuzzy Rule Approach

O. T. Arogundade[1], C. Atasie[1], Sanjay Misra[2(✉)], A. B. Sakpere[3],
O. O. Abayomi-Alli[4], and K. A. Adesemowo[5]

[1] Federal University of Agriculture Abeokuta, Abeokuta, Nigeria
arogundadeot@funaab.edu.ng, chibusanto@gmail.com
[2] Covenant University, Ota, Nigeria
sanjay.misra@covenantuniversity.edu.ng
[3] University of Ibadan, Ibadan, Nigeria
ab.sakpere@ui.edu.ng
[4] Kaunas University of Technology, Kaunas, Lithuania
olusola.abayomi-alli@ktu.lt
[5] Nelson Mandela University, Port Elizabeth, South Africa
kadesemowo@soams.co.za

Abstract. Decision making in agriculture affects both crops in all their phases (planting, management, costs, etc.) as well as the distribution and organization of crop production systems. Generating rules and connecting the rules into the fuzzy inference system for decision making is a very delicate task when associated with soil fertility test. Some of the constraints with previous study is the problem of uncertainty and imprecise complexity of experimenting and interpreting DSS system in real-life. The application of fuzzy-logic provides an effective decision-making tool for dealing the aforementioned challenges. This paper proposed a Mandani-type fuzzy inference System for testing soil fertility and increasing overall crop yield. This study was conducted in FUNAAB farm and seven inputs (nitrogen, phosphorous, potassium, organic matter, boron, zinc, and PH of water) with their nutrients percentage were fed into a fuzzy inference system. Three major inputs were varied based on their major role in soil constituents (nitrogen, phosphorous and potassium (NPK)). Our experimental result showed that irrespective of the level of the three major inputs (NPK) at every given time, the values of the output did not significantly change, it remained at 0.5 and it represents an average output on the crops considered for this purpose of this work. This study concludes that the application of fuzzy logic rule (mandani –type FIS model) in soil fertility test for cultivating four crops (Yam, Cassava, Maize and Cocoyam) have proven to be effective measure and thereby ensuring effective decision making.

Keywords: Soil fertility test · Fuzzy inference system · Mandani-type FIS model

© Springer Nature Singapore Pte Ltd. 2021
K. K. Patel et al. (Eds.): icSoftComp 2020, CCIS 1374, pp. 249–263, 2021.
https://doi.org/10.1007/978-981-16-0708-0_21

1 Introduction

Decision making is a task that everyone is involved in on a regular basis. It involves choosing between two or more options [12]. More interesting about the task is that its outcome can break or mar the stakeholders. As a result, there is a need to ensure that the art of decision making is improved upon so as to lead to a favourable outcome. For an agriculturist, decision making comes to play right from the early phase of planting up to the final stage of distribution of the farm produce. The advancement of Information Technology (Computer Science) has made it possible for this cumbersome process of decision making to be made possible even for an agriculturist. Also, fuzzy logic is a computing concept that provides an effective way by which conflict can be resolved especially when it involves multiple criteria and options [26].

In agriculture, there is a need to test for the fertility of soil before embarking on planting. The need for soil fertility test has become very crucial for profit maximization. Testing for soil fertility helps to understand the relationship between an estimated nutrient level needed for a given crop and the given nutrient of a soil to determine if there is any form of nutrient deficiency, sufficiency and/or toxicity for the crop in question [25]. The assessment of the quality/fertility of soil is a fuzzy classification problem [33]. Furthermore, soil map accuracy can be improved using fuzzy logic compared with conventional method [14]. As a result, in this research we attempt to use the concept of fuzzy logic to test the fertility of soil in an urban setting farm in Nigeria.

The term "fuzzy" implies vagueness. Hence, fuzzy logic can be defined as a model of logical reasoning with vague or imprecise statements [2]. Fuzzy logic assigns degrees of truth to propositions. Different variant of fuzzy logic has been used in agriculture or soil fertility testing. Mokarram, M. and Hojati, M. used fuzzy logic to evaluate soil fertility [13], order weighted average algorithm depended on fuzzy to specify some parameters. Other researches such as that of Moonjun, R. et al. [14], Prabakaran, G. et al. [18], Sami, M. et al. [21] and Davatgar, N. et al. [5] have also used one variant or the other of fuzzy logic. From all of these studies, it's obvious that Mandani-type fuzzy logic has not been widely explored. As a result, this study explores the use of manadani fuzzy logic for soil fertility testing in a University farm located in the South-Western part of Nigeria. This study is motivated by the need to enhance farmers' decision on the fertility state of the soil before planting begins. In addition, the need for early identification of deficient nutrients is also essential for proper planting growth and yield productivity.

The objectives of this study can be summarized as follows:

(i) develop a manadani fuzzy logic system for soil fertility testing
(ii) test and evaluate the effectiveness of the fuzzy logic system in decision making of soil fertility testing

The rest of this study is organized as follows: the reviewed related literature is reported in Sect. 2. Section 3 described the constructs of the proposed model. The implementation of the Mandani-type Fuzzy Inference System is reported in Sect. 2.2. Section 4 presents the implementation result while Sect. 5 concludes this study.

2   Background and Related Works

This section discusses in detailed the different state-of-the-art methods proposed and the contributions of previous literature in the testing for soil fertility. The impacts and roles of machine learning [37, 38] algorithms cannot be over-stressed as its applications cut across different areas. However, some of the applications of machine learning in soil test fertility include the studies from Moonjun et al. [14] that presented the impact of fuzzy logic for effective soil mapping. The study applied rule-based reasoning for efficient mapping of soil series and texture. Wang et al. [31] proposed a Takagli and Sugeno (T-S) fuzzy neural networks models for testing soil fertility of rice cultivation. Authors concluded on the impact of applying potassium and magnesium macronutrients in fertilizers can improve overall productivity in rice. In addition, Rodriguez et al. [20] proposed a fuzzy logic method using the T-S fuzzy interference method for developing an indexes for soil quality assessment. The proposed approach was able to determine the dynamics of soil quality for farming using physical, chemical and biological characteristics.

The application of novel adaptive neuro-fuzzy interference system (ANFIS) model was presented by Were et al. [34] for predicting and mapping soil uncertainty. Furthermore, Authors in [17] proposed the combination of ANN and fuzzy logic methods for soil samples classification using munsell colour approach. Similarly, Dang et al. [4] also presented a hybrid ANFIS system for rice cultivation prediction. The study integrated HyFIS system with GIS-based and the analysis of eight environmental variables was evaluated to assess the suitability areas for crop cultivation. Davatgar et al. [5] introduced the combination of principal component analysis and fuzzy cluster algorithm for the delineate of site specific nutrient management. The study was able to provide farmers the privilege of site specific nutrient management. Sirsat et al. [27] developed an automatic prediction system for measuring soil fertility indices. The study was used on four soil nutrients for soil organic carbon and four important soil (phosphorus pentoxide, iron, manganese and zinc. The study showed that the best prediction was achieved using extremely randomized regression trees (extraTrees). Prabakan et al. [18] developed a decision support system using fuzzy system to test for soil array, nutrients, water and climatic parameters thus improving crop productivity. Authors applied three types of graphical interference approach for determining the aggregation rule and their results showed improvement in the cost ratio. Wang et al. [33] also introduced a posterior probability support vector machine for assessing soil quality test for concentration of dangerous substance. Authors claimed from their study that emission from industries and vehicles, the use of phosphorus and potassium fertilizers have high effect in determining soil quality. Shekofteh et al. [24] presented a hybrid method using the combination of evolutional approach of ant colony organization algorithm and ANFIS method for predicting soil fertility. The method gave better efficiency and determination coefficient for predicting soil CEC. Seyedmohammadi et al. [23] demonstrated the application of fuzzy analytical hierarchy process for determining weight values in crop cultivation priority. The study further implemented the geographical information system and multi-criteria decision making techniques for enhancing soil suitability decision in crop cultivation. Agarwal et al. [1] proposed a soil fertility test method using principal of colorimetry and applied naïve bayes algorithm for prediction. Authors claimed that applying NB predicted a better accuracy and it can reduce time complexity for testing soil fertility. Authors in Sumiharto and Hardiyanto [28] designed a prototype NPK nutrient measurement using local binary pattern and back-propagation neural network for testing soil fertility.

Interestingly, authors in Ngunriji et al. [15] proposed a fuzzy logic soil mapping approach for determining the following: soil types, soil CEC, depth and drainage class. The results showed an improved prediction performance with field observations. Sun et al. [29] presented the impacts and the relationship of soil quality index in cultivation of A. monngholicus. Authors proposed five soil indicators namely organic matter, calcium, gallium, borom and magnesium for assessing soil quality. Sefati et al. [22] compared and evaluated different soil test models for assessing soil quality in urban areas. Li et al. [9] evaluated and assessed soil quality index using twenty soil properties based on physical, chemical and biological features for wheat-maize cultivation and increasing crop yield. The result analysis shows that alka;i-hydrolyzable nitrogen and organic matter are crucial elements in soil assessment compared to other elements. Leena et al. [8] developed a decision support system using GIS technologies for managing soil fertility. The study was able to enhance fertilizer recommendation distribution for soil nutrients and space variability thereby improving varieties of crop productivity. Some studies have introduced the use of sensors and other hardware devices to test and predict soil fertility. Authors in Rawankar et al. [19] presented a soil analysis approach for evaluating the characteristics of main soil samples nutrients for increasing crop cultivation yield. Similar study is from Authors in Masrie et al. [10] who also developed an optical transducer to effectively measure and predict macronutrients of nitrogen, phosphorus and potassium to test for soil fertility within soil samples.

Based on the findings from related work the application of fuzzy logic system in different soil test applications have shown that this method have the ability to understand and ease the representation and processing of human knowledge in computer. In addition, it has been shown in related study that the inputs, outputs, and rules of Fuzzy Logic [39, 40] are easy to modify. However, some of the drawbacks of existing studies includes failures with inference rule, and accumulated decision, time complexity of ML methods, problems with limited and constrained environmental models, leading to ineffective decision-making operations. Therefore, there is a need for a simple and effective methods to consider prior farmers' knowledge in agricultural system and best soil samples with emphasis on level of nutrients for variety of crop cultivation. Thus, this paper focussed on designing an effective fuzzy logic system based on mandami fuzzy interference for testing soil fertility thus improving crop yield.

2.1 Fuzzy Logic

This study presents a fuzzy logic algorithm with the ability to reduce inconsistency and costs of traditional soil mapping processes [14]. The application of fuzzy logic[] has been said to have resolve the difficulty between clear logical values and accuracy [18]. The use of fuzzy sets was initially introduced by Zadeh [35] as an extension of the classical notion of set. Lately, the adoption of fuzzy logic and fuzzy sets theory in environmental field has been on the rise as this method allows the integration of mathematical tools for dealing with uncertainty and imprecision [20]. Authors in [23] also defined fuzzy sets as a more general kind of structures called L-relations [6], which have been applied to various research domain, such as linguistics, decision-making and clustering [3, 16, 30]. [7] further defined fuzzy set μ of $X \neq \varnothing$ as a function from the reference set X to the unit interval, such that $\mu : X \rightarrow [0, 1]$ where $F(X)$ represents the set of all fuzzy sets of X, that is $F(X)^{\text{def}} = \{\mu | \mu : X \rightarrow [0, 1]\}$. In addition, fuzzy sets can be described by their characteristic/membership function and assigning degree of membership $\mu(X)$ to each element $x \in X$.

The basic logical operations are the OR, AND and NOT with operands A and B membership values with the interval [0, 1].

2.2   Fuzzy Inference System (Mamdani)

Fuzzy Interference is the process of mapping the given input variables to an output space using mechanism derived fuzzy logic which consist of If-Then rules, membership functions and fuzzy logical operations [32]. Mamdani fuzzy interference method is the most commonly used method which consist of different steps as depicted below and a typical example of a Mamdani inference system is depicted in Fig. 1.

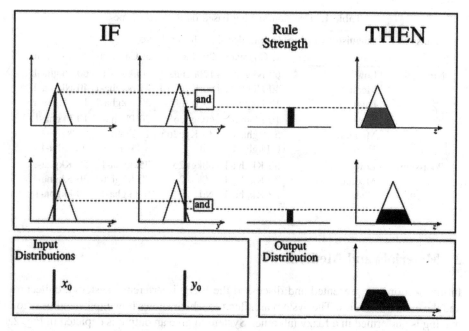

Fig. 1. A typical concept of the Mamdani-type Inference System

To compute the output of Mamdami-type FIS given the inputs, the following six steps must be carefully executed:

  i. A set of fuzzy rules must be established;
 ii. Apply input membership functions to fuzzify the inputs values;
iii. Establish a rule strength based on fuzzy rules and the combination of the fuzzified inputs in step (ii);
 iv. Identify the impacts of the rule by combining the rule strength in step (iii) with the output membership function;
  v. Integrate the impacts in step (iv) to get an output distribution;
 vi. To obtain a crisp output, result obtained in output distribution (step v) must be defuzzify.

2.3 Defuzzification and Decision Making

This is the last step of fuzzy interference process and it procedure here is the opposite of fuzzification operation. This study adopted the centroid method of defuzzification which is the most common and widely used method of defuzzification. The decision making for the four crops used in this study is summarized in Table 1.

Table 1. Decision making based on the Crop Type

Inputs	Linguistic variable	Output decisions for each crop			
		1: Cocoyam	2: Maize	3: Cassava	4: Cocoyam
Nitrogen	Low	60 Nkgha-1	120kgnha-1	90nkgha-1	60 Nkgha-1
	Medium	40 Nkgha-1	60 Kgnha-1	45 Nkgha-1	40 Nkgha-1
	High	10 Nkgha-1	39 Kgnha-1	20 Nkgha-1	10 Nkgha-1
Phosphorous	Low	10 Pkgha-1	60kgp2o5	20 Pkgha-1	10 Pkgha-1
	Medium	5 Pkgha-1	30 Kgp2o5	10 Pkgha-1	5 Pkgha-1
	High	0 Pkgha-1	Nil	5 Pkgha-1	0 Pkgha-1
Potassium	Low	50 Kkgha-1	60kgk2o	75kkgha-1	50 Kkgha-1
	Medium	30 Kkgha-1	30kgk2o	40 Kkgha-1	30 Kkgha-1
	High	20 Kkgha-1	Nil	0 Kkgha-1	20 kkgha-1

3 Materials and Methods

In this section, we presented and discussed the fuzzy interference system architecture and the evaluation rules. The system architecture which shows how inputs and decision making is performed in a fuzzy inference System to give an output is depicted in Fig. 2.

From Fig. 2, the rule base phase contains a number of fuzzy if-then rules and the database phase helps to define the membership function of the fuzzy set used in the fuzzy rules. The decision-making phase performs the inference operation on the rules generated. The fuzzification interface allows the transformation of the crisp input into degrees of match with linguistic values while the de-fuzzification interface produces the output by calculating the performance value with the help of suitable de-fuzzification method. The proposed Fuzzy interference process consist of the following steps as follows:

- i.   Fuzzification of the input variables
- ii. Application of the fuzzy operator (AND or OR) in the antecedent
- iii. Implication from the antecedent to the consequent
- iv. Aggregation of the consequents across the rules
- v.   De-fuzzification

3.1   Proposed Fuzzy Logic System Algorithm

With all the components, a fuzzy logic system can be built based on the following five steps as proposed by [11].

Input: {7 character set: PH water, Nitrogen, Phosphorus, Potassium, Organic Carbon, Zinc and Boron}

Output: {4 character set: Yam, Cassava, maize and Cocoyam}

Methods:

Step 1.   Independent variables which are the linguistic are inputted into the Mamdani Inference System as the key determinants or indicators of the dependent variable which are the Inputs.

Step 2.   Fuzzy sets are created for both independent and dependent variables with respect to the membership function. Such that for an input variable "Nitrogen" belongs to a membership function of either: "Very Low", "Low", "Moderately low", "Medium" and "Moderately high" which are then fixed in a respective ranges

Step 3.   The inference rules are then built within the system. A fuzzy hedge is used to tweak the membership function according to the description of the inference rules.

Step 4.   The output fuzzy set of the dependent variable is then generated based on the independent variables and the inference rules. After defuzzification, a numerical value is used to represent the output fuzzy set.

Step 5.   The result is then used for informed decision-making.

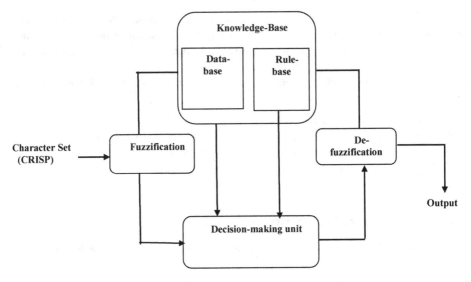

Fig. 2. System architecture of fuzzy inference system

3.2 Fuzzification and Rating for Soil Fertility Classes

Fuzzification is the process of combining the character set (Input value) used in a fuzzy value with an appropriate membership function/Linguistics variable. Seven inputs were used as input values which have the rating for soil fertility. Seven input variable with their respective linguistic variable and their corresponding linguistic values is presented in Table 2.

Table 2. Table showing the input variables and their linguistic values

Inputs 1: PH Water	
Strongly Acid	5.0–5.5
Moderately Acid	5.6–6.0
Slightly Acid	6.1–6.5
Neutral	6.6–7.2
Slightly Alkaline	7.3–7.8
Input 2: NITROGEN (Total N)	
Very Low	0.3–0.5
Low	0.6–1.0
Moderately Low	1.1–1.5
Medium	1.6–2.0
Moderately High	2.1–2.4

(*continued*)

Table 2. (*continued*)

Input 3: Phosphorous (BRAY-1-)MGKg-1	
Very Low	<3
Low	3–7
Moderate	7–20
High	>20 Mg
Input 4: Potassium (K)	
Very Low	0.12–0.2
Low	0.21–0.3
Moderate	0.31–0.6
High	0.61–0.73
Input 5: **ORGANIC CARBON** (gkg^{-1} O.M)	
Very Low	<4.0
Low	4.0–10.0
Moderate	10–14
High	14–20
Very High	>20
Input 6: ZINC (DPTA) **Mgkg–1**	
Low	<1.0
Medium	1.0–5.0
High	>5.0
Input 7: BORON (HOT H_2O SOL) Mgkg^{-1}	
Very Low	<0.35
Low	<0.35–0.5
Medium	0.5–2.0
High	<2.9

3.3   Rule Base and Expression

For the purpose of this study, MATLAB rule editor was used to generate fuzzy rules (if-then-rules). The rules defined were used for evaluating the rating for soil fertility test, thus each input membership function variable were assigned range of values. Eight IF-THEN rules (RI-RVIII) were generated as highlighted below:

R(I)   If (PH. Water is Neutral) and (Nitrogen is Medium) and (Phosphorus is Moderate) and (Potassium is Moderate) and (Organic. Carbon is Moderate) and (Zinc is Medium) and (Boron is Medium) then (YAM is MEDUIM) (1)

R(II)   If (PH. Water is Neutral) and (Nitrogen is moderately. High) and (Phosphorus is Moderate) and (Potassium is High) and (Organic Carbon is

Moderate) and (Zinc is Medium) and (Boron is Medium) then (YAM is HIGH) (1)

R(III)   If (PH. Water is Neutral) and (Nitrogen is moderately. High) and (Phosphorus is High) and (Potassium is High) and (Organic. Carbon is Moderate) and (Zinc is Medium) and (Boron is Medium) then (MAIZE is HIGH) (1)

R(IV)   If (PH. Water is Neutral) and (Nitrogen is moderately. Low) and (Phosphorus is Moderate) and (Potassium is High) and (Organic. Carbon is Moderate) and (Zinc is Medium) and (Boron is Medium) then (MAIZE is MEDIUM) (1)

R(V)   If (PH. Water is Neutral) and (Nitrogen is moderately. High) and (Phosphorus is Low) and (Potassium is High) and (Organic. Carbon is Moderate) and (Zinc is Medium) and (Boron is Medium) then (CASSAVA is MEDIUM) (1)

R(VI)   If (PH. Water is Neutral) and (Nitrogen is Medium) and (Phosphorus is High) and (Potassium is Low) and (Organic. Carbon is Moderate) and (Zinc is Medium) and (Boron is Medium) then (CASSAVA is MEDIUM) (1)

R(VII)   If (PH. Water is Neutral) and (Nitrogen is moderately. High) and (Phosphorus is Moderate) and (Potassium is Moderate) and (Organic. Carbon is Moderate) and (Zinc is Medium) and (Boron is Medium) then (COCOYAM is MEDIUM) (1)

R(VIII)   If (PH. Water is Neutral) and (Nitrogen is moderately. High) and (Phosphorus is High) and (Potassium is High) and (Organic. Carbon is Moderate) and (Zinc is Medium) and (Boron is Medium) then (COCOYAM is HIGH) (1).

4   Results and Discussion

This section presents the implementation of the model and the results obtained (Figs. 3, 4, 5, 6, 7, 8, 9, 10, 11 and 12) with discussions. The hardware and software requirement for effective implementation the proposed model are: Window OS (32 or 64-bits), 1 GB RAM, 250 GB HDD and Matlab R2008.

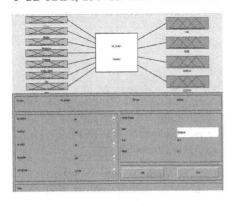

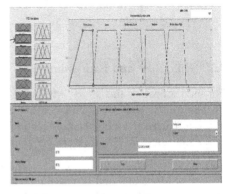

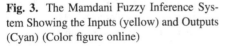

Fig. 3. The Mamdani Fuzzy Inference System Showing the Inputs (yellow) and Outputs (Cyan) (Color figure online)

Fig. 4. Membership Function editor for input variable "Nitrogen"

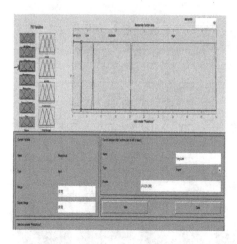

Fig. 5. Membership Function editor for input variable "Phosphorus"

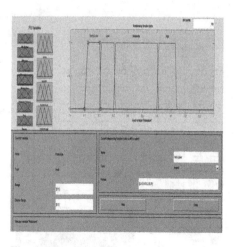

Fig. 6. Membership Function editor for input variable "Potassium"

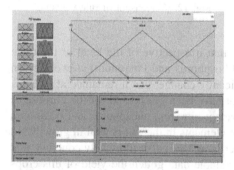

Fig. 7. Membership Function editor for output variable "Yam"

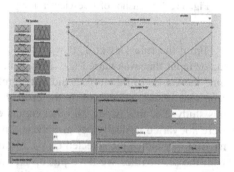

Fig. 8. Membership Function editor for output variable "Maize"

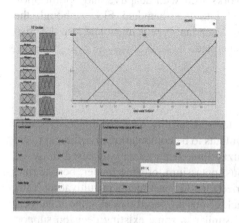

Fig. 9. Membership Function editor for output variable "Cassava"

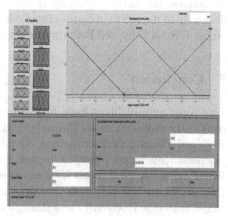

Fig. 10. Membership Function editor for output variable "Cocoyam"

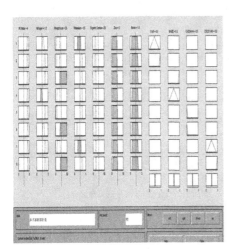

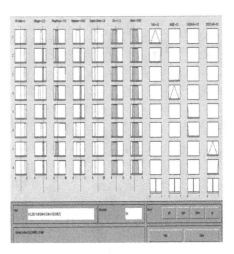

Fig. 11. Screenshot of rule viewer 1   **Fig. 12.** Screenshot of rule viewer 2

From the rule viewer 1, it was deduced that irrespective of the level of the three major input that was varied (i.e. Nitrogen, Phosphorus and Potassium) at every given time the values of the outputs did not significantly change, that it remained at 0.5, this represent an average output on the crops that have been considered for the purpose of this study. For this paper, all other inputs except nitrogen, phosphorus and potassium were not varied basically because these three elements in the soil is vital in growth and maximum yield of the selected crops. Furthermore, this paper ultimately conclude that with the set of rules we have put up and available data gotten the yield of this crops (Outputs) is a function of the availability of these three key element (i.e. Nitrogen, Phosphorus and Potassium) are not on a critical region. This study adopted Mamdani Fuzzy Inference System (FIS) because it works well with adaptive and optimization techniques, the seven inputs used was fed into the mamdani FIS. Although the designing of the FIS membership functions of Mamdani-type is linear and also the crisp output (Productivity and Performance) is generated.

5 Conclusion

This paper applied fuzzy logic rule to test for soil fertility using Mamdani-type FIS model. The proposed model allows Fuzzy Outputs to be computationally efficient to aid swift and effective decision making. Our fuzzy inference system was based on seven macronutrients inputs (nitrogen, phosphorous, potassium, organic matter, boron, zinc, PH of water) and three inputs NPK were varied for soil constituents in cultivating Yam, Cassava, Maize and Cocoyam. The drawback of our proposed model is the intelligent adaption to new discoveries and strategies. Similar to some existing decision support tool, fuzzy logic systems need to be reviewed and updated considering the dynamics of new discovery as a result of new research method or a change in the testing environment. Future recommendation is to effectively explore and adapt to dynamics deep learning methods in soil fertility test.

References

1. Agarwal, S., Bhangale, N., Dhanure, K., Gavhane, S., Chakkarwar, V.A., Nagori, M.B.: Application of colorimetry to determine soil fertility through Naive Bayes classification algorithm. In: 2018 9th International Conference on Computing, Communication and Networking Technologies (ICCCNT), pp. 1–6. IEEE, July 2018
2. Cintula, P., Fermüller, C., Noguera, C. (eds.): Handbook of Mathematical Fuzzy Logic, vol. 3, (Mathematical Logic and Foundations, vol. 58). College Publications, London (2015)
3. Coroiu, A.M.: Fuzzy methods in decision making process-a particular approach in manufacturing systems. In: IOP Conference Series: Materials Science and Engineering, vol. 95, no. 1, p. 012154. IOP Publishing (2015)
4. Dang, K.B., Burkhard, B., Windhorst, W., Müller, F.: Application of a hybrid neural-fuzzy inference system for mapping crop suitability areas and predicting rice yields. Environ. Model. Softw. **114**, 166–180 (2019)
5. Davatgar, N., Neishabouri, M.R., Sepaskhah, A.R.: Delineation of site specific nutrient management zones for a paddy cultivated area based on soil fertility using fuzzy clustering. Geoderma **173**, 111–118 (2012)
6. Hudedagaddi, D.P., Tripathy, B.K.: Clustering approaches in decision making using fuzzy and rough sets. In: Handbook of Research on Fuzzy and Rough Set Theory in Organizational Decision Making, pp. 116–136. IGI Global (2017)
7. Kruse, R., Moewes, C.: Fuzzy systems, Fuzzy set theory (2015). https://fuzzy.cs.ovgu.de/ci/fs/fs_ch02_fst.pdf. Accessed 11 Apr 2020
8. Leena, H.U., Premasudha, B.G., Basavaraja, P.K.: Sensible approach for soil fertility management using GIS cloud. In: 2016 International Conference on Advances in Computing, Communications and Informatics (ICACCI), pp. 2776–2781. IEEE, September 2016
9. Li, P., et al.: Soil quality assessment of wheat-maize cropping system with different productivities in China: establishing a minimum data set. Soil Tillage Res. **190**, 31–40 (2019)
10. Masrie, M., Rosman, M.S.A., Sam, R., Janin, Z.: Detection of nitrogen, phosphorus, and potassium (NPK) nutrients of soil using optical transducer. In: 2017 IEEE 4th International Conference on Smart Instrumentation, Measurement and Application (ICSIMA), pp. 1–4. IEEE, November 2017
11. Mazloumzadeh, S.M., Shamsi, M., Nezamabadi-Pour, H.: Evaluation of general-purpose lifters for the date harvest industry based on a fuzzy inference system. Comput. Electron. Agric. **60**(1), 60–66 (2008)
12. Majumder, M.: Multi criteria decision making. In: Majumder, M. (ed.) Impact of Urbanization on Water Shortage in Face of Climatic Aberrations, pp. 35–47. Springer, Singapore (2015). https://doi.org/10.1007/978-981-4560-73-3_2
13. Mokarram, M., Hojati, M.: Using ordered weight averaging (OWA) aggregation for multi-criteria soil fertility evaluation by GIS (case study: Southeast Iran). Comput. Electron. Agric. **132**, 1–3 (2017)
14. Moonjun, R., Shrestha, D.P., Jetten, G.: Fuzzy logic for fine-scale soil mapping: a case study in Thailand. CATENA **190**, 104456 (2020)

15. Ngunjiri, M.W., Libohova, Z., Minai, J.O., Serrem, C., Owens, P.R., Schulze, D.G.: Predicting soil types and soil properties with limited data in the Uasin Gishu Plateau Kenya. Geoderma Reg. **16**, e00210 (2019)

16. Novák, V., Štěpnička, M., Kupka, J.: Linguistic descriptions: their structure and applications. In: Larsen, H.L., Martin-Bautista, M.J., Vila, M.A., Andreasen, T., Christiansen, H. (eds.) FQAS 2013. Lecture Notes in Computer Science, vol. 8132, pp. 209–220. Springer, Heidelberg (2013). https://doi.org/10.1007/978-3-642-40769-7_19

17. Pegalajar, M.C., Ruiz, L.G.B., Sánchez-Marañón, M., Mansilla, L.: A Munsell colour-based approach for soil classification using Fuzzy Logic and Artificial Neural Networks. Fuzzy Sets Syst. **401**, 38–54 (2019)

18. Prabakaran, G., Vaithiyanathan, D., Ganesan, M.: Fuzzy decision support system for improving the crop productivity and efficient use of fertilizers. Comput. Electron. Agric. **150**, 88–97 (2018)

19. Rawankar, A., et al.: Detection of N, P, K fertilizers in agricultural soil with NIR laser absorption technique. In: 2018 3rd International Conference on Microwave and Photonics (ICMAP), pp. 1–2. IEEE, February 2018

20. Rodríguez, E., et al.: Dynamic quality index for agricultural soils based on fuzzy logic. Ecol. Ind. **60**, 678–692 (2016)

21. Sami, M., Shiekhdavoodi, M.J., Pazhohanniya, M., Pazhohanniya, F.: Environmental comprehensive assessment of agricultural systems at the farm level using fuzzy logic: a case study in cane farms in Iran. Environ. Model. Softw. **58**, 95–108 (2014)

22. Sefati, Z., Khalilimoghadam, B., Nadian, H.: Assessing urban soil quality by improving the method for soil environmental quality evaluation in a saline groundwater area of Iran. CATENA **173**, 471–480 (2019)

23. Seyedmohammadi, J., Sarmadian, F., Jafarzadeh, A.A., Ghorbani, M.A., Shahbazi, F.: Application of SAW, TOPSIS and fuzzy TOPSIS models in cultivation priority planning for maize, rapeseed and soybean crops. Geoderma **310**, 178–190 (2018)

24. Shekofteh, H., Ramazani, F., Shirani, H.: Optimal feature selection for predicting soil CEC: comparing the hybrid of ant colony organization algorithm and adaptive network-based fuzzy system with multiple linear regression. Geoderma **298**, 27–34 (2017)

25. Silvertooth, J.C.: Soil fertility and soil testing guideline for Arizona cotton (2015). https://cals.arizona.edu/crops/cotton/soilmgt/soil_fertility_testing.html. Accessed 25 Oct 2020

26. Singh, H., et al.: Real-life applications of fuzzy logic. Adv. Fuzzy Syst. (2013)

27. Sirsat, M.S., Cernadas, E., Fernández-Delgado, M., Barro, S.: Automatic prediction of village-wise soil fertility for several nutrients in India using a wide range of regression methods. Comput. Electron. Agric. **154**, 120–133 (2018)

28. Sumiharto, R., Hardiyanto, R.: NPK soil nutrient measurement prototype based on local binary pattern and back-propagation. In: 2018 IEEE International Conference on Internet of Things and Intelligence System (IOTAIS), pp. 23–28, November 2018

29. Sun, H., et al.: Effects of soil quality on effective ingredients of Astragalus mongholicus from the main cultivation regions in China. Ecol. Ind. **114**, 106296 (2020)

30. Wan, H., Peng, Y.: Fuzzy set based web opinion text clustering algorithm. In: 2015 4th International Conference on Mechatronics, Materials, Chemistry and Computer Engineering. Atlantis Press (2015)

31. Wang, H., Yao, L., Huang, B., Hu, W., Qu, M., Zhao, Y.: An integrated approach to exploring soil fertility from the perspective of rice (Oryza sativa L.) yields. Soil Tillage Res. **194**, 104322 (2019)

32. Wang, C.: A study of membership functions on mamdani-type fuzzy inference system for industrial decision-making. M.Sc. thesis from Department of Mechanical and Mechanics. Lehigh University (2015). https://preserve.lehigh.edu/cgi/viewcontent.cgi?article=2665&context=etd. Accessed 11 Apr 2020

33. Wang, H., Zhang, H., Liu, Y.: Using a posterior probability support vector machine model to assess soil quality in Taiyuan, China. Soil Tillage Res. **185**, 146–152 (2019)

34. Were, K., Tien, B.D., Dick, Ã., Singh, B.: Novel evolutionary genetic optimization-based adaptive neuro-fuzzy inference system and GIS predict and map soil organic carbon stocks across an Afromontane landscape. Pedosphere **27**, 877–889 (2017)

35. Zadeh, L.H.: Fuzzy sets. Inf. Control **8**, 338–353 (1965)

36. Zadeh, L.A.: Generalized theory of uncertainty: principal concepts and ideas. In: Fundamental Uncertainty, pp. 104–150. Palgrave Macmillan, London (2011)

37. Behera, R.K., Rath, S.K., Misra, S., Leon, M., Adewumi, A.: Machine learning approach for reliability assessment of open source software. In: Misra, S. (ed.) ICCSA 2019. LNCS, vol. 11622, pp. 472–482. Springer, Cham (2019). https://doi.org/10.1007/978-3-030-24305-0_35

38. Blessing, G., Azeta, A., Misra, S., Chigozie, F., Ahuja, R.: A machine learning prediction of automatic text based assessment for open and distance learning: a review. In: Abraham, A., Panda, M., Pradhan, S., Garcia-Hernandez, L., Ma, K. (eds.) IBICA 2019, vol. 1180, pp. 369–380. Springer, Cham (2019). https://doi.org/10.1007/978-3-030-49339-4_38

39. Alfa, A.A., Misra, S., Bumojo, A., Ahmed, K.B., Oluranti, J., Ahuja, R.: Comparative analysis of optimisations of antecedents and consequents of fuzzy inference system rules lists using genetic algorithm operations. In: Chillarige, R., Distefano, S., Rawat, S. (eds.) ICACII 2019. Lecture Notes in Networks and Systems, vol. 119, pp. 373–379. Springer, Singapore (2019). https://doi.org/10.1007/978-981-15-3338-9_42

40. Kumari, A., Behera, R.K., Shukla, A.S., Sahoo, S.P., Misra, S., Rath, S.K.: Quantifying influential communities in granular social networks using fuzzy theory. In: Gervasi, O. (ed.) ICCSA 2020. Lecture Notes in Computer Science, vol. 12252, pp. 906–917. Springer, Cham (2020). https://doi.org/10.1007/978-3-030-58811-3_64

Artificial Intelligence Applications to Tackle COVID-19

Devansh Shah$^{(\boxtimes)}$ and Santosh Kumar Bharti

Pandit Deendayal Petroleum University, Gandhinagar 382007, India
devanshah03@gmail.com

Abstract. The emergence of COVID-19 with grey areas about the cure and spread of the infection is a significant challenge for the 21st century world. The COVID-19 pandemic has prodigious consequences on human lives and the healthcare industry is constantly seeking support from modern decisive technology such as Artificial Intelligence (AI) to tackle this rapidly spreading pandemic. AI mimicking human intelligence plays a crucial role to predict and track patients, helps to analyze data for various aspects, including medical image processing, drug and vaccine development, and prediction and forecast of this disease. The present study aims to review the potentialities of Artificial Intelligence to diagnose COVID-19 cases and analyze the database to assess it for prevention and combat against COVID-19. We can extract the new insights in drug discovery through deep learning AI algorithms to speed up the process of drug and vaccine development. AI thus acts as a potential tool to quell COVID-19. Besides, this article provides the finest review of the contribution of AI and constraints to its impact against COVID-19. The potentiality of AI must be mobilized to tackle COVID-19 that is crucial in saving human lives and restricts the damages to the world's economy.

Keywords: Artificial Intelligence · COVID-19 · AI applications · Coronavirus · Pandemic

1 Introduction

COVID-19 disease was first revealed late in December 2019 in China and has been proclaimed a pandemic affecting almost all countries, having a significant effect on the healthcare industry. Apart from the colossal toll of human lives it has caused, the worst effect is on the global economy dragging many countries into recession. The application of new technologies has been sought by the healthcare industry for surveillance, prediction, drug development, and mitigation of the spread of this viral pandemic. Artificial Intelligence (AI) is a promising technology to handle the COVID-19 pandemic. AI applications such as Computer vision, Machine learning, and Natural Language Processing and others such as chatbot and facial recognition help the healthcare industry to show high-risk patients, predict and diagnose the infection, track the spread, and treat this infection [1, 2]. AI-based facial recognition cameras can track patients with infection. Robots and drones are used to deliver medication and food and to sanitize public areas [3]. AI aids in drug development and vaccines for the cure of the infection. The detection of the infection is done through radiological image processing through CT scan and x-ray image analysis, while thermal cameras and smartphone apps are used to detect fever [4]. To confront the circumstance, healthcare organizations have invested their huge endeavours in treating contaminated people and for investigating the general population for COVID-19 disease. The national government is putting forth a valiant effort to quell the disease and to meet the prerequisites for the healthcare organization. Also, lamentably, as of now neither medication nor a vaccine is available to counteract this novel coronavirus. Besides, nations have been attempting different treatment strategies. The preventive measures established by WHO is frequent hand-washing with soap and water or with a sanitizer, follow social distancing and, practice respiratory hygiene. Masks are known to safeguard individuals from infection. Aside from it, the best way to prevent the spread of the infection is to stay home and avoid social gatherings and isolation from infected people. Thus, it requires a joint effort of the healthcare industry, government and, public to help control the pandemic.

The literature survey is conducted utilizing Google Scholar, Scopus, PubMed, Elsevier and, IEEE databases and a concise review is done on data by evaluating different facets of AI technologies to fight COVID-19 pandemic. This study emphasizes the potentiality of AI applications to fight the COVID-19 pandemic, along with the restrictions and limitations of the technique. Section 2 discusses the potential role of Artificial Intelligence to fight COVID-19. Section 3 discusses constraints. The subsection showcases the importance of reliable and transparent data and guidelines for the whole of society approach towards pandemic preparedness. Section 4 proposes insight into novel approaches, and finally, a discussion of the impact made by these advances, current challenges, and anticipated future effects along with the conclusion is presented.

2   Potential AI Applications to Quell COVID-19 Pandemic

Various AI applications such as Natural Language Processing, Machine Learning, and Computer Vision utilizes colossal data-based models to predict, design, and portray the situation. To battle against COVID-19, AI applications emphasize mainly on the diagnosis through medical imaging, tracking and forecasting the disease, creating alerts, social control, and awareness Table 1.

Table 1. Applications of Artificial Intelligence

No	Application	Description	Implementation
1	Diagnosis using medical imaging	AI-based virus genome sequencing and lung segmentation applications for precise and quick diagnosis of COVID-19	Alibaba
		COVID-Net, a deep learning network used for diagnosis of COVID-19 disease from Ct images and X-rays	Wang et al. [6]
		An AI-based framework utilizing smartphone sensors to diagnose COVID-19	Maghdid et al. [4]
2	Disease Tracking	An epidemiological SIR model to track the spread of the infection and estimate the infected cases	Song et al. [36]
		An Epidemic Tracker-a forecasting model of the spread of the disease	Metabiota
		Abnormal respiratory pattern classifier to screen COVID-19 infected cases on large-scale	Wang et al. [37]
3	Prediction	AI driven infectious disease surveillance system to forecast the outbreak of Coronavirus	BlueDot
		U-Net, classifier based on CT images to predict hospital stay in COVID-19 patients	Qi 1 X et al. [38]
		XGBoost calculator provides a method to identify patients at high risk timely and accurately	Yan et al. [39]
4	Treatment	Deep learning model to predict available antiviral drugs that may act on novel Coronavirus	Beck et al. [24]
		AI algorithm to predict structure of virus protein to aid the development of new antiviral drug	Google's Deep Mind
		Machine learning algorithm to understand relationship between drug, disease and genes to expedite drug discovery	BenevolentAI
5	Awareness and Social Control	Infrared cameras and smartphone thermometer to scan public for raised temperature	Baidu
		Detection of cough type based on acoustic signals using smartphone's microphone for both patients and healthy controls	Nemati et al. [33]

2.1 Patient's Perspective

The COVID-19 pandemic has significantly challenged the healthcare industry. With confined clinical resources and many patients leading to the critical phase, it is important to find the infected people early to treat them effectively to diminish mortality. So far, the capabilities of AI to tackle COVID-19 are mainly focused on the diagnosis of the disease based on radiological imaging.

Early Detection and Diagnostic AI

An early, rapid, and a precise diagnosis of COVID-19 disease curb further spread of the infection thus helps save human lives. It helps to generate prolific data based on which AI models are trained to handle this crisis. Detection and analysis of symptoms with AI algorithms offer a quick and cost-effective diagnosis. AI utilizing radiological technologies such as X-rays, and CT scans help the diagnosis of infected cases faster and cheaper thus saving radiologist's time and can be as accurate as humans [5]. Alibaba's AI-based framework can predict COVID-19 in about 20 s with almost 96% diagnostic accuracy utilizing CT scan image analysis. A technique to scan CT images utilizing mobile phones has been proposed by Maghdid et al. [4]. A Deep learning model can aid radiologists for diagnosis of COVID-19 utilizing radiological image processing via X-ray and CT scan images. *COVID-Net* is an AI application that uses a deep convolutional neural network. Wang and Wong developed this tool to diagnose the virus from the chest X-ray images. An accuracy of 89.5% has been achieved with an AI migration neural network using CT scan images to diagnose COVID-19 disease [6]. This novel idea with an accuracy of 92% has been put forward by China's Paddle Paddle, Baidu's open-source deep learning platform.

The potential of AI in diagnosis has not been put in practice, though AI-assisted radiology technology has been practiced by the Chinese hospitals. But, due to the paucity of available data to train AI models and due to data being available only from Chinese hospitals may cause selection bias. Lastly, not all patients affected by COVID-19 need intensive treatment. Machine Learning assisted by a prognostic prediction algorithm for the prediction of the mortality risk factor in the patients affected by COVID-19 has been deployed by Yan et al., but the sample used is very small (only 29 patients) to train AI models [7]. To summarize, much research has been incited for AI applications for diagnosis and prognosis of the disease progression but is not yet in practice. The prompt diagnosis of COVID-19 is essential for the prevention, control and, treatment of the infection. Even though RT-PCR tests are proven to be optimal methods for the determination of COVID 19, it has certain limitations due to its low sensitivity; the time required for the examination and its implementation and performance of the RT-PCR test kit poses restrictions promoting AI-driven diagnosis from CT scan images [8] [Fig. 1]. Table 2 explains various AI applications in the CT scan diagnosis of COVID-19. As coronavirus tests are expensive and short in deftly, however, because of the easy availability of X-rays or CT scans, radiologists are able to diagnose COVID-19 with the aid of Deep Learning using X-ray or CT images. COVID-Net an artificial intelligence application is based on X-ray analysis from the data taken from patients having other lung conditions and COVID-19 disease.

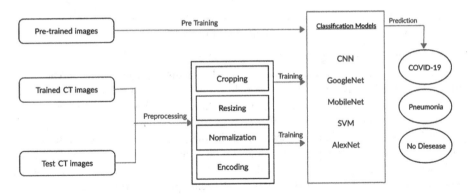

Fig. 1. Schematic architecture of AI for CT image classification

Table 2. AI Applications using CT scan for the diagnosis of COVID-19

AI Applications	Authors	Accuracy
2D Deep Convolutional Neural Network	Chen et al. [9]	Sensitivity-94.06% Specificity-95.47% Accuracy-94.98%
COVID-19 detection using neural network (COVNet)	Li et al. [10]	Accuracy-95%
COVID-Net: A Deep CNN	Wang, Lin, Wong. [11]	Accuracy-92.4%
3-dimensional deep learning model	Xu et al. [12]	Accuracy-86.7%

Chest CT scan is a non-invasive modality with typical CT features of peripherally distributed ground-glass opacity, crazy paving interstitial pattern, and multifocal pneumonic patches can predict disease early with accurate diagnosis [13, 14]. The performance of Chest CT scan by various authors is shown in Table 3 confirming that CT scan has higher sensitivity for the diagnosis of COVID-19.

Table 3. Analysis of Accuracy of Chest CT scan to RT-PCR

Study	Author	Performance
Correlation of Chest CT and RT-PCR Testing for Coronavirus Disease 2019 (COVID-19) in China: A Report of 1014 Cases	Ai et al. [15]	Sensitivity-97% Specificity-27% Accuracy-75%
Sensitivity of Chest CT for COVID-19: Comparison to RT-PCR	Fang et al. [16]	Sensitivity-98%
Diagnostic performance between CT and the initial real-time RT-PCR for clinically suspected 2019 coronavirus disease (COVID-19) patients outside Wuhan, China	He et al. [17]	Sensitivity-77% Sensitivity-96% Accuracy-88%
Diagnosis of the Coronavirus disease (COVID-19): rRT-PCR or CT?	Long et al. [18]	Sensitivity-97.2%

Disease Tracking and Predictive AI

AI is useful for tracking of COVID-19 disease and prediction of the disease and how it will spread with time and over space. A dynamic neural network is developed by Akhtar et al., and such models are retrained using COVID-19 pandemic data to predict its spread [19]. AI algorithms can easily find clusters and hot spots to analyze the level of infection. Various forecasting models of the disease spread have been made available: An *Epidemic Tracker*-a forecasting model of the spread of the disease has been provided by *Metabiota,* a San Francisco-based company and GLEAMviz epidemiological model by the Institute for the Future of Humanity at Oxford University to track the extent of the disease. The Robert Koch Institute in Berlin utilizes an epidemiological SIR model that assists the government to undertake containment measures such as quarantine, social distancing, etc. An analog extended SIR model, available in *R* format using Chinese data, has been deployed by Song et al. [20]. Tracking and prediction of the COVID-19 spread information are of the utmost importance for healthcare authorities to plan, structure, and manage with pandemic [21]. In this way, effective contact tracing is achieved, and a future course of the disease and its reappearance can be predicted. A Possible evaluation of the flattening of the epidemiological curve is achieved. It reflects how effective measures are to mitigate or curb the disease.

Prediction of Patient's Health

A huge increase in the number of infected cases during this pandemic has substantially increased the workload of the healthcare frontline warriors. AI with the help of the digital approach aids in the prompt diagnosis of the infection and facilitates treatment at an early stage. A novel forecast model based on XGBoost calculation has been proposed to show high-risk patients early, to predict mortality risk amongst the patients and thus improves the forecasting of the patients [22]. Another method, based on a U-Net subsidiary utilizing CT scan images, is used to forecast whether a long hospital stay is required or not. AI-based video monitoring has the potential to reduce the workload of the healthcare frontline warriors during this pandemic by observing the activities of the patient infected by the SARS-CoV-2 and to offer updates of the patients to bring clinical awareness amongst them.

2.2 Treatment and Curative AI

AI has been commended for its promising feature to contribute to drug discovery even long before the COVID-19 pandemic. COVID-19 being highly contagious with the resultant high mortality rate and its level of spread with no signs of slowing in comparison to other viral diseases, it is indispensable to develop antiviral drugs and vaccines for novel Coronavirus at the earliest to save human lives. Analysis of the available data on COVID-19 is being done by AI researchers to develop medicines and vaccines. The Developmental procedure of antiviral drugs, as well as screening and repurposing of the existing drugs, is being accelerated by AI algorithms to aid the treatment of the COVID-19. AI algorithms are trained based on the available information and the created AI model is used to screen prevailing medicines that can show efficiency to treat COVID-19.

Prediction of Protein Structure

In the context of antiviral drug development, a supercomputer SUMMIT by IBM based on AI is being used to treat SARS-CoV-2 [D 4]. Researchers are using a mathematical computation of the virus's spike (S-protein) of the virus that may interact with the human ACE2 receptor. Using SUMMIT, they can apprehend small molecules that can either bind to the protein-receptor complex, or the protein alone [23]. Google's Deep Mind, utilizing AlphaFold system- AI algorithm, has tried to predict the structure of virus proteins, the information that is valuable for the development of a new drug. But as these have not experimented, its accuracy cannot be made certain.

Drug Repurposing and Vaccine Discovery

AI is beneficial in vaccine development and treatment as it speeds up the process of drug testing, because standard testing methods are time-consuming [24]. *BenevolentAI* uses the machine learning to show existing already approved drugs that might be helpful to tackle novel Coronavirus infection. Using Machine Learning algorithms, an existing drug, maybe repurposed for treating COVID-19 [25]. Even though a vaccine is developed, it may not be of much use during this pandemic as enough scientific checks, medical trials, and controls are required for a vaccine approval. We estimate it that it may need over 18 months for a vaccine to come in the market for humans to use [26]. The brief detail of the organizations using AI for repurposing existing medicines for COVID-19 are shown in Table 4.

Table 4. Organizations using Artificial Intelligence for Drug repurposing.

BenevolentAI	The United Kingdom based association is known as a giant in the AI drug disclosure industry. The organization is using AI to repurpose all existing endorsed medicines against the novel coronavirus	Baricitinib, a drug for rheumatoid arthritis pain is supposed to have promising results for COVID-19 treatment
Gero	The Singapore based company distinguished 9 medicines using its AI framework	Niclosamide and Nitazoxanide are the molecules anticipated to have viability against coronavirus
Innoplexus	The Indo-German association started examining the effectiveness of therapies like Hydroxychloroquine and Remdesivir for novel coronavirus by utilizing information acquired from patients	Combination of chloroquine and tocilizumab, chloroquine and remdesivir, and the third mix of hydroxychloroquine with clarithromycin (an anti-microbial) or plerixafor (antiretroviral) has higher efficacy as suggested by AI

Potential Drugs for COVID-19

A few articles have proposed medications, conceivably effective to treat COVID-19 as shown in Table 5. The vast majority of these proposals rely upon in vitro investigations, virtual screenings and documentation of their impact on SARS and MERS. In expansion to these medicines, Tocilizumab has recently been recommended as a COVID-19 treatment. Studies have shown that IL-6 levels significantly corresponded with the severity of COVID-19, C-responsive protein (CRP), lactate dehydrogenase (LDH), and D-dimer levels and T cell checks, and recommended that Tocilizumab, with its inhibitory effect on IL-6, might be of success to treat COVID-19 [27]. Besides, no clinical research has shown the effects of Tocilizumab on COVID-19 and further investigations are very much needed.

Table 5. Promising drugs for COVID-19

Medicine	Description	Research work
Chloroquine Remdesivir	Reduction of viral duplication numbers in the cell supernatant and viral infection	Wang et al. [28]
Teicoplanin	Prevent the entry of SARS-CoV-2-Spike-pseudoviruses in the cytoplasm	Zhang et al. [29]
Baricitinib	Binding to AP2-associated protein kinase 1 (AAK1)	Richardson et al. [30]
Ikarugamycin molsidomine	Effective on the genes co-expressed with ACE2	Li et al. [31]
Formoterol Chloroquine	Binding to SARS-CoV-2 papain-like protease (PL^{pro})	Arya et al. [32]

2.3 Awareness and Social Control AI

Artificial Intelligence is useful for managing the pandemic by reinforcement of social distancing rules and lockdown maneuvers, using thermal imaging to find the infected people in public spaces. At Chinese air terminals and train terminals, thermal cameras are used to examine the vast crowd for raised temperatures, along with a facial recognition system to distinguish whether a person wears a facial mask [33].

A large Chinese AI and Internet company, *Baidu*, uses an infrared camera based on computer vision to scan the crowd for high temperatures. It can scan about 200 persons per minute. But the drawback is that it cannot distinguish whether the high temperature is due to COVID 19 or some other illness. Similar technology is used by the UK to monitor the people to follow the social distancing measures provided by the government. In the USA, "social distancing detection software" is being used to detect that such social distancing norms are not breached. Technologies such as cellular phones with Artificial Intelligence-controlled applications or wearables are also used to help their users to receive updated information about their health without having them visit hospitals. Such apps can notify individuals of the possible hotspot areas also. The information obtained from the cellular phone is used to detect the type of cough [34]. The available information based on AI algorithms promptly detects the patients at high-risk for quarantine purposes and thus allows to mitigate the spread of the infection. Drones are utilized to sanitize open spaces, broadcast guidance to the public and to track people not wearing face masks. A mobile application used to great effectiveness in India called the *Aarogya Setu* app tracks coronavirus cases nearby. It functions with mobile GPS and Bluetooth.

2.4 Early Warnings and Alerts

BlueDot, a Canadian AI model, is considered among the first in the world to identify the emerging risk from COVID-19, on 31st December 2019. It is a low-cost AI tool that has leveraged natural language processing and machine learning to track, predict the outbreak and spread of the infection much quicker than WHO and USA CDC. However, *HealthMap,* an AI model created at Boston Children's hospital, released an alert significantly before, on 30th December 2019. Additionally, as per Associated Press, just half an hour beyond, a researcher at the Program for Monitoring Emerging Diseases gave caution. Fundamentally, it required human understanding to perceive the menace. Kamran Khan, the founder of BlueDot, even clarified that the humans remain central in surveying and unraveling its yield. Thus, it makes clear that human contribution is required for the ideal application of AI. BlueDot predicted the outbreak even long before the World Health Organization issued an alert about the top 20 cities which could be likely at the cutting edge of the spread of the disease globally.

3 Constraints and Pitfalls

A significant hindrance to progress with AI is a lack of reliable data, and not able to understand its state of affairs is a significant risk to organizations. The research is ongoing to discover a vaccine against coronavirus and so will take a long way to abate this pandemic. A major issue of the pandemic is the lack of data and information sharing about transmission, clinical symptoms, diagnostic tests and preventive measures. A significant concern is the lack of reliable data to train an AI model. Also, 80% of the data is unstructured to train a model to analyze patterns. Transparent and accurate data sharing is the prime need of the present world to understand the impact of the disease and to battle against novel coronavirus. Either insufficient data or excessive data impose limitations on the applications of AI. While AI systems contribute something significant, Petropolous [35] and Bullock et al. have commented on its drawbacks at the current time in terms of operational maturity. There is inadequate data available to train AI models, insufficient open datasets to research upon, and yet other potential issues of large information hubris, and a piece of exceptional and torrential information, need assessment beforehand. About the need for more data on COVID-19, for multidisciplinary research to train AI models, more receptiveness and sharing of the data is in need. Most of the research available until now inclines to use very little, biased, and only Chinese data. Thus, need for more diagnostic testing is to ameliorate the tracking and prediction of the pandemic. Lack of data, huge data hubris, and noisy social media limit the AI-base prediction of COVID-19 spread to be precise and authentic. Because of this, forecasters prefers epidemiological SIR models over AI models.

The open-source dataset platforms are created for the collection and instant sharing of important data while preserving privacy. Various government organizations have strategically implemented to give transparent and accurate information to evade panic and distress among the public. Certain promising initiatives are given by various organizations to share datasets. WHO Global Research promises to share datasets on Coronavirus disease of the prevailing pandemic. *CORD-19* having articles is made accessible for data mining. It is a joint drive by Semantic Scholar, Microsoft, and Facebook, etc. *Kaggle* has released data competition, *CORD-19 Challenge*. Elsevier and Science Direct has made peer-reviewed research articles available for data mining. The Lens, have made accessible its patented data to reinforce the research on new and repurposed drugs. Few Universities have permitted their data and literature on COVID-19 for open access. Italy has adopted a transparent strategy to refrain the public from panic and confusion through overflowing social media. Not just insufficient data, but even excessive data may restrict AI applications. With the progress of the pandemic, the news and social media create huge data noise. With the daily overload of around over 100 scientific articles, the researcher deals with flooding of data. To overcome this, data analytic tools such as the *COVID-19 Evidence Navigator* by Gruenwald et al. imparts updates on computer-generated evidence maps daily of this pandemic [36].

Lack of awareness and misinformation of the pandemic creates panic and distress that is definitely more difficult to handle causing psychological effects on public health. The government should carry out awareness campaigns, offer education of the pandemic, and carry out protective measures to control panic. Transparent and reliable guidance to manage pandemic is of utmost importance to avoid panic and confusion and to encourage public compliance.

4 Future Scope

In future, Artificial Intelligence applications will be available to store potential data of medical industry that can be used for another comparable pandemic like COVID-19. The doctors, health care professionals, and staff could rapidly accept this turmoil, which can affect the treatment line of COVID-19 and other pandemics. In future, the health care industry would develop and needs to adjust to advanced innovations to make savvy health care framework and thus a need to change the programming devices and platform to the most recent ones. AI applications provide an automated answer to digital innovations to gather, store, investigate, and screen information system. Digital innovations can provide proper isolation of the diseased patient to minimize the mortality risk, acceleration of the drug production, treatment process and care. With these technologies, people can do work from home along with virtual offices and meetings. These technologies help better crowd management, transportation management, provide virtual clinic with use of telemedicine approach and adopt public safety measures.

5 Conclusion

Researchers are exploring the best possible method to quell Coronavirus pandemic, and Artificial Intelligence presents an alluring technique. It is a very useful upcoming tool for early detection of Coronavirus infection and helps to monitor the health of the infected patients. AI applications can offer proper isolation methods to reduce mortality in high-risk infected cases, help to plan treatment strategies for COVID-19, vaccine, and drug development by various useful algorithms. AI-based on analysis of available data can hasten the research on this novel SARS-CoV-2. Application of these technologies gear up the digital transformation, providing telemedicine solutions, limiting pointless hospital consultations. It enforces social distancing measures and allows better transportation management for ensuring the safety of the patients. This technology provides an online platform for distance education of COVID-19 in remote areas during the lockdown. Even though technology advancement is helping people battle against COVID-19, concerns are there of using these algorithms in a real-time environment. Despite achieving accuracy in diagnosing COVID-19 disease using radiological image processing through X-rays and CT scan image analysis, this technology is still unaccountable and lacks lucidity. To summarize, even though there lies a wide scope of utilizing AI applications to curb this pandemic; but, the development of these technologies is not enough to be operational. Only time will let AI applications to be utile to combat the emerging rampant diseases. There lies a threat to data privacy if the governments continue to surveil its nationals even after the pandemic is under control. The government authorities should take crucial steps in the analysis of the data to combat the pandemic with proper justifications because of public health concerns, otherwise, the public may lose trust in government and are less likely to follow health advice. Lastly, although use of AI to quell the pandemic is limited, it has led to the automation of human labor, has digitalized the economy and as a result of the current crisis, a proper policy may come into existence for the administration of Artificial Intelligence.

References

1. Javaid, M., Haleem, A., Vaishya, R., Bahl, S., Suman, R., Vaish, A.: Industry 4.0 technologies and their applications in fighting COVID-19 pandemic. Diabetes Metab. Syndr. Clin. Res. Rev. **14**, 419–422 (2020)
2. Vaishya, R., Javaid, M., Khan, I.H., Haleem, A.: Artificial Intelligence (AI) applications for COVID-19 pandemic. Diabetes Metab. Syndr. Clin. Res. Rev. **14**, 337–339 (2020)
3. Kumar, A., Gupta, P.K., Srivastava, A.: A review of modern technologies for tackling COVID-19 pandemic. Diabetes Metab. Syndr. Clin. Res. Rev. **14**, 569–573 (2020)
4. Maghdid, H.S., Ghafoor, K.Z., Sadiq, A.S., Curran, K., Rabie, K.: A novel AI-enabled framework to diagnose coronavirus covid 19 using smartphone embedded sensors: design study. arXiv preprint arXiv:2003.07434, 16 March 2020
5. Bullock, J., Pham, K.H., Lam, C.S., Luengo-Oroz, M.: Mapping the landscape of artificial intelligence applications against COVID-19. arXiv preprint arXiv:2003.11336, 25 March 2020
6. Wang, S., et al.: A deep learning algorithm using CT images to screen for Corona Virus Disease (COVID-19). MedRxiv, 1 January 2020
7. Yan, L., Zhang, H., Goncalves, J., et al.: A machine learning-based model for survival prediction in patients with severe COVID-19 infection. medRxiv Prepr 2020. https://doi.org/10.1101/2020.02.27.20028027
8. Yang, Y., et al.: Laboratory diagnosis and monitoring the viral shedding of 2019-nCoV infections. MedRxiv, 1 January 2020
9. Jin, C., et al.: Development and evaluation of an AI system for COVID-19 diagnosis. medRxiv. 1 January 2020

10. Li, L., et al.: Artificial intelligence distinguishes COVID-19 from community acquired pneumonia on chest CT. Radiology (2020)
11. Wang, L., Wong, A.: COVID-Net: a tailored deep convolutional neural network design for detection of COVID-19 cases from chest X-ray images. arXiv preprint arXiv:2003.09871, 22 March 2020
12. Xu, X., Jiang, X., Ma, C., et al.: Deep learning system to screen coronavirus disease 2019 pneumonia, p. 1e29 (2020). https://arxiv.org/abs/2002.09334.
13. Huang, P., et al.: Use of chest CT in combination with negative RT-PCR assay for the 2019 novel coronavirus but high clinical suspicion. Radiology 295(1), 22–23 (2020)
14. Lei, J., Li, J., Li, X., Qi, X.: CT imaging of the 2019 novel coronavirus (2019-nCoV) pneumonia. Radiology 295(1), 18 (2020)
15. Ai, T., et al.: Correlation of chest CT and RT-PCR testing in coronavirus disease 2019 (COVID-19) in China: a report of 1014 cases. Radiology 26, 200642 (2020)
16. Fang, Y., et al.: Sensitivity of chest CT for COVID-19: comparison to RT-PCR. Radiology 19, 200432 (2020)
17. He, J.L., et al.: Diagnostic performance between CT and initial real-time RT-PCR for clinically suspected 2019 coronavirus disease (COVID-19) patients outside Wuhan. China. Respiratory Med. 21, 105980 (2020)
18. Long, C., et al.: Diagnosis of the Coronavirus disease (COVID-19): rRT-PCR or CT? Eur. J. Radiol. 25, 108961 (2020)
19. Akhtar, M., Kraemer, M.U., Gardner, L.M.: A dynamic neural network model for predicting risk of Zika in real time. BMC Med. 17(1), 171 (2019)
20. Song, P., et al.: An epidemiological forecast model and software assessing interventions on COVID-19 epidemic in China. medRxiv. Epub, 3 March 2020
21. Naudé, W.: Artificial intelligence vs COVID-19: limitations, constraints and pitfalls. AI Soc. 35(3), 761–765 (2020). https://doi.org/10.1007/s00146-020-00978-0
22. Yan, L., Zhang, H., Goncalves, J., et al.: A machine learning-based model for survival prediction in patients with severe COVID-19 infection. medRxiv Prepr 2020. https://doi.org/10.1101/2020.02.27.20028027.
23. Smith, M., Smith, J.C.: Repurposing therapeutics for COVID-19: supercomputer-based docking to the SARS-CoV-2 viral spike protein and viral spike protein-human ACE2 interface Repurposing therapeutics for COVID-19: supercomputer-based docking to the SARS-CoV-2 viral spike protein and viral spike protein-human ACE2 interface
24. Sohrabi, C., Alsafi, Z., et al.: World Health Organization declares global emergency: a review of the 2019 novel coronavirus (COVID-19). Int. J. Surg. (2020)
25. Beck, B.R., Shin, B., Choi, Y., Park, S., Kang, K.: Predicting commercially available antiviral drugs that may act on the novel coronavirus (SARS-CoV-2) through a drug-target interaction deep learning model. Comput. Struct. Biotech. J. 18, 784–790 (2020)
26. Regalado A.: A Coronavirus Vaccine will take at least 18 months if it works at all
27. Liu, T., et al.: The potential role of IL-6 in monitoring coronavirus disease 2019. SSRN 3548761, 1 March 2020.
28. Wang, M., et al.: Remdesivir and chloroquine effectively inhibit the recently emerged novel coronavirus (2019-nCoV) in vitro. Cell Res. 30(3), 269–271 (2020)
29. Zhang, J., et al.: Teicoplanin potently blocks the cell entry of 2019-nCoV. BioRxiv, 1 January 2020
30. Richardson, P., et al.: Baricitinib as potential treatment for 2019-nCoV acute respiratory disease. Lancet (LondonEngland). 395(10223), e30 (2020)
31. Yang, L., Li, Z., Bai, T., Hou, X.: Discovery of potential drugs for COVID-19 based on the connectivity map

32. Arya, R., Das, A., Prashar, V., Kumar, M.: Potential inhibitors against papain-like protease of novel coronavirus (SARS-CoV-2) from FDA approved drugs

33. Chun, A.: In a time of coronavirus, Chinas investment in AI is paying off in a big way. South China Morning Post, 18 March 2020.

34. Nemati, E., Rahman, M.M., Nathan, V., Vatanparvar, K., Kuang, J.: A comprehensive approach for cough type detection. In: 2019 IEEE/ACM International Conference on Connected Health: Applications, Systems and Engineering Technologies (CHASE), 25 September 2019, pp. 15–16. IEEE (2019)

35. Petropoulos, G.: Artificial Intelligence in the Fight against COVID-19, Bruegel, 23 March 2020

36. Gruenwald, E., Antons, D., Salge T.: COVID-19 evidence navigator. Institute for Technology and Innovation Management, RWTH Aachen University (2020)

37. Wang, Y., Hu, M., Li, Q., Zhang, X.P., Zhai, G., Yao, N.: Abnormal respiratory patterns classifier may contribute to large-scale screening of people infected with COVID-19 in an accurate and unobtrusive manner. arXiv preprint arXiv:2002.05534, 12 February 2020

38. Qi1, X., Jiang, Z., Yu, Q., et al.: Machine learning based CT radiomics model for predicting hospital stay in patients with pneumonia associated with SARSCoV- 2 infection: a multicentre study. Pediatr. Clin. North Am. **13**(3) 2020. https://doi.org/10.1016/s0031-3955(16)31867-3

Throat Inflammation Based Mass Screening of Covid-19 on Embedded Platform

P. Dalal[1(✉)] ⓘ, M. Himansh[1] ⓘ, O. Ramwala[2] ⓘ, P. Parikh[3],
U. Dalal[2], M. Paunwala[4] ⓘ, and C. Paunwala[1] ⓘ

[1] Electronics and Communication Engineering, SCET, Surat, India
djpoojandalal18@gmail.com
[2] Electronics Engineering, SVNIT, Surat, India
[3] Gujarat Adani Institute of Medical Science, Bhuj, Kutchh, India
[4] Electronics and Communication Engineering, CKPCET, Surat, India

Abstract. The upsurge of the COVID-19 pandemic and its fatal repercussions make non-invasive and automated mass screening inevitable to ensure that the suspected cases can be quarantined, and the dissemination of the disease can be controlled during the incubation period of the coronavirus. Currently, thermal screening being the only non-invasive mass-screening technique with the drawback of concealing the feverish symptoms by the consumption of paracetamol, developing an efficient alternative for mass-screening becomes essential. Throat inflammation is a vital perceivable symptom of COVID-19 for early detection and mass screening of COVID. This paper proposes the identification of Tonsillitis and Pharyngitis by detecting the Region of Interest, followed by performing HSV segmentation on the region around uvula for Pharyngitis detection and template matching using tonsil gland followed by Canny and HOG transform on the ROI cropped image for Tonsillitis detection. The proposed method can be administered without direct contact with the infectious patients, thereby reducing the burden on the medical and paramedical fraternity. Quantitative and qualitative evaluation showcase promising results and indicate the reliability of the proposed method. Moreover, the proposed technique can be implemented on the cost-effective, power-efficient, and parameter-constrained embedded platforms, including NVIDIA Jetson Nano.

Keywords: COVID-19 · Early detection · Embedded platform · HSV segmentation · Inflammation · Pharyngitis · Template matching · Tonsillitis

1 Introduction

The novel coronavirus disease is a highly contagious disease that rapidly spread across the world and has become a concern for public health and welfare, with WHO declaring it as a pandemic [1]. Many symptoms such as reduction in WBC (White Blood Cells) count, fever, pneumonia are known to be the clinical characteristics of SARS-CoV-2 (Severe Acute Respiratory Syndrome Novel Corona Virus). Recently, it has also been noted that Tonsillitis and Pharyngitis may also be potential symptoms, which appear in very early stages.

© Springer Nature Singapore Pte Ltd. 2021
K. K. Patel et al. (Eds.): icSoftComp 2020, CCIS 1374, pp. 277–288, 2021.
https://doi.org/10.1007/978-981-16-0708-0_23

Hence, mass screening of potential coronavirus infected patients in necessary to contain the spread of this contagious virus while also resuming all the necessary activities. Mass screening based on body temperature has been employed to identify potential coronavirus patients; however, this isn't reliable as the thermal IR Guns which are being used only measure the surface temperature of the body and has little to no correlation with fever. Moreover, fever is a symptom that varies from person to person and fluctuates multiple times in a day. Also, it has been known that fever can be easily circumvented by consuming paracetamol. Hence another characteristic needs to be identified and addressed, which may be useful for mass screening.

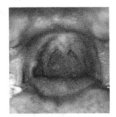 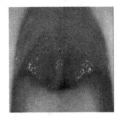

Fig. 1. Infected throat images. Best viewed in color.

Coronavirus is known to spread through cough droplets in which it can live for around 3 h, and its incubation period is known to be from 2 to 14 days. The virus enters the body from the upper respiratory tract, and it multiplies in the mucosa of nasopharynx and oropharynx, and hence a person may feel irritation in the throat for the first few days. Redness in the throat and inflammation of the tonsils gland may be observed, as shown in Fig. 1. This serves as the motivation for this research because if this can be diagnosed in early stages, then the segregation of potential coronavirus patients from the rest of the population can be done, which may help to control the spread of this virus.

2 Related Work

Thermal screening is the common method identified for the mass screening for the COVID-19 disease as fever is a common symptom. Due to the high contagiousness of the disease, an early identification requirement arises. But the accuracy of thermal screening is affected by human, environmental, and equipment variables. Also, fever is not constant for the infected patients and it fluctuates. Hence, techniques better than thermal screening are required [2]. Another process identified for early detection of the SARS-COV-2 is using chest radiography or X-Rays, along with Deep-learning models for detection of consolidation areas, and nodular opacities for infected patients.

Following a major drawback is the detection from X-Rays is successful only if the infected person has pneumonia symptoms else the method fails [3–5].

Tonsillitis and Pharyngitis are identified as major throat infections, which are also symptoms of the other virus of the coronavirus family. Due to the unavailability of a good throat dataset, classification using artificial neural networks may seem irrational. Tonsillitis can be detected from throat images by traditional image processing methods. For the identification of tonsillitis by the fuzzy logic system [6], a 3-Channel image is input to the system. After the preprocessing, the red channel boundary was identified for tonsil size extraction. From the extracted image, tonsil size, area, feature, and color were extracted which was given input to a fuzzy-based inference system. This method is said to give 80% accuracy. Another method ascertained was to use a green channel image for tonsil extraction, followed by mean value calculation and using a Sobel edge detector [7]. In this, the RGB image and Tonsil extracted area are input for the extraction of red color intensity and tonsil area in pixels. So, early diagnosis can be performed.

For fast implementation, this research is focused to develop better techniques for early diagnosis which can be easily computed on edge devices without compromising heavy processing power. As image segmentation and localization plays an important role in the detection of tonsillitis and pharyngitis from the throat, a multistage algorithm which uses template matching is found useful for faster detection of tonsillitis [8]. In this cited work, template matching compares a match between two images using correlation which is found to be beneficial in faster implementation of the proposed method. For the detection of pharyngitis, which can be identified as from redness of the throat, HSV based segmentation is applied. An auto-crop and unsupervised clustering method are identified [9] which works on segmentation based on HSV colour space. The object is separated from the background followed by pixel processing and calculation.

3 Proposed Method

Medical diagnosis from the throat is a complex task in the absence of a medical professional. Using Artificial Neural Networks (ANNs) for image processing requires a lot of processing power as well as a good dataset, which increases the cost factor required for a portable device that could aid in mass-screening. So, a method that involves low computation cost, as well as a better on-device performance with ready to deploy methodology is needed. Moreover, this research endeavors to diagnose symptoms of Tonsillitis and Pharyngitis, which may indicate the possibility of an individual being infected with COVID-19.

Hence, a technique is required, which can help in mass screening to reduce the computation and processing cost factor with good reliability. Using traditional image processing methods, which include a series of segmentation, transformation, filtering, and equalization along with correlation coefficient based template matching [10] has performed profitably for the faster and cost-effective mass screening (Fig. 2).

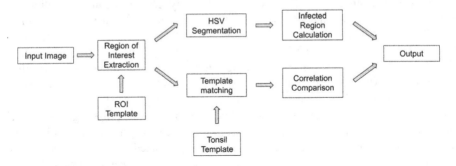

Fig. 2. Proposed methodology

3.1 Region of Interest Detection (ROI)

Region of interest can be defined as a subset of the original image on which the major computations are performed. The Region of Interest (ROI) detection is vital to locate tonsils accurately and must be robust to subtle features of the throat. The input throat image has some features that are irrelevant for the diagnosis, along with different orientations. For the detection, we are interested in the region around uvula and tonsillitis, omitting other regions like tongue, hard palate, and soft palate. Redness around uvula and swelling of tonsil glands are points of interest. So an auto-cropping method resulting in ROI is designed using a template match method that scans the input image cropping it into a feature-rich region.

As being the primary step, it ensures the effectiveness of the latter. For ROI, we provide a sample template image and the input image followed by Template Matching Algorithm. Canny and Hough transform are applied to both- template image and the input image. Applying template matching using edges rather than on raw images gives a substantial boost to accuracy.

The process of ROI detection is, as shown in Fig. 3. A mask is created from the template image, which has our area of concern- the uvula and tonsil glands. The mask is slid over the input image, mask size is varied accordingly, and the correlation is calculated. Coordinates are selected where there is a maximum correlation coefficient between the mask and image.

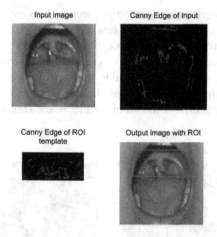

Fig. 3. Region of interest detection

3.2   Segmentation

A color image can be represented in different ways, through different color models. The most common color models are RGB, HSV, YCrCb, and all these models have different applications. RGB is an additive color model, which means that different colors can be represented by the addition of color pixels of Red, Green, and Blue. Different proportions of these colors can be used to represent different colors. This model is essentially used by display devices such as monitors, television to display different colors. However, even the slight variations in color, in the form of brightness, saturation, or illumination is strongly dependent on the three colors mentioned above, which make this model less ideal for image processing applications.

HSV color space is more commonly used for image processing applications, such as segmentation [11]. HSV color space closely matches the perception of how humans understand the colors. This model is good at isolating color information such as hue and saturation from grayscale information such as intensity or brightness. Hence, the values of hue and saturation are not affected by different levels of brightness and illumination conditions, which make it ideal for image processing applications such as image segmentation. Moreover; conversion HSV color space to RGB can be easily done using the following equations

$$B = V(1 - S) \tag{1}$$

$$R = V\left[1 + \frac{S\cos H}{\cos(60 - H)}\right] \tag{2}$$

$$G = 3V - (R + B) \tag{3}$$

Here H, S, and V stand for Hue, Saturation, and Value respectively, and B, G, and R stand for Blue, Green, and Red, respectively.

Segmentation of colors can be done by selecting a range of colors and isolating these colors from the rest of the image. Using HSV color space, a range of colors can be easily decided. In this research, the susceptible pharyngitis pixels are required to be segmented from the rest of the image. As symptoms of Pharyngitis are indicated by redness near the uvula, a range for isolating these pixels were decided after careful experimentation and deliberation. The upper limit of HSV is (170, 170, 100), and the lower limit is (180, 255, 255). As shown in the Fig. 4, the susceptible pixels have been isolated.

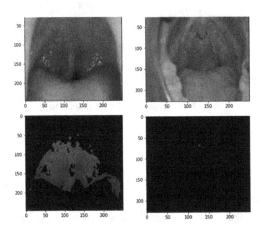

Fig. 4. HSV segmentation (infected image: left; normal image: right)

3.3 Template Matching

Many sophisticated methods like keypoint detectors, local invariant descriptors such as SIRF, SURF, and keypoint matching techniques like RANSAC or LMEDs are mainly used in object detection in image processing. A keypoint detector can be appropriate where there is a significant gradient difference in the image. SIRF, SURF algorithms have performed poorly on this throat medical dataset. Hence, this study shows the use of the Template Matching technique in medical diagnosis and object detection.

Template Matching can be said as a method for searching and finding the location of a template image in a larger image [12]. It simply slides the template image over the input image (as in 2D convolution) and compares the template and patch of input image under the template image. The value of the correlation between the template and image is calculated based on the correlation coefficient. The template matching function slides through the image, compares the overlapped regions of size w × h against template using the specified method, and stores the comparison. If we consider a template T, and the image I, then correlation at each stride is calculated using:

$$R(x,y) = \sum x', y'(T'(x',y') \cdot I'(x+x',y+y')) \tag{4}$$

Where,

$$T'(x', y') = T(x', y') - 1/(w \cdot h) \cdot \sum x'', y'' T(x'', y'') \qquad (5)$$

$$I'(x + x', y + y') = I(x + x', y + y') - 1/(w \cdot h) \cdot \sum x'', y'' I(x + x'', y + y'') \qquad (6)$$

(I denotes image, T template, R result). This summation is done over the template and the image patch: $x' = 0...w - 1$, $y' = 0...h - 1$.

For the detection of tonsillitis, a template image of Tonsil transformed using canny-edge and Histogram of Gradients (HoG) is used. Canny edge and HOG are applied to the image obtained after the ROI cropping step, and the correlation coefficient is compared using the Eq. (4). When the input image is tonsillitis positive, the correlation coefficient has high value than a threshold, and lower in case of tonsillitis negative. By comparing the correlation coefficient, the presence of swollen tonsil glands can be computed.

3.4 Hardware Implementation

NVIDIA Jetson Nano [13] is a cost-effective, power-efficient, and parameter-constrained embedded development board developed by NVIDIA that is useful for inferencing deep learning and computer vision models. It consists of 4GB system-wide memory that is used by CPU as well as GPU. The CPU is quad-core ARM Cortex A57 clocked at 1.43 GHz. GPU consists of 128 CUDA Supported cores. Moreover, all necessary ports are included, such as ethernet port, USB, HDMI port, and also a connector for Raspberry Pi camera. For our experiment, we have used a USB Webcam.

Jetson Nano can be operated in two ways, i.e., by connecting a monitor via HDMI port, or completely headless mode. Connecting a monitor through HDMI gives access to the graphical user interface of Ubuntu OS.

The inference time for our model on Jetson Nano was 0.7 s, which is instantaneous and can be considered as real-time for the desired purpose.

4 Experiments and Results

This section elaborates on the experiments conducted and the dataset preparation process. The metrics used to evaluate performance have been explained briefly.

4.1 Dataset Preparation

As no well-defined datasets for throat images were available, the images were manually obtained through web crawling. Over 200 images were downloaded, out of which a medical professional [14] identified around 180 images, and these images were then labeled and categorized into three categories - normal, Pharyngitis, and Tonsillitis. Appropriate preprocessing techniques were then applied, such as Gaussian blurring for removing noise, and then these images were used for processing.

4.2 Testing Details

The first task for finding optimal HSV range for proper identification of Pharyngitis was done with due observations and experimentation of the dataset. The primary assumption that all the input images captured from similar devices and after applying histogram equalization to the input images, HSV range of [170, 170, 100] to [180, 255, 255] was found beneficial. This segmentation resulted in the infected region from the throat which then was clustered and calculated to provide pharyngitis infection percentage. Then the experiments were made by fuzzy logic to define a threshold for the pixel percentage to classify the input images (Fig. 5).

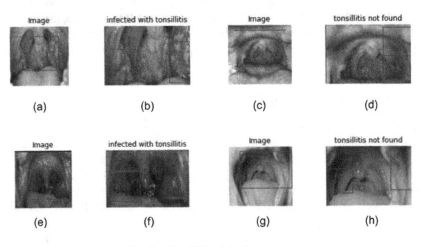

Fig. 5. Tonsillitis detection output

After the segmentation, the foremost step was to select a template image for ROI detection as well as tonsil gland identification. Testing through various template images for Region of Interest, a template image was selected that was converted to grayscale and different image transforms like Canny, Histogram of Gradients (HOG) were applied. The best results were obtained with a combination of Canny Edge on the grayscale template, followed by HOG. The same transforms are carried out on the input image on which the template matching is performed. The main advantage of this resulted that the proposed method was successful in determining the images which belonged to both the classes, i.e., there were chances that a patient is infected with Pharyngitis as well as tonsillitis, multi-class classification became possible.

4.3 Evaluation Metrics

For evaluating medical models, choosing the right and sufficient evaluation metrics is essential because these metrics play an imperative role in ascertaining the practical performance. In this section, various evaluation metrics are described.

Confusion Matrix

This metric is useful to derive all other metrics described henceforth. This metric tabulates all the possibilities of predictions that can be given by the model based on some particular input (Table 1).

Table 1. Confusion matrix

	Normal	Pharyngitis	Tonsillitis
Predicted normal	20	4	13
Predicted Pharyngitis	2	14	0
Predicted Tonsillitis	7	2	115

Sensitivity

This metric measures the proportion of the correctly predicted positives to the actual positives. This metric is especially useful to determine the model's performance on cases pertaining to the infectious samples. It is denoted as given in Eq. (7).

$$\text{Sensitivity} = \frac{True\ Positive}{True\ Positive + False\ Negative} \tag{7}$$

Specificity

This metrics gives a proportion of correctly predicted negatives to the total number of negatives. This metric is especially useful to determine the model's performance on cases pertaining to the normal samples. It is denoted as given in Eq. (8).

$$\text{Specificity} = \frac{True\ Negatives}{True\ Negatives + False\ Positives} \tag{8}$$

Positive Predictive Value (PPV)

PPV gives the probability that a patient is infectious, given that the prediction by the model was given as positive. It may be denoted as in Eq. (9).

$$\text{PPV} = \frac{True\ Positive}{True\ Positive + False\ Positive} \tag{9}$$

Negative Predictive Value (NPV)

NPV gives the probability that a patient is healthy, given that the model predicted it to be healthy. It may be denoted as given in Eq. (10).

$$\text{NPV} = \frac{True\ Negative}{True\ Negative + False\ Negative} \tag{10}$$

False Positive Rate (FPR)

It is a measure that gives the ratio of the number of negative samples incorrectly recognized as positives to the total number of negative samples. This is especially necessary because it is important not to identify normal patients as positive as denoted in Eq. (11).

$$FPR = \frac{False\ Positive}{False\ Positive + True\ Negative} \tag{11}$$

False Negative Rate (FNR)

It is a measure that gives the ratio of the number of positive samples tested as negative to the total number of positive samples. This metric is especially necessary because it is important to not identify the infected patient as normal. In that case, the patient falsely identified as healthy may infect other patients. It should be as low as possible as denoted in Eq. (12).

$$FNR = \frac{False\ Negatives}{False\ Negatives + True\ Positives} \tag{12}$$

Accuracy

It is the overall accuracy of the system, a ratio of samples identified correctly to the total number of samples. Let TP denote True Positive, TN denotes True Negative, and FP denote False Positive and FN denote False Negative. Accuracy may be denoted as in Eq. (13).

$$Accuracy = \frac{TP + TN}{TP + FP + TN + FN} \tag{13}$$

F1 Score

F1 score is the harmonic mean of precision and recall and is one of the indicators that give the overall performance of a model. It may be denoted as in Eq. (14).

$$F1\ Score = \frac{2 * Precision * Recall}{Precision + Recall} \tag{14}$$

Matthews Correlation Coefficient (MCC)

This metric gives a very balanced view of model performance in case of several class imbalance in testing data (Table 2).

$$MCC = \frac{TP * TN - FP * FN}{\sqrt{(TP + FP)(TP + FN)(TN + FN)(TN + FP)}} \tag{15}$$

Table 2. Evaluation metrics

Metric	Pharyngitis	Tonsillitis
Sensitivity	0.78	**0.90**
Specificity	0.91	**0.74**
PPV	0.87	**0.94**
NPV	0.83	**0.60**
FPR	0.09	**0.25**
FNR	0.22	**0.10**
Accuracy	0.85	**0.87**
F1 score	0.82	**0.92**
MCC	0.70	**0.60**

5 Conclusion

This paper proposes a unique method for early detection and mass screening of potential coronavirus patients based on Tonsillitis symptoms. The proposed technique aims to identify the symptoms of Pharyngitis and Tonsillitis in the throat that occur in the early stages of coronavirus infection. Detection of Region of Interest is the pivotal step in for identification of Tonsillitis and Pharyngitis which is accomplished using Template Matching algorithm. HSV segmentation on the region around the uvula is performed for Pharyngitis detection. Template matching using tonsil gland followed by Canny and HOG transform on the ROI cropped image is performed for Tonsillitis detection. The proposed method can be implemented on power-efficient, parameter-constrained, and cost-effective NVIDIA's Jetson Nano embedded platform. Quantitative and qualitative evaluation showcase promising results and indicate the reliability of the proposed method. Future improvements can be achieved by using better dataset and by overcoming the high distribution of dataset source.

References

1. https://www.who.int/emergencies/diseases/novel-coronavirus-2019. Accessed 15 June 2020
2. Tan, L., Wang, Q., Zhang, D., et al.: Lymphopenia predicts disease severity of COVID-19: a descriptive and predictive study. Signal Transduct. Target. Ther. **5**, 33 (2020). https://doi.org/10.1038/s41392-020-0148-4
3. Wang, L., Lin, Z.Q., Wong, A.: COVID-Net: a tailored deep convolutional neural network design for detection of COVID-19 cases from chest X-ray images. arXiv:2003.09871 (2020)
4. Oh, Y., Park, S., Ye, J.C.: Deep learning COVID-19 features on CXR using limited training data sets. IEEE Trans. Med. Imaging **39**, 2688–2700 (2020). https://doi.org/10.1109/TMI.2020.2993291
5. Fan, D., et al.: Inf-net: automatic COVID-19 lung infection segmentation from CT images. IEEE Trans. Med. Imaging **39**, 2626–2637 (2020). https://doi.org/10.1109/TMI.2020.2996645

6. Phensadsaeng, P., Chamnongthai, K.: The design and implementation of an automatic tonsillitis monitoring and detection system. IEEE Access **5**, 9139–9151 (2017). https://doi.org/10.1109/ACCESS.2017.2699665

7. Phensadsaeng, P., Kumhom, P., Chamnongthai, K.: A computer-aided diagnosis of tonsillitis using tonsil size and color. In: 2006 IEEE International Symposium on Circuits and Systems, Island of Kos, pp. 4, pp.-5566 (2006). https://doi.org/10.1109/ISCAS.2006.1693895

8. Spiller, J.M., Marwala, T.: Medical image segmentation and localization using deformable templates. In: Magjarevic, R., Nagel, J.H. (eds.) World Congress on Medical Physics and Biomedical Engineering 2006. IFMBE Proceedings, vol. 14. Springer, Heidelberg (2007). https://doi.org/10.1007/978-3-540-36841-0_578

9. Khattab, D., et al.: Color image segmentation based on different color space models using automatic GrabCut. Sci. World J. (2014). https://doi.org/10.1155/2014/126025

10. Gao, T., Sun, X., Wang, Y., Nie, S.: A pulmonary nodules detection method using 3D template matching. In: Wang, Y., Li, T. (eds.) Foundations of Intelligent Systems. Advances in Intelligent and Soft Computing, vol. 122. Springer, Heidelberg (2011). https://doi.org/10.1007/978-3-642-25664-6_73

11. Bora, D.J., Gupta, A.K., Khan, F.A.: A new efficient watershed based color image segmentation approach. In: 2016 International Conference on Data Mining and Advanced Computing (SAPIENCE), Ernakulam, pp. 134–144 (2016). https://doi.org/10.1109/SAPIENCE.2016.7684157

12. Luo, Q., et al.: Stochastic fractal search algorithm for template matching with lateral inhibition. Sci. Program. J. (2017). https://doi.org/10.1155/2017/1803934

13. https://www.geforce.com/hardware/desktop-gpus/geforce-gtx-1050-ti/specifications. Accessed 15 June 2020

14. Parikh, P.: Gujarat Adani Institute of Medical Science, Bhuj, Kutchh, India

Predicting Novel CoronaVirus 2019 with Machine Learning Algorithms

Umang Soni[(⊠)] [iD], Nishu Gupta[iD], and Sakshi[iD]

Netaji Subhas University of Technology, New Delhi, India
umangsoni.iitd@gmail.com,
{nishug.mp.17,sakshi.mp.17}@nsit.net.in

Abstract. The 2019 coronavirus pandemic which started infecting the people of Wuhan, China during December 2019 has affected many countries worldwide within a span of 4–5 months. This has forced the countries to close their borders resulting in a global lockdown. The World Health Organization declared the disease as a pandemic during early March this year. As of 15th April 2020, nearly 3 months since the spread of the disease, no vaccine has been developed and preventive measures such as social distancing and countrywide lockdown seem to be the only way to prevent it from spreading further. The rising death toll indicates the need to carry out extensive research to aid medical practitioners as well as the governments worldwide to comprehend the rapid spread of the disease. While many research papers have been published explaining the origin and theoretical background of the disease, further research is needed to develop better prediction models. The data for the problem was generated from the sources available during the course of this study. This paper extensively analyzes the medical features of 269 patients using various Machine Learning techniques such as KNN, Random Forest, Ridge classifier, Decision Tree, Support Vector Classifier and Logistic Regression. The paper aims to predict the fatality status of an individual diagnosed with COVID-19 by assessing various factors including age, symptoms, etc. The experimental results from the research would help medical practitioners to identify the patients at higher risk and require extra medical attention, thereby helping the medical practitioners to prioritize them and increase their chances of survival.

Keywords: COVID-19 · Prediction · Machine Learning · Healthcare · Data Mining · Pandemic

1 Introduction

1.1 Origin and Cause

During December 2019, many residents of Wuhan, China started presenting severe health conditions at various local hospitals. Their examination revealed that they suffered from severe pneumonia but the medical practitioners failed to recognize the cause of their health condition. Most of the cases were known to be exposed to the Huanan wholesale seafood market which is known to trade live animals as well. The number of cases soon started rising and resulted in an outbreak. The samples from the Huanan

© Springer Nature Singapore Pte Ltd. 2021
K. K. Patel et al. (Eds.): icSoftComp 2020, CCIS 1374, pp. 289–300, 2021.
https://doi.org/10.1007/978-981-16-0708-0_24

market tested positive indicating the origin of the virus. On 31st December 2019, the Government of China alerted the World Health Organization upon which the Huanan market was ordered to be closed until further investigation. On 7th January 2020, the cause of the outbreak was identified by the Chinese Center for Disease Control and Prevention (CDC) which was later named 2019-nCoV by the World Health Organisation. It emerged as a coronavirus that shared more than 95% homology with the bat coronavirus and more than 70% homology with SARS-CoV. As of date, 6 coronavirus species are known to exist which cause human disease, 4 of which i.e. 229E, OC43, NL63, and HKU1 cause common cold symptoms. During late January this year, people worldwide were returning to their hometowns after visiting Wuhan to celebrate the Chinese New Year. This accounts for one of the largest travel activities worldwide. Soon people worldwide started getting infected and this resulted in the outbreak becoming a pandemic, as termed by the World Health Organisation during early March this year. The number of cases has increased exponentially over the past few months which suggests the occurrence of human-to-human transmission. The hospital-related transmission was identified when clusters of doctors or patients were found to be infected at a particular point of time and a potential source of infection could be tracked [4]. Studying various patients globally, the early symptoms shown by the patients include fever, difficulty in breathing, dry cough, diarrhea, and fatigue [6]. This is followed by the gradual development of dyspnea. In severe cases, patients experience inflammatory shocks, septic shock, MODS, etc. leading to death [6]. The uncontrolled spread of the disease can be attributed to the respiratory and extra respiratory routes. As of 15th April 2020, a total number of 1,914,916 people have been infected by COVID-19 with 123,010 deaths. The mortality rate is 3.4% as estimated by the World Health Organization and the incubation time for this disease is 1–14 days.

1.2 Prevention

The disease is known to transmit through large droplets released when a person coughs or sneezes [9]. The person transmitting the infection may be asymptomatic as well, making the spread of this disease difficult to contain [9]. Studies are indicative of the presence of higher viral loads in the nasal cavity as compared to the throat, making it imperative for the person to cover his/her mouth or nose when traveling in public places [12]. Many prevention techniques have been employed by various nations which include restricted movement of people, preventing large gatherings, scanning suspected individuals, quarantining patients with a travel history and in many cases, country-wide lockdown. The best possible preventive measures that exist as of 15th April 2020 include self-sanitation with special emphasis on hand sanitation and not touching one's face.

1.3 Treatment

To date, no effective vaccine or therapy has been developed for COVID-19. According to the guidelines laid by the National Health Committee, patients are currently receiving oxygen therapies such as a nasal catheter, mask oxygen and high-flow oxygen therapy [6]. Treatment methodology is dependent on the severity of the case. Many factors such as symptomatic treatment, prevention of complications and secondary infections, play a key role in determining respiratory and circulatory reports [6]. Lopinavir and ritonavir are reported to have the potential to treat SARS infections and may be a contributing factor in treating patients infected with COVID-1. In cases where the patient experienced reduced lymphocyte count and thrombocytopenia, symptomatic treatment was given [6]. It is imperative that drugs and vaccines are developed as soon as possible. Currently, the usage of intravenous immunoglobulin has also been recommended to improve the ability of anti-infection for extreme cases. The use of steroids (methylprednisolone 1–2 mg/kg per day) has been recommended for patients suffering from ARDS. Overall, no particular treatment has been recommended for coronavirus infection except for meticulous supportive care.

As of date, there have been no reports regarding the mention of any methodology which distinguishes patients requiring instantaneous medical attention and their fatality status. Therefore, the task to identify the patients at imminent risk becomes a difficult task.

1.4   Research in Context

Evidence Before this Study: Prior to conducting this research, the authors searched online for articles related to COVID-19 fatality status for articles and publications up to 15th April 2020 with the keywords "coronavirus prediction", "coronavirus ML model", "COVID-19", and "coronavirus classifier". The authors found many publications predicting the geographical spread of the disease but very few papers that predicted the severity of the disease. The authors found 1 paper that employed Machine Learning methods to detect the severity of the disease, however, it utilized a very small dataset and it achieved lower accuracy in comparison to this study.

Additional Significance of this Study/ Research:

1. Dataset generation from various sources available.
2. Fatality status prediction technique with the highest accuracy which could be employed for patients worldwide
3. Recommendation for medical practitioners to optimize medical attention according to the sensitivity and fatality status of the patient

In this research paper, various ML techniques have been employed on a self-generated dataset. Our proposed methodology includes the use of ML-based techniques to predict the fatality status of a patient. This study utilizes various classification techniques including KNN, Random Forest, Ridge classifier, Decision Tree, Support Vector Classifier and Logistic Regression. All the resources used in the study have been made publicly available to further research and expedite response action in case of outbreaks such as COVID-19. The remaining paper is structured into various sections. The section of the Literature Review assesses the previous works related to COVID-19 that were published since the outbreak of the disease. The Methodology section gives details of the dataset and algorithm used. Results and Discussion section provides and analyzes the key findings obtained while conducting this research. The Recommendations section provides recommendations to medical practitioners based on the findings analyzed in the previous section. The Conclusion section summarizes the methods, algorithms, and further scope of the research.

2   Literature Review

Fong, S. J., Li, G., Dey, N., Crespo, R. G., & Herrera-Viedma, E. (2020). Finding an Accurate Early Forecasting Model from Small Dataset: A Case of 2019-nCoV Novel Coronavirus Outbreak. arXiv preprint arXiv:2003.10776. The authors propose a methodology that encompasses the process of augmenting the existing data, distinguishing the best forecasting model from other models, and improving the model to achieve higher accuracy. The newly constructed algorithm namely polynomial neural network with corrective feedback (PNN + cf) is capable of forecasting the disease with decreased prediction error.

Zhang, N., Zhang, R., Yao, H., Xu, H., Duan, M., Xie, T.,... & Zhou, F. (2020). Severity Detection For the Coronavirus Disease 2019 (COVID-19) Patients Using a Machine Learning Model Based on the Blood and Urine Tests. The paper studied the application of machine learning algorithms to build the COVID-19 severity detection model. The paper showed that SVM or support vector Machine showed an accuracy of 0.8148 on the test dataset. The study included data of 137 patients identified with COVID-19. This study included the binary classification problem between 75 severely ill and 62 other patients with mild symptoms.

Jia, L., Li, K., Jiang, Y., & Guo, X. (2020). Prediction and Analysis of Coronavirus Disease 2019. arXiv preprint arXiv:2003.05447. This paper applied the Logistic model, Bertalanffy model and Gompertz model. The validity of the models was proved by fitting and analyzing the trends of SARS. In general, the Logistic model proved to be the best model in this study. The paper analyzed the number of people infected in Wuhan, non-Hubei and China.

3   Methodology

Machine Learning Techniques
A number of machine learning algorithms are being used by researchers worldwide to enhance the accuracy of their findings and results. One of the widely used classification techniques is the k-Nearest Neighbor (k-NN) classifier where the class is determined by the nearest neighbors. It is also known as Memory-based Classification based on the requirement of training examples in memory at run-time. Also, since this technique is based on training examples, it is also known as Example-based Classification. The selection criteria for k nearest neighbors are dependent on the distance metric. The widely used approach to determine the class of query is to assign the majority class to the query.

$$\sqrt{\sum_{k}^{i=1} (x_i - y_i)^2} \quad \text{Distance calculation in KNN}$$

In a tree classifier, unwanted computations are eliminated since it uses only particular subsets against which the sample is tested. This is in contrast with traditional single-stage classifiers. The decision tree classifier is based on a multistage decision-making approach. It works on the approach of breaking a complex decision into a culmination of various simpler decisions with the goal that the final result would resemble the desired result. The building of a Decision Tree involves the calculation of entropy using the frequency of one attribute and two attributes, both.

$$E(S) = \sum_c^{i=1} -p_i p_i \quad \text{Mathematical Formula for Entropy}$$

Another classifier, known as the Random Forest classifier, is widely used in machine learning applications. The classifier constructs each tree by utilizing a different boot-strap sample of the dataset. Standard trees involving each node are split using the best split wears in Random Forest node splitting is carried out by using the best among a subset of predictors chosen randomly at that point. This classifier is known to perform better than many existing classification techniques. Random Forest classifier also involves the use of Gini Impurity which is defined as the probability of a chosen sample being incorrectly labeled if it was labeled by the distribution of samples in the node.

$$I_G(n) = 1 - \sum_j^{i=1} (p_i)^2 \quad \text{Gini Impurity of a node n}$$

Ridge Regression or Tikhonov regularization employs the use of a new parameter which determines to what extent the solution varies from the ordinary least squares regression. This helps to improve the conditioning of the problem. Many advanced methods require the use of gradient-based and suboptimal optimization processes whereas, in the case of ridge regression, the existence of a closed-form solution makes it fast to be trained. Support Vector classifier is similar to SVM. It is considered appropriate for unsupervised learning and builds on kernel functions. The regularization parameter, C, is able to control the trade-off between low testing error and low training error. Logistic regression as a classifier is used to predict the probability of a particular outcome variable that is different from other predictor variables. It is also used to ensure that the assumption of linearity is not violated.

$$\frac{p}{p-1} = exp(b_0 + b_1 x) \quad \text{Equation for Logistic Regression}$$

PRECISION, RECALL, ACCURACY, F1 SCORE

Accuracy is defined as the ratio of correctly predicted observation of the total observation.

$$Accuracy = \frac{TP + TN}{TP + FP + FN + TN}$$

Precision is used to quantify the number of positive class predictions that belong to positive cases. It is given by:

$$Precision = \frac{TP}{TP + FP}$$

Recall is also known as sensitivity, determines the number of correctly identified actual positives.

$$Recall = \frac{TP}{TP + FN}$$

F1 Score takes into consideration the false positives and false negatives into account.

$$F1Score = 2 \times \frac{Precision \times Recall}{Precision + Recall}$$

Data Source

The data samples used in this study were collected from Kaggle source (link: https:// www.kaggle.com/sudalairajkumar/novel-corona-virus-2019-dataset?select=COVID19 _line_list_data.csv) and they were further processed to generate a new dataset. Initially, the primary dataset was filtered in MS Excel to obtain the required columns and row entries. Data entries containing the description of the symptoms in the 'symptom' column were chosen. This was followed by the removal of unwanted features, considering the primary purpose of this study. The features which were irrelevant for our analysis were removed. All the features were assigned the value '1' in case they were present in the clinical features of a patient and '0' wherever they were absent. For example, the value '1' was assigned to the column named 'cough' if the particular patient showed cough as one of the symptoms, otherwise 0. The feature 'Days taken by the doctors to confirm' was obtained by the difference between symptom onset date and reporting date. The value assigned to 'male' and 'female' in the 'Gender' column was '1' and '0' respectively. The dataset was further split into training and testing data into two separate CSV files on the basis of the attributes -'death' and 'recovered'. The training dataset contained the feature named 'death status' of the patient. It was given the value '1' if the patient had died. Another feature named 'recovery status' was created wherein the patients who recovered were given the value '1'. These two columns were merged into one column named 'fatality status' which was given '1' if the person had died and '0' if the person had recovered. The previous two attributes were removed. There were 50-row entries and 24 attributes in our train dataset. The test dataset contained the entries for which the 'death' and 'recovered' attributes both were '0' implying that those patients were under-recovery and their death status was not declared, hence we needed to predict the death status for these entries. There were 219-row entries and 24 attributes in our test dataset. **All the attributes contained in the dataset are explained below in the table** (Table 1):

Table 1. Description of the attributes

Attribute	Description
Fatality status	1: death, 0: recovered
Gender	1: male, 0: female
Age	The age of the patient
Days taken by the Hospital to report	Time taken by doctors to confirm if the person suffered from the disease or not
If_onset_approximated	If the date of onset of symptoms was exact: 0, if it was approximated: 1
Visiting Wuhan	If the patient had a travel history to Wuhan:1 else 0
From Wuhan	If the patient was a resident of Wuhan:1, else 0
Diarrhea	Patient infected with diarrhea: 1, else 0
Fever	Patient experiencing fever: 1, else 0
Cough	Patient experiencing cough: 1, else 0
Difficulty in breathing	Patient experiencing difficulty in breathing: 1, else 0
Running nose	Patient experiencing running nose: 1, else 0
Malaise	Patient experiencing malaise: 1, else 0
Chills	Patient experiencing chills: 1, else 0
Joint pain	Patient experiencing joint pain: 1, else 0
Sputum	Patient infected with sputum: 1, else 0
Pneumonia	Patient experiencing pneumonia: 1, else 0
Vomiting	Patient experiencing vomiting: 1, else 0
Sore throat	Patient experiencing sore throat: 1, else 0
Dyspnea	Patient infected with dyspnea: 1, else 0
Muscle pain	Patient experiencing muscle pain: 1, else 0
Chest discomfort	Patient experiencing chest discomfort: 1, else 0
Abdominal pain	Patient experiencing abdominal pain: 1, else 0
Loss of appetite	Patient experiencing loss of appetite: 1, else 0

Method

The prediction model is primarily based on Machine Learning techniques involving classifiers. Initially, libraries such as Pandas, NumPy and TensorFlow were used. Train. csv (containing the training data) was read in a Pandas DataFrame named 'train' and Test.csv (containing the testing data) was read in a Pandas DataFrame named 'test'. A Pandas Series named 'Y' stored the label fatality status for training data. An array named 'X' contained all the training data except the fatality status attribute. An array named 'X_test' contained all the testing data except the death status attribute (which is to be predicted). There were missing values in X and X_test which were imputed with the mean along each column using SimpleImputer. From X, a cross-validation set was prepared using train_test_split with the cross-validation set size being 0.3(30%) of X and the rest i.e. 0.7(70%) of X was treated as the training set thereafter. After this, several ML classifiers were fit on the training data. The metrics used for comparison between the classifiers and choosing the best option for prediction of the fatality status for the testing data were accuracy, precision, recall and F1 score of the cross-validation set.

Certain classifiers parameters were set which are as follows:

KNN: n_neighbors = 5,
Logistic regression: C = 2,
Support Vector Classifier: kernel = 'linear', C = 1,
Decision Tree: random_state = 0,
Random Forest: random_state = 1,
Ridge Classifier: no change, sticking to the default values.

4 Results and Discussion

The study showed that KNN Machine Learning Algorithm could predict the fatality status of a patient most accurately with a 100% performance. KNN showed the highest precision, recall and F1 score thereby showing that the algorithm is the most reliable one to predict the health of an individual. The model implied can be used to test patients who are at a higher risk of dying. This would allow medical practitioners to optimize their efforts and time so as to save more patients. In such precarious times when the shortage of medical staff and medical resources has become a contributing factor in the death of large numbers of people, the application of this method would help the medical practitioners to identify patients at higher risk so as to save more lives. The accuracy, precision score, F1 score and Recall score for each Machine Learning Algorithm is shown below (Table 2 and Fig. 1):

Table 2. Comparison of machine learning techniques

Machine learning algorithm	Accuracy	Precision	Recall	F1 score
KNN	1.0	1.0	1.0	1.0
LR	0.93	1.0	0.5	0.66
SVC	0.87	0.5	1.0	0.66
DT	0.8	0.4	1.0	0.57
RF	0.93	1.0	0.5	0.66
RC	0.93	0.66	1.0	0.8

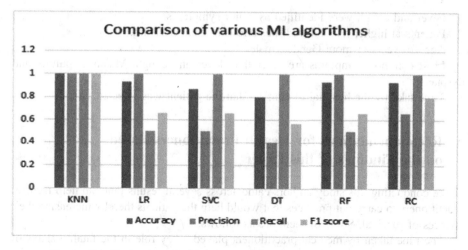

Fig. 1. Graphical representation of the comparison of various ML algorithms

The number of male deaths that occurred accounted for 72.2%. Similarly, the number of female deaths that occurred accounted for 27.77% of the cases respectively. The number of cases where the hospital took more than 7 days (1week) to confirm that the person was infected or not, accounted for 66.67% of the total number of cases (Table 3).

Table 3. Percentages of cases experiencing a particular symptom

Symptom	Percentage
Diarrhea	5.56%
Fever	61.11%
Cough	61.11%
Difficulty in breathing	0%
Running nose	0%
Malaise	16.67%
Chills	0%
Joint pain	0%
Sputum	27.78%
Pneumonia	0%
Vomiting	0%
Sore throat	0%
Dyspnea	16.67%
Muscle pain	0%
Chest discomfort	5.56%
Abdominal pain	0%
Loss of appetite	5.56.%

Fever and cough were identified as major symptoms.

Patients at higher risk showed the following characteristics:

Age: 70 years or more Gender: male.

Most common symptoms are other than fever and cough: Malaise, sputum, and dyspnea.

Time take by the hospital to confirm that the patient was infected: >7.

5   Recommendations for Health Practitioners Based on the Findings of this Paper

While conducting this study authors came across several results that can help medical practitioners to carry out practices that would help the patients thereby increasing their chances of survival. Some of them are as follows:

The time taken by medical practitioners played a key role in the fatality status of male patients of the age group of >70 years and hence they should be tested on a priority basis. It is imperative for medical practitioners to take extra care while checking multiple patients since patients of age < 30 years old can act as carriers of the virus for patients of age >70 years who are at a higher risk of getting infected and not recovering. This could lead to mass community transmission even when the patients are being treated and tested simultaneously. The appointment of separate doctors for testing of each age group should be practiced to minimize the chances of transmission between young and old people. Male patients of age >45 years old experienced higher chances of being infected with Malaise. Hence, medical resources used to cure pneumonia need to be made available to this age group. Male patients of age >43 years old had higher chances of being infected by Diarrhea. Hence, medical resources used to cure pneumonia need to be made available to this age group. Female patients of age >50 years old had higher chances of being infected by Sputum. Hence, medical resources used to cure sputum need to be made available to this age group. Male patients of age above 65 years old had higher chances of being infected by Dyspnea. Hence, medical resources used to cure pneumonia need to be made available to this age group. The immune system of a human body becomes weak with age and hence doctors with age >40 should take extra precaution while treating and testing patients. With the scarce number of ventilators, medical resources and healthy medical practitioners worldwide, it is imperative for hospitals to strategize methods for the quick recovery of the patients and the successful protection of the medical staff. This study would help them to do the same.

Limitation of this Study

While our model achieves high performance, other models with higher performance can be obtained with the increase in data available. The data available online is scarce as compared to the information available from hospitals, which as of 15th April 2020, cannot be accessed due to the rising risk of infection. Therefore, this study can be further improved in the future if more symptom centric data is made available by various hospitals and organizations. Look forward to subsequent large sample and multi-centered studies.

6 Conclusion

The study primarily aims to predict the fatality status of a patient using Machine learning algorithms. This would not only enable early intervention but it would also play a key role in decreasing the mortality rate in patients who are at a higher risk of dying due to COVID-19. This paper employed KNN as the technique showing higher performance as compared to other algorithms in terms of F1 score, precision, recall and accuracy. The experimental findings further revealed that Malaise, sputum, and dyspnea were the major symptoms apart from fever and cough. The model employed by the paper is believed to prove beneficial in detecting high-risk patients. The key significance of this study is the recommendations for medical practitioners which would not only help them to optimize their efforts and medical resources towards the patients but also be instrumental in decreasing the cases of community transmission. Though the study employed a dataset of 269 patients, it is, however, the largest dataset on symptoms available as of date. COVID-19 is a worldwide pandemic and requires further research to enable effective prevention and treatment.

References

1. Huang, C., et al.: Clinical features of patients infected with 2019 novel coronavirus in Wuhan, China. Lancet **395**(10223), 497–506 (2020)
2. Wax, R., Christian, M.: Practical recommendations for critical care and anesthesiology teams caring for novel coronavirus (2019-nCoV) patients. Can. J. Anesth./J. canadien d'anesthésie **67**(5), 568–576 (2020). https://doi.org/10.1007/s12630-020-01591-x
3. Chen, Z.-M., et al.: Diagnosis and treatment recommendations for pediatric respiratory infection caused by the 2019 novel coronavirus. World J. Pediatrics **16**(3), 240–246 (2020). https://doi.org/10.1007/s12519-020-00345-5
4. Wang, D., et al.: Clinical characteristics of 138 hospitalized patients with 2019 novel coronavirus–infected pneumonia in Wuhan, China. Jama **329**, 1061–1069 (2020)
5. Holshue, M., et al.: First case of 2019 novel coronavirus in the United States. New Engl. J. Med. **382**(10), 929–936 (2020). https://doi.org/10.1056/NEJMoa2001191
6. Pan, Y., Guan, H.: Imaging changes in patients with 2019-nCov (2020)
7. Ruan, Q., Yang, K., Wang, W., Jiang, L., Song, J.: Clinical predictors of mortality due to COVID-19 based on an analysis of data of 150 patients from Wuhan, China. Intensive Care Med. **46**, 846–848 (2020). https://doi.org/10.1007/s00134-020-05991-x
8. Wang, M., et al.: Remdesivir and chloroquine effectively inhibit the recently emerged novel coronavirus (2019-nCoV) in vitro. Cell Res. **30**(3), 269–271 (2020)
9. Corman, V.M., et al.: Detection of 2019 novel coronavirus (2019-nCoV) by real-time RT-PCR. Eurosurveillance **25**(3), 2000045 (2020)
10. Zhao, S., et al.: Preliminary estimation of the basic reproduction number of novel coronavirus (2019-nCoV) in China, from 2019 to 2020: a data-driven analysis in the early phase of the outbreak. Int. J. Infect. Dis. **92**, 214–217 (2020)
11. Gong, F., et al.: China's local governments are combating COVID-19 with unprecedented responses—from a Wenzhou governance perspective. Front. Med. **14**(2), 220–224 (2020)
12. Sabino-Silva, R., Jardim, A.C.G., Siqueira, W.L.: Coronavirus COVID-19 impacts to dentistry and potential salivary diagnosis. Clin. Oral Invest. **24**(4), 1619–1621 (2020). https://doi.org/10.1007/s00784-020-03248-x

13. Zhou, T., et al.: Preliminary prediction of the basic reproduction number of the Wuhan novel coronavirus 2019-nCoV. J. Evid.-Based Med. **13**(1), 3–7 (2020)

14. Zhan, C., Tse, C., Fu, Y., Lai, Z., Zhang, H.: Modelling and prediction of the 2019 coronavirus disease spreading in china incorporating human migration data. Available at SSRN 3546051 (2020)

15. Xie, J., Tong, Z., Guan, X., Du, B., Qiu, H., Slutsky, A.S.: Critical care crisis and some recommendations during the COVID-19 epidemic in China. Intensive Care Med. **46**(5), 837–840 (2020). https://doi.org/10.1007/s00134-020-05979-7

16. Cunningham, A.C., Goh, H.P., Koh, D.: Treatment of COVID-19: old tricks for new challenges. Crit. Care **24**, 91 (2020). https://doi.org/10.1186/s13054-020-2818-6

17. Arabi, Y.M., Murthy, S., Webb, S.: COVID-19: A novel coronavirus and a novel challenge for critical care. Intensive Care Med. **46**, 1–4 (2020). https://doi.org/10.1007/s00134-020-05955-1

18. Ni, L., Zhou, L., Zhou, M., Zhao, J., Wang, D.: Combination of western medicine and Chinese traditional patent medicine in treating a family case of COVID-19. Front. Med. **14**(2), 210–214 (2020). https://doi.org/10.1007/s11684-020-0757-x

19. Chung, M., et al.: CT imaging features of 2019 novel coronavirus (2019-nCoV). Radiology **295**, 202–207 (2020)

20. Lai, C.-C., Shih, T.-P., Ko, W.-C., Tang, H.-J., Hsueh, P.-R.: Severe acute respiratory syndrome coronavirus 2 (SARS-CoV-2) and coronavirus disease-2019 (COVID-19): the epidemic and the challenges. Int. J. Antimicrob. Agents **55**(3), 105924 (2020). https://doi.org/10.1016/j.ijantimicag.2020.105924

21. Backer, J., Klinkenberg, D., Wallinga, J.: Incubation period of 2019 novel coronavirus (2019-nCoV) infections among travellers from Wuhan, China, 20–28 January 2020. Eurosurveillance **25**(5), 2000062 (2020). https://doi.org/10.2807/1560-7917.ES.2020.25.5.2000062

22. Ji, L.-N., et al.: Clinical features of pediatric patients with COVID-19: a report of two family cluster cases. World J. Pediatrics **16**(3), 267–270 (2020). https://doi.org/10.1007/s12519-020-00356-2

23. Salzberger, B., Glück, T., Ehrenstein, B.: Successful containment of COVID-19: the WHO-Report on the COVID-19 outbreak in China. Infection **48**(2), 151–153 (2020). https://doi.org/10.1007/s15010-020-01409-4

24. Lu, H.: Drug treatment options for the 2019-new coronavirus (2019-nCoV). Biosci. Trends **14**(1), 69–71 (2020)

25. Guo, Y.R., et al.: The origin, transmission and clinical therapies on coronavirus disease 2019 (COVID-19) outbreak–an update on the status. Military Medical Research **7**(1), 1–10 (2020). https://doi.org/10.1186/s40779-020-00240-0

26. Wang, H., Wang, S., Kaijiang, Y.: COVID-19 infection epidemic: the medical management strategies in Heilongjiang Province, China. Crit. Care **24**(1), 107 (2020). https://doi.org/10.1186/s13054-020-2832-8

27. Li, B., et al.: Prevalence and impact of cardiovascular metabolic diseases on COVID-19 in China. Clin. Res. Cardiol. **109**(5), 531–538 (2020). https://doi.org/10.1007/s00392-020-01626-9

28. Riou, J., Althaus, C.: Pattern of early human-to-human transmission of Wuhan 2019 novel coronavirus (2019-nCoV), December 2019 to January 2020. Eurosurveillance **25**(4), 2000058 (2020)

29. World Health Organization: Novel Coronavirus (2019-nCoV): Situation Report, 3 (2020)

30. Wu, A., et al.: Genome composition and divergence of the novel coronavirus (2019-nCoV) originating in China. Cell Host & Microbe **27**, 325–328 (2020)

Evaluation of Image Filtering Parameters for Plant Biometrics Improvement Using Machine Learning

Taiwo Olaleye[1] ⓘ, Oluwasefunmi Arogundade[2] ⓘ, Cecelia Adenusi[2],
Sanjay Misra[4(✉)], and Abosede Bello[3]

[1] Computer Centre and Services, Federal College of Education,
Abeokuta, Nigeria
agsobaolaleyetaiwo@gmail.com
[2] Department of Computer Science, Federal University of Agriculture,
Abeokuta, Nigeria
arogundadeot@funaab.edu.ng, ceceresearch@gmail.com
[3] Biology Department, Federal College of Education, Abeokuta, Nigeria
bose4ung@yahoo.com
[4] Department of Electrical and Information Engineering, Covenant University,
Ota, Nigeria
sanjay.misra@covenantuniversity.edu.ng

Abstract. The need to improve on the existing performance metrics of plant biometric researches in literature is more than addendum but a critical juncture towards the path of enhancing classification accuracies hence the purpose of this work aimed at establishing yardsticks for improved image processing phase precursor to machine learning. In this study, we applied seven dissimilar filtering iterations on three distinct plant image datasets and appraise their influence on plant biometrics to evaluate the implications of five image filtering parameters. The supervised machine learning classification was conducted on Sequential Minimal Optimization algorithm with 10-fold cross validation after oversampling of minority classes was conducted to reduce level of classification biasedness. Classification enhanced with 1.2739% improvement through inter-filter mixture over highest single filter result while insignificant poorer result was achieved with intra-filter mixture returning 0.637% decline when compared with inter-filter. Larger attribute-extraction filters returned a 4.1402% classification improvement over filters with lower attributes extraction and a 1.3169% improvement was recorded by colour-attribute-based filter over texture-based on a coloured image dataset. Image pixel representations and dataset sizes are other parameters that influence the accuracy level of image predictive analytics. The experimental results establishes the advantage of *intra-filter combination* over inter option and the prominence of the size of extracted image attributes over obtaining good results. Nature of image dataset in terms of colour or greyscale likewise must inform the choice of filter to be deployed according to experimental results obtained from this work.

Keywords: Image filtering · Machine learning · Minority oversampling · Image features · Image attributes

© Springer Nature Singapore Pte Ltd. 2021
K. K. Patel et al. (Eds.): icSoftComp 2020, CCIS 1374, pp. 301–315, 2021.
https://doi.org/10.1007/978-981-16-0708-0_25

1   Introduction

Machine learning (ML) has continued to enjoy wide range of patronage as a flexible data mining tool and a repository of several building-block learning algorithms for conceptualizing thoroughbred skillful models focused on different domains of research interests. Its vast application in the area of content based image retrieval system is noteworthy as research works continued to discover leverages offered by the artificial intelligence use case subcategory. Machine Learning can be viewed as a way through which algorithms performance is enhanced with time based on feedback with two primary approaches including supervised and unsupervised machine learning approaches. In supervised learning, there exist a model of both input and output training dataset such that the algorithm is executed until it can arrive at the desired output goal and these set of algorithms could either fall into classification or regression category [1]. Classifications algorithms simply classify input to match desired output while Regression analysis is a statistical method for approximating the relationships among variables. Both are used in predictive and forecasting tasks. Unsupervised machine learning algorithms unravels structures from dataset by clustering or grouping data points for spotting patterns. The essence of machine learning descriptions in literature suggests the study of mining information from a pool of data thereby making it possible to learn some information from data that were hitherto not obvious. ML wide acceptance and high applicability trend has enjoyed wide spread acceptance from end users such that the moral burden of profound explainability lies on the researcher each time to enhance transparency of proposed ML model [2]. Transparency is believed to involve different efforts to offer stakeholders, especially end users, with necessary information about functionalities of a model and ways may include publishing algorithm's code, disclosing properties of the training method and most importantly datasets used [3] which further underscores the paramount relevance of the nature, scope and composition of data deployed for predictive analytics. However, data available for mining could be textual, numeric or image and ML algorithms targets patterns encapsulated within data by training a subset of the data and classification follows based on the initial pattern-seeking training and the correlation observed between independent data attributes and dependent output class category [4].

While several elements continued to serve as dataset for machine learning tasks, images sometimes referred to as pictures, has been objects of data mining in other research tasks in the areas of biometrics [5], identity management [6], image processing [4], medical data mining tasks [7], handwriting detection [8], including agriculture related research works [9] etc. Aforementioned notwithstanding, image preprocessing, segmentation, filtering etc. comes before classification for a seamless ML task which yields image attributes that forms the numeric composition of the featured metadata and these attributes are transformed into applicable data types and forms the pool of the instances deployed for the predictive analytics of intended research interest. A single image filter can be used on the set of images or a group approach all targeted at better output performance. The applied additional filters, if more than one, add new numeric data to each instance of the dataset which eventually influences the classification learning precursor to the testing phase. The collection of image filtering algorithms available for plant biometrics with their unique parameters, characteristics, target features etc. and variable nature of image datasets for machine learning tasks motivated this work in a bid to establish best practices for enhanced classification.

The aim of this paper therefore is to determine the effect of combining filters for processing image dataset, importance of size of feature attributes extracted from images, the size of each image instances, type of features extracted by filters, and the size of dataset itself through the deployment of synthetic minority oversampling technique (SMOTE) for an enhanced performance accuracy metrics. The Waikato environment for knowledge analysis (WEKA) tool was used for the preprocessing and classification phases of the proposed model. The organization of the rest of the paper is as follows: Sect. 2 of this paper reviewed several image filtering and preprocessing literatures that offered related models to this study while Sect. 3 describes the methodology deployed in this research work. Section 4 discusses results and Sect. 5 concluded this work with recommendations and possible future works.

2   Related Works

The source of image dataset deployed for filtering processes differ and a germane factor in the overall intention of having a reliable classification process of training and testing. Sources include online image laboratories [10–12], modified copies of field images targeting spots of interests across images to suit purpose and intent [13, 14], and field images directly taken from the use case or natural habitat [15, 16] but for the online laboratory images, they are already often categorized along use cases to cater for unique application domains or area of interest [17] while the field images are at best for image identification and returns better classification result [15].

In an image classification attempt, [4] applied random forest ML algorithm to discover the effect of different filters on four distinct categories of image dataset to further determine roles played by category of image dataset on output accuracy. The study discovers that filter combinations got better presentation than a single filter-approach while filter combinations on artworks returned a lower 83.42% accuracy result in comparison to a 99.76% output on natural image dataset. Morphological features of images are often targets of image preprocessing or segmentation tasks while experiments could center on greyscale or colored images depending on the purpose of filtering but the work of [18] targets image contour disparities popularly characterized by amoebas. Experiments on grayscale and color images demonstrate that amoeba filters outdo orthodox morphological operations with a fixed structured element for noise reduction tasks. Tests on artificial 3D images shows the high noise-decline capability of amoeba-based filters.

Authors of [19] opines that of all factors contributing to good image quality in single-photon emission computed tomography (SPECT), image filtering is an important, but mostly partially applied, image-processing factor. An overview of currently available SPECT filtering choices was done and discussed in this work to offer guidance on choice. It discovered *Hann* and *Butterworth* filters allow precise estimates to most filter types while suggesting the use of limited filter types in an effort to regulate image-processing methods, which may lead to improved predictability. The work of [20] describes new discovery on segmentation of textured gray-scale images through pre-filtering of image inputs and fractal features. The work uses fractal-based features which rely on textural characteristics, not intensity elements and to reduce number of features deployed for segmentation, significance of features is observed using a test similar to the F-test, while less significant features were exempted in the clustering process. The authors used a variable window size to extend the K-means algorithm while ensuring preservation of details of boundary.

A preliminary study on four variables augmentation method, augmentation rate, size of basic dataset per label, and method combination was conducted by [21] herein to unravel influence of the variables on deep learning tasks noting that combination of two geometric methods reduces performance while combinations with at least one photometric method improves performance especially pairing geometric and photometric methods. Order of methods in combination is discovered to have no impact on performance. In the first half of this work, [22] proposes fast algorithms for bilateral image filtering (BLF) and nonlocal means (NLM) as against the kernel filtering discussed in their work. They achieved state-of-the-art fast algorithms for BLF of grayscale images and extended idea of quick color filtering which involves calculation of a three-dimensional kernel. Second half of the work features introduction of a scale-adaptive variant of BLF used for defeating fine surfaces in images by developing swift execution of a symmetrized variant of NLM that used for regularization within the plug-and-play structure for image refurbishment.

[23] proposes a computerized proactive discovery of rice plant diseases using image processing and SVM and random forest classification algorithms. An 82.41% performance accuracy was recorded by SVM which is far better than the random forest classification algorithm. The classification of rice plant is the research focus of [24] by converting videos of rice plants into images before preprocessing and subsequent classification of needed morphological regions. Features extracted from the images through the #D technology serves as inputs of their 250 dataset by extracting 18 color and 21 texture features. Researchers in [25] makes use of CNN by image processing to discover the maturity level of Banana (Cavendish), Mango (Carabao), and Calamansi/Calamondin, through categorization into pre-matured, matured, and over-matured. The model is written in Spyder in Anaconda Navigator, which applies Tensorflow-GPU and Keras coupled with the usage of CUDA and CUDDN to process the data and determine results. RGB and grayscale datasets were used for classification returning a state-of-the-art accuracy in output.

The work of [26] concerns the use of image processing to assess the reabsorption rate of the implanted HA, and β-TCP commercial granules in bone flaws after a granuloma removal in oral and maxillofacial surgery. Cone-beam computed tomography dimensions were gathered at baseline and at 12-month. Result on 2D images shows good reabsorption of the granules. Edge detection in road markings during image preprocessing and segmentation was deployed in the work of [27] to aid automatic patrol robots to identify road boundaries without errors. The experimental results show that proposed method is efficient in reducing the edge features of road marking lines while [28] deployed Superpixel segmentation for image preprocessing in an attempt to diagnose age-Related Macular Degeneration (AMD) as a foremost retinal disease that causes vision loss. Digital image preprocessing and other ML algorithms were deployed in this work to diagnose AMD-fundus in images. The fundus images went through intensity alteration and two-sided filtering followed by optic disc removal and Superpixel dissection using Simple Linear Iterative Clustering. Intensity-based statistics and Texton-map Histogram attributes were extracted from images for subsequent classification by chosen ML. Work of [29] is an image retrieval system premised on manifold feature fusion. The multi attribute approach first combines the global and local features images by setting weights differently, and then retrieval based on adaptive coefficients of the fusion features. Result shows single retrieval extraction outcome trails the model of the authors and likewise improves the query proficiency with impressive P-R curve and good application value. In [30], an overview of machine learning theories and algorithms describes the thoroughbred expertise inherent in the machine learning subfield of artificial intelligence while establishing the truism of machine learning being the future of technological and scientific advancements. The paper describes the 'what', 'how 'and 'why 'of its applications. There are several other related works available in literature [31–34].

Technical Gaps in Literature: Two major technical gaps prominent in most literatures consulted are (1) the failure to factor in the prejudice of classification results when imbalanced class dataset is deployed for training phase of predictive analytics which inadvertently affects predictive result; and (2) the need to unravel the implication of mixing filters of different classes (intra-filtering) for preprocessing of image datasets as against the adoption of related filters (inter-filtering) deployed in literatures. These gaps led to the design of the proposed work for subsequent intervention. Intervention: Oversampling of minority classes is adopted to reduce level of classification partiality while both inter-filtering and intra-filtering approaches were conducted to compare accuracy outcomes as reported in (2).

3   Methodology

Four phases defines the scope of this work including the plant image capturing and categorization, image preprocessing and filtering, synthetic minority oversampling technique application, and the machine learning classification phases. The output of each phase directly serves as inputs into the immediate subsequent phase and the pipeline is as described by the activity diagram on Fig. 1.

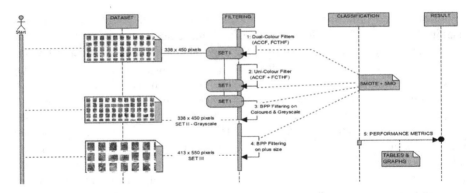

Fig. 1. Activity diagram modeling the study pipeline

3.1 Dataset Capturing

A set of thirteen different herbal plant images is captured for this work and is further unbundled into three distinct datasets including *DS_1* (coloured version), *DS_2* (grayscale version of *DS_1*) and *DS_3* (bigger size of *DS_1*). The varying degree of imbalanced class distribution in the three newly built dataset is as presented in Fig. 2.

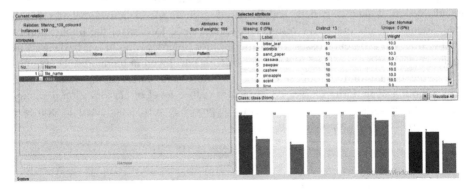

Fig. 2. Imbalanced class distribution of image instances across the three datasets

3.2 Image Filtering

The second phase of image filtering is in seven iterations and carried out on all three datasets used in this study. Since the *arff* file deployed for WEKA work tool is numeric data type, filters simply extracts characteristic distinct features from the images at each iteration and adds the extracted numerical attributes into the existing *arff* file dedicated for each database of *DS_1, DS_2* and *DS_3* depending on which one is being filtered at any point in time (Figs. 3, 4 and 5). The filters deployed include Auto Colour Correlogram Filter (*ACCF*), Fuzzy Colour and Texture Histogram filter (*FCTHF*), and Binary Pattern Pyramid Filter (*BPPF*), which are all used as either single filters or as combined filtering tools. Table 1 gives the filters and the number of extractions from each 109 instances across datasets, while noting that the combined filtering abilities and number of attributes add up for the combined categories. Figure 6 is the *arff* file of dataset after filtering showing numeric values of features extracted. These filter combinations adopted gave the best results even though results of others are close enough for adoption meaning the image filters deployed in WEKA are highly efficient without significant inferiority in the processing of plant images chosen for this work. The application order is also insignificant because with each filter, WEKA extracts unique numeric data as attributes for each instance before machine learning classification phase.

Table 1. Filtering iteration with attribute nature and sizes

S/N	Filter	Features extracted	Filter_id	Active dataset	# of attributes	ARFF_id	Instance/ attribute ratio
1.	ACCF	Colour	F_1	DS_1	1024	Arf_1	109:1024
2.	FCTH	Colour + texture	F_2	DS_1	192	Arf_2	109:192
3.	ACCF + FCTH	Colour + Texture	CF_1	DS_1	1216	CArf_1	109:1216
4.	BPPF	Patterns	F_3	DS_1	756	Arf_3	109:756
5.	ACCF + BPPF	Colour + Patterns	CF_2	DS_1	1780	CArf_2	109:1780
6.	BPPF	Patterns	F_3	DS_2	756	Arf_4	109:756
7.	BPPF	Patterns	F_3	DS_3	756	Arf_5	109:756

Fig. 3. Image input DS_1 with corresponding filtered output Arff_1

Fig. 4. Image input DS_2 with corresponding filtered output Arff_4

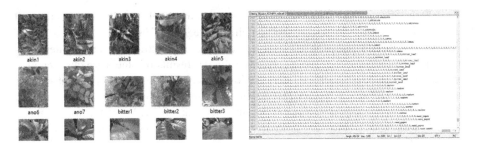

Fig. 5. Image input DS_3 with corresponding filtered output Arff_5

3.3 Sequential Minimal Optimization (SMO) Algorithm

The SMO deployed in this evaluation study is an improvement on the traditional secure vector machine (SVM) which is aimed to address the optimization problem of the latter. SMO is an effective method for training SVM on classification tasks especially on sparse data sets and it is different from SVM algorithms as it does not entail a quadratic programming solver. Research showed that SVMs can be optimized via the decomposition of a large quadratic programming problem into smaller mini-problems. Optimizing individual mini-problem therefore minimizes the initial quadratic programming problem once no further progress is possible on all of the sub-problems. The original quadratic programming problem is thereby solved. Since individual sub-problem can have stable magnitude, optimization through decomposition is possible with a permanent size. Decomposition in SMO therefore is far more efficient than the quadratic programming approach of SVM. Since SMO deploys a sub-problem of dual size, each sub-problem therefore has a methodical solution. While other methods towards solving the quadratic programming problem of SVM hold great promise, SMO is the only optimizer that explicitly exploits the quadratic form of the objective function and simultaneously uses the analytical solution which is therefore applied in our methodology for a better result.

3.4 SMOTE Application

In the aforementioned and as evident in Fig. 2, species of plants in the datasets with smaller class representations of instances will affect the accuracy of the classification owning to the biased composition of the datasets. Hence, *cassava, fruit, akintola, orange,* and *lemon* species with their *5, 5, 6, 7,* and *7* are minorities and their poor representations will skew precision of the machine learning towards the other plants. *Lime,* with *9* representations, may not necessarily affect since it's only short of *1* to make up with the *10* representations recorded by the majority class. SMOTE is therefore applied in three iterations on the seven *arff* files to address the under sampling of the minority class by generating synthetic instances to scale up the representations of the minority. SMOTE is configured to search 5-k nearest neighbor of any member of the minority class and then generate attributes along the line formed between the neighbors in such an highly efficient manner inheriting the exact characteristic nature of the parent minority. The new synthetic data generated along the line connecting each minority sample scales up the minority class with the new synthetic versions as captured on Fig. 6 below. Upon SMOTE application, the machine learning classification phase ensues to determine the experimental result.

3.5 Machine Learning Implementation

The last three phases of this proposed work is implemented on the WEKA platform including image preprocessing, minority oversampling through SMOTE, and classification by SMO after the first phase of plant image capturing. The image preprocessing is done across seven filtering phases with intra and inter combinatorial filtering approach using ACCF, *FCTH and BPPF* filters on the *WEKA* preprocessing submenu. The resulting *Arf_1, Arf_2, Arf_3, Arf_4, Arf_5 and CArf_2 numeric arff* files representing the seven filtering categories actualized from the distinct datasets are deployed for the next phase of the minority oversampling to address class imbalance as represented on the three image datasets presented in Fig. 2 above. The synthetic minority oversampling technique is a plug-in applied as incorporated in the preprocessing submenu of the WEKA application. With class imbalance addressed through minority oversampling, the SMO classification algorithm, an improvement on the SVM, is deployed for the machine learning training phase via the Classifier tab of the WEKA application across the seven filtered *arff* files. The classification accuracy and results are as presented I the next session of this work.

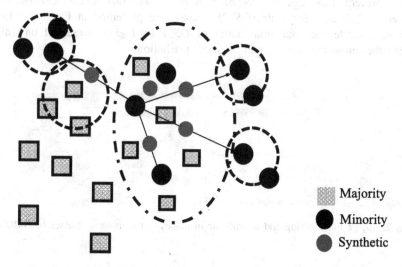

Fig. 6. Depiction of the SMOTE application for minority oversampling

4 Result and Discussion

Upon successful image filtering sessions on the *DS_1*, *DS_2* and *DS_3*, a corresponding seven versions of *arff* file were generated including *Arf_1*, *Arf_2*, *Arf_3*, *Arf_4 and Arf_5* on single filters and *CArf_1* and *CArf_2* on combined filtering tasks. The seven *arff* files were deployed for the subsequent machine learning classification using Sequential Minimal Optimization (SMO) function algorithm as an improved version of SVM, designed to solve the high quadratic programming problems of SVM. SVM is widely used in image classification predictive analytics in literature and with an improved SMO, classification is sure to return an improved accuracy by simply breaking the optimization problem into a series of smaller possible sub-problems, which are then solved methodically.

With the generation of the seven *arff* files prior to classification by SMO, they are presented for oversampling of minority classes and the resulting synthetic additions for balancing through SMOTE application on *DS_1* is presented in Fig. 7 thereby increasing the representations of the minority classes immediately after the 109th instance while Fig. 8 shows the projection plots of the three SMOTE iterations on *DS_1* which improved minority classes in the process. Table 2 shows the performance accuracy of SMO machine learning on *Arf_1*, *Arf_2* and *CArf_1* which seeks to discover the combinatorial advantage or otherwise of filters and the influence of attribute size while Table 3 shows the effect of dataset nature, effect of kind of features extracted from filter and combinatorial effect and Table 4 shows performance on dataset of bigger size to discover the impact of image sizes on classification accuracy. Having recorded same performance accuracy figures on a larger dataset (474 instances), the graph of weighted averages of *Precision, Recall, F-measure* and *ROC areas* of the coloured *(DS_1)* and grayscale *(DS_2)* datasets are presented in Fig. 9 for further clarification while the confusion matrix of *DS_1 by F_3* is presented on Table 5 showing the number of correct and incorrect predictions.

Fig. 7. *arff_1* file showing added synthetic instances of the minority classes by SMOTE

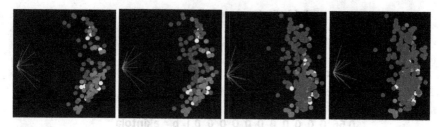

Fig. 8. Projection plots of three SMOTE iterations on *DS_1* showing synthetic additions for class balancing

Table 2. Classification performance of filters over attribute size and combinatorial effect

S/N	Experimental parameters				Performance (%)			
					Initial inst. size	SMOTE iterations		
	Filter_id	Datset_id	Arff_id	Size of Attr.	109	134	244	314
1.	F_1	DS_1	Arf_1	1024	66.9725	73.1343	88.9344	91.4013
2.	F_2	DS_1	Arf_2	192	50.4587	62.6866	83.1967	87.2611
3.	CF_1	DS_1	CArf_1	1216	68.8073	74.6269	88.9344	92.6752

Table 3. Classification performance over dataset nature, filter features, and filter combination

S/N	Experimental parameters				Performance %				
					Initial size	SMOTE iterations			
	Filter_id	Dataset_id	Arff_id	Attr.size	109	134	244	314	474
1.	F_3	DS_2	Arf_4	756	38.5321	52.9851	76.2295	84.7134	90.0844
2.	F_3	DS_1	Arf_3	756	33.0275	49.2537	77.8689	83.4395	90.0844
3.	F_3	DS_1	Arf_3	756	33.0275	49.2537	77.8689	83.4395	90.0844
3b	F_1	DS_1	Arf_1	1024	66.9725	73.1343	73.1343	88.9344	91.4013
4.	CF_2	DS_1	CArf_2	1780	70.6422	74.6269	88.1148	92.0382	95.1477

Table 4. Classification performance over size of dataset images

S/N	Experimental parameters				Performance %				
					Initial size	SMOTE iterations			
	Filter_id	Dataset_id	Arff_id	Attribute size	109	134	244	314	474
1.	F_3	DS_3	Arf_5	756	38.5321	53.7313	77.459	85.0318	90.5063
2.	F_3	DS_1	Arf_3	756	33.0275	49.2537	77.8689	83.4395	90.0844

Table 5. Confusion matrix of ds_3

= Confusion Matrix =

a b c d e f g h i j k l m <-- classified as

4 1 0 0 1 1 0 0 0 0 3 0 0 | a = bitter_leaf

0 66 0 0 0 0 0 0 0 0 0 0 0 | b = akintola

2 0 4 0 2 0 0 1 0 0 0 1 0 | c = sand_paper

0 0 0 30 0 0 0 0 0 0 0 0 0 | d = cassava

2 1 0 0 5 2 0 0 0 0 0 0 0 | e = pawpaw

0 0 0 1 2 1 2 0 2 1 1 0 0 | f = cashew

1 1 0 1 0 1 5 0 1 0 0 0 0 | g = pineapple

0 0 3 0 1 0 0 4 1 1 0 0 0 | h = scent

0 0 0 0 0 0 0 0 99 0 0 0 0 | i = lime

1 0 0 2 1 0 1 1 2 0 2 0 0 | j = plantain

0 0 0 0 0 0 0 0 0 0 77 0 0 | k = lemon

0 0 0 0 0 0 0 0 0 0 0 77 0 | l = orange

0 0 0 0 0 0 0 0 0 0 0 0 55 | m= green_grass

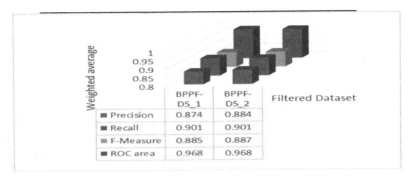

Weighted average	BPPF-DS_1	BPPF-DS_2	Filtered Dataset
Precision	0.874	0.884	
Recall	0.901	0.901	
F-Measure	0.885	0.887	
ROC area	0.968	0.968	

Fig. 9. Performance metrics of F_3 over DS_1 and DS_2

On Table 2, an insignificant improvement of 1.2739% was recorded on inter-filter CF_1 over single filter F_1 with 91.4013% accuracy probably largely due to the smaller dataset size as a better 95.1477% accuracy was recorded by intra-filter CF_2 on a bigger dataset DS_1 but both results better than individual performances of F_1, F_2 and F_3 that extracts colour and texture features separately. Hence, combination of filters performs better. The size of attributes extracted from images influences eventual performance as noticed on Tables 2 and 3. The *832* difference between attributes of f_1 and f_2 contributed to the *4.1402%* improvement recorded on their classification accuracies having worked on the same DS_1. Improvement on Table 3 is however not remarkable with 1.3169% between f_1 and f_3 with a *268* differences in attribute size. The bigger image sizes of *413 × 550* pixels of DS_3 returned a 0.4219% improvement over the size of DS_1 with a lower dimension of *338 × 450*. The type of feature extracted from images influences performance as colour extracted features from coloured DS_1 performed better than texture extracted features hence better to deploy filters with common colour-ground with dataset for classification. But having recorded same accuracy on Table 3 in the fourth SMOTE iteration, the weighted averages of both classification in *Recall, Precision, ROC area*, and *F-measure* shows the grayscale dataset performed slightly better as noted on the graph of Fig. 8 with the harmonic mean of *F-Measure* parameter even though their diagnostic abilities are at par with same ROC value recorded. Dataset size improves performances along the line of improved number of instances from 109 to 474 reiterating the disadvantages of under-sampling and inclusion of minority classes in the dataset.

5   Conclusion

The tests intend to discover through experimental results, the effect of combining filters for processing image dataset, importance of size of feature attributes extracted from images, the size of each image instances, type of features extracted by filters, and the size of dataset itself. Experimental results after the machine learning phase by SMO reveals significant improvements when filters are combined from 91.4013% accuracy to 95.1477%. Bigger sizes of extracted image attributes likewise returned a 4.1402% improvement at one instance and a 1.3169% improvement at another instance of classification. A 0.4219% improvement was recorded on bigger input image sizes of 413 × 550 pixels over 338 × 450 pixels. Extracted features that aligns with the nature of dataset also improved classification accuracy compared to attributes of less similarity with the characteristic nature of image dataset. Across all classifications and iterations, a bigger dataset size returns better classification accuracies. As a future work to this study, distinct datasets of different sources and texture are recommended for further evaluation as against dataset of same nature used in this work.

Acknowledgement. The authors profoundly express gratitude to Covenant University for her support through CUCRID.

References

1. Mirza, S., Mittal, S., Zaman, M.: Decision support predictive model for prognosis of diabetes using SMOTE and decision tree. Int. J. Appl. Eng. Res. **13**(11), 9277–9292 (2018)
2. Bhatt, U., et al.: Explainable machine learning in deployment. In: Proceedings of the 2020 Conference on Fairness, Accountability, and Transparency, pp. 648–657 (2020)
3. Mitchell, M., et al.: Model cards for model reporting. In: Proceedings of the Conference on Fairness, Accountability, and Transparency, pp. 220–229. ACM (2019)
4. Abidin, D.: Effects of image filters on various image datasets. In: Proceedings of the 2019 5th International Conference on Computer and Technology Applications, pp. 1–5 (2019)
5. Greitans, M., Pudzs, M., Fuksis, R.: Palm vein biometrics based on infrared imaging and complex matched filtering. In: Proceedings of the 12th ACM Workshop on Multimedia and Security, pp. 101–106 (2010)
6. Khan, S., Javed, M.H., Ahmed, E., Shah, S.A., Ali, S.U.: Facial recognition using convolutional neural networks and implementation on smart glasses. In: 2019 International Conference on Information Science and Communication Technology (ICISCT), pp. 1–6. IEEE (2019)
7. Alghamdi, M., Al-Mallah, M., Keteyian, S., Brawner, C., Ehrman, J., Sakr, S.: Predicting diabetes mellitus using SMOTE and ensemble machine learning approach: the Henry Ford ExercIse Testing (FIT) project. PLoS ONE **12**(7), e0179805 (2017)
8. Kato, N., Suzuki, M., Omachi, S.I., Aso, H., Nemoto, Y.: A handwritten character recognition system using directional element feature and asymmetric Mahalanobis distance. IEEE Trans. Pattern Anal. Mach. Intell. **21**(3), 258–262 (1999)
9. Zahara, M.: Identification of morphological and stomatal characteristics of Zingiberaceae as medicinal plants in Banda Aceh, Indonesia. In: IOP Conference Series: Earth and Environmental Science, vol. 425, no. 1, p. 012046. IOP Publishing (January 2020)
10. Wang, Z., Chi, Z., Feng, D.: Shape based leaf image retrieval. IEE Proc.-Vis. Image Signal Process. **150**(1), 34–43 (2003)
11. Mokhtar, U., Ali, M.A.S., Hassanien, A.E., Hefny, H.: Identifying two of tomatoes leaf viruses using support vector machine. In: Mandal, J.K., Satapathy, S.C., Sanyal, M.K., Sarkar, P.P., Mukhopadhyay, A. (eds.) Information Systems Design and Intelligent Applications. AISC, vol. 339, pp. 771–782. Springer, New Delhi (2015). https://doi.org/10.1007/978-81-322-2250-7_77
12. Prasvita, D.S., Herdiyeni, Y.: Medleaf: mobile application for medicinal plant identification based on leaf image. Int. J. Adv. Sci. Eng. Inf. Technol. **3**(2), 5–8 (2013)
13. Kumar, M., Gupta, S., Gao, X.Z., Singh, A.: Plant species recognition using morphological features and adaptive boosting methodology. IEEE Access **7**, 163912–163918 (2019)
14. Priyankara, H.C., Withanage, D.K.: Computer assisted plant identification system for android. In: 2015 Moratuwa engineering research conference (MERCon), pp. 148–153. IEEE (April 2015)
15. Thomas, V., Chawla, N.V., Bowyer, K.W., Flynn, P.J.: Learning to predict gender from iris images. In: 2007 First IEEE International Conference on Biometrics: Theory, Applications, and Systems, pp. 1–5. IEEE (September 2007)
16. Hossain, J., Amin, M.A.: Leaf shape identification based plant biometrics. In: 2010 13th International Conference on Computer and Information Technology (ICCIT), pp. 458–463. IEEE (December 2010)
17. Lee, S.H., Chang, Y.L., Chan, C.S., Remagnino, P.: Plant identification system based on a convolutional neural network for the LifeClef 2016 plant classification task. In: CLEF (Working Notes), pp. 502–510 (2016)

18. Lerallut, R., Decencière, É., Meyer, F.: Image filtering using morphological amoebas. Image Vis. Comput. **25**(4), 395–404 (2007)

19. Van Laere, K., Koole, M., Lemahieu, I., Dierckx, R.: Image filtering in single-photon emission computed tomography: principles and applications. Comput. Med. Imaging Graph. **25**(2), 127–133 (2001)

20. Kasparis, T., Charalampidis, D., Georgiopoulos, M., Rolland, J.: Segmentation of textured images based on fractals and image filtering. Pattern Recognit. **34**(10), 1963–1973 (2001)

21. Hu, B., Lei, C., Wang, D., Zhang, S., Chen, Z.: A preliminary study on data augmentation of deep learning for image classification. arXiv preprint arXiv:1906.11887 (2019)

22. Ghosh, S.: Kernel-based image filtering: fast algorithms and applications. In: SIGGRAPH Asia 2019 Doctoral Consortium, pp. 1–3 (2019)

23. Pascual, E.J.A.V., Plaza, J.M.J., Tesorero, J.L.L., De Goma, J.C.: Disease detection of Asian rice (Oryza Sativa) in the Philippines using image processing. In: Proceedings of the 2nd International Conference on Computing and Big Data, pp. 131–135 (October 2019)

24. Buenaventura, J.R.S., Kobayashi, J.T., Valles, L.M.P., De Goma, J.C., Balan, A.K.D.: Classification of varietal type of Philippine rice grains using image processing through multi-view 3D reconstruction. In: Proceedings of the 2nd International Conference on Computing and Big Data, pp. 140–144 (October 2019)

25. Ayllon, M.A., Cruz, M.J., Mendoza, J.J., Tomas, M.C.: Detection of overall fruit maturity of local fruits using convolutional neural networks through image processing. In: Proceedings of the 2nd International Conference on Computing and Big Data, pp. 145–148 (October 2019)

26. El Byad, H., Hakim, S., Ezzahmouly, M., Ed-Dhahraouy, M., El Moutaouakkil, A., Hatim, Z.: Application of image processing in dentistry: evaluation of bone regeneration. In: Proceedings of the 4th International Conference on Big Data and Internet of Things, pp. 1–5 (October 2019)

27. Chen, S., Liu, Z.: An image processing method reducing road marking line edge features for patrol robots identifying road boundaries. In: Proceedings of the 2019 3rd International Conference on Advances in Image Processing, pp. 29–33 (November 2019)

28. De Goma, J.C., Binsol, O.J.D., Nadado, A.M.T., Casela III, J.P.A.: Age-related macular degeneration detection through fundus image analysis using image processing techniques. In: Proceedings of the 2019 3rd International Conference on Software and e-Business, pp. 146–150 (December 2019)

29. Han, X., Li, Y., Zheng, Q., Huang, Y., Zhang, Z., He, Z.: A multiple feature fusion based image retrieval algorithm. In: Proceedings of the 2019 8th International Conference on Networks, Communication and Computing, pp. 103–108 (December 2019)

30. Alzubi, J., Nayyar, A., Kumar, A.: Machine learning from theories to algorithms: an overview. In: Journal of Physics: Conference Series, vol. 1142, no. 1, p. 012012 (November 2018)

31. Temiatse, O.S., Misra, S., Dhawale, C., Ahuja, R., Matthews, V.: Image enhancement of lemon grasses using image processing techniques (histogram equalization). In: Panda, B., Sharma, S., Roy, N. (eds.) Data Science and Analytics. REDSET 2017. Communications in Computer and Information Science, vol. 799. Springer, Singapore (2018). https://doi.org/10.1007/978-981-10-8527-7_24

32. Dhawale, C.A., Misra, S., Thakur, S., Jambhekar, N.D.: Analysis of nutritional deficiency in citrus species tree leaf using image processing. In: 2016 International Conference on Advances in Computing, Communications and Informatics (ICACCI), pp. 2248–2252. IEEE (September 2016)

33. Patil, M.Y., Dhawale, C.A., Misra, S.: Analytical study of combined approaches to content based image retrieval systems. Int. J. Pharm. Technol. **8**(4), 22982–22995 (2016)

34. Singh, S.K., Dhawale, C., Misra, S.: Past, present and future research direction for Camoufor camouflage image detection. Int. J. Control Theory Appl. **9**(22), 335–340 (2016)

Glaucoma Detection Using Features of Optic Nerve Head, CDR and ISNT from Fundus Image of Eye

Kartik Thakkar[1]([⊠]) [iD], Kinjan Chauhan[2], Anand Sudhalkar[3],
Aditya Sudhalkar[4], and Ravi Gulati[5]

[1] BCA Department, Vivekanand College, Surat, India
thakkar.kartik@hotmail.com
[2] Department of Computer Science, Shree Ramkrishna Institute of Computer
Education and Applied Science, Surat, India
kinjan.chauhan@srki.ac.in
[3] Medical Research Foundation, Sudhalkar Eye Hospital and Retina Centre,
Vadodara, India
sudhalkar@hotmail.com
[4] Sudhalkar Eye Hospital and Retina Centre, Vadodara, India
aditya@sudhalkareyehospital.com
[5] Department of Computer Science, Veer Narmad South Gujarat University,
Surat, India
rmgulati@vnsgu.ac.in

Abstract. Human eye suffers from many diseases. If patients have peripheral,
partial or blur vision, there are chances of Glaucoma. Glaucoma causes no pain
and show no symptoms unless noticeable vision loss occurs. Glaucoma is the
2nd most leading cause of blindness. Retinal Fundus images (photograph of the
back of the eye i.e. fundus using specialised fundus cameras) contain features
like Optic Cup, Optic Disc, Blood Vessels, Neuro Retinal Rim (NRR), Macula
and Retinal Nerve Fibre Layer (RNFL). These features change in shape, size and
colour if the eye is Glaucomatous. An approach is to analyse Optic Nerve Head
(ONH) for any changes occurred due to glaucoma. Optic Disc and Optic Cup
was analysed in images taken by normal Ophthalmoscope (Fundus Camera).
Cup to Disc Ratio (CDR) and Inferior (I), Superior (S), Nasal (N) and Temporal
(T) distance was calculated from extracted Optic Cup to Optic Disc. These ISNT
distances are significant signs of Glaucoma. We have proposed an algorithm to
segment Optic Disc and Optic Cup from retinal fundus image and analyse CDR
and ISNT values to classify whether the eye is Glaucomatous or Healthy. The
Algorithm was tested on 108 private image dataset achieving Sensitivity of 90%
and Specificity of 97%. The Algorithm achieved 94.48% accuracy using different types of images compared to other algorithms that works only on specific
image. In this context the proposed Algorithm gives satisfactory result in terms
of accuracy.

Keywords: Glaucoma · Notching · ONH · Optic Disc · CRD · ISNT · Neuro
Retinal Rim · Optic Cup

© Springer Nature Singapore Pte Ltd. 2021
K. K. Patel et al. (Eds.): icSoftComp 2020, CCIS 1374, pp. 316–327, 2021.
https://doi.org/10.1007/978-981-16-0708-0_26

1 Introduction

Human eye suffers from many disorders, most of them have noticeable symptoms, but Glaucoma is not one of them. From different types of Glaucoma like Open-Angle, Angle-Closure or Normal-Tension, Open-Angle Glaucoma is said to be a "Silent Theft of Vision" because it does not cause any pain or has no symptoms. Glaucoma is an irrevocable disease which leads to partial or complete vision loss. According to study by A. Issac et al. [1], Glaucoma is the 2nd leading cause of blindness. Ophthalmologist can detect Glaucoma using different eye tests which are expensive and require expert observation [2]. Another approach that is used to detect Glaucoma in its very early stage is by analysing Retinal Fundus Images. Analysing structural changes that occur in ONH area can be used with Image Processing Techniques to diagnose Glaucoma. According to a study by Atheesan S. et al. [3], Retinal Fundus Images contain features like 1) Optic Cup, 2) Optic Disc, 3) Blood Vessels, 4) Neuro Retinal Rim, 5) Macula and 6) Retinal Nerve Fibre Layer as shown in Fig. 1. These features change in shape, size and colour if the eye is Glaucomatous.

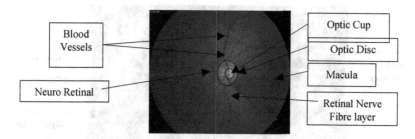

Fig. 1. Fundus image of right eye (source: our sample images)

A Healthy Eye and a Glaucomatous Eye are shown in Fig. 2(A) and Fig. 2(B) respectively. We can detect, segment and analyse these features using different Image Processing Techniques to check whether the eye is Glaucomatous or Healthy.

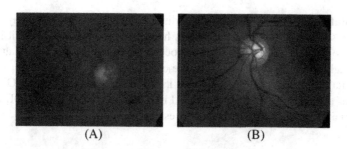

(A)   (B)

Fig. 2. (A) - Healthy eye (source: our sample images) (B) - Glaucomatous eye (source: our sample images)

Accurate segmentation of Optic Cup and Optic Disc is a vital step in image processing to detect Glaucoma from fundus images. The area of Optic Cup can be compared with the area of Optic Disc. The ratio of Optic Cup and Optic Disc is called CDR. According to Ophthalmology if the CDR is more than 0.3 (CDR > 0.3), then there are high chances of Glaucoma Al. Bandar et al. [2]. But we can't rely on only one parameter for accurate result. Circular area between Optic Cup and Optic Disc is known as NRR. The thickness of NRR from all four sides are known as Inferior (bottom), Superior (top), Nasal (nose side), Temporal (other side). The distance between Optic Cup and Optic Disc from each side is known as ISNT distance. ISNT distance are larger to smaller from Inferior to Temporal respectively. This is called ISNT Rule according to which Inferior > Superior > Nasal > Temporal. If an eye does not obey this rule, it is most likely to have Glaucoma as shown in Fig. 3. In our proposed algorithm, we have used detection of features like OC and OD to calculate CDR and ISNT which is then used to classify eyes into Healthy and Glaucomatous. We have used Image processing techniques like Transformation, Segmentation, Edge detection and Image Correction to achieve our goal.

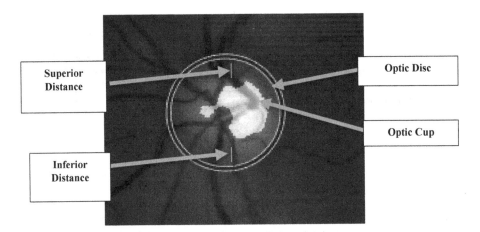

Fig. 3. Fundus image showing NRR and ISNT distances

Problem Statement. Glaucoma is a silent disease which does not leave any symptoms or pain. It results in irreversible vision loss hence it is required to detect it in its very early stage to prevent vision loss before it occurs. OD and OC are first features to get affected by glaucoma in its early stage. We can check whether the patient is likely to get glaucoma or not by checking CDR and ISNT features obtained using OD and OC. The Goal of this study is to attain a method to detect glaucoma using CDR and ISNT features obtained using Digital Image Processing techniques.

The Organization of Paper is as Follows

- In Sect. 2 we have discussed work already done by other researchers on the same area with their result and gap analysis.
- Section 3 defines step by step working of each phase of proposed.
- In Sect. 4 we have discussed pseudo code for the proposed algorithm with input output of all 4 phases.
- Section 5 discusses Experiments and Analysis of the proposed algorithm with explanation of how GUI tool is executing each step of the Algorithm.
- In Sect. 6 we have given result of the proposed algorithm and accuracy of the algorithm compared to other previous researches.
- In Sect. 7 we conclude our work with achieved result and discussed how the current work can be extended or improved.

2 Literature Survey

Some work has been done in the field of Glaucoma detection using computerized image processing techniques.

Anindita Septiarini et al. 2020 [4] proposed statistical approach on fundus images to detect gaulcoma by extracting ONH features using correlation feature selection method and classifying with k-nearest neighbour algorithm on 84 fundus images. Proposed method measured in terms of accuracy with 95.24% but the paper only provides accuracy of feature extraction.

Juan Carrillo et al. 2019 [5] present a computational tool for improving Glaucoma detection in comparison with earlier work using thresholding. Result were obtained by taking fundus image with accuracy of 88.5%. Research have not defined size of dataset and also accuracy is low compare to other earlier researches.

Khalil et al. 2018 [6] proposed a novel method to detect Glaucoma from Spectral Domain Optical Coherence Tomography (SD-OCT) image. Algorithm was used to improve precision of the Inner-Limiting-Membrane (ILM) layer extraction and to refine contour of ILM layer. The system showed clear improvement over its contemporary systems in terms of accuracy by getting 90% accuracy. Proposed method works on OCT images only which is expensive and hence less desirable compared to fundus image.

Cheriguene et al. 2018 [7] proposed a CAD system-based Twin Support Vector Machine (TWSVM) and three families of feature extraction named Gray Level Co-occurrence Matrix, Central moments and Hu moments. System was experimented on 169 images for classification in Glaucomatous and healthy. Paper shows that classification accuracy obtained by TWSVM is very promising compared to the SVM results. Result accuracy of 94.11% is based on comparison of TWSVM and SVM, but it did not clearly state that the image is Glaucomatous or not.

Nirmala et al. 2017 [8] diagnosed Glaucoma using wavelet based contourlet transform with the help of Gabor filters. They used Naïve Bayes classifiers for Classification images which gave 89% of classification accuracy. It can be improved by improving the method or by adding more features of fundus image.

Thangaraj et al. 2017 [9] proposed supervised learning and compared with other techniques of Glaucoma detection. Nonlinear transformation of Support Vector Machine (SVM) was used for classification and it was compared with Level set based method and Fused method. Classification accuracy was 93% on public databases like DRIONS, STARK and RIM-ONE. Papers did not state which features were used to detect Glaucoma and how those images were processed before classification.

Al-Bander et al. 2017 [10] used Deep Learning approach to detect Glaucoma by proposing a fully automated system based on Convolutional Neural Network (CNN). Features were extracted automatically from raw image and classified using SVM classifier. Accuracy, Specificity and Sensitivity were demonstrated as 88%, 90% and 85% respectively. Results are lower compared to previous researches reviewed in this paper.

Kartik Thakkar et al. 2017 [11] proposed an algorithm to segment OD and OC to analyse CDR and ISNT values from retinal fundus image and classify whether the eye is Glaucomatous or Healthy. Researchers found that ISNT and CDR both feathers can give more accurate result by giving accuracy of 94.48%.

Dr. Kinjan Chauhan et al. 2016 [12] developed data mining technique using Decision Tree, Linear Regression and Support Vector Machine for diagnosis of glaucoma in the retinal image. OCT image have been used in each technique to find out their performance in term of accuracy, sensitivity and specificity. Researcher found that Decision Tree and Linear Regression Model performs much better than SVM giving accuracy of 99.56%. Here OCT images are used which is expensive and less available.

We also considered techniques used for calculation of CDR and ISNT in [13–15] for our research to obtain high accuracy.

From above literature study, we can observe that no method has been proposed to detect glaucoma from fundus images using features of OC and OD with a good accuracy. We have observed that detection of Glaucoma can be improved by using only fundus images and detecting it in its early stage.

3 The Proposed Glaucoma Detection Algorithm

The researchers in literature review worked on different image processing techniques to detect Glaucoma. By reviewing all techniques, we conclude that ONH plays a very crucial role in diagnosing the health of an eye. By analysing Optic Cup (OC) and Optic Disc (OD), two most important features of ONH, we can identify whether the patient's eye is Glaucomatous or healthy. In this paper, we have proposed a novel algorithm that uses these two features and classify an image into Glaucomatous or Healthy. The proposed algorithm calculates CDR and ISNT Distances, obtained from shape and size of OC and OD. The proposed Algorithm consists of four phases. These phases process a retinal fundus image to locate and segment region of interest from the image. Figure 4 shows block diagram of our proposed algorithm distributed in four distinct phases.

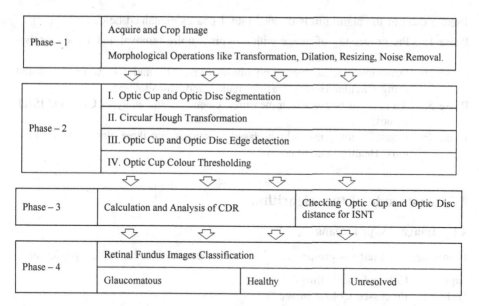

| Phase – 1 | Acquire and Crop Image | | | |
| | Morphological Operations like Transformation, Dilation, Resizing, Noise Removal. | | | |

Phase – 2	I. Optic Cup and Optic Disc Segmentation			
	II. Circular Hough Transformation			
	III. Optic Cup and Optic Disc Edge detection			
	IV. Optic Cup Colour Thresholding			

| Phase – 3 | Calculation and Analysis of CDR | Checking Optic Cup and Optic Disc distance for ISNT |

| Phase – 4 | Retinal Fundus Images Classification | | |
| | Glaucomatous | Healthy | Unresolved |

Fig. 4. Block diagram of proposed methodology

The following Figs. 5 and 6 show images taken during each phase of the algorithm.

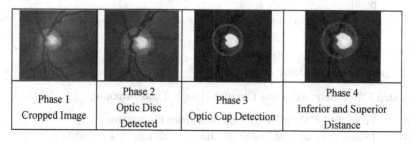

| Phase 1 Cropped Image | Phase 2 Optic Disc Detected | Phase 3 Optic Cup Detection | Phase 4 Inferior and Superior Distance |

Fig. 5. Result images of the proposed algorithm for Glaucomatous right eye

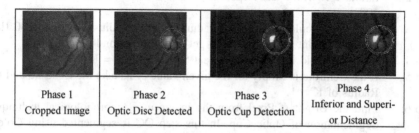

| Phase 1 Cropped Image | Phase 2 Optic Disc Detected | Phase 3 Optic Cup Detection | Phase 4 Inferior and Superior Distance |

Fig. 6. Result images of the proposed algorithm for Normal left eye

Pseudo code of the algorithm is divided into 4 phases explained below.

Phase 1:   Pre-processing of image with cropping, noise removal and some morphological operations.

Phase 2:   Detection and Segmentation phase where OC and OD were segmented using Circular Hough Transformation and Thresholding.

Phase 3:   An analysis phase which measures, calculates and analyses CDR and ISNT values.

Phase 4:   Classification phase which classifies images into three classes, Glaucomatous, Healthy and Abnormal.

4   Pseudocode of the Algorithm

4.1   Image Pre-processing

In this step the Image is pre-processed to make them feasible for further processing.

Input: Colour Fundus Image
Output: Processed Colour Image

Step 1:   Acquire Colour Fundus Image taken by Ophthalmoscope.
Step 2:   Crop 1% area of the image from all sides to remove tags and/or noise from the image.
Step 3:   Take the centroid into consideration, crop the image further to get required pixels.
Step 4:   Perform Dilation and Erosion with scale factor 10 to remove blood vessels.

4.2   Segmentation of Optic Disc

In this step OD is detected using Circular Hough Transformation.

Input: Processed Colour Image obtained from the previous step
Output: Image with detected edge of OD with all regional Properties

Step 1:   Extract Red Channel of the pre-processed image
Step 2:   Initialize K with 0 and Repeat Steps 3 and 4 for K having values from 0 to 100.
Step 3:   Calculate circular area having radius with K (Radius Value) to 100 (last reachable point in the image) to get the Centroid and the Radius.
Step 4:   If the Centroid is not empty repeat Step 3 with K = K + 1.
Step 5:   If the Centroid is Empty for the given value of K, take the Centroid and the Radius of K − 1.
Step 6:   Find the Brightest Pixel from the image using morphological technique. Segmentation of Optic Cup. In this step OC is segmented using Colour Thresholding technique.

Input: Image with detected edge of OD with all regional Properties obtained from the previous step
Output: Image with highlighted OC area with its region Properties.

Step 1:   Extract Green Channel of the pre-processed image.
Step 2:   Fetch the Highest Intensity Pixel from Segmented Optic Disc Circular Area.
Step 3:   Calculate Graythresh Value using the Highest Intensity.
Step 4:   Segment area of Optic Cup using the following formula.
            CupArea: = (Intensity_of_pixel_inside_OD > Threshold ? PixelValue: null)
Step 5:   Use dilation morphological operation to smoothen the segmented Cup area.
Step 6:   Perform morphological operation to get accurate Cup area using the imfill
            function in Matlab.

4.3 Analyse Image for CDR and ISNT

In this step we analysed the Segmented OD and OC to get CDR and ISNT Measurements and provide classification according to the analysis.

Input: Measurements of the OD and OC, Image with highlighted OC area with its
            region properties as obtained from the previous step
Output: Value of CDR, ISNT and Classification Results

Step 1:   Measure Region properties of the segmented OC and OD
Step 2:   Calculate CDR using the area of OC and OD fetched by Region Properties
Step 3:   Check the value of CDR
Step 4:   If CDR is greater than 0.3, the Image is classified as Glaucomatous.
Step 5:   Fetch Centroid, Height and Width of both OC and OD.
Step 6:   Calculate distance between OC and OD from Inferior(I), Superior(S), Nasal
            (N) and Temporal(T) sides.
Step 7:   Analyse values of ISNT
Step 8:   If I > S > N > T then
            The Result is Normal.
            else
            The Result is Glaucomatous.
Step 9:   If the result of Steps 4 and 8 is Glaucomatous,
            The Image is classified as Glaucomatous else it is classified as Normal.
            If the Result of Step 4 is Glaucomatous
            but that of Step 8 is Healthy then the Result is considered as there are High
            Chances of Glaucoma.
Step 10:   If the algorithm fails to identify the OC or OD, the image is classified as an
            Abnormal Image.

5 Experiment and Analysis

To effectively execute all the steps of the proposed Algorithm, we have developed a GUI Tool using MATLAB. GUI includes separate procedural functionalities for each phase of the Algorithm. Figure 7 shows the functionality of the algorithm in our GUI Tool.

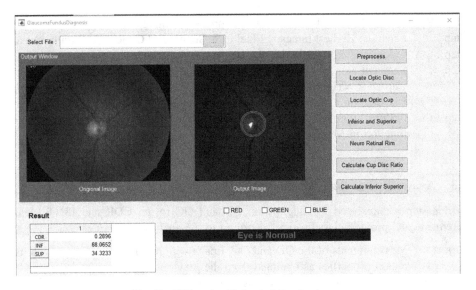

Fig. 7. GUI tool with loaded Fundus image

The algorithm was tested on 108 Private Dataset images of size 720×576 pixels from the patients of Sudhalkar Eye Hospital, Raupura Main Road, Vadodara, Gujarat, India. The algorithm was applied on these 108 images from which 3 images were classified as Abnormal, 60 images were classified as Glaucomatous and 48 as Normal.

The results were compared with the results of OCT and Perimetry which gave 90% Sensitivity which means 90% of images were correctly identified with Glaucoma, 97% Specificity which means 97% of images were correctly identified without Glaucoma and 94.48% F-Score specified that overall accuracy of the algorithm. Detailed results with True Positive (TP), True Negative (TN), False Positive (FP) and False Negative (FN) are described as follows.

Technically it can be defined as.

True Positive (TP)	The image is Glaucomatous, and it is detected as Glaucomatous using the proposed model. Our Experiment showed TP value as 60, that means out of 108 images the proposed algorithm detected 60 images as Glaucomatous which were Glaucomatous as diagnosed through the Perimetry Test
True Negative (TN)	The image is Normal, and the system also detects it as Normal using the proposed model. Our Experiment showed 38 TN Value, which means out of 108 images the proposed algorithm detected 38 images as Normal which were Normal as diagnosed through the Perimetry Test
False Positive (FP)	The image is Normal, but it is detected as Glaucomatous image using the proposed model. Our Experiment detected 1 Normal image as Glaucomatous which gives FP value 1
False Negative (FN)	The image is Glaucomatous, but the system detects it as Normal image using the proposed model. Experiment detected 6 Glaucomatous images as

	Normal and that was due to false detection of the OC hence FN value was 6
Precision	Quantity of Glaucomatous images (TP) detected from the cases of Glaucomatous images (TP + FP) $Precision = \frac{TP}{(TP+FP)}$ From our experiment this ratio was 0.98 and hence the Precision was 98%
Specificity	True Negative Rate. Proportion of Correctly Identified Images without Disease $Specificity = \frac{TN}{(TN+FP)}$ Proportion of Normal images were calculated as 0.9743, which gives Specificity as 97.43% by our experiment
Sensitivity (Recall)	True Positive Rate. Proportion of Correctly Identified Images with Disease $Sensitivity(Recall) = \frac{TP}{(TP+FN)}$ 91% image were found correctly with Glaucoma
F-Score	It measures Test's Accuracy. It is an average of Precision and Recall $F - Score = 2 \times \frac{Precision \times Recall}{Precision + Recall}$ Overall accuracy of our experiment was 94.49%

The obtained result seems to be very promising where proposed Algorithm is implemented without any pre-processed or OC centred images.

6 Result and Discussion

We used NVIDIA 520 HD Graphic GPU for implementation. MATLAB toolboxes were used to script and implement the proposed algorithm. GUI Tool was developed to accelerate the image acquisition and Glaucoma detection process as shown in Fig. 7. GUI works separately for all 4 phases on given image and shows result of each phase so that it can be helpful for doctors to cross check the result. GUI also provide facility to view image in different colour scale with marked OC, OD and ISNT which help doctors to manually diagnose the image. The proposed Algorithm was evaluated on 108 images and we achieved 94.49% accuracy. We have achieved our goal of detecting glaucoma using only fundus image with high accuracy compare to other techniques Table 1 shows comparison of results obtained by previous researchers and current research.

Table 1. Comprehensive Analysis of Algorithm with other Techniques

No	Author name and year	Techniques and features used	Accuracy
1	Khalil et al. 2018 [6]	Spectral Domain OCT	90%
2	Cheriguene et al. 2018 [7]	Gray Level Co-occurrence Matrix	94.11%
3	Nirmala et al. 2018 [8]	Wavelet Based Contourlet Transform	89%
4	Thangaraj and Natarajan 2017 [9]	Nonlinear Transformation of SVM	93%
5	Al-Bander et al. 2017 [10]	Convolutional Neural Network (CNN)	88%
6	**Proposed Algorithm**	**CDR and ISNT**	94.48%

The graphical representation of the comparison of results obtained from our research with the results obtained from earlier research is shown in Fig. 8.

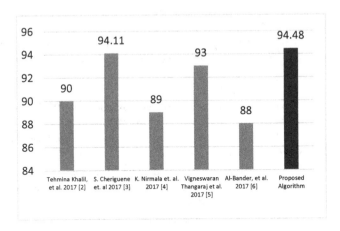

Fig. 8. Comparison chart of researches

7 Conclusion and Future Work

By experimenting and analysing different approaches by researchers we conclude that structural changes in ONH can be considered as a concrete parameter to detect whether the eye is Glaucomatous or not.

In our proposed method we have considered OC and OD to analyse CDR and ISNT as features of ONH to detect Glaucoma for retinal fundus images using four-phased algorithm. We implemented our proposed algorithm on 108 images and got 94.48% accuracy. We also developed a GUI based application which works on our proposed algorithm and checks whether an input retinal fundus image is Glaucomatous or not. Our future enhancement is to improve the Algorithm by adding more parameters like Notching, Parapapillary Atrophy and Brightness features of OC to get more concrete result.

Acknowledgements. We would like to express our gratitude and deep regards to Dr. Prashant Chauhan, Ophthalmologist/Eye Surgeon, Shree Arvind Eye Hospital, Surat for his constant support and encouragement. We would also like to give our sincere gratitude to Prof. Alpa Shah, Sarvajanik Institute of Engineering and Technology, Surat for her invaluable suggestions and support.

References

1. Agarwal, A., Gulia, S., Chaudhary, S., Dutta, M.K., Travieso, C.M., Alonso-Hernandez, J. B.: A novel approach to detect glaucoma in retinal fundus images using cup-disk and rim-disk ratio. In: Proceedings of the 2015 International Work Conference on Bio-Inspired Intelligence: Intelligent Systems for Biodiversity Conservation, IWOBI 2015, pp. 139–144 (2015). https://doi.org/10.1109/IWOBI.2015.7160157

2. Schacknow, P.N., Samples, J.R.: The glaucoma book: a practical, evidence-based approach to patient care (2010)
3. Lowell, J., et al.: Optic nerve head segmentation. IEEE Trans. Med. Imaging **23**(2), 256–264 (2004). https://doi.org/10.1109/TMI.2003.823261
4. Septiarini, A., Harjoko, A., Pulungan, R., Ekantini, R.: Automated detection of retinal nerve fiber layer by texture-based analysis for glaucoma evaluation. Healthcare Inform. Res. **24**(4), 335–345 (2018). https://doi.org/10.4258/hir.2018.24.4.335
5. Carrillo, J., Bautista, L., Villamizar, J., Rueda, J., Sanchez, M., Rueda, D.: Glaucoma detection using fundus images of the eye. In: 2019 22nd Symposium on Image, Signal Processing and Artificial Vision, STSIVA 2019 - Conference Proceedings, pp. 1–4 (2019). https://doi.org/10.1109/STSIVA.2019.8730250
6. Khalil, T., Akram, M.U., Raja, H., Jameel, A., Basit, I.: Detection of glaucoma using cup to disc ratio from spectral domain optical coherence tomography images. IEEE Access **6**(c), 4560–4576 (2018). https://doi.org/10.1109/ACCESS.2018.2791427
7. Cheriguene, S., Azizi, N., Djellali, H., Bunakhla, O., Aldwairi, M., Ziani, A.: New computer aided diagnosis system for glaucoma disease based on twin support vector machine. In: Proceedings of EDIS 2017 - 1st International Conference on Embedded and Distributed Systems, vol. 2017-Decem, pp. 1–6 (2018). https://doi.org/10.1109/EDIS.2017.8284039
8. Nirmala, K., Venkateswaran, N., Kumar, C.V., Christobel, J.S.: Glaucoma detection using wavelet based contourlet transform. In: Proceedings of the International Conference on Intelligent Computing Control, I2C2 2017, vol. 2018-Janua, pp. 1–5 (2018). https://doi.org/10.1109/I2C2.2017.8321875
9. Thangaraj, V., Natarajan, V.: Glaucoma diagnosis using support vector machine. In: Proceedings of the 2017 International Conference on Intelligent Computing and Control Systems, ICICCS 2017, vol. 2018-Janua, pp. 394–399 (2017). https://doi.org/10.1109/ICCONS.2017.8250750
10. Al-Bander, B., Al-Nuaimy, W., Al-Taee, M.A., Zheng, Y.: Automated glaucoma diagnosis using deep learning approach. In: 2017 14th International Multi-Conference System Signals Devices, SSD 2017, vol. 2017-Janua, pp. 207–210 (2017). https://doi.org/10.1109/SSD.2017.8166974
11. Thakkar, K., Chauhan, K., Sudhalkar, A., Gulati, R.: A novel approach for glaucoma detection using features of optic nerve head. Int. J. Trend Sci. Res. Dev. (2017)
12. Chauhan, K., Chauhan, P., Sudhalkar, A., Lad, K., Gulati, R.: Data mining techniques for diagnostic support of glaucoma using stratus OCT and perimetric data. Int. J. Comput. Appl. **151**(8), 34–39 (2016). https://doi.org/10.5120/ijca2016911855
13. Agarwal, A., Gulia, S., Chaudhary, S., Dutta, M.K., Burget, R., Riha, K.: Automatic glaucoma detection using adaptive threshold based technique in fundus image. In: 2015 38th International Conference on Telecommunications and Signal Processing, TSP 2015, pp. 416–420 (2015). https://doi.org/10.1109/TSP.2015.7296295
14. Singh, A., Dutta, M.K., ParthaSarathi, M., Uher, V., Burget, R.: Image processing based automatic diagnosis of glaucoma using wavelet features of segmented optic disc from fundus image. Comput. Methods Programs Biomed. **124**, 108–120 (2016). https://doi.org/10.1016/j.cmpb.2015.10.010
15. Kotowski, J., Wollstein, G., Ishikawa, H., Schuman, J.S.: Imaging of the optic nerve and retinal nerve fiber layer: an essential part of glaucoma diagnosis and monitoring. Surv. Ophthalmol. **59**(4), 458–467 (2014). https://doi.org/10.1016/j.survophthal.2013.04.007

Crop Yield Estimation Using Machine Learning

Nihar Patel[1]([✉])[iD], Deep Patel[1][iD], Samir Patel[2][iD], and Vibha Patel[3][iD]

[1] Computer Department, Vishwakarma Government Engineering College,
Ahmedabad, India
niharpatel1999@gmail.com

[2] Computer Science and Engineering, Pandit Deendayal Petroleum University,
Gandhinagar, India

[3] Information Technology, Vishwakarma Government Engineering College,
Ahmedabad, India

Abstract. The recent area of interest for computer scientists and data analysts working on precision farming has been the use of machine learning and deep learning algorithms to recommend crops to the farmers and predict yield. Improving crop yields not only helps farmers but also seeks to address global problems such as food shortages. Predictions can be made taking into account forecasts of climate, soil and its mineral content, moisture, crop historic performance, rainfall and others. Crop Data from six states of India for five crops from 2009–2016 has been used for training and validation of different machine learning regression algorithms to produce a comprehensive study of crop yield estimate. The yields are estimated using Linear models, Support Vector Regressor, K Neighbors Regressor, Tree-based models, Ensemble models and Shallow Neural Networks with R-squared score for evaluation. Test accuracy showed promising results in ensemble models and neural networks. Extra Trees Regressor is the best model with Mean Absolute Error of 351.10 and maximum accuracy of 99.95%. This paper aims at providing state of art implementation on machine learning algorithms to facilitate farmers, governments, economists, banks to estimate the crop yields in Indian states based on specific parameters.

Keywords: Machine learning · Precision farming · Yield prediction · Crop recommendation

1 Introduction

As estimated by the **United Nations**, the global population is estimated to reach 9.8 billion by 2050. This would create large need for Food and Agriculture products to maintain the demand. **Harvard Business Review** reports that the market for food is projected to rise between 59 % and 98 % by 2050. **UN FAO** claims that almost one-third of the total food produced i.e 1.3 billion tonnes goes

© Springer Nature Singapore Pte Ltd. 2021
K. K. Patel et al. (Eds.): icSoftComp 2020, CCIS 1374, pp. 328–342, 2021.
https://doi.org/10.1007/978-981-16-0708-0_27

missing or discarded, while 795 million people are starving. Consumers in rich countries waste almost as much food annually (222 million tonnes) as the whole of sub-Saharan African net food production (230 million tonnes). Currently, almost 9 million people die of starvation and hunger-related diseases each year as analysed by **theworldcounts**. This is greater than the cumulative effects of AIDS, Malaria and TB. Hence it must be matter of concern to the world governments to overcome this challenge faced by the entire human race. The actions of governments, farmers, experts and technology together could solve this situation.

The fast pace of technology has opened new arenas for better human life. Trending technologies like Machine Learning, Internet of Things, Augmented and Virtual Reality, Data Analytics, Cryptocurrency, etc has been in news for a while. Machine Learning is an emerging computer science domain that attracts millions of computer scientists' attention to it. It is a fast growing field which subsequently has led to Computer Vision, Deep Learning, Natural Language Processing, and others. Machine learning means providing the ability to computers to learn themselves rather than to program them explicitly. This groundbreaking concept has lead to the development of smart recommendation and prediction systems which has exceptional results in product recommendations used by multi-national E-Commerce companies, Movies and Video Recommendation used by Online Video streaming platforms, Stock Price Prediction, etc. The wide spread use of machine learning in various domains has eventually started and industries are already benefiting from it. Machine learning and Deep learning is heavily being used in domains like Medical Science and Drug Development, Agriculture, Self Driving automobiles, Speech controlled Home Automation, Educational services, Space and Aviation, Recommendation Systems, Archaeology, Deep Space Exploration, etc. This has benefited mankind to a great extent and would continue to do so in future.

This paper aims to discuss a yield-estimation method using state-of-the-art machine learning regression techniques to approximate crop yields according to the specified conditions and the available historical evidence. Factors influencing crop's production include rainfall, temperature, altitude, soil and moisture content, field emissions, crop diseases, fertilizer application, irrigation timing, etc. Average Rainfall for the Indian subcontinent as forecasted by The Indian Metro logical Department (IMD) is 300–650 mm (11.8–25.6 in.). Because rainfall is quite unpredictable and distributed unequally among the sub continent, many farmers need to rely on irrigation canals and bore wells. Though there is quite variance in the irrigation facilities available to the farmers in different states. The soil and its mineral content are another major factor. In India, 9 major soil types are alluvial soil, red and yellow soil, sandy and alkaline soil, peaty and marshy soil, woodland and mountain soil. These soils differ in their chemical composition and mineral content. Depending on their genetics, crops require different soils to grow. Weather and Climate heavily affects the crop, some are crops of Rabi season (July–October), while others are crops of Kharif season (October–March).

The soil's moisture content also plays a major role in influencing crop yield and nutrient content. Since the Industrial Revolution, pollution has been ever rising. Pollution influences not only crop yield, but also decreases crops' nutritional value. The possible consequences of plant pollution could be calculated as: interference in enzyme processes, alteration in chemistry and physical structure, growth slowdown and decreased production due to metabolic structural changes, rapid acute tissue degeneration. Weeds are undesirable grass/plants that grow together with the main crops that usually use most of the soil nutrients and therefore the main crop does not grow healthy. Every year, millions of dollars are wasted in weed prevention and removal. The next most significant factor impacting crop yield is fertilizer. They generally consist of three major macronutrients, the nitrogen (N), the phosphorus (P) and the potassium (K). Calcium, magnesium, and sulfur are also present as the secondary macro-nutrients. The required fertilizer dosage produces an improvement in crop yield. If a random amount of fertilizers is used, the crop can have serious tissue deterioration resulting in less yield and could degrade the quality of the soil hence making the soil unfit for future plantations. It is therefore necessary to provide a proper dose of fertilizers at regular intervals. This paper discusses at length how different parameters affect crop yields and how different algorithms could be used to predict agricultural produce. This paper uses data from various states as a whole to predict their agricultural production. Other work were either too specific for a region or a factor affecting yield. Hence, this paper aims to provide a novel approach to data of different states considering the affecting factors.

Section 2 contains literature survey of the existing methods used and implemented for different factors affecting crop yield. Section 3 contains our implementations of different approaches and their results assimilated together. Section 4 contains the possible future work and conclusion.

2 Background and Related Work

2.1 Precision Agriculture

Precision Agriculture (PA) or Site Specific Crop Management (SSCM) is a principle of agriculture management focused on the observation, estimation and reaction of inter and intra-field crop variability. Precision agriculture research seeks to establish a Decision Support System (DSS) for the entire management of the farm with the objective of maximising input returns while preserving resources. Precision farming is a modern farming technique that uses analysis data on soil characteristics, soil types, data collection of crop yields, and recommends the best crop to farmers based on their site-specific parameters. Therefore, by picking the correct crop, the farmer's productivity is increased.

Authors' work [24] suggests use of machine learning algorithms such as K nearest neighbors, Naive Bayes, Random Tree and Chi-squared Automatic Interaction Detection (CHAID) to recommend crops for precision farming. The rules were generated in the form of if-then statements. The prediction accuracy achieved was about 88%. Work by authors [3] propose an IoT based Artificial

Neural Network system which would be taking into account data like Humidity, Temperature, Wind speed and Sunlight for Crop Monitoring. Paper by [21] addresses an application named RSF that recommends crops to farmers. The system detects user position and selects top N related upazillas (sub-region of a district) taking into account agro-climatic and agro-ecological data. Based on it, the application recommends top C crops to the user. It reported an average precision of 0.72 and an average recall of 0.653.

A thorough review on crop yield prediction has been done by [14]. Authors selected 80 papers out of which 50 used machine learning and the rest used deep learning. The main finding was that temperature, rainfall, and soil type were the most used features. Work by authors [11] suggests the use of Deep Neural Networks rather than Shallow Neural Networks and Regression Tree for yield estimation. Their studies have shown that environmental variables had a greater influence than genotype on crop yields. Extending their work, authors [12] proposed a CNN-RNN based model, which focused on the time dependency of environmental variables.

Authors [19] worked on how to apply machine learning to farm data. A case report on the culling of dairy herds has been clarified and data mining has been applied. In [16], the authors discussed forecasting crop yields using machine learning and deep learning for corn in Illinois using **Caffe** - a Deep Learning framework developed by University of California - Berkeley. Two InnerProduct-Layer's network model gave the best results, achieving Root Mean Square Error (RMSE) of 6.298 (standard value). While single InnerProductLayer and Support Vector Regressor gave RMSE of 7.427 and 8.204 respectively. The authors [7] explore the use of machine learning methods in order to derive new information in the form of generic decision rules for efficient use of capital and manpower. In [6], authors used various algorithms such as SVM, C4.5, CHAID, KNN, K-means, Decision Tree, Neural Network and Naive Bayes to provide a method for smart agriculture. Their analysis also included a paper that used the Hadoop system to carry out rigorous calculations. Work by [20], summarizes the different Machine Learning algorithms used for crop production estimation.

2.2   Rainfall

Rainfall is a major factor for agriculture. In a country like India with such diverse lands, some states like Punjab have enough water via irrigation, but considering the majority, most farmers have to be dependent on rainfall. Sowing crop solely relying on rainfall could prove disastrous for the farmers. Authors [28] have worked on the disparity in rainfall in the Indian sub continent for a period of over 150 years. The trends on rainfall vary measurably because India is a mix of different terrains. Concentrated on the long-term patterns of extreme monsoon rainfall deficiency and abundance in Indian areas, [23] analysed 135 years (1871–2005) of climate change using the non-parametric Mann-Kendall methodology. The analysis covered nearly 90% of the Indian subcontinent. Authors [9] calculated Standard Precipitation Index (SPI) using Mann Kendall trend test for 14 agro-climatic zones over a period of 56 years (1951–2006) out of which only 6 agro - climatic zones have a significant trend in summer season.

Work by author [29] describes the correlation of sowing season with rainfall and type of crop. For calculating the relationship between rainfall, crop area and productivity, methods such as mean, standard deviation, coefficient of variance and Karl Pearson's method of correlation were used. Their study determined the distribution of annual and seasonal rainfall and their association with crop area, crop production and productivity of Jowar, Rice, Wheat and Maize crops in Maharashtra, India for a period of 15 years from 2000–2001 to 2014–2015. The rainfall variability was measured by Oliver's Precipitation Concentration Index (PCI). Paper by [31] discusses about the trends of rainfall and its effect on crop production in the Indian state of Bihar where 70% of rural population is employed in Agriculture. Authors present that though the rainfall decreased in about 85% of districts, there has been a positive relationship between Standardized Precipitation Index (SPI) and rice production.

2.3   Weather and Climate Change

Weather is an important factor considering crop production. Weather and climate are usually considered synonyms, though it isn't true. The weather is the day-to-day state of the atmosphere, and in minutes to weeks its short-term variance. The mixture of temperature, humidity, precipitation, cloudiness, visibility, and wind over an area over a brief period of time is generally the weather. While climate refers to the temperature of an area spread over a period of time, typically 30 years. Plants do get affected by the weather in which they are sown. [18] analyses the impact on agriculture of climate change. As predicted by them, the world's agricultural production is estimated to decline between 3% and 16% by 2080 due to global warming and disturbed weather trends. Papers [17] and [13] discuss about newer approach of Climate Smart Agriculture (CSA). The effects of increased CO_2 has already risen the average global temperatures and the sea levels are ever rising. Work of author [34] refer a software which uses data mining and provides an overview of how different climatic parameters affect the crop yield and eventually decision rules are developed based upon predicted and actual crop production and threshold values of different features were set.

2.4   Pollution and Fertilizers

Pollution has been affecting animals and plants adversely since the Industrial Revolution. Various chemicals when left in the atmosphere, react with other elements and produce harmful toxins. These pollutants mix with water droplets and in form of rain come back to earth. Acid rain combines with soil and so the hazardous chemicals get mixed with the soil decreasing its fertility. Authors [2] clearly indicate that pollution affected the yield. They deployed numerous sensors to create a Wireless Sensor Network (WSN) to monitor pollution. The results indicated that the areas where pollution was more, yield obtained was significantly less. Excessive use of fertilizers result in water and soil pollution.

Agricultural runoff consists of fertilisers, pesticides, animal waste, or fragments of soil that lead to soil deterioration. The key to increased crop yield with adequate nutritional value depends in the amount and type of fertilizers applied. Authors [37] worked on decision making based on fertilization for increased yield and better nutritional value for which they developed an ArcGIS based web application.

2.5   Soil and Minerals

Soil affects considerably in crop production. Various types of soils found in India are Red, Black, Brown, Alluvial, Laterite and Sandy. The soils rich in mineral content is the best suitable for crops to grow as well as to have proper nutritional value. Soil includes number of parameters like pH, moisture content, mineral content, temperature, humidity, water retainment capacity, ground water level, etc. Authors [5] suggests using Artificial Neural Networks to predict crop yield considering soil parameters like temperature, pH, humidity, etc. Mineral content of iron, copper, manganese, sulphur, magnesium, calcium, potassium, nitrogen, phosphate, organic carbon, etc. were taken into consideration. In order to train their Artificial Neural Network model, the algorithm proposed by them uses back propagation.

2.6   Plant Diseases

Diseases reduces crop yield as well as nutritional value in crops. Currently about 10% to 30% of the total production is damaged due to pests, diseases and weeds. [33] facilitates a method which provides a correlation between crop – weather – pest—diseases for ground nut crop. Data processing methods have been used and the actual surveillance data have been trained in mathematical models. Data set was trained using Regression Mining technique which is used developing Multivariate equation. The authors observed that the association between relative humidity and Bud Necrosis Virus (BNV) was strongly positive whereas with crop age was strongly negative. While for thrips, Evapotransipiration and Age of Crop were found to be strongly correlated. Another work by [25] developed a system which predicted fungal diseases on vegetable, fruit, cereal and commercial crops. Algorithms for extraction and classification of features based on image processing techniques have been designed. The purpose of their work is to establish a technique for the identification and classification of fungal disease symptoms caused by horticulture and agricultural crops. The average classification accuracy was a promising 80.83% when all the image types used color features and 85% when all the image types used shape features. Using leaf-level classification, [32] used neural convolution networks to recognize crop disease. With an overall accuracy of 96.3%, their model was able to categorise 13 different plant diseases.

2.7   Remote Sensing and Internet of Things

Remote Sensing is the acquisition of information about an object or phenomenon without any physical contact with an object and therefore in contrast to on-site observation. Images are captured using drones, satellites, air crafts or Unmanned Aerial Vehicles (UAVs) and Convolution Neural Networks (CNN) are applied on it for further analysis. An IoT-based agricultural measuring stick was proposed by the authors [22] to capture live data such as temperature and soil moisture. They achieved an accuracy over 98%. The use of drones and UAVs to help track crops and avoid any harm is discussed in depth by [26]. Similar study is presented by [30], which include the recent developments in agricultural robots and their novel applications. Authors [4] used CNN for plant classification on panchromatic images from GF-1 satellite of China. After parameter tuning, accuracy of 99.66% was obtained. [36] worked on a Gaussian Process applied to CNN for estimating Crop yield. The process was scale-able, accurate and inexpensive as compared to the prevailing manual survey method. This paper is used as a basis by the authors [35] for deep transfer learning and extending the former method to regions of Brazil and Argentina with satisfactory results. [1] worked for plant health for maize crop using CNN on Remote sensing data. The VGG16 model was used for feature extraction and ConvNet was used for training. The average accuracy was reported by 99.58%. Work by authors [8], used the classic Googlenet and its minor modified CNN architecture to classify the leaves with minor to 30% damage. The accuracy obtained was 94%, considering 30% leaf damage. [38] used Long Short Term Memory (LSTM) and Conv1D based architectures for multi-temporal crop classification. Similar work by [10] used 3D Convolution Neural Networks for mutli temporal crop classification. 3D CNN showed a significant improvement over 2D CNN. Authors [27] proposed a hybrid CNN - HistNN deep neural network which was able to classify 22 categories of crops with almost 90% accuracy. Another work by [15] used Ensemble of 1D and 2D CNNs Crop and Land Cover classification achieving an accuracy of 85% for major crops.

3   Implementation and Results

3.1   Methodology

Figure 1 illustrates the working of training and evaluation the system. Different parameters are provided to various Regression Models to evaluate the best performance based on test accuracy and Mean Absolute Error (MAE) for estimating crop yield. Maximum accuracy with minimum MAE would be the ideal model for prediction. Also necessary care has to be taken for the model not to overfit the training data. All the hyper-parameters have been fine tuned for best results. For the purpose of training, variety of models like Linear Models, SVR, KNR, Tree based Models, Ensemble Models and Neural Networks have been studied and implemented.

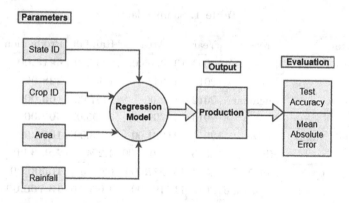

Fig. 1. System flow

3.2 Data Preprocessing

The most important task of any machine learning problem is to gather accurate data. The quality of data determines performance of the model. The current problem requires data such as area, rainfall, state/region, climate, soil, temperature, etc to train. However it is not possible to obtain consistent data for all parameters. The current dataset includes data from **Government of India** website. Different features like Rainfall, Year, State, Area, Production are available for different crops and has been used for preparing this dataset. Table 1 shows the sample data. The dataset consisted of five major crops Rice, Wheat, Maize, Sugarcane, Cotton for six states Odisha, Kerala, Tamil Nadu, Gujarat, Bihar, Uttar Pradesh for seven years (2009–2016). The states and crops are designated numbers rather than strings while training. The values of Area are in Thousand Hectares, Rainfall in millimetres and Production in Thousand Tonnes. Some parameters of the data were not available, hence such entries were removed from the dataset before training. Data was divided as 90% training data and 10% testing data.

3.3 Implementation

Predicting crop yield essentially remains a regression problem. The sklearn library in python has many implementations of different regression models. Linear models include LinearRegression, LassoRegression, RidgeRegression, SGDRegressor, ElasticNetRegressor, MultiTaskElasticNetRegressor, LassoCV, etc. Models like SupportVectorRegressor (SVR) and KNeighborsRegressor (KNR) are much complex than the linear models and could fit the data better, hence improving accuracy. Another category of algorithms are the Tree based and Ensemble models. Tree models include DecisionTreeRegressor and Random Forests. Another approach is to use the ensemble technique, wherein number of weak models are trained to obtain a strong model. Ensemble methods are further divide into Bagging and Boosting. Bagging is using different models in

Table 1. Sample data

State	Crop	Year	Area	Rainfall	Production
Odisha	Rice	2009–10	4365.00	1397.80	**6918.00**
	Maize	2012–13	94.00	1,430.20	**228.00**
Kerala	Sugarcane	2012–13	2.00	2187.00	**166.00**
	Rice	2013–14	200.00	3,255.00	**509.00**
Tamil Nadu	Maize	2011–12	281.00	1013.00	**1696.00**
	Rice	2015–16	2,037.00	1,204.00	**7,983.00**
Gujarat	Cotton	2014–15	2773.00	630.10	**10500.00**
	Sugarcane	2010–11	190.00	1,066.90	**13,760.00**
Bihar	Rice	2015–16	3215.00	875.50	**6489.00**
	Maize	2009–10	632.00	993.70	**1,479.00**
Uttar Pradesh	Wheat	2010–11	9637.00	718.20	**30001.00**
	Sugarcane	2015–16	2,169.00	595.00	**1,45,385.00**

parallel, while Boosting is using different models sequentially. BaggingRegressor, ADABoostRregressor, VotingRegressor, ExtraTreesRegressor, GradientBoosting and XGBoostRegressor are the methods available in ensemble approach. This technique increases the accuracy to great extent and provides better results. Though, sometimes these models may overfit the training data, and could highly underfit the testing data. This problem can be mitigated by tuning the hyper-parameters appropriately. Neural Networks are literally used in all tasks as they are highly complex and easy to build using high-end python libraries like Tensorflow, Keras, Pytorch, etc. Though Deep Neural Networks can not be used in the current implementation due to scarcity of large amount of data, Shallow Neural Networks could be a better option.

Accuracy was measured using R^2 Score. Values closer to 1 indicate higher accuracy.

$$R^2 Score = 1 - \frac{\sum_i (Y_i - \hat{Y}_i)^2}{\sum_i (Y_i - \bar{Y})^2}$$

$$MeanAbsoluteError = \frac{1}{n} \sum_{i=1}^{n} |Y_i - \hat{Y}_i|$$

Y_i indicates True value,
$\hat{Y}_i$ indicates Predicted value,
$\bar{Y}$ shows the mean of True values.

3.4   Results

Table 2 summarizes the accuracy and MAE obtained for different models and the detailed discussion of results are covered in subsequent subsections.

Linear Models, SVR and KNR. Linear models in a regression problem tries to fit a line to the given data points, minimizing the loss. The most basic is the Linear Regression model. Ridge Regression and Lasso Regression are minor variations of the Linear Regression. Elastic Net and MultiTask Elastic Net are the combination of Ridge and Lasso Regression. As the data had four features and continuous values as output, it was expected that linear models would not be the perfect choice for it and the accuracy confirmed it. The maximum accuracy of linear models was 32.89% by Lasso Regression. Linear models sometimes estimated the yield to be negative as shown in Fig. 2a. The models failed to predict the output accurately ending in large mean absolute error of 11686.79. K Neighbors Regressor which works similar to K Nearest Neighbors (KNN), showed a great improvement in terms of accuracy over the linear models. The MAE was 1592 and accuracy obtained was significantly higher. The reason of it working better than linear models was because it used its nearest neighbors to predict output. Support Vector Regressor like Support Vector Machines creates decision boundaries for the parameters and predicts output based on it. Figure 2b shows how well SVR performed, however it estimated one negative value and so the MAE was more than KNR. Though SVR proved to be a significant improvement over KNR with highest accuracy of 99.38%.

Table 2. Accuracy comparison

Model type	Model	Test accuracy	MAE
Linear	LinearRegressor	32.89	11722.50
	RidgeRegressor	32.89	11686.79
	LassoRegressor	32.90	11719.32
	LassoCV	31.73	11418.88
	SGDRegressor	32.65	12052.44
	ElasticNetRegressor	32.89	11722.50
	MutiTaskElasticNet	32.89	11722.50
KNN	KNeighborsRegressor	99.00	1592.00
SVM	SVR	99.38	1646.27
Tree based/ensemble	DecisionTree	99.84	754.76
	RandomForest	99.87	1004.18
	AdaBoostRegressor	99.86	524.29
	BaggingRegressor	99.75	757.11
	VotingRegressor	98.10	1291.67
	ExtraTreesRegressor	99.95	351.10
	GradientBoosting	99.57	1568.03
	HistGradientBoosting	93.53	3660.00
	XGBRegressor	99.63	706.96
Neural network	Neural Network	99.91	863.31

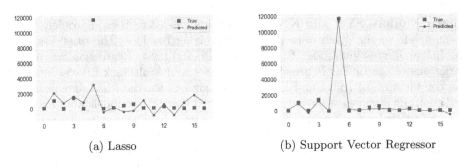

(a) Lasso   (b) Support Vector Regressor

Fig. 2. Predicted vs true

Tree-Based Models and Ensemble Approach. Decision Tree Regressor as the name suggests uses tree based model to make decisions and classify inputs. A collection of many Decision Trees is called a Random Forest, a type of ensemble model. Other ensemble approaches are Adaboost, Bagging Regressor, Extra Trees, XGBoost, etc. Ensemble models penalize the incorrect output while training it and try to minimize the loss. This method gives a great improvement in accuracy. The best accuracy obtained was 99.95% and the corresponding MAE was 351.10. Figure 3a shows the Predicted values and True values for Extra Trees Regressor (ETR) and it is evident from it that, ETR was the best model. The reason Tree based model performed better was because the data was such that it could be divided into hierarchies and could be classified by parameters like state and rainfall.

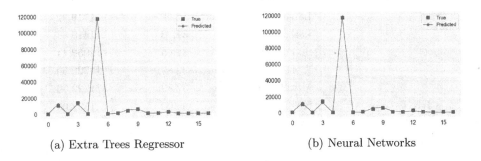

(a) Extra Trees Regressor   (b) Neural Networks

Fig. 3. Predicted vs true

Neural Networks. Neural Networks (NN) are inspired from the human brain and tries to mimic it. Many neurons are inter connected to each other so as to create a complex network. A neural network of 2 hidden layers with 60 and 10 neurons was trained for 20000 epochs with adam optimizer and a learning rate of 0.0253. Mean absolute error was set as the loss criterion. Overall accuracy obtained was 99.91% which indicates how well the model performs. Figure 3b shows the predictions of the final model. After many attempts, this neural network was finally created with precise hyper-parameters.

4 Future Work and Conclusion

It is evident from analysis of different models that Extra Trees Regressor gave the best accuracy of 99.95% with least MAE of 351.1. From Fig. 4 and Fig. 5, it is clear that Extra Trees Regressor has outperformed all other models. Though MAE value is the least of all models, it is quite high in real world as the unit is Thousand Tonnes. Future work includes more data, better models and development of Ensemble based algorithms which could help to achieve better results and deeper insights. Assimilating more diverse parameters could help to obtain more accurate models and precise predictions. Moreover, newer technologies like Hyper-spectral/Multi-spectral Imaging, Drone technology could provide even better results when synchronized together. Based on above analysis a crop, best suitable for the soil, with its estimated yield could be obtained. Further possible outputs of the system would be to give details about timing for irrigation, amount of fertilizers, time of waning and waxing, market details such minimum support price, loan rates, etc. This large system would require more complex data sets, efficient algorithms, larger connectivity and readiness of farmers to use it. Hence, this system would facilitate a 21st century farmer with 21st century technology for betterment and prosperity of his/her life.

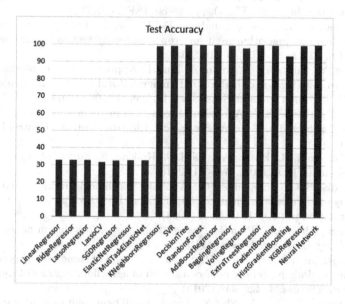

Fig. 4. Accuracy vs model

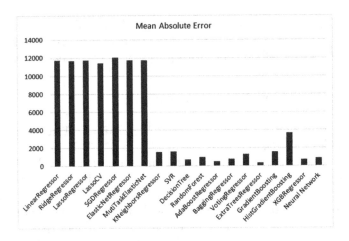

Fig. 5. MAE vs model

References

1. Abdullahi, H.S., Sheriff, R., Mahieddine, F.: Convolution neural network in precision agriculture for plant image recognition and classification. In: 2017 Seventh International Conference on Innovative Computing Technology (Intech), pp. 1–3. IEEE, Londrés (2017)
2. Affrin, K., Reshma, P., Kumar, G.N.: Monitoring effect of air pollution on agriculture using WSNs. In: 2017 IEEE Technological Innovations in ICT for Agriculture and Rural Development (TIAR), pp. 46–50. IEEE (2017)
3. Chandgude, A., Harpale, N., Jadhav, D., Pawar, P., Patil, S.M.: A review on machine learning algorithm used for crop monitoring system in agriculture. Int. Res. J. Eng. Technol. **5**(04), 1470 (2018)
4. Chunjing, Y., Yueyao, Z., Yaxuan, Z., Liu, H.: Application of convolutional neural network in classification of high resolution agricultural remote sensing images. Int. Arch. Photogramm. Remote Sens. Spat. Inf. Sci. **42**, 989 (2017)
5. Dahikar, S.S., Rode, S.V.: Agricultural crop yield prediction using artificial neural network approach. Int. J. Innov. Res. Electr. Electron. Instrum. Control Eng. **2**(1), 683–686 (2014)
6. Dighe, D., Joshi, H., Katkar, A., Patil, S., Kolkate, S.: Survey of crop recommendation systems. IRJET **05**, 476–481 (2018)
7. Dimitriadis, S., Goumopoulos, C.: Applying machine learning to extract new knowledge in precision agriculture applications. In: 2008 Panhellenic Conference on Informatics. pp. 100–104. IEEE (2008)
8. Jeon, W.S., Rhee, S.Y.: Plant leaf recognition using a convolution neural network. Int. J. Fuzzy Logic Intell. Syst. **17**(1), 26–34 (2017)
9. Jha, S., Sehgal, V.K., Raghava, R., Sinha, M.: Trend of standardized precipitation index during Indian summer monsoon season in agroclimatic zones of India. Earth Syst. Dyn. Discuss. **4**, 429–449 (2013)
10. Ji, S., Zhang, C., Xu, A., Shi, Y., Duan, Y.: 3D convolutional neural networks for crop classification with multi-temporal remote sensing images. Remote Sens. **10**(1), 75 (2018)

11. Khaki, S., Wang, L.: Crop yield prediction using deep neural networks. Front. Plant Sci. **10**, 621 (2019)
12. Khaki, S., Wang, L., Archontoulis, S.V.: A CNN-RNN framework for crop yield prediction. Front. Plant Sci. **10**, 1750 (2020)
13. Khatri-Chhetri, A., Aggarwal, P.K., Joshi, P.K., Vyas, S.: Farmers' prioritization of climate-smart agriculture (CSA) technologies. Agric. Syst. **151**, 184–191 (2017)
14. van Klompenburg, T., Kassahun, A., Catal, C.: Crop yield prediction using machine learning: a systematic literature review. Comput. Electron. Agric. **177**, 105709 (2020)
15. Kussul, N., Lavreniuk, M., Skakun, S., Shelestov, A.: Deep learning classification of land cover and crop types using remote sensing data. IEEE Geosci. Remote Sens. Lett. **14**(5), 778–782 (2017)
16. Kuwata, K., Shibasaki, R.: Estimating crop yields with deep learning and remotely sensed data. In: 2015 IEEE International Geoscience and Remote Sensing Symposium (IGARSS), pp. 858–861. IEEE (2015)
17. Lipper, L., et al.: Climate-smart agriculture for food security. Nat. Clim. Change **4**(12), 1068–1072 (2014)
18. Mahato, A.: Climate change and its impact on agriculture. Int. J. Sci. Res. Publ. **4**(4), 1–6 (2014)
19. McQueen, R.J., Garner, S.R., Nevill-Manning, C.G., Witten, I.H.: Applying machine learning to agricultural data. Comput. Electron. Agric. **12**(4), 275–293 (1995)
20. Mishra, S., Mishra, D., Santra, G.H.: Applications of machine learning techniques in agricultural crop production: a review paper. Indian J. Sci. Technol. **9**(38), 1–14 (2016)
21. Mokarrama, M.J., Arefin, M.S.: RSF: a recommendation system for farmers. In: 2017 IEEE Region 10 Humanitarian Technology Conference (R10-HTC), pp. 843–850. IEEE (2017)
22. Nayyar, A., Puri, V.: Smart farming: IoT based smart sensors agriculture stick for live temperature and moisture monitoring using Arduino, cloud computing & solar technology. In: Proceedings of the International Conference on Communication and Computing Systems (ICCCS-2016), pp. 9781315364094–121 (2016)
23. Pal, I., Al-Tabbaa, A.: Regional changes in extreme monsoon rainfall deficit and excess in India. Dyn. Atmos. Oceans **49**(2–3), 206–214 (2010)
24. Pudumalar, S., Ramanujam, E., Rajashree, R.H., Kavya, C., Kiruthika, T., Nisha, J.: Crop recommendation system for precision agriculture. In: 2016 Eighth International Conference on Advanced Computing (ICoAC), pp. 32–36. IEEE (2017)
25. Pujari, J.D., Yakkundimath, R., Byadgi, A.S.: Identification and classification of fungal disease affected on agriculture/horticulture crops using image processing techniques. In: 2014 IEEE International Conference on Computational Intelligence and Computing Research, pp. 1–4. IEEE (2014)
26. Puri, V., Nayyar, A., Raja, L.: Agriculture drones: a modern breakthrough in precision agriculture. J. Stat. Manag. Syst. **20**(4), 507–518 (2017)
27. Rebetez, J., et al.: Augmenting a convolutional neural network with local histograms-a case study in crop classification from high-resolution UAV imagery. In: ESANN (2016)
28. Saha, S., Chakraborty, D., Paul, R.K., Samanta, S., Singh, S.: Disparity in rainfall trend and patterns among different regions: analysis of 158 years' time series of rainfall dataset across India. Theor. Appl. Climatol. **134**(1–2), 381–395 (2018)
29. Shinde, K., Khadke, P.: The study of influence of rainfall on crop production in Maharashtra state of India (January 2017)

30. Singh, P., Kaur, A., Nayyar, A.: Role of Internet of Things and image processing for the development of agriculture robots. In: Swarm Intelligence for Resource Management in Internet of Things, pp. 147–167. Elsevier (2020)

31. Singh, S., Singh, K.M., Singh, R., Kumar, A., Kumar, U.: Impact of rainfall on agricultural production in Bihar: a zone-wise analysis. Environ. Ecol. **32**(4A), 1571–1576 (2014)

32. Sladojevic, S., Arsenovic, M., Anderla, A., Culibrk, D., Stefanovic, D.: Deep neural networks based recognition of plant diseases by leaf image classification. Comput. Intell. Neurosci. **2016**, 1–11 (2016)

33. Tripathy, A., et al.: Data mining and wireless sensor network for agriculture pest/disease predictions. In: 2011 World Congress on Information and Communication Technologies, pp. 1229–1234. IEEE (2011)

34. Veenadhari, S., Misra, B., Singh, C.: Machine learning approach for forecasting crop yield based on climatic parameters. In: 2014 International Conference on Computer Communication and Informatics, pp. 1–5. IEEE (2014)

35. Wang, A.X., Tran, C., Desai, N., Lobell, D., Ermon, S.: Deep transfer learning for crop yield prediction with remote sensing data. In: Proceedings of the 1st ACM SIGCAS Conference on Computing and Sustainable Societies, pp. 1–5 (2018)

36. You, J., Li, X., Low, M., Lobell, D., Ermon, S.: Deep Gaussian process for crop yield prediction based on remote sensing data. In: Thirty-First AAAI Conference on Artificial Intelligence (2017)

37. Zhang, H., et al.: Design and implementation of crop recommendation fertilization decision system based on WEBGIS at village scale. In: Li, Daoliang, Liu, Yande, Chen, Yingyi (eds.) CCTA 2010. IAICT, vol. 345, pp. 357–364. Springer, Heidelberg (2011). https://doi.org/10.1007/978-3-642-18336-2_44

38. Zhong, L., Hu, L., Zhou, H.: Deep learning based multi-temporal crop classification. Remote Sens. Environ. **221**, 430–443 (2019)

Embedded Linux Based Smart Secure IoT Intruder Alarm System Implemented on BeagleBone Black

Jignesh J. Patoliya, Sagar B. Patel[✉], Miral M. Desai, and Karan K. Patel

Electronics and Communication Department, Charotar University of Science and Technology, Anand, Gujarat, India
sagarp3199@gmail.com

Abstract. With the tremendous growth in the Embedded Linux Applications in the profuse sectors, the integration of Internet of Things with the Embedded Linux would be very fruitful. The utmost reason for the use of Embedded Linux are open source, platform independent as it can be used on any platforms like Advanced RISC Machine (ARM), x86, PowerPC, Microprocessor without Interlocked Pipeline Stages (MIPS). The integration of IoT, Embedded Linux and Amazon Web Services (AWS) required secure isolated environment for better work. The ubiquitous way to validate the system probity and authorization is to authenticate the OS during the boot process. The use of AWS Cloud Technologies would be very efficacious for the applications for real time monitoring of the system. The proposed paper relates to the implementation of Smart Secure Intruder System using PIR motion sensor integrating with AWS Cloud Technology with Android App Monitoring using device driver statically loaded onto the BeagleBone Black (ARM Platform) for this IoT application along with the use of Trusted Platform Model (TPM) Security for OS level entry security in the BeagleBone Black Booting Process. The Linux OS is running on the BeagleBone Black Platform. The device driver is the piece of software whose aim is to control and manage the particular hardware device and part of the kernel for efficient applications.

Keywords: Embedded Linux · IoT · Device driver · Beagle Bone Black Board · Cross-compilation · GPIO · AWS Cloud · Trusted Platform Model (TPM) · Crypto Cape

1 Introduction

Today Linux has been installed on many different microprocessors and runs on many platforms that don't contain any hard disk. Simply, running Linux on Embedded Systems is called Embedded Linux. Embedded Systems are resource constrained; battery operated, some of them require real time performance, based other than the x86 architecture like ARM, Alf-Egil Bogen Vegard Wollan RIS (AVR), PowerPC, MIPS and so on. Using Embedded Linux reduces cost of hardware by taking the advantage of multitasking operating system brings to embedded devices. By its quirky benefits,

© Springer Nature Singapore Pte Ltd. 2021
K. K. Patel et al. (Eds.): icSoftComp 2020, CCIS 1374, pp. 343–355, 2021.
https://doi.org/10.1007/978-981-16-0708-0_28

Embedded Linux is mostly used in these applications like Smartphones, Routers, Robotics, Tablets, Development Boards and many more.

Device driver is simply the black box between the hardware and software for implementing the specific function written in C language. Device drivers are loadable kernel modules which flourishes the speed of loading them into the embedded devices. Device Drivers are flourished to efficiently use device memory. To develop a device driver, we need an Operating System that should properly work in the target architecture [1]. There are three main types of device drivers namely Character, Block and Network. Character Device Driver deals with the byte wise data transfer and keyboard, mouse, camera are some examples of character devices. Block Device Drivers deal with the block wise data transfer like in chunks of data where back and forth communication is possible and pen-drives, hard-disks are some examples of block device drivers. Network devices communicate with the use of packets on the system request and deals with the routing like Ethernet and Wi-Fi.

The Internet of Things technology is the interconnection of the physical objects in the surroundings which correlates to the human-to-human, machine-to- machine and machine-to human interaction easily and smartly. The IoT Technology is very demanding in the current scenario as it helps the remote monitoring of the system, smartly controlling the applications and many more benefits of IoT are inculcated. IoT with Cloud Technology is also very fruitful as it gives us better results in data analysis and remote monitoring in the plethora of applications.

OS level Security can be applied to the Embedded Linux Platform like BeagleBone Black using TPM secure crypto-coprocessor. It is used as the checking of the hashes at the time of booting the own kernel for the BeagleBone black. TPM is complex crypto-controller used for storing the Rivest-Shamir-Adleman (RSA) keys, generating random generation and also used for secure storage for authenticating the platform. This encryption keys are also known as artefacts and this can include passwords, certificates or encryption keys. fTPMs (firmware TPMs) and vTPMs (virtual TPM) are also used in the industry for its specific applications like in Google Authenticator and Last-Pass Authenticator in smartphones.

Amazon Web Services (AWS) is the leading cloud platform for providing the various robust services like Storage, Network, Database and compute. AWS Security for efficient connection between Cloud and hardware device is quite worthy as it uses Security Certificates like Transport Level Security (TLS). The monitoring of the sensor data can be easily completed using AWS Application formed using various services for its specific applications like AWS Dynamo DB NoSQL (Not Only Structured Query Language) and AWS Instance.

BeagleBone Black (BBB) is the robust open-source low-power single-board computer platform for embedded linux development produced by Texas Instruments. It boots the Linux in very few seconds and being the open source for developers adds the usage of it in many projects. It has very high expandability supporting the plethora of Capes (Additional modules for specific applications). These boards are showing the flourishing growth in the field of various applications like Internet of Things (IoT), Drones, Robotics, High end Industrial Applications, Smart Homes [2] (Fig. 1).

Fig. 1. BeagleBone Black

The BeagleBone Black has TI Sitara AM3358BZCZ100 Processor with 1 GHz and 2000 MIPS speed. 512 DDR3L 800 MMHz SRAM Memory and 4 GB with 8 bit Embedded mmc Onboard flash is present in this Single Board Computer. It works on 1 GHz ARM Cortex A8 and has GPU of PowerVR SGX530. It has total external 92 pins in two headers (P8 and P9 with 46 each). It has Ethernet (10/100 RJ45), SD, MMC, USB, micro HDMI Connectors on the board. It has enormous peripherals connectivity possible like 4 x UART (Universal Asynchronous Receiver Transmitter), LCD (Liquid Crystal Display), MMC1 (MultiMedial Card), 2 x SPI (Serial Peripheral Interface), 2x I2C (Inter-Integrated Circuit), ADC (Analog to Digital Converter), 4 Timers, 8 PWMs (Pulse Width Modulation) and 2x CAN (Controller Area Network). Three on-board buttons are there namely reset, power and boot. The Software Compatible with BBB is Linux, Android, and Cloud9 IDE (Integrated Development Environment) with Bonescript.

2 Related Work

We have referred some of the papers. The following are the references mentioned from the papers.

R. Dinakar et al. implemented the smart sensoring mechanism with notifying if intruder is detected using PIR Sensor. The Raspberry Pi being robust Single-Board Computer (SBC) is used as the platform for implementing the Home Security System. The notification is inculcated by means of time constraint of certain minutes of detection by PIR Sensor, if it detects then it sends the message of presence of intruder [3]. S. Osmin et al. developed the Intrusion Detection System using Raspberry Pi for securing the home and office. The ARM based Raspberry Pi platform is used for operating and controlling the motion detection in the office or home which is deployed using Raspberry Pi Camera Module. The Telegram Application is integrated with the project for giving the alert to the user for any intruder notified by the camera module on the certain time basis [4].

R. Nadaf et al. deployed the Home Security System for intruder detection using Raspberry Pi using the Raspberry Pi Camera module. The Python and Nodejs framework is used for implementation of the system. The opencv library in python is used to process the image captured by Raspberry Pi Camera for face detection of intruder in the office or home. If the intrusion is detected using Camera module, the alert will be sent to the owner's smartphone [5]. N. Surantha et al. designed the Smart Home Security system using Raspberry Pi and Arduino as the platform for the system. The Webcam is mounted on the Pi for the continuous monitoring of the home and PIR sensor senses the movement if any invader is entered. SVM is used for the verification of object or human. The alert is generated in case of the detection of suspicious movement and it is sent to the owner about its existence [6].

B. Ansari et al. implemented Character Device Driver on Raspberry Pi characterizing the platform as ARM and customized kernel. The Implementation of interrupt based GPIO control of raspberry Pi using character device driver is done. The Cross-compiler is inculcated for converting the code written and compiled in x86 platform and used for running in ARM based platform. The interrupt handling mechanism is used for toggling the LED in the device driver using gpio API in kernel space [1]. C. Profentzas et al. analyzed the performance of secure boot in Embedded Systems. The Performance of the secure booting time is compared and analyzed among the single board computers like Raspberry Pi and BeagleBone Black. The hardware cryptographic based and software-based techniques are verified in both the embedded linux ARM based platform. The use of the specific Single Board Computer is categorized on the basis of the requirement of the speed of the Secure booting, the efficiency and the application required to be built for the Industrial Internet of Things (IIoT) [7]. K. Patel et al. implemented the IoT based Security System using Raspberry Pi (ARM Platform). PIR Sensor is used for monitoring the motion in the home. The detection of intruder by the PIR Sensor strikes the email alert to the owner of the house. The Email Alert by SMTP Protocol is implemented using Raspbian OS framework [8] (Fig. 2).

3 Proposed Work

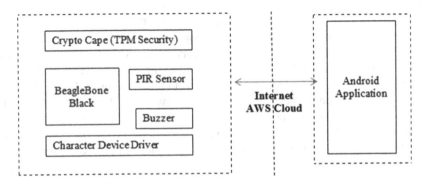

Fig. 2. Architectural diagram

The working of the system is briefly explained below:

1. BeagleBone Black is the platform used for the proposed secure system. The OS level security is offered by TPM (Trusted Platform Module) with Crypto Cape used onto the BeagleBone Black Board.
2. The secure own kernel image is made and verified using Crypto Cape which can't be easily intruded by any attacker.
3. Physically, The PIR Sensor monitors the motion inside the room, if it detects some unusual movement, buzzer would be on, and Alert would be sent to Android Application.
4. AWS Cloud is used for remotely monitoring the data received by the sensor and analyzing the movement in the room continuously with the specific time gap of 15 s.

4 Mathematical Model

A mathematical model is an abstract model that utilizes the mathematical language like Input, Process and output elements to denote the system behavior.

4.1 Mathematical Model for Hardware Structure

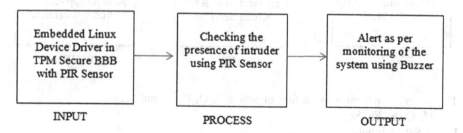

The complete system is collection of sets of I, O, F, Fc and Sc.

S = {**I, O, F, Fc, Sc**}

I   : Set of Inputs
O   : Set of Outputs
F   : Set of functions
Fc : Set of failure cases
Sc : Set of success cases

Input:

- Character Device Driver
- PIR Sensor interfaced with BBB
- Buzzer interfaced with BBB
- Crypto Cape on BBB

Processing: Monitoring the system using PIR Sensor
Output:

- Buzzer Alert by intruder detection
- Monitoring status sent to AWS Cloud continuously

Functions:

- Buzzer On/Off

Failure Cases:

- PIR Sensor not working properly.
- Buzzer is not responding.
- Device Driver has compilation/run-time error.

Success Cases: Successfully monitored the system and alert is sent if intruder is detected to the AWS Cloud [9].

4.2 Mathematical Model of Cloud Application

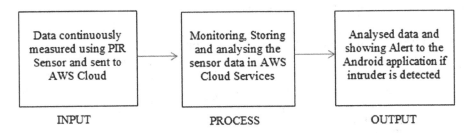

| INPUT | PROCESS | OUTPUT |

The complete system is collection of sets of I, O, F, Fc and Sc.
S = {**I, O, F, Fc, Sc**}
I   : Set of Inputs
O   : Set of Outputs
F   : Set of functions
Fc   : Set of failure cases
Sc   : Set of success cases

Input: Data sensed by PIR Sensor.
Processing: Remote Monitoring, Storing and analyzing of the data for the smart IoT System.
Output:

- Alert in the Mobile Application if Intruder detected by PIR Sensor
- Data analyzed by AWS Cloud for the secure system

Functions:

- Alert message on Mobile Application

Failure Cases:

- AWS Cloud is not connected properly
- Mobile Application is not working.
- Internet Connectivity is not there in all the places.

Success Cases: Successfully received the alert in the mobile application if the intruder is there in the house using AWS Cloud platform as the mediator.

5   Experimental Setup

The overall experimental setup is bifurcated into major four classes.

5.1   Secure Kernel Image

Regularly, the boot-up process is split into different stages by the manufacturers of Embedded Devices. The main motive for the stage division of the boot process is to efficiently use the memory of the internal device and using the external memory for getting the efficient embedded system with minimal memory and robust application. The preliminary ROM Bootloader loads the OS and kernel execution is started. It sets the system and prepares the memory for loading the secondary stage bootloader SPL and MLO. The secondary stage of the boot sequence is the bootloader of the specific operating system. The process of trusted and secure boot has to validate the rectitude of the Linux Kernel and application code before executing the secondary stage [7]. The Security in the boot process is ensured by Trusted Platform Module (TPM). Crypto Cape (plug-in board extendable capability) is used onto the BeagleBone Black for acquiring the OS level security. The AT97SC3204T from crypto cape is used for the purpose of the secure boot. TPM can protect our identity, validate the operating system, provide the secure two factor authentication and significantly reduce the attacking service. To protect the unwanted breaking of the OS by an intruder, the OS level security is very important. Hence, TPM is used for providing very robust hashing verifying mechanism for securing OS.

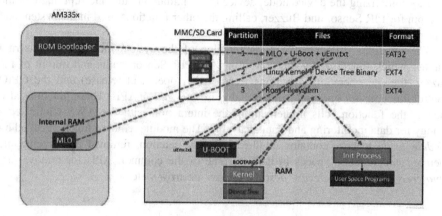

Fig. 3. Booting Process of BeagleBone Black

As shown in Fig. 3, The first stage of the boot process is to execute the code in Boot ROM. This code will run automatically after power up the device as manufacturer has hard-coded the code in the ROM, so we can't change it. Boot ROM configures the CPU and initializes the essential peripherals. The Boot ROM passes SHA-1 hash to the TMP module in Crypto Cape for verifying. Then device has been prepared to execute the Secondary Program Loader. The CPU starts the execution of the SPL program after passing the control from Boot ROM to SPL into the RAM. Then, MLO is controlling the second phase of the boot sequence by preparing the device to execute the U-Boot. Again to securely confirming the completion of the sequence and authenticating, hash is transferred to TMP Module. After only successful verification, it will be letting us to move to the next step. Finally, the SPL will try to find the U- Boot Image, load it into the RAM and pass the control of CPU to U-boot. Then, U- boot is the robust OS bootloader providing the ability to configure the booting options using command prompt. By setting the environmental and configuration variables, U- boot will load and pass the execution flow to the kernel. The final hash file of kernel and boot parameters is transferred to the TPM. The TPM is now free to decrypt the blob file of data. As the attacker does not know the contents of the decrypted blob file, they can't be intruding into the OS even they can tampered the Boot TOM. Hence, this decrypted blob file can be used as disk encryption key or can be shown to the sysadmin for trusting the safety of the hardware of any intrusion. Then, kernel image can be binary file or zipped like uImage or zImage. It contains the architecture of the kernel to be compiled. This way the kernel image is secure.

5.2 Writing the Device Driver Code

Device Driver is the black box in which there is a piece of code written to fulfil the condition of interfacing with the hardware and software. The device driver is the loadable kernel module with robust application. It must contains two functions for maintaining the inserting and removing the module by *module_init()* and *module_exit()* macros.

The main definition which needs to be firstly executed must be present in *module_init()* macro. The function is passed to these macros. In this system, this function is used for initializing the device node, device class, initializing the interrupt, naming the gpio pin for PIR Sensor and Buzzer, calling the other functions used in the system and declaring the file operations object.

The functions called in the main function of the system includes the interrupt handler which functions for the controlling the PIR Sensor status and output of the buzzer, the file operations functions (read, write, open and release) and the GPIO control functions for *gpio_set_value()* and *gpio_get_value()* APIs. These functions also include the function calls implementing the interaction with the AWS Cloud technology for data monitoring and data analysing. The module removal function called by *module_exit()* macros contains all the necessary deletion, removal and freeing the memory and function spaces in it. The some of the common APIs for removal are *gpio_free(), free_irq(), device_destroy(), class_destroy()*, etc.

5.3   Cross Compilation of Device Driver

The Device Driver can be compiled using two ways: Dynamic and Static. The Static Compilation is secure as we have to edit the configuration file in the Devices file in the main kernel file and enable it to compile. This will add the additional security for the cross-compilation of Device Driver. The Cross-compilation is needed because the system on which we are compiling and writing the device driver is x86 and for which the driver is being compiled, that platform is ARM.

Here, the Embedded Linux Target Platform is BeagleBone Black (ARM Platform). The Applications are running on BBB after cross-compiling in x 86 platforms and transferring it to BBB using Serial Protocol.

The Character device driver file written for the system can be statically cross-compiled for BBB by following steps:

- First, copying the.c character device driver file into linux-kernel (BBB) /drivers/char folder and editing the KConfig File by adding the name of the driver inside it.
- Then add obj-$(CONFIG_MY_DRIVER) + = IOT_Intrusion_System.o in the Makefile in the same folder of /chars.
- After adding this lines, make menuconfig and we would get Iot Intruder Alarm System Driver in it in Device Drivers > Character Devices successfully, there we need to add '*' to it.
- The completion of making menuconfig will automatically add 'y' in the CONFIG_IOT_INTRUDER_SYSTEM_DRIVER in.config file in linux (BBB) kernel directory.
- The most important step after completing the configuration settings is to make kernel Image and updating the kernel in the board.
- After rebooting the BBB, the module would be successfully loader for its use (Fig. 4).

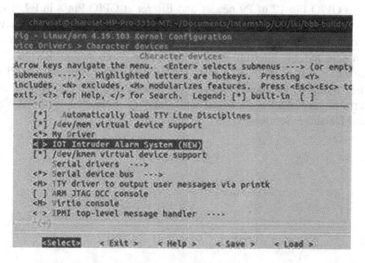

Fig. 4. Menuconfig options for configuration settings

5.4 BeagleBone Black Setup

The statically cross-compiled driver in BeagleBone Black is inserted via insmod. The PIR Sensor has been called via interrupt handler. Whenever there is the detection of intruder, the interrupt handler is executed and PIR Sensor sends the appropriate alert to the AWS Cloud and powers on the buzzer. The interrupt generated by PIR Sensor is shown in /proc/interrupts file in the BeagleBone Black with the name "INTRU-SION_DETECTED_BY_PIR_SENSOR".

6 Overall Hardware Setup

6.1 Hardware Implementation

As shown in the Fig. 5, Crypto Cape (red color) is attached on top of the BeagleBone Black for implementation of OS level Security for the proposed system. PIR Sensor is connected to GPIO Pin 12 of P9 header and Buzzer at GPIO Pin 8 in P9. The device driver inserted into the BBB is executed and the functioning of the system starts. There is the interrupt mechanism for the PIR Sensor functioning in this system. When there is any motion detected, the interrupt is generated at the mentioned GPIO pin of the PIR Sensor, the data is sent to the AWS Cloud and also the buzzer is raised. The PIR Sensor continuously monitors the motion around it and sends the data regularly to the AWS Cloud Platform. The data is analyzed and remotely monitored in the AWS Cloud Storage and Database Services.

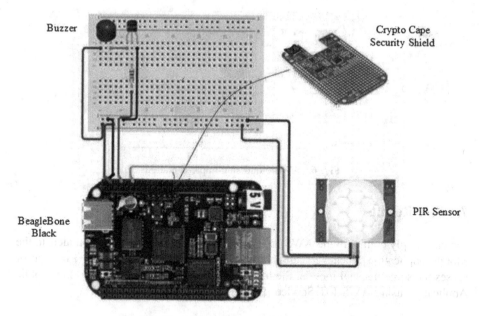

Buzzer

Crypto Cape
Security Shield

BeagleBone
Black

PIR Sensor

Fig. 5. Hardware implementation of the system

6.2   Interface Between AWS Cloud and Mobile Application

AWS Iot service establishes the connection between the cloud and the BeagleBone Black. A proper SDK and a security certificate are being installed in the device for the proper receiving of messages in the IoT. The robust Node.js SDK are the best suited for the hardware support for Cloud. These SDKs also provide commands for receiving and sending the MQTT messages from the AWS Cloud Services for remote monitoring using the Internet. The associated certificate for AWS IoT Service connectivity is needed for the secure establishment of connection with cloud from the BeagleBone Black. For proper functioning of the system, the application is also set up on the cloud side which allows messages to be sent from the physical Node.js gateway through the service to be published on the representation of the gateway digitally. Physical device sends the messages to the AWS DynamoDB NoSQL database regularly. AWS IoT Rules Engine is connected to the digital gateway for determining the location of the storage of the messages. By using Rules Engine and DynamoDB, there is no need of software coding for the dashboard application. The AWS Iot Dashboard is developed in Angular.js which sends the continuous queries to the DynamoDB database for performing the action related to the system (Fig. 6).

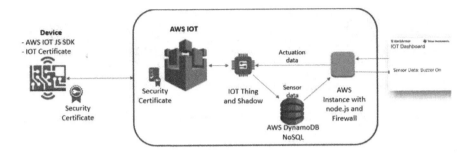

Fig. 6. AWS cloud side implementation

7 Test Results

We can simply configure the AWS IoT service for sending the notification alert to the Mobile application whenever certain triggering is there. So, when the PIR Sensor senses the some unusual motion, the triggered message is sent remotely to the Mobile Application using AWS IoT Service (Fig. 7).

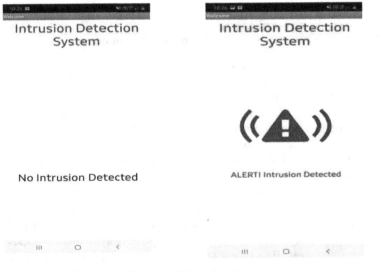

Fig. 7. Mobile application

8 Conclusion

Smart Secure IoT Intrusion Detection System with BeagleBone Black is presented here which included TMP Module Crypto Cape, PIR Sensor, Interface between Mobile Application and AWS Cloud. Security is the most indispensable for the embedded applications. So, our main objective was to secure the kernel of the running system and acquire the data remotely. TMP module and AWS Cloud Services added the fruitful factor in the smart Intrusion Detection system using PIR Sensor. The BeagleBone Black is very robust and effective for customized secure kernel in which intruder can't be easily attacking the system. If any intruder is detected by PIR Sensor, the alert is sent to the Mobile Application remotely via the Cloud Platform and Buzzer turns high. The time taken for the secure boot and transfer of data to the Cloud and mobile application is quite reliable using this ARM Platform based BeagleBone Black. The deployed system is the most beneficial among the discussed related work and other system of Intrusion detection is that BeagleBone Black is robust platform which encapsulates the customized kernel security with efficient timing. It provides better performance than Raspberry Pi. The future extension of the developed system would be to add the real time camera monitoring for the Intrusion Detection and providing better efficiency and authenticity by trusted boot.

References

1. Ansari, B., Kaur, M.: Design and implementation of character device driver for customized kernel of ARM based platform. In: International Conference on Current Trends in Computer, Electrical, Electronics and Communication (ICCTCEEC) (2017)
2. Nayyar, A., Puri, V.: A comprehensive review of BeagleBone technology: smart board powered by ARM. Int. J. Smart Home **10**(4), 95–108 (2016)
3. Dinakar, R., Singh, D., Abbas, M., Alex, M., Yadav, A.: IoT based home security system using Raspberry Pi. Int. J. Innov. Res. Comput. Commun. Eng. **6**(4), 3835–3842 (2018)
4. Osmin, S.: Smart intrusion alert system using Raspberry Pi and PIR sensor. Spec. Issue J. Kejuruteraan **1**(1) (2017)
5. Nadaf, R., Hatture, S., Bonal, V., Naik, S.: Home security against human intrusion using Raspberry Pi. In: International Conference on Computational Intelligence and Data Science (ICCIDS) (2019)
6. Surantha, N., Wicaksono, W.: Design of smart home security system using object recognition and PIR sensor. In: 3rd International Conference on Computer Science and Computational Intelligence (2018)
7. Profentzas, C., Gunes, M., Nikolakopoulos, Y., Landsiedel, O., Almgren, M.: Performance of secure boot in embedded systems. In: IEEE Conference (2018)
8. Tanwar, S., Patel, P., Patel, K., Tyagi, S., Kumar, N., Obadiat, M.: An advanced internet of thing based security alert system for smart home. IEEE J. (2017)
9. Agarwal, N., Paul, S., Gujar, P., Gite, V.: Internet of Things (IoT) based switchox using MQTT protocol. Int. J. Res. Eng. Technol. (IJRET) **5**(4) (2016)

Author Index

Printed in the United States
By Bookmasters

Printed in the United States
By Bookmasters